EXPERIENCE AND IDENTITY

JOHN MONEY

EXPERIENCE AND IDENTITY
Birmingham and the West Midlands 1760–1800

Manchester University Press

Published by Manchester University Press
Oxford Road, Manchester M13 9PL

ISBN 0 7190 0672 4

 British Library Cataloguing in Publication Data

Money, John
    Experience and identity.
    1. Midlands - History
    I. Title
    942.4'07'3   DA670.M64

    ISBN 0-7190-0672-4

Printed in Great Britain by
Western Printing Services Ltd, Bristol

CONTENTS

PREFACE

This book has three justifications. The first is that the study of British political history during the later eighteenth century has usually taken relationships among the Great and the situation within the orbit of St James's, Westminster and Whitehall as its principal concerns. The second is that although it is true that much work has also been done on extra-parliamentary politics, accounts of these too tend to be organised about certain features, most notably the development of popular radicalism in London and Middlesex, and the history of the Yorkshire-based County Association movement, which, prominent though they were, should not be regarded as the only possible points of reference. The third is that when enquiry does move beyond these to the general relationship between popular political consciousness and social change, especially during the last decade of the century, it is the situation in the north, in industrial Lancashire and the West Riding of Yorkshire, which generally consumes the most attention. By taking a stance which requires events to be viewed not only from outside the central context of established politics but also from outside the standpoints usually occupied in the study of extra-parliamentary politics, and of the interaction between political consciousness and social change, I hope to have contributed to the series of particular studies of provincial activity—social and cultural, informal and non-parliamentary, as well as explicitly political—that will be needed before 'the world beyond Westminster', which, from the 1760s onwards, began to challenge the conventions and alter the fabric of existing political society, is fully illuminated.

My chief business is therefore with one part of England only; but this does not mean that the grand chapter of events is ignored. It could hardly be left out of a study which derives much of its point from the increasing sensitivity of provincial affairs to the larger issues of national policy and, conversely, from the fact that at least some of the former were themselves becoming matters of national concern. But though Birmingham and its surrounding counties can supply abundant examples for a general account of the ways in which Englishmen responded to all the great episodes of the later eighteenth century, and especially to the deep dilemmas of the War of American Independence, it is not these reactions in themselves but the ways in which they were assimilated, and the part which that process played in the formation of the region's own indigenous political culture, that are the heart of the matter. In pursuit of this, I am more concerned with the activity and use of ideas than with their abstract nature or their ultimate validity: with what people thought was happening and the service to which this was put, rather than with what they ought to have thought, or whether they were 'in fact' right or not; with opinions and attitudes, the ways in which they were formed, exchanged and adapted to different purposes in the course of argument, and with the institutions, ephemeral as well as permanent, that gave them actual embodiment; with the ways in which particular circumstances could bring views on subjects apparently quite discrete to impinge on each other, and with the results of those conjunctions. One practical result of this is that my argument runs as much across and between the different parts of the book that follows as it does within each of them in turn. This means that in many places, the narrative is heavily cross-referenced: for what a study of this kind may lack in spatial extent it more than recovers in the interdependent variety of its material, very little of which proved to be so simple that all its different aspects could be fully dealt with under a single head.

Another consequence is that this book could not have been written without the help of many people. I have to thank the Controller of Her Majesty's Stationery Office for permission to make use of material in the Public Record Office, and I acknowledge similar debts to the Assay Master and Trustees of the Birmingham Assay Office, and to Josiah Wedgwood & Sons Ltd, of Barlaston. I wish also to record my thanks to Francis Pipe-Wolferstan, Esq., of Statfold, for making available to me the diary of his forebear, Samuel Pipe-Wolferstan, and to the librarian of the Birmingham Book Club for allowing me to consult the club's surviving records. In addition I would like to express my appreciation to Miss D. M. Norris and the staff of the Central Reference Library, Birmingham; to Mr F. B. Stitt of the Staffordshire Record Office and the William Salt Library, Stafford, and also to the archivists and librarians of the John Rylands Library, Manchester; of the Coventry and North Warwickshire Collection, Coventry; of the Lichfield Joint Record Office, and of the Northamptonshire and Warwickshire Record Offices. My research in all these places has been made possible by grants from the Canada Council during the summers of 1968, 1969, 1971 and 1973, and I have also been generously supported, both in my research and in the publication of this book, by the Faculty Research Committee of the University of Victoria. For the preparation of a long and complicated manuscript, which passed through several different versions before it reached the present one, I owe everything to the speed, the accuracy and, not least, the forbearance of Joan Whitfield and Mary Adamson.

Not all of my debts are so material, however. I owe much to Professor I. R. Christie of the University of London, and to Neil McKendrick of Cambridge, who examined this work in its earliest, half-formed state as a Cambridge Ph.D. thesis, and much also to Frank O'Gorman of the University of Manchester, who read an intermediate draft of the present book, and made criticisms and suggestions from which the final version has drawn incalculable benefit. Above all others, however, my greatest duty is to Professor J. H. Plumb of Cambridge, who has given me his guidance, advice and encouragement at every stage of my work. My debt to him grows only greater as time passes. Finally, I dedicate this book to the memory of my father: there could have been no other choice.

ABBREVIATIONS

A.O.P.: Boulton & Watt MSS, the Assay Office, Birmingham
Aris: *Aris's Birmingham Gazette*
A.Q.C.: *Ars Quatuor Coronatorum*
  Transactions of the Quatuor Coronati Lodge, No. 2076
Barl.: Wedgwood MSS, Barlaston
B.R.L.: Birmingham Reference Library
Garbett–Lansdowne Letters: Letters and papers, chiefly from Samuel Garbett to the
  Earl of Shelburne, later Marquess of Lansdowne, 1766–1802: four volumes of
  photostats in B.R.L. of original MSS, now in William L. Clemens Library, Ann Arbor,
  Michigan
Hill, *Bookmakers*: Joseph Hill, *The Bookmakers and Booksellers of old Birmingham*
  (Birmingham, published privately, 1907)
History of Birmingham: William Hutton, *History of Birmingham* (Birmingham, 1781,
  and later editions where specified)
Hist. Parl.: Sir Lewis Namier and John Brooke, *The History of Parliament, the House
  of Commons, 1754–90* (3 vols, London, 1964)
Jopson: *Jopson's Coventry Mercury*
Langford, *Birm. Life*: J. A. Langford, *A Century of Birmingham Life: a Chronicle of
  Local Events, 1741–1841* (2 vols, Birmingham, 1868)
Newdigate: Newdigate MSS, Warwickshire County Record Office, CR 136
Parliamentary History: W. Cobbett; J. Wright, *The Parliamentary History of England
  from the Earliest Period to 1803* (London, 1806–20)
Ryl. Eng. Mss: MS copies of Wedgwood correspondence in John Rylands Library,
  University Library of Manchester; English MSS 1101–10
Swinney: *Swinney's Birmingham and Stafford Chronicle*
T.B.A.S.: *Transactions of the Birmingham Archaeological Society*
U.B.H.J.: *University of Birmingham Historical Journal*
Whitley: T. W. Whitley, *The Parliamentary Representation of the City of Coventry*
  (Coventry, 1894)

INTRODUCTION

In these Midland districts, the traveller passed rapidly from one phase of English life to another; after looking down on a village dirty with coal dust, noisy with the shaking of looms, he might skirt a parish all of fields, high hedges and deep rutted lanes; after the coach had rattled over the pavement of a manufacturing town, the scene of riots and trades union meetings, it would take him in another ten minutes into a rural region where the background of the town was only felt in the advantage of a near market for corn, cheese, and hay, and where men with a considerable banking account were accustomed to say that 'they never meddled with politics themselves'.

The passage is from the preface to George Eliot's *Felix Holt the Radical*. In its particular detail it describes the northern parts of Warwickshire at the time of the first Reform Act, but its general sense would have been equally appropriate to the West Midlands as a whole during the later years of the previous century. Here answers to the early problems of life and work in manufacturing towns were being worked out alongside older patterns of order. At the same time the region's own affairs were becoming increasingly sensitive to the course of national events, and were bringing it more and more frequently into contact with other parts of the country which were likewise experiencing the effects of social and economic change. The growth of popular consciousness, the responses of public opinion and the evolution of the wider aspects of politics which accompanied these developments were therefore of more than local significance. This study examines their evolution during the last forty years of the eighteenth century, and attempts to show how they contributed to the formation of common attitudes to shared experience from which the region derived a sense not only of its own special identity but also of the part it had to play in the larger course of the nation's history.

The most obvious single feature of the West Midlands' experience was the growth of Birmingham. In 1750 the town's population was estimated at 23,688, more than double what it had been thirty years earlier. By 1778 the figure had risen to 42,400; seven years later it had been swelled by another ten thousand, and by the time of the first census in 1801 it had reached 73,670.[1] For all that Edmund Burke might refer to it already as 'the Great Toy Shop of Europe',[2] however, eighteenth century Birmingham was not yet the provincial metropolis which it has since become. Although the main focus of this study lies in the town itself and in its immediate surroundings, it is therefore necessary to resist the temptation to think simply in terms of the rise of one centre. Birmingham's situation, not at the hub of any previously recognisable area of its own but at the meeting point of the three counties of Warwickshire, Worcestershire and

Staffordshire, meant that, even as it grew, so there developed a balancing tension between the new centre and the older influence and example of the county capitals, the cathedral cities of Lichfield and Worcester and the city of Coventry.[3] The results of this were as conspicuous a feature of regional consciousness as was the simple growth of Birmingham, and an even more characteristic one.

Nor was the busy world of manufacture and commerce of itself anything new to the West Midlands. The Severn gorge at Coalbrookdale had long been a centre of iron production, and the manufacture of a wide range of metal tools and other hardware had been established in the villages and towns of north Worcestershire and south Staffordshire since the sixteenth century.[4] For many years, too, landed families such as the Earls of Dartmouth at Patshull, near Wolverhampton, or the Viscounts Dudley, had been as interested in the industrial as they were in the agricultural profits of their estates.[5] The Foleys, now Lords Lieutenant of Herefordshire, had laid the foundations of their fortune as Black Country ironmasters in the seventeenth century, and the intimate conjunction of contrasting 'phases of English life' which exercised such a formative influence on George Eliot was nowhere better personified than in the family of Francis Parker-Newdigate, of Arbury, near Nuneaton, whom her father served as agent from 1806 onwards.[6] The Newdigates had lived at Arbury since the sixteenth century, and there had been more than a touch of the high-flyer about Francis's cousin and immediate predecessor. Notorious until 1784 as the diehard Member of Parliament for Oxford University, and founder there of the prize for English verse which still bears his name, Sir Roger Newdigate, fifth Baronet, had been in many ways the quintessence of traditional independence. In 1762 he had thought it 'best not to lose the country gentleman in the courtier'; in 1773 he had led the House of Commons in its rejection of Sir Henry Houghton's Bill for the relief of dissenting ministers and schoolmasters in the matter of subscription to the thirty-nine articles; in old age he had castigated *bon ton*, the Frenchified craze for novelty which he believed to be at the root of every evil that had befallen the nation in his lifetime, in terms which at once recall that other Sir Roger immortalised by Joseph Addison and foreshadow William Cobbett's 'Conservatism of the flesh'.[7] Yet Sir Roger Newdigate, appropriately described in 1780 as 'a rank Tory, with an affectation of honesty and independence', had also been one of the prime movers behind the Coventry and Oxford canals. As one of the principal mineowners in the north Warwickshire coalfield, he had followed the example of the Duke of Bridgwater by building one of the longest private waterways in the kingdom to join his collieries at Chilvers Coton and Arley to the main navigation. And in his library Watson's *Chemistry* and a full set of the *Encyclopaedia* in French found a perfectly compatible place alongside the treatises on classical antiquities and the works of solid divines like Archdeacon Paley, Dr Horsley and Beilby Porteus, which reflected his reputations as a connoisseur and as a guardian of the established Church.[8]

Birmingham itself contained the same mixture of old and new. Alongside the great factory at Soho the small businesses survived. If it is true that by the end of the century a distinction was beginning to appear in common parlance between 'great' manufacturers on one hand and 'working' manufacturers on the other,[9] it is of more significance as a reflection of the way in which Birmingham's social scale was still more usually visualised that 'John Nott, Button Burnisher' and

'Job Nott, Bucklemaker', the two fictitious exemplars of virtue and patriotism whose advice was purveyed to the town's artisans under various titles from 1790 onwards,[10] were both cast as small independent masters in their own right. The pattern of development in Birmingham and the West Midlands was in fact one of short-distance migration, readjustment and adaptation. In the formation of its characteristic attitudes the region therefore owed as much to tradition and to the influence of existing communities as it did to innovation and the rise of the new manufacturing centre itself.

The book as a whole is divided into four parts. The first establishes the outlines of the local and regional issues through which the people of Birmingham and the West Midlands were discovering where their common interests lay, with regard both to their own affairs and to those of other parts of the country. It is, however, the second part of the work which is its real core. 'Popular consciousness', 'public opinion' and 'the wider aspects of politics' are imprecise terms. Under examination, their content at any time splinters into separate fragments. Since this is especially true of their state in the second half of the eighteenth century, when the permanent significance of all three had barely begun to be recognised, it would not be enough simply to record successive reactions to a long series of particular issues. If this alone were done, the subject of the book, which relies heavily enough on the accumulation of local detail as it is, would dissolve altogether into a multitude of separate items, which could be pursued indefinitely down divergent paths without bringing closer any understanding of their total sum. In order to avoid this the second part of the study is concerned not with reactions to this or that specific question but with the actual means which existed in the West Midlands for providing news and information, exchanging ideas and influencing opinion of all kinds. By examining not only the different character-istics and roles of the newspapers which served the region but also the full range of opportunities for social meeting which were part of its normal life, the wide variety of its concerns can be placed in a context much closer to that in which they were originally discussed than would be the case if each issue were treated in isolation. By doing this it is not only possible to see how separate issues affected each other and influenced the whole way in which the people of the West Midlands were disposed to think about themselves; it is also possible to examine the institutions which gave form to this developing sense of identity, and to trace the activities and attitudes of the overlapping groups of individuals which were the principal agents in the most significant aspect of 'the means of communica-tion and the creation of opinion'—the progressive broadening of articulate popular consciousness which became apparent in Birmingham and the Black Country from the late 1760s onwards.

With the means by which the region's experience was assimilated thus estab-lished, Part three turns more specifically to its political affairs, and to the inter-play which developed between the pursuit of its own particular concerns and its reactions to the major events in the nation's history. In this the central feature was the close mutual relationship that developed between Birmingham and the parliamentary constituencies of the West Midlands. This was most clearly demonstrated in the contested election for Warwickshire in 1774. The overthrow of the county's time-honoured political arrangements by the unexpected return of Sir Charles Holte on this occasion has normally been regarded as one of the earliest and clearest examples outside London and Middlesex of the effects of urban penetration on the old representative system. In broad terms this was the case, and it is certainly true that the victory of 1774 was the most conspicuous single achievement in the political experience of the Birmingham area before the beginning of the nineteenth century. The triumph of Sir Charles Holte was not, however, the result of deliberate planning by Birmingham's leaders. It was brought about in the first instance by a generalised 'opposition' movement, expressing itself in the traditional language of independence and freeholders' rights, which reflected the indirect repercussions of Wilkes and Liberty. This movement had developed in many parts of the West Midlands during the years before the election, even though it came to fruition only in Warwickshire. Here it actually upset the calculations, such as they were, of the Birmingham manufacturers, who were also prevented from turning the result of the election immediately to their own account by the serious divisions which had arisen among them over the dispute with the American colonies. Not until the later stages of the War of Independence, when these differences had either been resolved or ceased to be of immediate importance, was it possible for a formed 'Birmingham interest' to take systematic advantage of the position won by Sir Charles Holte. The place of the 1774 election in the political experience of the region thus remained ambivalent. On one hand, the contest had taken place against a background of considerable popular interest which could claim with some truth to have affected its result, and which was clearly capable of radical development. On the other, even though it was delayed, the eventual outcome of the election was to incorporate Birmingham, with every appearance of complete satisfaction to all concerned, into the existing 'structure of politics', and therefore to strengthen the arguments against hazarding real assets for the sake of speculative reforms. It was this mixed tradition which formed the background to the region's reactions to the French revolution and to the ambiguous part which it played in the democratic agitation of the early 1790s. With this the third part of the book ends; but the appreciable impact which the emissaries of the Sheffield Society for Constitutional Information did make when they came south in 1792 and 1793 only makes it harder to explain their ultimate inability to turn Birmingham into a stronghold of artisan Jacobinism similar to that from which they had come. They had good reasons to expect complete success: at many points the sociological characteristics of the town's trades closely resembled those of Sheffield; the political awareness of its artisan population had been a proven fact since the 1770s at least, and its own reformers had in their own recent past provided a heroic example of beleaguered resistance to Old Corruption by surviving the severe damage inflicted on their movement by the Priestley riots. Yet in the last analysis Birmingham's response was uncertain. The final part of the book seeks the reasons for this in the ways in which the underlying transition from rural to urban and industrial society was perceived in the West Midlands, and in the efforts which were made to mitigate the most divisive manifestations of the revolutionary crisis by explaining this transition in terms adapted from traditional ideals of social order, which, whatever their theoretical shortcomings may have been, could still be effectively supported for practical purposes by appealing to the experience which Birmingham and its surroundings had shared during the previous thirty years.

NOTES

1 *V.C.H. Warwicks.*, VII, 7–8.

2 In his speech on the first reading of the Birmingham Playhouse Bill, as reported in *Aris*, 31 March 1777.

3 For Birmingham's relationship with other West Midlands centres earlier in the century see M. J. Wise, 'Birmingham and its trade relations in the early eighteenth century', *U.B.H.J.*, II, No. 1 (1949), 54–79.

4 W. H. B. Court, *The Rise of the Midlands Industries, 1650–1838* (London, 1938, repr. Oxford, 1953).

5 See in particular T. J. Raybould, *The Economic Emergence of the Black Country: a Study of the Dudley Estate* (Newton Abbot, 1973).

6 For the circumstances in which the novelist grew up see Walter Allan, *George Eliot* (London, 1965), ch. 1, and, at greater length, Gordon S. Haight, *George Eliot, a Biography* (Oxford, 1968).

7 *Cf.* Crane Brinton, *English Political Thought in the Nineteenth Century* (London, 1933, repr. New York, 1962), pp. 62, 75. Sir Roger's remarks are quoted in full below, p. 259.

8 For Sir Roger Newdigate see Sir Lewis Namier's 'Country gentlemen in Parliament, 1750–84', in his *Crossroads of Power* (London, 1962), from which (pp. 41, 44) Sir Roger's views in 1762 and his character in 1780 are taken; Richard B. Barlow, *Citizenship and Conscience: a Study in the Theory and Practice of Religious Toleration in England during the Eighteenth Century* (Philadelphia, 1963), pp. 184–9; *Hist. Parl.*, III, 196–9, and Antony C. Wood, 'The diaries of Sir Roger Newdigate, 1751–1806', *T.B.A.S.*, 78 (1950), 40–54. For Sir Roger's involvement in the Coventry and Oxford Canals see *Newdigate Mss*, B 2199, 2369, 2374, 2375; for his library, B 2429a; 2460; 2461a–f; 2462a and c; 2466c, d, e, k.

9 See below, p. 267.

10 For the Nott pamphlets, which continued to appear in different guises until 1850, see *The Catalogue of the Birmingham Collection* (Birmingham, 1918), pp. 696–700, and R. K. Webb, *The British Working Class Reader: Literacy and Social Tension, 1790–1848* (London, 1955), pp. 43–44, 57–58.

PART ONE

THE REGION AND THE NATION

I

NEW CENTRE AND
OLD COMMUNITIES

However much Birmingham may have owed to the closeness of its relationships with the older communities and interests of the West Midlands, the processes of accommodation on which this asset rested were not automatic. Birmingham still had to take the initiative in addressing its own problems, and the differences it provoked by doing so were not always satisfactorily resolved. Two examples in particular illustrate the ways in which the new centre's needs impinged on existing circumstances. In the first, the results provided an important means of expression for Birmingham's sense of accord with its surroundings; in the second, they exposed the serious shortcomings which still attended the relationship. The most conspicuous case of successful initiative and assimilation is provided by the Birmingham General Hospital, one of the town's first and most important communal projects, which not only supplied a pressing need but also acted as an important channel for the social, political and cultural connections of its more prominent inhabitants. The collaboration between Birmingham's leaders and their country neighbours which worked so well in this case seemed to be equally effective in the ordering of the town's government; but though Birmingham people liked to draw attention to the fact that their working arrangements with the local members of the county bench left them free from the trammels of superfluous officialdom, the increasing complexity of the town's business really needed expert management and agencies better adapted to the task than those which already existed. When measures to meet this need were proposed during 1789 and 1790, however, they not only became entangled in a dispute with the Warwickshire Court of Quarter Sessions over Birmingham's share of the county rate but were also baulked by bitter resistance in the town itself. Thanks to the fact that the opposition was led by William Hutton, Birmingham's historian and a prominent member of the congregation at the Old Meeting, the quarrel which followed added considerably to the widening rift in the town between Church and Dissent, and it was still smouldering on the eve of the Priestley riots in 1791. The dispute, which centred on rating proposals intended to pay for a comprehensive plan for policing the town, was the more remarkable because, despite his obstruction on this occasion, William Hutton was himself a self-proclaimed reformer. He had been actively involved in Birmingham's internal government for the past twenty years, and he had recently advanced novel ideas, based on his own experience and on eclectic gleanings from more theoretical sources, for regulating the petty disputes among working people which were the most frequent cause of disturbance in the town. Taken individually, none of these matters was of momentous significance, though Hutton's attitude to law and government did foreshadow on a small scale the larger position developed by reformers during the following century; but they establish the outlines of Birmingham's immediate relations with its surroundings; they illustrate what was achieved in solving the problems which these presented, as well as its limits, and together they form the background of local issues, without an appreciation of which the town's reactions to larger events, particularly after 1789, can be only partly understood.

The early history of the General Hospital, which was founded and built between 1765 and 1779,[1] shows very clearly how Birmingham's new institutions helped to consolidate and determine its relations with the surrounding region as they were assimilated into the existing round of life. Proposals for the new foundation were first made public in a letter on behalf of the Overseers of the Poor which the *Birmingham Gazette* carried for three successive weeks during September and October 1765.[2] This rejected the more conventional alternative of a county infirmary similar to those recently established at Stafford, Shrewsbury and Chester, on two grounds. As the examples of Liverpool and Manchester showed, such institutions were ill suited to the needs of 'large populous towns', and in any case Birmingham's situation at the very edge of Warwickshire meant that a new infirmary for the town could hardly be presented as a 'county' enterprise. Joint action with the Warwickshire authorities would be continually hampered by irreconcilable conflicts of interest, and Birmingham would therefore have to make its own plans. The fact that the normal course of collaboration was thus rejected did not, however, remove the need for understanding between the town and its surrounding communities. On the contrary, it pointed to the importance of finding a new accommodation between them. As 'the Nobility and Gentry of the neighbouring country and the Principal Inhabitants of the Town' were told in a second letter,[3] the need for a new hospital arose from the preponderance of immigrants among Birmingham's working population who did not qualify for relief from the existing workhouse infirmary. Most of the newcomers came from neighbouring parishes, and it was to provide for their needs that the original proposal had suggested that outlying communities should be able to subscribe to the new hospital on a scale graded according to their own poor rates and the number of beds they wished to control. This suggestion was adopted in the hospital's first set of rules, which provided that the 'Head Magistrate, or other officer . . . of any township, body corporate, or society subscribing two guineas yearly shall be a trustee'.[4] In this way Birmingham's immigrants were provided for, and the new foundation was incorporated into the existing structure of local government and charitable relief in the area.

To begin with, the new foundation made little headway. It had to compete for money with the counter-attractions of more profitable investment in canals and more pleasurable subscription to theatrical entertainments, and its progress was further hampered by financial stringency during the first years of the American war. By degrees, however, the General Hospital began to receive an increasing share of attention. Among its early benefactors and officers were many familiar names. Samuel Garbett, Dr John Ash, Matthew Boulton, Dr William Small and the elder Samuel Galton were all on the hospital's first committee, elected on 24 December 1765, and all became trustees for its property.[5] In 1777 Ash, whose name was particularly associated with the hospital, and who became its first senior physician, thanked Lord and Lady Dartmouth for their donations to the charity, and for recommending it to Lords Clarendon and Warwick.[6] Together with Lord Craven, of Combe Abbey, near Coventry, Dartmouth headed the list of subscribers published in 1779, when an annual appeal was launched. Others who concerned themselves with Hospital affairs at this time included Robert Augustus Johnson, Esq., of Kenilworth; the Reverend Dr Spencer, the leading magistrate in the Birmingham area; Sir Charles Holte, Member of Parliament for the county, and Robert Lawley, of Canwell Priory, Shropshire, who was already cultivating the connections which led to his election to Parliament for Warwickshire in 1780, when Holte retired. Lawley, who inherited the family baronetcy in November 1779, was chairman of the annual meeting of the General Board of the Hospital in 1780, the record of which shows that the same wide patronage continued. The meeting was attended by Sir George Shuckburgh, Warwickshire's other new Member of Parliament, by Sir Henry Gough of Edgbaston, by Robert Augustus Johnson, and by many more. The Earl of Dartmouth was elected as president for the following year, with the Warwickshire members as vice-presidents; a call of ten guineas was made on all parish subscriptions, and churches and chapels of all denominations were asked to recommend the charity, especially on the Sunday nearest midsummer.[7]

As this wide attention suggests, the full significance of the new foundation in the life of the region now extended well beyond its immediate purpose. It played an important part, for example, in the early history of the Lunar Society of Birmingham, the most remarkable of the elite groups of provincial intelligentsia which played a crucial part in the application of science to the problems of technological improvement and social change during the early industrial revolution. Medicine was a major interest of a society which, in William Small, William Withering and Erasmus Darwin, included three of the most eminent practitioners of the day among its members, and the General Hospital was one of the chief concerns which first drew the Lunar circle together. Two members of the group, Boulton and Small, and the elder Galton, father of a third, were involved in Hospital business from the start. When William Withering was prompted by Erasmus Darwin to come to Birmingham and fill the gap left in the circle by the death in 1775 of William Small, his permanent removal from Stafford, where he had been physician to the county infirmary, was confirmed by his appointment in 1779 as John Ash's colleague on the staff of the General Hospital. Similarly, it was probably the part played in Hospital affairs by Robert Augustus Johnson, combined with his relationship by marriage to Lord Craven, one of the foundation's leading patrons, which explained how this worthy but otherwise obscure man found his way into the exalted intellectual company of his fellow Lunaticks.[8] In other ways, too, the General Hospital acted as a valuable medium in Birmingham's relationship with its surrounding area. During the mid-1770s the town's own leaders were divided, and their connections with the nobility and gentry of the neighbouring counties were disrupted, by differences arising out of the Warwickshire election of 1774 and reaction to the early stages of the American war.[9] The revival of interest in the General Hospital from 1777 onwards was one of the developments which helped to repair this dislocation, and during the following decade the new foundation played a prominent part in consolidating the recognised place which the 'Birmingham interest' was by then anxious to assume in the established structure of regional society and politics. This was particularly so because in addition to the reputation which it acquired through its practical work the hospital also became widely known as a fashionable charity. Though ten years passed between the first of its benefit seasons of concerts and oratorios in 1768 and the second in 1778, the hospital's music festivals established themselves from then onwards as major occasions for the gathering of the West Midlands' leading families. In this way the hospital and its associated activities played a substantial part in attracting the patronage of wealth and rank so assiduously cultivated by Birmingham's leaders, while at the same time they helped to realise the town's own cultural ambitions. The results of this process can be seen not only in the hard-headed appreciation of 'our music meeting' shown by men like Samuel Garbett, who valued it chiefly as an opportunity to advance Birmingham's material interests, but also in the significance which the triennial festivals acquired, through their full-scale performances of sacred music, as symbolic expressions of the town's higher and less tangible aspirations to greatness.[10]

The development of local authority in Birmingham,[11] like that of the General Hospital, seemed to show that the town could act on its own behalf without forfeiting the relationship which it enjoyed with its surroundings. With the securing of its first Improvement Act in 1769, Birmingham joined Manchester as one of the first of the new provincial centres to remedy the deficiencies of its ancient manorial and parochial administration by establishing a statutory authority with specific powers.[12] Despite subsequent adjustments to its composition and functions, the body of commissioners which the Act empowered to supervise the cleaning, paving, lighting and policing of Birmingham's streets remained responsible for the greater part of the town's government until the middle of the following century. The Lamp Act, as the legislation of 1769 was usually called, is therefore significant as a major independent innovation in Birmingham's development. Like the General Hospital, however, it was intended to assist rather than to supersede existing arrangements, and it was no mere chance that the two undertakings should both have been proposed at the same time. They engaged many of the same men, and they shared the same general motives. As the regulations of the hospital facilitated its liaison with neighbouring communities in order to make good the deficiencies of the old workhouse infirmary, so the role of the Street Commissioners complemented that of Birmingham's own manorial Court Leet and Parish Vestry on one hand, and of the local members of the Warwickshire and Staffordshire Commissions of the Peace on the other. In this way it was hoped that the town's special administrative problems could be solved without disturbing established relationships and without the restrictions which, according to common belief, would have been inherent in seeking a charter of incorporation. It was therefore not so much the simple passage of the Lamp Act, or its first extension in 1773, which gave Birmingham particular cause for self-congratulation as the fact that these measures nevertheless left 'Government' more conspicuous in the town by its absence than by its presence. 'A town without a charter is a town without a shackle,' wrote William Hutton, who, like the compiler of Pearson and Rollason's *Birmingham Directory* of 1777, regarded the combination of relative order and freedom from obtrusive authority as an important cause of the town's growth.[13] Thanks to this happy condition, Hutton believed, Birmingham people were too busy making constructive use of their natural energies to think of making mischief. It was 'easy to point out some places only one third the magnitude of Birmingham, whose frequent breaches of the law, and quarrels among themselves, find employment for half-a-dozen magistrates and four times that number of constables . . .'. The business of Birmingham, on the other hand, had been, and still could be, carried on perfectly well by the county Justices who happened to live in the area.[14]

William Hutton wrote of this providential arrangement as one of the brightest single gems in the 'grand lustre' of the British constitution.[15] The conceit may have flattered his local readers, but it was as misleading as it was obvious: no such metaphor could disguise the facts that effective treatment of the difficulties created by Birmingham's growth required specialised experience and powers; that the acquisition of these, both by the town's own agencies and by the local magistrates, was bound to alter the nature of the relationship which Hutton's cliché took for granted, and that no matter how it was modified the existing accommodation between Birmingham and its surroundings would eventually hinder as much as it helped the solution of the town's problems. During the later 1780s these realities were made quite plain by difficulties of internal police and criminal jurisdiction which emphasised Birmingham's special situation with regard to its neighbouring communities. One reaction to these difficulties was to seek ways to maintain the services of Joseph Carles, Esq., the magistrate on whom the town particularly depended for the expert handling of its affairs. Associated with this *ad hominem* solution were proposals to provide Birmingham with an effective police agency of its own, and to regularise Carles's unique personal position by making permanent provision for a specialist magistracy in the town. A radically different response to the same general problem was that favoured by William Hutton, who proposed to keep the peace in Birmingham not by reinforcing the conventional authorities and procedures but by direct intervention in the minor quarrels of the town's tradesmen in order to eliminate the supposed causes of disorder at their source. In the event these different reactions succeeded only in frustrating each other and in adding to the tensions which caused the Priestley riots; and after these, Birmingham had to rest content with a partial solution to its problems in the shape of local additions to the Warwickshire bench—a remedy which may have satisfied the form, but no longer properly fulfilled the substance, of the old relationship between town and county.

Joseph Carles, of Handsworth, Staffordshire, is usually remembered as the justice who may have condoned, and certainly lost control of, the mob which hounded Joseph Priestley and his fellow Unitarians out of Birmingham in July 1791. It comes as a surprise, therefore, to discover that this man, whose part in the Priestley riots has marked him as a disgraceful example of illiberal and incompetent reaction, had previously earned such universal esteem as a magistrate that on 12 March 1791 a testimonial on his behalf had been sent to William Pitt, signed by all the leading inhabitants of the Birmingham area, including Joseph Priestley, William Russell, William Withering and James Keir, the chief victims of the mob only four months later.[16] Despite appearances Carles, who was on the Commissions of the Peace for Staffordshire and Warwickshire, was far from being an ordinary country magistrate. More than any other Justice in the area, he had devoted his time and energy to Birmingham's problems, even at the risk of his personal fortune, so that he was in danger of exchanging his position on the bench for a debtor's prison. The efforts made by the town's leaders to keep their most expert magistrate from ruin produced a correspondence which not only bespeaks their concern for him personally but also reveals their awareness of the general difficulties which Birmingham's growth was producing.

As early as 1782 Samuel Garbett had told the Earl of Shelburne that Carles was 'of great importance to the neighbourhood of Birmingham, and really doth much more than his share of public duty', and on at least one occasion after that, Garbett used his political connections to seek special powers for the Justice so that he could act effectively in cases which extended well beyond the normal scope of a local magistrate's authority.[17] In 1787 interests in Birmingham, Walsall and Wednesbury made a more general application to government on Carles's behalf, acting through the Marquess of Stafford and the Members of Parliament for Warwickshire. This produced no result, but in May 1790 Garbett again took up the subject by reminding Matthew Boulton of the earlier request and urging him to speak to William Pitt and Lord Stafford about the possibility of finding a place for Carles which would relieve his financial straits. A suitable opportunity arose later in the year when one of the general receiverships for Warwickshire fell vacant, and the Birmingham leaders made a concerted effort to obtain it for their 'worthy active and effective magistrate'. Once more they sought the help of Sir Robert Lawley, the Warwickshire Member who was regarded as Birmingham's particular representative; Garbett spoke to George Rose, Pitt's Under-secretary of the Treasury, and the Marquess of Stafford again put the case to the Minister himself. 'Several other gentlemen' were also enlisted, among them Thomas Gilbert, the Member for Lichfield, who was one of the acknowledged experts on the problems of the new manufacturing areas, particularly with regard to the Poor Law, and who, as agent to Lord Stafford, was himself deeply involved in the development of the West Midlands.[18] Gilbert must have been in a particularly good position to appreciate the value of Carles's work in the Birmingham area; but despite his advocacy, despite the other efforts which were made and despite the testimonial of March 1791, the application was again unsuccessful.

'Our Birmingham Gentlemen', whom Boulton had never known 'so unanimous and anxious', were 'much disappointed',[19] but they did not let the matter rest. After the Priestley riots, it is not surprising that the government was reluctant to become directly involved in Carles's personal situation, but nevertheless the magistrate's plight did demonstrate that special arrangements were needed to keep competent officers in the town, and this was more generally recognised in the plans for a police Bill which were discussed at intervals in Birmingham between 1789 and 1793. Under the terms of the Bill, magistrates were to be appointed with specific responsibility for the town's government. As Samuel Garbett pointed out in no uncertain terms, this was not work for untried strangers. It would require expert knowledge and continuous attention. One magistrate should be available in the town at all times; two should attend at the Public Office on three days in every week, and the inhabitants should bear their own part by soliciting the patronage of William Pitt once more 'so far as to enable the town to make proper compensation to Gentlemen who will give such attendance'. On this plan, the police Bill would work; but Garbett warned that he himself would have nothing to do with 'any new plan for taxing the town to pay salaries to anybody that Country Gentlemen may appoint to do their duty as Justices of the Peace', and he ended by repeating his conviction that

Joseph Carles was 'probably much (very much) better than anybody we can expect to be forced upon us'.[20]

If the police proposals had been put into effect Carles's particular relationship with Birmingham would probably have been put on a regular footing; for he had been actively involved in the first exploration of the scheme in 1789, and he was closely consulted on the terms of appointment for the special Justices in 1793.[21] As it was, however, the measure was abandoned, partly because its prospective cost aroused opposition from the town's smaller ratepayers, partly because it fell victim to the more general divisions of the 1790s and partly because additions to the Warwickshire Commission of the Peace in 1794 made it seem unnecessary. Though Carles himself became a stipendiary magistrate of sorts when his friends took their own steps to maintain his services by subscribing to pay his debts,[22] the final result of Birmingham's attempt to rectify the deficiencies of its local government was therefore not commensurate with the effort involved. Nevertheless the attempt itself is significant. Recognition that the supervision of the town's affairs was fast becoming a full-time task which could no longer be left to the chance abilities of country Justices was bound to affect the nature of the existing relationship between Birmingham and its surrounding area. Tension in this not only delayed prompt action on the police Bill when it was first proposed; it also helped indirectly to deepen the more fundamental differences in Birmingham itself on which the measure eventually foundered.

Of the difficulties which provoked Birmingham's efforts to retain the services of Joseph Carles and to obtain its own specialist magistrates, that which brought the town into most direct conflict with the existing centre of government in the area, was the problem of criminal administration. As the *Birmingham Gazette* warned on 16 February 1789, the town was fast becoming a criminal asylum, particularly now that the enforcement of the vagrancy laws in the neighbouring country districts was driving undesirables of every kind to seek refuge in the anonymity of its streets. The corollary of this was that Birmingham began to account for an increasing number of the offenders who crowded the county gaol at Warwick. This was being extended at the time; but, to judge from the number of times the Home Office was urgently asked to relieve Warwick gaol of its mounting backlog of convicts awaiting transportation, the strain on the county must have been considerable, and it was apparently increased by the fact that, thanks to their ingenuity with even the most rudimentary of tools, Birmingham men were harder to keep under lock and key than the common run of country convicts. The county was in debt, and it seemed wrong that, since the county rate was levied on landed property only, the commercial wealth of Birmingham should continue to make no contribution to the common good. At its Epiphany meeting in 1790 the Warwickshire Court of Quarter Sessions therefore resolved to petition Parliament for relief from the expense of moving Birmingham prisoners to Warwick and keeping them there pending trial.[23]

In Birmingham discussion of the proposals in which Joseph Carles's personal affairs were later to be involved was already several months old. During November 1789 James Watt junior had sent detailed reports to Matthew Boulton of the way in which the problems of internal police were being faced in Manchester, and had pressed strongly for close co-operation between Birmingham and the northern centre in the prosecution of felons and receivers of stolen goods, 'as it is highly probable that the greatest part of the goods stolen here find a market in

Birmingham and vice versa'. Watt reported that Manchester was preparing a police Bill for submission to the next session of Parliament,[24] and his implicit advice that Birmingham should do likewise was reflected in the findings which the town's leaders presented to a public meeting on 8 December. These drew attention to the increase in prostitution in the town, the disposal of stolen metal through pawnbrokers, the proliferation of gin shops, the inadequacy of Birmingham's own prison accommodation and the insufficient powers of the Street Commissioners. As a temporary measure, nightly patrols were proposed, to be financed during the coming winter by voluntary subscription. Permanent remedy was to be sought in legislation to make the patrols a permanent charge on the town and to establish a 'regular office for receiving information' about criminal activities. The proposed Bill also contained clauses to replace private pawn-brokers by a proper agency for receiving pledges and making small loans, to license dealers in metal and to provide Birmingham with separate prison accommodation, 'adapted as far as possible to culprits of every class'. In addition, special attention was paid to lodging houses. Quite apart from the need to keep track of a shifting population, some attempt to regulate the living conditions of the town's working people was necessary if the social causes of crime were to be treated as well as its consequences. Control of the houses which sheltered the majority of Birmingham's transient inhabitants was one possible way of achieving this, particularly as they took in 'lewd women and men of the vilest character' and were a corrupting influence on the increasing number of apprentices who lived apart from their masters' families. In future, therefore, lodging-house keepers were to be licensed and were to keep a register of their boarders; and among the later refinements to the original proposals which the Police Committee considered was a suggestion that the town should provide special hostels for out-apprentices, built and supervised at public expense.[25] Whether these comprehensive provisions would have been very effective in practice is doubtful; but the extensive internal regulation they implied is a measure of the extent to which concerned opinion on Birmingham's local government had moved beyond the complacency of the past, and they do show that the town's leaders were well aware of the changing social circumstances which lay at the root of the problem that was occupying the Warwickshire Court of Quarter Sessions.

The Warwick resolution seemed to threaten Birmingham's plans, and at a public meeting held to discuss it on 22 February 1790 the town emphasised its own measures. A committee, led by Joseph Carles and his colleague, the Rev. Dr Spencer, was instructed 'to enquire what is done in the like cases at Manchester, Liverpool, Sheffield, Leeds, or any other considerable towns or manufacturing neighbourhoods, as Wolverhampton, Walsall, Wednesbury, Bilston, Willenhall, Darlaston, Newcastle under Lyme, and places in Lancashire that have become populous of late years in consequence of manufactures'. The county magistrates were to be informed of the action taken, and a strong representation was to be made of Birmingham's objections to their intentions. The meeting pointed out that the town's own poor rates had soared in recent years, that many of its residents were already moving out to the neighbouring parishes to avoid the burden, and that this check to Birmingham's own growth would ultimately be to the disadvantage of the neighbouring landowners, the value of whose property had been 'much increased by the manufactures lately established . . . by the industry and ingenuity of our fathers'. In short, Birmingham had enriched the whole area by its growth and was already carrying more than its share of the cost. The county was therefore asked to suspend its application to Parliament until the town had completed its own investigation of the police problem.[26]

The outcome was entirely unconstructive. Despite its own professed intent to pursue the police enquiry to a conclusion, the meeting of 22 February ended by resolving to postpone further discussion of the proposals of the previous December until the difference with the county had been settled. Action on Birmingham's own measures was thus delayed, and during the following months the issue became submerged in a series of related quarrels within the town itself. The source of these disputes was the same in all cases: gathering discontent at the mounting burden of the parish rate, which found expression, first in opposition to the police Bill, second in furious objection to the rating of tenement houses, and third in criticism of supposed malpractice and lack of initiative in the use of the existing revenues. The police proposals themselves were thus quickly superseded as the immediate focus of attention; but the grounds on which they were opposed, and the ways in which these were taken up in the later phases of the controversy, exposed differences in outlook which rapidly acquired religious and political overtones, with the result that the alignment of conflicting interests produced by the whole series of disputes contributed at least as much to the local prelude to the riots of 1791 as did the better known difference between Joseph Priestley and the Churchmen over the admission of controversial theology to the Birmingham Library.

Despite its apparent necessity and the thoroughness of its provisions, the police Bill was not entirely welcome. Among the smaller property owners it was regarded not as a measure required by the public interest but as an attempt by a few prominent individuals to impose themselves on the town by forcing through without proper consultation a proposal whose cost they would themselves escape, since the houses of the rich were now predominantly outside the administrative boundaries of Birmingham proper, and therefore did not pay the parish rate.[27] On the face of it this was an understandable objection. In fact it was less legitimate than it seems, because the movement of the wealthy to residential areas outside the town, coupled with shortage of building space and the demand for cheap accommodation within it, meant that only a fraction of the property in Birmingham itself was sufficiently substantial to be ratable under current assessments.[28] Many of those who complained of the evasions of the rich were therefore themselves equally able to avoid payment to the public good, while the difficulties of mounting costs and insufficient revenue which beset the town's government went unsolved. On 27 September 1790 this was pointed out in a notice from the Vestry which announced that, since only 1,300 of the 8,000 houses built in Birmingham during the last thirty years paid the existing rate, the parish proposed to levy a special charge on the landlords of property let at under £10 a year. The result was redoubled opposition from the small owners, whose case was stated by William Hutton in a justification of slum landlordism which turned against the Vestry a modification of the same argument that had been used earlier by the town in general against the Warwick resolution on the county rate: that by housing the human raw material on which Birmingham's prosperity depended the speculators in tenement property were already making a vital contribution to the community. Hutton objected that

No town in Britain has equalled Birmingham in the rapidity of its growth. This is owing to the increase of its manufactories, for they will rise and fall together; both originate from the commercial spirit of the inhabitants; whatever therefore tends to damp this rising flame will be found in the end destructive.

The amazing increase of trade and of houses are not so much owing to the natives as to aliens. . . . Every person who is to subsist by industry has a certain portion of labour to sell. There are thousands of places within fifty miles around us where such persons hawk this valuable commodity, but cannot procure a purchaser. Birmingham is a market everlastingly open for this kind of traffic, and the more free the market, the more it will abound with customers, hence the article is purchased at an easy rate. . . . Apprentices make but a small part of our laborious hands. The desolate wanderer, the disbanded soldier, the broken tradesman, the discarded liveryman, the people of either sex and of every description, without money and without employment, find both in the shops. . . . Although this ingress of people fills the town with paupers, which become a heavy burden on the inhabitants, yet the profits of their labour in the aggregate is infinitely an over-balancer. As it is our interest to receive them, so it is equally our interest to furnish them with accommodations, therefore small houses are necessary, and instead of mulcting the man who ventures his fortune upon so slender a basis, he merits the thanks of his neighbours.[29]

Small wonder that in the course of preliminary discussion of the police proposals during the previous November Samuel Garbett had deplored the indifference of 'the busy people of this place' to anything beyond their immediate profits.[30] Though Hutton's letter was not provoked by the same particular issues, both its overall argument and its detailed assessment of conditions in Birmingham reflected an outlook completely different from the paternalism of the Police Committee's attempt to extend the formal means of social control in the town. This suggests that behind the immediate quarrels which troubled Birmingham lay a more fundamental conflict of ideas. It is therefore worth pausing to consider Hutton's attitude to the problems of the town's government in more detail.

Had it been made half a century later Hutton's attack on the rating proposals might have come straight from one of Thomas Carlyle's 'Respectable Professors of the Dismal Science', and his advocacy of *laisser-faire* on this occasion seems entirely in keeping with the earlier remarks on local government in his *History of Birmingham. Pace* Samuel Garbett, however, Hutton was abused by his opponents in the rating quarrel not for his callous indifference to Birmingham's problems but as an interfering busybody who had made a nuisance of himself in several of the town's administrative offices during the past seventeen years. This seems inconsistent, and the case of the small landlords was not the first issue in which Hutton's attitude to public affairs had shown the same apparent contradiction. In 1768 he had taken a leading part in the opposition to the Lamp Act, basing his stand on the same mixture of principle and self-interest which marked his reactions in 1790; yet once he had himself become a Street Commissioner in 1773 there was none more zealous in the work nor louder in denunciation of his colleagues' apathy. Despite his declared antipathy to officious authorities of any kind, Hutton took his work as a Commissioner of the Birmingham Court of Conscience sufficiently seriously to write an illuminating book about it, and it was his very efficiency in this capacity that made him a victim of the riots in 1791. Strangest of all, perhaps, in view of his attitude to the issues of the previous three years and his reputation as one of Birmingham's better known Dissenters, Hutton offered his services as a possible member of the Warwickshire Commission of the Peace in July 1792 because he believed he had precisely the kind of expert knowledge the town needed in its magistrates.[31]

Hutton's attitude to the problems of local government in Birmingham was more consistent than it seems. In his history of the town, written when its problems were still manageable without drastically disturbing the existing arrangement of authorities, he had certainly taken pride in the apparent spontaneity with which its affairs regulated themselves; and as his defence of the small landlords shows, he continued to oppose what he regarded as misplaced interference with the freedom of private enterprise. But when Hutton's *History* went on to declare that 'we oft behold a pompous corporation which sounds well in history over something like a dirty village. This is a head without a body. The very reverse is our case. . . . We are a body without a head'[32] it was not so much reinforcing its earlier remarks by denying absolutely the need for control in Birmingham as suggesting more specifically that the forms and procedures of traditional authority would be worse than useless because they bore no relation to the town's real circumstances. Hutton's criticisms during 1790 and 1791 therefore stemmed not from the simple belief that Birmingham's government needed no attention but from the conviction that the remedies proposed by orthodox opinion mistook the nature of the problem, would affect the wrong people and would do more harm than good because they were not based on sound principles. It is Hutton's desire to rectify this that explains the apparent contradiction between his negative attitude to the rating proposals and his own intense involvement in local affairs. His reaction was the same as it had been seventeen years earlier, when he became a Street Commissioner: 'this also I relished, and considered a large field for reform'.[33]

Hutton's positive reaction to the situation in Birmingham is best illustrated by the ideas he developed and put into practice as a commissioner of the town's Court of Conscience. Instituted by Act of Parliament in 1752, this was one of a number of similar agencies in other towns whose main purpose was to arbitrate in common disputes among tradesmen. The courts seem to have functioned only spasmodically, for their reputation suffered from a common misconception about their origins, which were confused with the conciliar jurisdiction in poor men's causes first brought to prominence under Cardinal Wolsey and therefore associated with the trappings of arbitrary power abolished by the Long Parliament.[34] To Hutton, however, who believed that manufacturing towns required a means of maintaining order and dispensing routine justice different from traditional practice in kind as well as degree, a court of conscience seemed to be the ideal way of handling the causes of disturbance among working people.

Hutton developed this opinion in his *Courts of Requests, their Nature, Utility and Powers Determined, with a Variety of Cases Determined in that of Birmingham*.[35] For the most part the book is devoted to some two hundred examples of the way in which the court worked; but important though these are for the light they shed on conditions in the town, the most interesting parts of the work are the more general observations which introduce and accompany the individual cases. It would be misleading to suggest that these advanced a distinctive and systematic philosophy of human nature. Hutton, who had first come to Birmingham as a runaway apprentice from Nottingham and had raised himself to moderate wealth as a stationer, bookseller and circulating library owner, was a self-taught man who had picked up a working knowledge of new ideas, not an original thinker in his own right. His general remarks do, however, show his concern to justify the work of the Court of Conscience in terms of what he believed to be the basically 'economic' motives of human conduct. 'Man in a state of nature has but few wants, and these are ill satisfied,' wrote Hutton: hence the value attached to possession, and the proposition that the dynamic of increasing expectations which powered the economic progress of society was also responsible for much of the petty crime committed by its members:

> The grand struggle of life is to grasp it. . . . Man's wishing to *keep* indicates a wish to *increase*. . . . No man can circumscribe his wants to a shilling. If he can, it must be a *shilling more*. This desire after property puts a man upon undue means to obtain it.[36]

By itself this was not particularly startling: by 1787 the ideas of the new political economy had been widely received, and few, even among Hutton's most conservative critics, could have quarrelled on practical grounds with his association between crime and covetousness. From his general position, however, Hutton was led to views on the social operation of the law which were more controversial. Since the straightforward equitable jurisdiction of a court of conscience was based on common sense and dictated by practical need, it could not only reach down to sections of society beyond the scope of the other petty courts, whose procedures and powers were bound by years of precedent; it could also be related directly to the real principles of social development. In this way the higher courts would be relieved of their burden of nugatory cases, and a more rational form of control, which would help trade rather than hinder it, would be brought to the manufacturing towns. In the whole enormous literature of the law, however, Hutton complained, there was not one work on this neglected subject. 'Equity,' he wrote with almost Benthamite impatience, 'lies dormant as a science without profit. The straight, the easy, the concise road to justice is blocked up and the traveller is led through the dark, long, and intricate windings of the law.'[37] Yet the special value of a court of conscience, which Hutton portrayed as a kind of probation agency rather than as a judicial body in the conventional sense, lay in its ability to supervise the poor for their own real good by deploying the 'science of equity', properly based on 'economic' fundamentals. This was particularly true of cases involving the handling of small debts, the aspect of their affairs in which working people were most in need of guidance,[38] but it was emphasised in all the examples Hutton discussed, and in *A Dissertation on Juries*, published in 1789 as an appendix to his main work, he summarised his opinions by pointing out the 'amazing difference' between a court of law, which could only inflict prescribed penalties for offences already committed, and a court of conscience, which could both settle disputes by suiting its actions to particular circumstances and prevent their recurrence by binding the future behaviour of all those concerned.[39]

Despite his apparently selfish obstruction of the rating proposals in 1790, Hutton's attitude to Birmingham's problems was thus as constructive, according to its own lights, as that of his opponents. His thought was neither original nor consistent in the strict sense, but it did reflect the interaction between the conditions of a rapidly growing commercial and manufacturing centre and a mind which was trying to find a practical application for new ideas. The result, which was to be characteristic of much of the development of English government at all levels during the coming century, was an empirical combination of tendencies which in theory remained incompatible; for the *laisser-faire* position Hutton adopted as champion of the small landlords was joined to an advocacy of reform which was just as interventionist as the legalistic interference of the traditional authorities he condemned. The difference between the two sides of the argument lay, of course, in their respective views of the principles on which authority should act. Had the debate on these remained impersonal much bitter recrimination might have been avoided, and the subsequent course of events in Birmingham might have been less damaging to the town. This did not happen, either with regard to the discussion of courts of conscience or with regard to the rating proposals. In the former case, Hutton's *Dissertation on Juries*, which was written specifically in reply to charges that *Courts of Requests* contained a threat to the future of the jury system,[40] not only made general comparisons between the efficiency of courts of conscience and the cumbersome procedures of their common-law alternative, the hundred court; it also cited particular examples of the time-wasting and money-spinning practices of the attorneys who frequented the latter, drawn from first-hand experience. This cannot have endeared Hutton to the lawyers among his fellow townsmen. In the case of the dispute over small houses, however, the offence he gave was still wider, because after stating his general objection to the rating proposal he went on to support his implicit claim that, properly administered, the existing rates were sufficient for Birmingham's needs by mounting a personal attack on the ethics and competence of the Parish Vestry and the Overseers of the Poor.

These were charged in particular with partiality in their handling of two schemes for contracting for the labour of the able-bodied poor which had been proposed during the autumn of 1789. After some confusion the Overseers had awarded the contract to the inferior of the two plans, ostensibly because it did not entail such an extensive future commitment as its competitor, and because the author of the rejected plan had asked for an excessive guaranteed return on the venture.[41] Now, however, Hutton reopened the question by claiming that one of the Overseers had told him 'that no man would be suffered to transact Parochial business who did not believe in the Trinity'.

> Unable to withhold a smile, I remarked as religion had long since ceased to meddle in the Vestry, it would be absurd to refer the Question to a perfect stranger; that when I turned Catholic, and he turned Priest, I would make my confession. The real motive still lay hid, but under so flimsy a covering that the dimmest eye might see it. 'If we adhere to the Agreement,' says one officer to another, 'We shall be reduced to servants. We may collect the levies, but not be suffered to finger them. Our authority and our consequence will vanish together; and we, like the guardians, shall be reduced to cyphers. While we hold the purse, we hold the power; we will part with neither.'[42]

These insinuations were returned in kind, and Hutton was portrayed as the leader of a Presbyterian conspiracy to grasp exclusive control of Birmingham's government. Each side rejected the public resolutions of the other; motions for an impartial investigation of the Overseers' accounts came to nothing, and so did a suggested compromise in the form of a more flexible scale of assessments on small property. In Liverpool, Manchester, Bristol and Leeds a similar solution had been accepted; in Birmingham the small landlords gave the mob a powerful pretext for its traditionalism the following July by trying to pass the liability for the proposed rate on to their tenants, on the spurious grounds that to do otherwise would deprive them of 'that Benefit . . . which by the common Rights of Man, the dictates of Humanity and Justice, and by the existing Laws of this Country [they] ought to enjoy, namely, gaining a settlement in the Parish'. During the early months of 1791 the attack on the Overseers was extended into opposition to any attempt to change the Guardian Act of 1783, which was the statutory basis of the administration of poor relief in Birmingham, and it was not until May 1791, when an amended Act was passed and small houses were rated in spite of opposition, that the quarrel ended.[43]

In the case of the General Hospital a major initiative on the part of Birmingham was assimilated into the existing round of regional life, and the town's connections with the surrounding area were correspondingly strengthened. In the case of the town's domestic government the relationship was neither so smooth nor so edifying. Despite appearances, the complicated affairs of a rapidly expanding manufacturing town could not be handled indefinitely by a combination of medieval village institutions, *ad hoc* statutory authorities and a non-resident magistracy, the whole still loosely related to the county administration centred on Warwick. Birmingham was lucky to have, in Joseph Carles, a magistrate who lived reasonably near the town and who was prepared to devote himself to its problems. This, however, was a full-time job, and the efforts made to relieve Carles's personal difficulties admitted as much. So also did the police proposals discussed between 1789 and 1793. These were the result of careful deliberation and comparison of conditions in Birmingham with those in other manufacturing areas, and they might well have provided the town with a more adequate framework of order. Unfortunately, however, discussion of the measures coincided with a clash between Birmingham and the Warwickshire county administration. As a result, further action was postponed and became entangled in a prolonged quarrel within the town itself, which was made more acute by the deeper conflict of ideas which underlay it. In the months before the Priestley riots Birmingham's local concerns thus produced a confusion of issues in which personalities, their material interests and their prejudices were all involved. This denied all precedents for harmonious co-operation among the town's leaders, damaged the relationship between them and the inhabitants in general, and frustrated practical action on measures which, had they been adopted, might have enabled the violence of 1791 to be contained more effectively without the intervention of the Home Office and the Dragoons.

Three more years passed before the town found a remedy of sorts in the additions which were made in 1794 to the Warwickshire Commission of the Peace in order to give it greater strength in the Birmingham area.[44] But though Matthew Boulton was 'happy to see such an addition to the Warwickshire Justices' the solution to the problem was more apparent than real. If it demonstrated once more the relationship between Birmingham and its surrounding districts it also exposed the limitations of that relationship. Every aspect of the discussion of local government during the preceding years had pointed to the fact that the conditions which existed in Birmingham needed special consideration. Yet the proposed police Bill never materialised; Hutton's offer of his services on the Warwickshire Commission of the Peace was not taken up; and as for the Court of Conscience, after his experiences in 1791 Hutton expressed himself as 'likely to distribute justice while sitting on a bench in the moon' as to resume its direction.[45] In the changed political climate of the 1790s the extension of the Warwickshire commission, far from treating Birmingham's problems in their own terms, merely emphasised a connection between the rulers in town and county which left the real interests of the former out of account. It is hardly surprising that by 1795 local pamphleteers were complaining that there was not much to choose after all between Birmingham's own leaders and country gentlemen.[46]

NOTES

1 For full details see Langford, *Birm. Life*, I, 154–74.
2 *Aris*, 30 September, 7, 14 October 1765.
3 *Aris*, 18 November 1765.
4 *Aris*, 2 December 1765.
5 Langford, *Birm. Life*, I, 155, 157.
6 *H.M.C. Dartmouth*, III, 235: Ash to the Earl of Dartmouth, 3 April 1777.
7 *Aris*, 9 August, 20 September 1779, 25 September 1780; *Hist. Parl.*, III, 24.
8 Robert E. Schofield, *The Lunar Society of Birmingham, a Social History of Provincial Science and Industry in Eighteenth-century England* (Oxford, 1963), pp. 88, 121–4, 227–230.
9 See below, pp. 199–210.
10 The development and significance of the oratorio festivals are considered in their own right below, pp. 84–5.
11 For this see Conrad Gill, *History of Birmingham*, vol. I, 'Manor and Borough to 1865' (Oxford, 1952), pp. 154–77; the same author's 'Birmingham under the Street Commissioners, 1769–1851', *U.B.H.J.*, I, No. 2 (1948), 255–87; and *V.C.H. Warwicks.*, VII, 318–27.
12 See Sidney and Beatrice Webb, *English Local Government*, vol. 4, Statutory Authorities for Special Purposes (London, 1922, repr. 1963), ch. 4. Manchester secured its Cleaning and Lighting Act in 1765.
13 *V.C.H. Warwicks.*, VII, 4.
14 William Hutton, *History of Birmingham* (3rd edn, Birmingham, 1793), p. 140.
15 *Op. cit.*, p. 139.
16 Public Record Office, Home Office Papers, H.O. 42/18.
17 *Garbett–Lansdowne Letters*, I, Garbett to Shelburne, 29 November 1782; II, Garbett to Sir George Shuckburgh, 5 December 1787. Garbett was seeking special authorisation from the Attorney General for Carles to arrest an Austrian national who was suspected of arranging for the forgery in Birmingham of a large quantity of specie for circulation in the Empire.
18 *A.O.P.*, Garbett to Boulton, 30 May 1790, Boulton to Gilbert, 21 October 1790, Gilbert to Boulton, 30 October 1790. For Gilbert see *D.N.B.* and *Hist. Parl.*, II, 499–501.
19 *A.O.P.*, Boulton to Gilbert, 20 November 1790.
20 *A.O.P.*, Garbett to Boulton, 7 April 1793.
21 *A.O.P.*, Carles to Boulton, 17 February 1793; Aris, 18 February 1793.
22 *A.O.P.*, John Brooke (attorney, magistrate and coroner for Warwickshire) to Boulton, 16 February 1792; correspondence between Carles, Boulton and John Collins, banker, of Stafford, February–March 1793.
23 Home Office Papers, H.O. 42/3–14, *passim*; H.O. 42/15, lists of convicts awaiting transportation, 14 October 1789, giving name, sentence and place of conviction for the

years 1786–89, which show Warwick Assizes second only to Gloucester as the leading source of convicts, apart from Middlesex and the Old Bailey; H.O. 42/21, Walter Landor to Henry Dundas, 9 September 1792; P. M. Styles, 'The development of county administration in the late eighteenth and early nineteenth centuries, illustrated by the records of the Warwickshire Court of Quarter Sessions, 1773–1837', *Dugdale Society Occasional Papers*, No. 4 (1933), pp. 11, 12, 25, 26.

24 *A.O.P.*, Watt to Boulton, 16, 17 November 1789. Manchester obtained its Act in 1792: A. E. Redford, *History of Local Government in Manchester*, 3 vols (London, 1939), I, 97.

25 *Aris*, 14 December 1789, 8 February 1790.

26 *Aris*, 1 March 1790.

27 *Aris*, 15 March 1790.

28 *V.C.H. Warwicks.*, VII, 321.

29 *Aris*, 11 October 1790.

30 *Garbett–Lansdowne Letters*, II, Garbett to Lansdowne, 27 November 1789.

31 'The Life of William Hutton, written by Himself' in Llewellyn Jewitt, *The Life of William Hutton and History of the Hutton Family* (London, 1872), pp. 181–7; Langford, *Birm. Life*, I, 184. B.R.L., Hutton-Beale MSS, draft quoting Hutton's offer to serve as a magistrate, 19 July 1792; Home Office Papers, H.O. 43/4, Dundas to Sir Robert Lawley, 26 July 1792, asking him to check Hutton's credentials.

32 Hutton, *History of Birmingham*, p. 141.

33 'Life... written by Himself', in Jewitt, *op. cit.*, p. 187.

34 See Giles Jacob, *A New Law Dictionary* (7th edn, 1756), which gives a concise history of courts of conscience and goes to some length to distinguish them from the conciliar Court of Requests. The former were derived from a statute of 9 Henry VIII which established the Court of Conscience of the City of London to hear civil disputes between freemen involving sums under forty shillings. In the eighteenth century similar courts were established in Southwark, Westminster and the Tower Hamlets and, outside the capital, in Lincoln, Birmingham, St Albans, Liverpool and Canterbury—a mixture of different types of community which suggests that the courts' function was not clearly defined and was probably different in each particular instance. Coventry toyed with the idea of establishing a court of conscience during 1781 but seems to have dropped it. See *Jopson*, 12 November 1781.

35 1787.

36 *Courts of Requests*, p. 2. For the sources of Hutton's method *cf.* David Hume's derivation of the idea of justice from 'the selfishness and confined generosity of man, along with the scanty provision nature has made for his wants', *Treatise of Human Nature*, Book III, part 2, section ii, 'of the origin of Justice and Property' (Everyman edition, vol. II, p. 22); and, at a more distant remove, Adam Smith's explanation of the 'propensity to truck, barter and exchange one thing for another', which gave rise to the division of labour, in terms of man's dependence in a state of nature on the help of others, 'which it is vain for him to expect ... from their benevolence only': *Wealth of Nations* (ed. E. Cannan, London, 1904), p. 14.

37 *Courts of Requests*, p. 6.

38 *Courts of Requests*, pp. 23–4.

39 *Dissertation on Juries*, pp. 53–4.

40 *Dissertation on Juries*, p. 2. Hutton had exposed himself to this charge not only by the content of his ideas but by calling his original book *Courts of Requests* when he meant Courts of Conscience, and by referring to their 'first rise under Wolsey', which not only revealed confusion in his own mind but perpetuated the common misconception of the courts' origins.

41 *Aris*, 31 August, 7 September, 26 October, 2–23 November 1789.

42 *Aris*, 11 October 1790.

43 *Aris*, 18, 25 October, 1, 15, 22 November, 6, 13 December 1790, 28 February, 7, 14 March 1791; Langford, *Birm. Life*, I, 472.

44 *A.O.P.*, Heneage Legge to Boulton, 16 December 1793, 23 January 1794; Boulton to Legge, 2 February 1794.

45 B.R.L., Hutton-Beale MSS, William Hutton to Catherine Hutton, 30 October 1791.

46 See below, p. 267.

II

THE CHALLENGE
TO THE CAPITAL

When Samuel Aris first thought of issuing a 'Miscellany' supplement to the *Birmingham Gazette* he must have spent some time planning the contents of his new venture. 'Feature' articles, of more lasting interest than the passing news in the main paper, would obviously supply most of his copy, but he really needed something both topical and permanent with which to launch the project. He could hardly have chosen better than the 'Account of Canals' which headed the first Miscellany on 30 November 1772. After reporting the progress of the Trent and Mersey canal this passed to a description of the country that would be served by the navigation and the other projects associated with it. The Staffordshire Potteries in particular were depicted as good common man's country with plenty of opportunities for those willing to work, a place well supplied with provisions where children could earn their keep and a numerous offspring was not a burden. A spirit of emulation was abroad; men of genius and fortune strove for the honour of themselves and their country; the imitative arts were conducted with assiduity and success. The account ended with some sound advice. A more direct link with the capital than that provided by the rather circuitous route of the projected Coventry and Oxford canals would soon be needed, not so much by Midlanders as by Londoners. The latter could not afford to miss the chance of remaining in contact with a region of England which, thanks to its new outlets to Liverpool, Bristol and Hull, was fast becoming capable of sustaining its own independent development and of setting the pace for the rest of the country.

Nothing that happened to them during the later eighteenth century captured the imagination or so continuously retained the attention of West Midlanders as the fact that their home country was becoming the nodal point in a new system of communications and transport. Quite apart from the material benefits conferred by the canals themselves, their building exerted a major influence on the developing self-consciousness of the region. It made the interdependence of different parts of the West Midlands impossible to ignore; it made the region as a whole increasingly aware of its relationships with other parts of England; and it produced a continuous exchange of views on a subject of both regional and national importance, which reflected not merely the rise of one centre, but rather the need for particular interests in different places to learn to co-operate with each other, and with more distant areas, for the sake of mutual advantage.

The problems involved in the successful promotion of a canal navigation are well illustrated by the campaign conducted during 1765 by Josiah Wedgwood and others on behalf of the Trent and Mersey canal,[1] the first of the major enterprises which stimulated and complemented the development of the region's internal navigations by linking the West Midlands with other parts of the country.[2] Wedgwood and his fellow backers had to do four things: to recruit support from the different towns and interests that would be affected; to present their scheme in a way which would generate informed public discussion; to coax the landowners into agreeing to the necessary invasion of their property, and to develop political connections strong enough to ensure a safe passage for the requisite Act of Parliament. They showed themselves equally adroit at all four, and Wedgwood in particular made skilful use of the instinct for social susceptibilities which served his other enterprises so well.[3]

Wedgwood outlined his strategy early in April 1765 in a letter to Erasmus Darwin of Lichfield, whom he described as 'Generalissimo in this affair'. Thomas Bentley and his Liverpool friends were in contact with Sir William Meredith, their Member of Parliament, and advised an approach to John Tarleton, the mayor of the port. Accordingly, great importance was attached to formal overtures to Liverpool from the inland cities and towns which would have a stake in the canal, 'as we apprehend an address will come with a better grace from one Mayor and Corporation to another than from an individual'. Newcastle under Lyme, which was also seeking the patronage of the Earl of Stafford, was to lead the way; Darwin was asked to persuade Lichfield corporation to follow suit, and 'if we had something of the same sort from Birmingham, sign'd by some Gentn. who are known in Liverpool, it must still have the greater weight there ...'. Later in the month the press campaign which was to support these overtures was also taking shape. In London two pieces a week were to appear in the *St James's Chronicle*, and in the provinces similar coverage was planned in the Liverpool, Manchester, Chester, Derby, Nottingham and Birmingham papers.[4]

Despite these extensive plans, however, Wedgwood was well aware that the courtship of public approval was a delicate business, best conducted 'by degrees and by stealth as it were', and he took care not to advertise the canal too importunately, lest 'individuals of this Public' should think 'that instruction is offered them *without their asking for it*', and 'counteract rather than coincide with any measures intended for their benefit'. When Samuel Garbett suggested that the promoters should earn some extra publicity by arranging for a facetious attack on the canal in order to stir up 'some judicious skirmishing in the Birmingham Gazette' Wedgwood's reaction was therefore cautious. He saw the point himself, of course, but nevertheless felt that men were 'too foolish to be jested with in that manner'. After this, occasional pieces for the press were still used to stimulate and maintain curiosity about the canal, but Wedgwood now advised his colleagues not to 'write much in the Publick Papers, but to draw up one plain Pamphlett upon the subject'.[5] The result was Thomas Bentley's *View of the Advantages of Inland Navigation*, drafted with punctilious care during the late summer of 1765 lest inelegancies of style, a misplaced word or an unintentional innuendo should offend the fastidious, anger the owners of property or make enemies among the politicians. Eventually even Wedgwood found it hard to have 'the Uniting of seas & distant countrys' held up for the sake of Erasmus Darwin's more egregious corrections, but nevertheless several of Darwin's amendments were real ones. A landowner imbued with the principles of Capability Brown might well have been offended by the prospect of a canal 'as straight as *Fleet Ditch*' at the bottom of his meadow: to have his lawn terminated or divided by water was quite another matter. Too obsequious an address to the great would only diminish the stature of the promoters, and Darwin insisted that 'nobody writes Grace & Rt. honourable, but Taylors and such like folks . . .'. Particular care was taken over the dedication of the work to both Houses of Parliament, where the wrong choice of words might well have proved fatal. The entire political world of the 1760s was hypersensitive to criticism, no section of it more so than that which was held responsible for the severe damage currently being inflicted on the English economy by American reaction to the Stamp Act. An apparently innocent reference to the 'design for reviving our (decayed) manufactures and commerce' was therefore removed from the dedication lest it should be construed as an affront to the recently fallen administration of George Grenville, 'on some of whom we chiefly depend'. However much the politicians might deserve reproach, it was they who would decide the future of the Trent and Mersey canal, and Wedgwood was taking no chances.[6]

Though he knew the risks involved in its creation, however, Wedgwood was convinced that 'a bustle, a popular bustle must carry' the navigation 'through all difficultys at last', and in his reactions to the drafting of Bentley's work caution was balanced by impatient insistence that 'a Pamphlet we must have, or our design will be defeated'.[7] It is this urgent but sophisticated awareness of public opinion which is the most striking feature of the campaign for the Trent and Mersey canal. This is not to say that the tasks of rousing the towns and cities on the route, making friends in the right places and constructing a lobby within the 'structure of politics' were neglected; but they were not conceived in isolation, and they were secondary to the main objective. The proposed canal was to be vindicated in the first instance by informed public controversy. After it, those who persisted in opposing the scheme would stand revealed as retrogressive obscurantists, and the passage of the necessary Bill through an enlightened legislature would be merely the logical conclusion of a rational argument. Though canal navigation was not a matter of national politics—at least, not in the eighteenth century's conventional understanding of the term—it was becoming a subject of wide concern, and in the strategy adopted by the navigators can be seen the genesis of a relationship between politics and public opinion more characteristic of nineteenth century England than of the age of oligarchy.

Nevertheless Wedgwood and his associates had to spend much of their time countering or conciliating the opposition of particular groups. Especially intransigent were the 'Cheshire Gentlemen'—the proprietors of the older Weaver and Sankey river navigations, whose offers of concessions, alternating with threats to build their own canal, combined with hints from the Duke of Bridgwater about the extension of his Lancashire works to cast a cloud of uncertainty over the support of Liverpool and over the actual disposition of the western end of the Grand Trunk.[8] Nor were older vested interests the only obstacles to be overcome. Though Samuel Garbett enlisted the support of the Society of Arts for the canal and offered his own technical criticisms of Bentley's pamphlet in October 1765,[9] his initial ardour cooled noticeably thereafter. By December he was being very difficult. The £300 subscription confidently promised from Birmingham earlier in the year had not materialised, and Garbett, who was now raising all sorts of spurious objections to the proposed government of the Grand

Trunk and to its plans for a southward branch to the Birmingham area, announced that he was 'determined to be neuter'.[10] The truth, however, was not that Garbett and his local colleagues had lost interest in canals but that the ideas on inland navigation propagated earlier in the year had struck independent roots. If there was to be a branch from Birmingham to the Grand Trunk, then it should pass through Wolverhampton and the south Staffordshire coalfield, not through Tamworth and Lichfield, as originally planned, and the men of the Black Country wanted control over its construction and management to be in their own hands. The result was that so far as direct participation was concerned the Birmingham area was lost to the promoters of the Trent and Mersey canal, who gave up the idea of including branches in their petition to Parliament and confined themselves to proposing a route which would facilitate junctions with other ventures at a later date.

During the second major period of canal activity in the 1780s the problem of particular opposition was more complex. By then most people were convinced in principle of the advantages of inland navigation, and discussion of canals was predominantly concerned not with the presentation of a general argument but with the reconciliation of conflicting interests. The way in which this made different parts of the West Midlands aware of each other's existence and helped to weld them together to form a wider sense of regional identity is well illustrated by the course of the dispute of 1783 between the proprietors of the original Birmingham canal, opened in 1770, which joined the town to the Staffordshire and Worcestershire canal at Aldersley, and the promoters of a new canal from the Wednesbury collieries to the lower part of Birmingham, and thence to the Coventry canal at Fazeley. A letter in *Aris's Birmingham Gazette* on 13 January 1783 pointed out that this local quarrel involved the future of the entire region's connection with the rest of the country. The Coventry and Oxford companies, delayed by internal disagreement and by financial setbacks during the American war, had exhausted their original capital without achieving a junction with either the Grand Trunk or the river Thames.[11] A link, such as that proposed, between Wednesbury and the Coventry canal at Fazeley would help considerably to lower the cost of carrying coal to Oxford. This would increase the volume of traffic on the Coventry and Oxford canals, which in turn would relieve the financial pressure on the companies concerned. With this in mind, a joint meeting of the proprietors of the Grand Trunk, the Coventry and Oxford companies and the promoters of the Birmingham New Navigation had guaranteed to complete the Coventry and Oxford canals, provided that the canal from Wednesbury to Fazeley was built. Once this had been done the connections between the whole of the West Midlands and the rest of the country, particularly with London and Hull, would be vastly improved. The letter complained that, after obstructing such an important development, the proprietors of the original Birmingham canal were now trying to steal the new company's idea by offering to build the proposed canal themselves. A settlement was eventually reached when 'The Company of the Proprietors of the Birmingham and Fazeley Canal Navigation', incorporated by Act of Parliament in 1783, was amalgamated with the original Birmingham Canal company to form 'The Company of the Proprietors of the Birmingham and Birmingham and Fazeley Canal Navigations'. This acted with the Grand Trunk company to complete the Coventry canal's connection to the Trent and Mersey canal in 1785.[12]

Before this solution was achieved, however, obstruction had to be met from another sectional interest. Early in 1785 the mine owners in north Warwickshire, fearing that higher-quality coal from the Wednesbury pits would be brought down the new canal to deprive them of their local monopoly on the Coventry market, mounted an opposition to the Bill for confirming the agreement with the Grand Trunk and the Birmingham companies. Instead they tried to instigate an independent proposal on the part of the Coventry company to extend the Trent (Burton) canal and to make the Tame and Anker rivers navigable as far as Atherstone.[13] This move, which was not in the interests of the other shareholders, split the Coventry company and filled the columns of *Jopson's Coventry Mercury* between January and March 1785 with correspondence on the issue. On 3 January the paper reported two meetings. One, held in Coventry by the main body of shareholders, endorsed the original agreement and offered in addition to reduce the tonnage on Wednesbury coal from $1\frac{1}{2}d$ to $1d$ per mile over the new canal. The other, held by the mine owners at Atherstone, repudiated the Coventry resolutions and in turn resolved to petition against any preferential treatment of Wednesbury coal. How, asked a second contributor to Jopson's paper, could Wednesbury coal, from a water distance of fifty-three miles, be expected to compete in Coventry with the product of the Warwickshire pits, none of which was more than eight miles from the city? As this letter pointed out, the Birmingham companies could hardly be expected to spend some £80,000 on their own project, still less complete the Coventry canal, without the encouragement of some preference. In any case, even if Wednesbury coal did pay a reduced tonnage, that from the local pits would still be far cheaper.

Though they did not press the Tame and Anker plan, the Warwickshire mine owners certainly seemed to be obstructing the completion of an important and wide-ranging design for the sake of their own local monopoly. Nevertheless, as the prime movers of the original Coventry canal and as one of its main sources of capital, they were entitled to some consideration, especially as they had also committed large sums of money to opening new collieries[14] on the understanding that the tonnage rates would be the same for everyone. From this point of view the final position of the Warwickshire mine owners—that they too should share the benefits of any cut in the rates—seems quite reasonable; for any permanent effects on the proprietors' profits which might follow a general reduction of charges could be forestalled by provision for a review of the rates after the completed canal had been in use for a time.[15] The case for conciliation was put by 'An Old Observer' on 24 January. Collieries and canals were essentially interdependent, and developments in both were justified only if they served the public. Both parties to the dispute were guilty of an unthinking, uncompromising local solidarity which served no useful purpose. The proprietors, who had not distinguished themselves in the past for breadth of vision, had only themselves to blame for the opposition of the mine owners, among whom there had never previously been 'so much agreement . . . as to bring them into the same room together'. Even if they carried their Bill without meeting the mine owners' reasonable demands the proprietors alone would stand little chance of raising the capital needed to complete the canal. The dispute ended in July 1785 when the Coventry company finally gave a firm undertaking to complete its line to Fazeley under the terms originally stipulated in the agreement with the Grand Trunk and the Birmingham companies. The Oxford company now felt able to complete its line below Banbury, and the next five years saw the completion of the remaining sections of the continuous water route joining Lancashire to the Midlands, and the Midlands to the Thames, which Josiah Wedgwood had foreseen twenty-five years earlier.[16]

Despite the happy result in this instance, however, the overall usefulness of canal navigations was in danger of being impaired by the uncontrolled multiplication of individual projects. The open debate which this situation provoked exerted a powerful influence on the practical formation of public attitudes in the West Midlands. In particular, the competing claims of rival projects brought practical men face to face with important aspects of parliamentary responsibility. The questions that were raised in this way may not have been so extensive as those which attended the proposals of the political reformers, but because they were more tangible their influence on the outlook of those who confronted them was at least as great, and certainly more immediate. Those who had committed themselves to the original navigations, which had secured parliamentary approval during the first period of canal activity before the American war, now found their commitment threatened by newer schemes which seemed to be inspired less by enlarged views than by the prospect of gain for particular interests. As supporters of the original Staffordshire and Worcestershire canal pointed out in 1785, to give *carte blanche* to this process would discourage genuine initiative in the national interest because it would destroy public trust in the permanence of canal legislation.[17] In this particular dispute, in which the point at issue was the application of the Stourbridge and Dudley companies for a new cut between the Severn and Viscount Dudley's collieries at Tipton in Staffordshire, extensive private interests were clearly engaged on both sides. The opposition's appropriation of all the public virtue involved should therefore not be taken literally. More significant than the particular rights and wrongs of the question is the fact that 'the Public Faith held in Parliamentary Establishments' to which the Staffordshire and Worcestershire men appealed became a standard invocation in discussion of competing canal proposals. By virtue of their scale and the large quantities of capital involved, these directed greater attention than any previous development had done to the role which the legislature ought to play as mediator between the public interest on the one hand and private property and enterprise on the other. This was well demonstrated in 1786, when the Stourbridge and Dudley companies extended their designs of the previous year to include a Bill for a direct line from Stourbridge to Diglis, on the Severn below Worcester. Opposition, again led by the Staffordshire and Worcestershire company, condemned this as 'a cruel infringement of private property and a base violation of the sacred faith of Parliament'; the *Birmingham Gazette* carried a long discussion of the difference between canal companies as potential private monopolies and turnpike trusts as an 'estate of the Public', and the defeat of the Stourbridge and Dudley Bill was greeted by bells, bonfires and feasting along the entire line of the Staffordshire and Worcestershire canal. Similar controversy on a still larger scale accompanied the promotion of the Worcester and Birmingham canal between 1789 and 1791, which, though supported by more than 6,000 petitioners from Birmingham itself, obtained its Act only at the second attempt after opposition from the Staffordshire and Worcestershire, from the original Birmingham navigations and from other interests as far away as Oxford.[18]

In these ways the building of the canals opened up an important new field in which the engagement of public policy was a simple matter of practical prudence, quite apart from any principles which might be involved. As Samuel Garbett pointed out in 1793, inland navigation should be seriously investigated as a 'national political object'. Instead of 'allowing speculators to make partial patches as private jobs, and thereby to obtain possession of ground and water that will counteract the great lines for public accommodation', canal projectors should have been directed by authority to the best overall routes, and no more time should be lost in initiating official plans for a direct trunk connection between London and the Midlands. From this Garbett turned to the far-reaching social, economic and political effects of canal developments in the Birmingham area itself, in particular those between Birmingham and Worcester, Warwick and Stratford, and between Dudley and Netherton. All these he considered superfluous, especially the last, and he feared that by providing more outlets for coal than could be adequately supplied without straining the present and foreseeable future capacity of the south Staffordshire collieries they would force up the local price of the fuel and thereby do serious damage to the industries of the hardware district. Under different circumstances Garbett would probably have set little store by this last concern. On this occasion, however, he was concerned with the possible repercussions of a sudden increase in the demand for coal on a specific political situation. 'The colliers,' he wrote,

> have lately advanced their wages, and they know that the country is dependent upon them, which is an important consideration. For they do not want either sagacity or disposition to avail themselves of it, and combinations among them are frequently severely felt by the proprietors of coal. . . . Consequently, it is highly requisite to be cautious of adopting any measure that will evidently increase their power and inevitably bring difficulties upon many thousands of manufacturers, who have certainly less deference for the law than they had before the riots which lately disgraced us.[19]

Whether Garbett's call for more rational planning was entirely consistent with his own earlier prevarication over the Trent and Mersey canal, or where the balance was struck in his own mind between his concern for the hardware district in particular and his zeal for the accommodation of the public at large, only he could say. But from his appreciation of the part which the canals were playing in the development of the Birmingham area, not only in economic but also in social and political terms, and from his concern to establish direct long-distance connections between London and the Midlands as a whole, it is clear that the moral of Samuel Aris's 'Account of Canals' of 1772 had not gone unheeded.

The similarities between canal and turnpike development are obvious. There was the same need in both cases for co-operation between the different places which would be affected. In both cases, too, initiative was subject to the processes of eighteenth century legislation, and success depended not only on the reconciliation of opinion but also on skilful use of the available means of political influence. The differences, though perhaps less conspicuous, are equally important. The improvement of road communications was neither such an innovation nor so particularly associated with the region as the canals could claim to be.[20] Because the scale on which most turnpike trusts operated was smaller than that of the canal navigations they tended to be eclipsed in popular consciousness by the newer, more exciting form of transport. The turnpikes did not produce anything like the same amount of correspondence in the newspapers as did the canals, and the routine notices inserted by officers of existing trusts caused little comment. People were used to turnpike activities and therefore took less notice of them. The first part of the road between Birmingham and Coventry had been turnpiked in 1723, and the rest of it was treated in the same way during the next thirty years,[21] but the fact that in 1781 William Hutton could still describe it, together with the Dudley road, as 'despicable beyond description'[22] suggests that turnpiking had not made much difference to the quality of roads in the West Midlands.

It is, however, precisely in the more commonplace nature of attempts to improve the roads that their value lies for the present purpose, for they draw attention to the elements of continuity in the development of the West Midlands. If the improvements in Staffordshire, which took Josiah Wedgwood to London on turnpike business in 1763, mounted him once more on the same 'hobby horse' in 1765, and in July of that year received extensive notice in the *Birmingham Gazette*, invite comparison with the excited reaction to the canals, the Overseer of the Highways at Netherseal, who four years later cited sixteenth century legislation to remind local magistrates of their responsibilities for the maintenance of the roads, drew attention to the problem of adapting long-established practice to changing circumstances.[23] The closer integration of the turnpike trusts into the ordinary fabric of life also meant that it was they rather than the canals which acted as a ground for the first awareness of the region's potential development, particularly in its smaller towns and villages. Here they had a direct effect on property values by offering the prospect of improved communications. For the same reason they interacted, both as incentive and as result, with the process of enclosure. Though financed on a different basis and from more localised sources than the canals, they attracted support from a wider social range, which included not only the landowners but also tenant farmers, tradesmen and a variety of other small investors.[24] And they became one focus for the tensions that accompanied the processes of social and economic change.

The latter was particularly true of the irksome regulations which governed the use of the roads. The various Broad Wheel Acts,[25] passed between 1753 and 1773 in an attempt to preserve travelling surfaces by prescribing the width of waggon wheels, were widely regarded as an unfair burden on the small freeholder, whose position was already precarious. As 'A Lover of his Country' put it in 1774 in the course of a letter which was mainly concerned with the general complaint about the disappearance of the English yeoman, 'The Maxims of the Broad Wheeled and Rolling Plans' were

> Calculated so very severe on the lower class of Farmers (Who are not able to purchase such expensive machines) as to render them incapable to gain a comfortable livelihood, or even a support; and unless some set of expedients can be thought of to relieve them, that useful set of men will soon be lost in the commonwealth.[26]

Turnpike legislation thus became associated with more widely based misgivings. Efforts to enforce the regulations had indeed produced sporadic agitation among

the farmers during the years before 'A Lover of his Country' wrote to the
Birmingham Gazette. In November 1762 the farmers of Worcestershire announced that

> A *much esteemed*, and very industrious set of *gentry*, from no other motive *to be
> sure* than the *good of their country*, having of late made a trade of informing
> against some hundreds of farmers etc. in Worcestershire and these parts, for
> drawing with more horses on the public roads than the law allows, very many
> contributions have been raised. But we hear, an application will be made to
> Parliament the ensuing session for redressing so manifest a grievance to the
> Farmers in general etc., who otherwise must lay aside business, or submit to a
> kind of perpetual taxation from the above set of worthies.

This was followed in January 1763 by a resolution to petition against the Broad
Wheel Acts.[27] The farmers were up in arms again in June 1768. This time
they met at Warwick to oppose a Bill to enforce the universal use of broad-
wheeled waggons, and their appeal for support from other counties and parishes
was answered by the Staffordshire farmers, who met at Stafford early in July.[28]
When the issue involved was not confined to any single trust, but concerned
rather the effects of general legislation, turnpike business could thus provoke
extensive reactions. Whether it appeared as laws to increase the efficiency of
highway maintenance, or, more visibly, in the form of officials whose zeal for
the rules threatened the customary accommodation between the law as it was
written and the law as it was locally enforced, the demonstrations of 1762 and
1768 expressed widespread suspicion of any interference with habitual practice.
When, at their summer assizes of 1763, the High Sheriff and Grand Jury of
Worcestershire condemned the cider tax, which was 'to be collected in a manner
equally odious and offensive to the country, and unprofitable to the public
revenue',[29] they spoke a language which the farmers of the county already
understood because they had used it themselves during the previous winter. Six
years later Worcestershire was prominent among the counties which petitioned
after the Middlesex election dispute; Warwickshire came close to following its
neighbour's example, and unwonted stirrings were reported among the freeholders of Staffordshire. If the importance of these activities is to be measured
solely by their repercussions among the great, the farmers' meetings at Worcester
in 1762 and at Warwick and Stafford in 1768 may not have amounted to much;
but they contributed nonetheless to the rising groundswell of resentment which
influenced local events during the formative period in the political experience of the West Midlands consummated by the Warwickshire election of
1774.[30]

The canals and turnpikes multiplied the West Midlands' connections with a
wider world. On 4 July 1768 the *Birmingham Gazette* noticed the improvement
in the postal services. The Anglo-Irish post now ran six times a week, and letters
could be sent direct to destinations in other parts of the country via the cross-
posts, 'by which means, correspondence between this town and many other
commercial parts of both kingdoms will be greatly accelerated'. By 1777 fifty-
two coaches a week, each carrying up to six passengers, left Birmingham for
London, a journey of about nineteen hours; sixteen coaches a week went to
Bristol, four to Coventry and four to Sheffield.[31] By the end of the American

war Birmingham had established its own links with the world and was no longer so dependent on London for its news. Of the two Birmingham papers, Myles Swinney's *Birmingham and Stafford Chronicle* in particular had made considerable use of direct contacts in the out-ports as sources for the latest developments overseas during the war,[32] and as far as commercial matters were concerned, reactions in the West Midlands to events in other countries were now far quicker than those of the capital. When Joseph II of Austria closed his dominions to British goods in 1784, for example, Samuel Garbett knew of it from the Birmingham firm of Oakridge & Marindin, which had business contacts in Prague, months before the news made any impact on official circles in London, and it was only after the Birmingham Commercial Committee had alerted its counterparts in the other manufacturing centres that the Ministry began to take notice. William Pitt's first intimation that something was amiss seems to have come from the urgent memorandum which the Manchester Chamber of Trade sent to the Treasury as a result of Birmingham's warning. Not until the memorandum had itself been authenticated by the copy of the Emperor's edict which Garbett had sent to Manchester did the Minister begin to take the situation seriously; and even after this the attitude of Whitehall, based on official estimates of trade with the Empire and on the assumption that the edict was unlikely to be enforced, remained one of polite disbelief. It is not surprising that Garbett found the reaction of George Rose, Pitt's under-secretary at the Treasury, quite intolerable:

> If Mr. Rose thinks the amount of the trade between England and the Emperor's dominions is to be known by the duties paid, he judges at random. ... I have not the smallest doubt that Mr. Rose's attention to this business is like his answer, and like the attention of the Minister in Vienna, who sent no account of the Edict. The whole is "Sir, your most obedient and most humble servant etc. etc. ... ".[33]

Garbett's anger at the diplomatic persiflage and masterly inactivity of the central government in this incident is one indication of the way in which manufacturing interests in the provinces were beginning to chafe under the conventional leadership of the politicians in London. It was in these circumstances that a distinctive attitude to public affairs was most clearly articulated among those who were leading the development of the West Midlands.

The affair of the Imperial Edict was but one episode among many in the development of the manufacturers' associations which, in 1785, culminated in the formation of the General Chamber of Manufacturers of Great Britain under the leadership of Josiah Wedgwood and Samuel Garbett, in order to oppose William Pitt's proposed treaty of commerce with Ireland.[34] The ideas which produced this first full-scale attempt to bring the pressure of industrial opinion in the provinces to bear on the political process at Westminster had been conceived and canvassed by Samuel Garbett as early as 1766, but it was only in the more propitious economic and political conditions of the 1780s that the Birmingham leader's suggestions became feasible. Because the importance of industrial interests in the economy had increased, the manufacturers no longer felt the need to make their own actions dependent on those of the merchants; some of the leaders of the new interest, particularly in the north, had gained political experience in Christopher Wyvill's county association movement, and after the crisis of the American war the political process itself was more responsive to organised lobbying on a large scale. A further stimulus to united action on the part of the manufacturers came from the growing burden of taxation on a wide range of industrial raw materials. In 1784 a proposed excise on bricks, increases in coal duties and taxes on fustians and calicoes provoked widespread opposition in the Midlands and Lancashire. All this reinforced the growing conviction that the politicians were abysmally ignorant of the problems of industry and dangerously unaware of the latter's importance to the nation. Resistance to the receipts tax of 1783 had already produced widely publicised proposals for a national association of Guardians of Commerce; at the same time Samuel Garbett had revived his scheme for a national lobby, and provincial commercial committees had been founded in Glasgow, Birmingham, Sheffield, Manchester, Norwich and Liverpool.[35]

Faced with these portents, it is tempting to leap to the conclusion that when the General Chamber of Manufacturers was organised during the early months of 1785 supporters in the provinces sprang up spontaneously, ready armed to challenge the circumscribed views of men whose only skill in 'Subjects that regard Society' lay in the 'narrow Cunning which is ridiculously called Politicks'.[36] In fact the reactions of the manufacturers during the preceding three years had been marked as much by mutual recrimination as by a steadily growing sense of common interest. They had disagreed over the importance to be attached to erstwhile colonial markets in the negotiations which ended the American war. Despite Samuel Garbett's efforts to co-ordinate responses to the Imperial Edict, Manchester and Sheffield had acted on their own, with the result that neither their appeal to the British government, nor Garbett's own attempt to seek a postponement of the edict through the good offices of Lord Shelburne and the diplomats, achieved anything. When the Irish proposals did finally provoke something like a united response the General Chamber was brought into being only with great difficulty, and the original intention to make it into a positive political agency with full powers to influence Parliament on behalf of the manufacturers had to be abandoned, so that the chamber remained a loose federation of separate interests. Even this did not take its intended form. The provincial chambers, which were supposed to exercise the real power of policy making, were never established, and the important decisions continued to be taken by the existing commercial committees.[37] The fissiparous tendencies which were to cause the General Chamber's disintegration in February 1787 all had to be overcome at every stage, even in the 'separate strongholds'[38] of the new manufacturers themselves.

To anyone who was inclined to doubt the fact the columns of *Aris's Birmingham Gazette* during the years before the foundation of the General Chamber of Manufacturers offered ample proof that the times did indeed 'open a new aera in the commercial world'.[39] As early as 1778 William Gibbons of Bristol, one of the leading ironmasters, had warned the men of the hardware district of the consequences they could expect if Lord North persisted in his intention of easing some of the restrictions on Irish trade and setting it on the same basis as that of England in colonial markets.[40] In 1780 another address from Bristol, this time to the users of brass and other copper alloys, set out to rouse its readers 'from supine neglect to a state of active attention'. This was followed by the formation of the Birmingham Brass Company, a co-operative enterprise intended to defeat the designs of a price-fixing combination among the miners and smelters of copper, which in turn led to a price war during 1781 between the new company and the warehouse of the Parys Mine Company of Anglesea, the existing monopolist. Between March and June 1782 meetings were held in Birmingham and Stourbridge to draw up petitions against proposed taxes on land and water carriage. The following year the *Birmingham Gazette* reported action to oppose the receipts tax in Birmingham, Wolverhampton, Walsall, Worcester and Shrewsbury, and printed a lengthy discussion by Lords Mansfield and Kenyon of the legal aspects of the proposal.[41] All these individual concerns combined with growing anxiety about the effects of alterations in the customs regulations on the town's overseas trade to bring about the foundation in August 1783 of the Birmingham Commercial Committee.[42]

Despite this mounting activity, however, all the difficulties which beset the General Chamber of Manufacturers as a whole were present in the West Midlands. The very nature of private enterprise and the extent of the risks taken by individuals to further their own projects meant that co-operation was to be achieved only after patient persuasion, and then with the minimum of disclosure, either to potential rivals or to the public at large. The manifesto of the Birmingham Commercial Committee against the taxation of industrial raw materials equated freedom with secrecy and proclaimed that every manufacturer had a natural right to demand both.[43] In the same vein Samuel Garbett described 'liberality among traders of real ability' as never going further,

> even to a brother, than giving him a preference when terms are equal.... This
> is the first and settled principle amongst the more settled and respectable charac-
> ters, and any trader, who in commerce requires more from his friend or brother,
> acts illiberally.[44]

The problem of co-ordinating the reactions of men who only half trusted each other clearly called for special abilities. Though his presence may have been missed at the General Chamber's meetings in London, it was therefore probably a blessing in disguise that Garbett took offence at the Ministry's unwillingness to recognise the provincial commercial committees and refused to go up to the capital. By staying in Birmingham Garbett, who was virtually the only person whom individuals were prepared to trust, and who alone was prepared to devote his time to controlling local reactions, performed a vital service to the chamber. Even he was unable to persuade the Birmingham committee to co-operate fully with the delegates from Sheffield and Staffordshire;[45] but without his untiring efforts the General Chamber might well have found itself without any support at all from the West Midlands.

The greatest difficulty Garbett faced was that of overcoming the fluctuation of local reactions between fevered enthusiasm and apathy. Associated with this was the need to co-ordinate the activities of the Birmingham Commercial Committee with those of the ironmasters, who were meeting at West Bromwich. Once these problems had been solved, and a sustained expression of opinion had been created, it had to be supported by personal representation and directed so as to exert the greatest possible influence at Westminster. During May and June 1785 the question of choice which was thus raised, between association with the political opposition and open disclosure of information at the bar of the House of Commons, or more confidential approaches to the government itself, was to produce a revealing disagreement within the General Chamber between Wedgwood and the Manchester men, who favoured the first alternative, and Garbett and his fellow Midlanders, who preferred the second.

When Garbett first wrote to Matthew Boulton in London at Wedgwood's request during the last week of February 1785 plans for the General Chamber of Manufacturers had only just begun to take definite shape. In Birmingham, however, the Commercial Committee had already considered the Irish commercial proposals, and Garbett was able to supply Boulton with copies of its resolutions on them for circulation at a preliminary meeting of manufacturers in the capital. At West Bromwich, too, the West Midland ironmasters had considered the Irish measures in detail, and were preparing independently to enlist their own political support.[46] Garbett's immediate concern was therefore to avoid going too far too fast. At this stage, for example, the Birmingham committee wanted to widen the issue by discussing a paper on policy towards the West Indian plantations. As Garbett said, this might conceivably fall within the scope of a general committee meeting in London, but it would be very foolish for any provincial body to exceed the bounds of its own competence in such a way. Action on the Irish proposals ought not to be carried further than obtaining time for a thorough investigation of the question, and even petitions for this would achieve little if they were sent up before the chamber in London had organised itself properly. In early March, when the Birmingham area was 'in a flame', Garbett found it hard to prevent this happening.[47]

Nevertheless, of course, petitions of the right kind, signed and supported in person by the right people, would be essential when the time came, and too much restraint would cause potential supporters to lose interest at the crucial moment. The variable mood of the manufacturers in different parts of the region had first to be caught at its peak in each place and then synchronised with reactions elsewhere. On 12 March Garbett, together with Thomas Russell, James Watt, John Wilkinson and Thomas Gibbons of Wolverhampton, was arranging for a petition to be signed by the ironmasters at West Bromwich on the 18th. For the moment, however, he hesitated to take similar steps in Birmingham, for despite mounting concern in the surrounding district the town itself was still 'very cool about the Irish business'.

> They would sign a petition, but they will neither give money or go from home on the occasion, nor voluntarily meet two or three times in a morning, and if I was to leave Town, I don't believe a tolerable meeting would be procured on the subject, for I don't see a man that would give himself the trouble to ask Gentlemen to come, nor do I see one that would conduct what is absolutely necessary at public meetings. Those who deal to Ireland say they dare not appear. Those who do not deal to Ireland say it don't relate to them, so that we are in an unpleasant situation—the best chance we now stand is from the meeting at West Bromwich on Friday, and therefore pray don't fail to send me a draft of a petition for them to sign. . . .
>
> The truth is I shrink and heartily wish you was well at home, for I see our neighbours will neither support nor thank us, for in speaking of it they are as cool as tho it was a circumstance that happened 100 years since or that might possibly occur 100 years hence. Mr. Galton and Mr. Russell don't seem so sanguine as to give me any expectation of their willingness to go to London. I hope one or both of them will go with me to W. Bromwich on Friday tho I am almost afraid to ask as they will see their declining offends me.[48]

During the week before the West Bromwich meeting, however, a letter from Wedgwood 'containing the wonderfull information Dr. Prettyman gave him' changed the situation dramatically. Wedgwood's letter arrived on 15 March; by seven o'clock on the evening of the 16th a petition from the Birmingham Commercial Committee was on its way to Boulton in London, and copies of both letter and petition had been sent to Gibbons at West Bromwich. The handwriting of Garbett's letters at this time wanders all over the page and shows every sign of extreme haste. He himself noted that he had not even washed his face for three days and was working harder than was 'consistent with health and prudence'. Despite his anxiety to take advantage of the moment, however, Garbett was still moving carefully. The Birmingham petition had only 152 signatures, but they were all 'either of the commercial committee or Merchant or Manufacturer, not Gentlemen, Clergy or other inhabitants'. To have hawked the petition from house to house, to have called the town together by handbill or to have 'set the cryers about . . . would have looked like blowing the flame'.[49] When he took the chair at West Bromwich on the 18th Garbett again confined the signing of the ironmasters' petition to those who actually attended the meeting, although

> If it was not imprudent to ring an alarm in the country many thousand hands might be obtained, and if the Ministry persist, certainly will be obtained in a manner that may easily prove extremely disagreeable to us all.

This caution was entirely justified. Behind the calculated risk of calling public meetings lay the threat of violence if the men of the nailing villages took matters into their own hands, and the manufacturers would lose whatever political credit they had if they seemed to be flirting with that danger. As it was, Sir John Wrottesley, one of the Members of Parliament for Staffordshire, tried to suppress the West Bromwich petition and changed his opinion of it only when he realised that it had not in fact been handed through the county to raise a clamour.[50]

After 18 March Garbett could afford to relax a little. The Birmingham and West Bromwich petitions had been supported by three more from Wolverhampton, Dudley and Stourbridge, and a fourth was expected from Shrewsbury. But the struggle was not over yet. In Birmingham a reaction had already set in after the hectic activity of the 15th and 16th. Despite his hopes to the contrary, Garbett had had to go alone to the West Bromwich meeting, and his colleagues on the Commercial Committee were losing interest once more. Mr Palmer and Mr Russell were not manufacturers in the strict sense of the word, and the former was in any case too busy with his own affairs to stir abroad. Samuel Galton, 'quite a domestic man', had been 'exceedingly soured by attending in London upon Navigation business'; nor was there any chance of persuading Charles Lloyd, another 'constant attendant upon his wife and little family', to go up. Garbett was very much afraid, therefore, that the Birmingham and West Bromwich petitions, though satisfactory enough in themselves, would be unsupported by expert personal testimony. He could and did suggest the names of men who could answer for the petitions, but 'nothing less than compulsion will bring some of these'.[51]

Besides this indifference on the part of individuals Garbett was also worried by more general aspects of the situation. He knew only too well that the coolness of the region as a whole sprang from the fact that 'we are not yet [as] oppressed as our Manchester brethren'. But while adversity might produce the sustained reaction which had hitherto been missing in the West Midlands it would also make opinion much more difficult to control, and Garbett, who had taken care to exclude all but essential information from the Birmingham and West Bromwich petitions, deplored the necessity the Lancashire men felt themselves under 'to publish to all the world the state and extent of their trade', even if they had been driven to it. He could, of course, have supplied the lack of personal support for the petitions by yielding to the persuasion of his colleagues in the General Chamber and by going up to London himself. To have done this, however, would have been to abandon completely the precarious situation in the West Midlands. Garbett therefore remained in Birmingham, dispersing papers sent down by Boulton and persuading the manufacturers of the region to write to the Members of Parliament for Staffordshire, Worcestershire and Shropshire, asking for their help in postponing any decision on the Irish proposals and in establishing a standing committee of the House of Commons 'to attend to representations of manufacturers from the great establishments'. After a long drafting session with his colleagues on the Birmingham Commercial Committee, however, he had to admit that even these letters would not be 'as forcible as I hoped'.[52]

Garbett continued to complain that his neighbours saw 'what is passing as cooly as tho it was a subject that related to the Antediluvians',[53] and towards the end of April Wedgwood too began to be worried. It was surprising, he thought, 'that such a manufacture as Iron, with three or four petitions in the House, should not have a single person to attend it in the Chamber of Manufacturers or to speak a word on its behalf at the bar of the House of Commons'. Pitt, who was anxious to be finished with the Irish proposals, was asking 'very earnestly why none of the Gentn. in that business were in town', and Wedgwood, who was trying to prolong the question beyond the end of the parliamentary session, told Boulton that 'If all our labour is at last thrown away, I must with many others attribute it to their standing aloof'. The ironmasters were quite wrong to think that nothing was to be gained by appearing before the House, and their fear of exposing details of their trade was groundless. Such action was 'the only thing wanted to prevent a resolution taking place', and embarrassing questions could easily be averted either by the intervention of a friendly Member or by frankly admitting that an answer 'would expose their trade'. Even at the end of May, however, when he was in sight of his objective, Wedgwood was still waiting for a response from the West Midlands and wondering, 'if we must not expect the best things from Birmingham, from whence must we expect them?'[54]

Since his own letters ceased in mid-April, it is difficult to say for certain what Garbett thought of this apparent failure on the part of the West Midlands. Despite his earlier efforts to rouse the region, however, he probably now condoned its silence, for Wedgwood was urging the Birmingham leaders to adopt a course of action which ran directly counter to his own ideas on the management of opinion:

> The general answer of such members as mean to vote with the Minister ... is that they do not understand much of the Resolutions themselves and have not heard anything from their constituents. Now you know what *we* have done in

this business. If the Gentlemen of Birmingham or the country round it can open the eyes of their constituents, all within their reach, or whom they can write to, if they will be so kind as to exert themselves, they will thereby render an essential service.[55]

This was precisely what Garbett had tried to avoid in March with the Birmingham and West Bromwich petitions; and though he had organised the writing of letters from the manufacturers to Members of Parliament at the beginning of April there was all the difference in the world between such letters and the kind which Wedgwood was advocating. When in May Wedgwood joined Lord Sheffield and William Eden in public agitation against the government the Birmingham men began to fear that further association with such a campaign would do them more harm than good. While Wedgwood was calling for more visible support for the General Chamber, the ironmasters were acting on their own. On 11 May Boulton joined William Gibbons of Bristol and Richard Reynolds of Coalbrookdale for an interview with George Rose, and the three men were confident 'that if the Irish Proposition pass into Law, we shall have a Bounty on Iron Ware to equalize us with Ireland'. At this point Garbett himself decided that the time had at last come to go up to London. On 19 May he met Pitt together with Sir Robert Lawley and Isaac Hawkins-Browne, the Members for Warwickshire and Bridgnorth, to discuss the prospective iron bounty. When the ironmasters did finally meet again at West Bromwich on 31 May the context of the petition they drew up was very different from that of its predecessor in March.[56]

Garbett certainly seems to have come close to 'sacrificing the independence of the General Chamber to secure special concessions for the iron trades',[57] but he himself did not see the situation in that light. On the contrary, he was very sensitive to the imputation of ulterior motives and tried to forestall it by avoiding any contact with his own political patron, the Marquess of Lansdowne, during his visit to London. It can also be argued in Garbett's defence that the way in which the Irish proposals were finally averted—concessions and amendments from Pitt until the measures as they eventually passed proved unacceptable in Dublin—owed as much to the approach adopted by the Birmingham men as it did to Wedgwood's plan to filibuster the proposals by 'throwing in many petitions and having good evidences at the Bar'. Nor did Garbett's preference for confidential negotiation with the Ministry mean that he set any less store by the chamber, whose survival at a time when tempers were hot owed a good deal to his personal powers of conciliation.[58]

The difficulties Garbett had to overcome in the West Midlands led him in fact to an attitude to the General Chamber just as sanguine in its own way as Wedgwood's, and it is instructive to compare the positions of the two men in May 1785 with their positions a few weeks earlier. Then it had been Garbett who was breathing fire and Wedgwood who had advised caution. Although internal divisions threatened its future for a time during May, the General Chamber had already faced a more fundamental test. It had been summoned into existence within the space of a few weeks; yet it was presuming to exert direct influence on the policies of the Ministry. It had no charter, therefore no legal existence, therefore no strict right to be heard; yet it made bold to intervene in the deliberations of Parliament. With the dismissal of the infamous Fox–North coalition and the general election of 1784 still fresh in memory, with the final bid of Christopher Wyvill's Yorkshire Association still to be played out, Pitt's own Bill for parliamentary reform still to be brought in[59] and the Minister only in the precarious first stages of his long career, it was by no means certain that the aspirations of the General Chamber of Manufacturers would be recognised at all, let alone shown any sympathy. This, of course, was why Garbett was so careful with the West Midlands petitions; but it was also why he wished to see the chamber assert itself on its proper ground to the fullest possible extent.

In the campaign against the Irish proposals the General Chamber itself submitted only one petition, asking in general terms for any decision to be postponed until the matter had been fully investigated. This seems careful enough; but Wedgwood, who had read in the *English Chronicle* on 29 March of Mr Cochrane's appeal to the House of Commons to delay the Irish debate pending information from the chamber, had misgivings. 'It seems to me,' he wrote to Matthew Boulton on 4 April,

> as if we were getting upon new ground, and such as will not be very safe for us to travel in. What! (our adversaries will say) does this infant institution already call upon Parliament to stop its operations till it has received information from the C of M? What may be expected (they will declare) from such an institution if it is suffer'd a few years longer? I confess myself very apprehensive from this step.... We may no doubt publish our resolutions and propositions voluntarily to the public, but I always understand it to be our idea that we should wait to be called upon before we did anything that could, even by our enemies, be construed into giving information immediately to Parliamt. itself....[60]

Garbett, on the other hand, thought that a direct request for postponement was an essential step towards securing the 'station we are entitled to', provided always that the petition confined itself strictly to the Irish proposals and their effects on manufactures. He was therefore very far from sharing the fears of his colleagues on the Birmingham Commercial Committee that 'the Minister may chuse to occasion the Petition to be rejected altogether as coming from a self-created body without legal authority'. On the contrary, while Garbett did not think Pitt would take such a step, he confessed that he 'should not be sorry if he did', and rejoiced at the thought of the chamber petitioning Parliament, since 'it will bring your stability to an issue, ... and if the House of Commons should treat the petition with contempt it will rouze the languid'.[61]

No doubt Wedgwood was more aware than Garbett of the finesse needed to handle a delicate situation, but what was the purpose of expressing opinions if there was no way of bringing the politicians to the point? When Parliament did take up the challenge by refusing to hear the chamber as a body and by reviving archaic regulations to question the credentials of its individual members, Garbett became yet more aggressive. 'Depend upon it,' he wrote, 'the Chamber sinks if, when the delegates meet, they go no further than wording good resolutions at a tavern to put into newspapers.... The difficulty that may attend their petition being accepted is too trifling to embarrass, much less to stop such men from advancing.' In the objections that were being raised to the chamber Garbett saw not a setback but an opportunity: such 'oppression' was exactly what was needed to jolt the hesitant men of the Black Country into action. If Pitt wanted credentials, credentials he should have. The General Chamber should create its own by challenging both Parliament and the Minister in the forum of public opinion. Garbett did not think Pitt would dare to send eminent men back to the country to report that they had been fobbed off with 'the flimsy operation of an insignificant form'. Therefore he urged the members of the chamber to call the Minister's bluff by petitioning individually. Once this had been done, Birmingham and the other manufacturing districts could petition on their own account, designating the members of the chamber as their delegates, thus providing them with credentials enough and establishing the chamber on grounds which could hardly be questioned.

> The world [Garbett wrote] will form its opinion of the General Chamber of Manufacturers by the manner in which they treat the little shuffling device that was probably concerted to prevent your petitioning. But if any minister can support himself after refusing a petition from such persons, we shall see our situation is become desperate and rouze accordingly.[62]

The points at issue between Garbett and Wedgwood during April and May 1785 were the role which 'public opinion' ought to play in the affairs of the chamber and the distinction between politics and party politics. Though he had second thoughts in May about his earlier militancy, Garbett's attitude remained basically consistent throughout. If he harped constantly upon 'The necessity of exercising politicks in cultivating, protecting and extending our manufactures'[63] the thought of doing anything which might jeopardise the political position of the irreplaceable Pitt never entered his head,[64] and when he expressed his opinion on the petition question in April Garbett had no intention of getting embroiled in party politics. The forum he wished to appeal to was that of 'eminent men', and the purpose of the appeal was to authenticate and reinforce the 'lobby', not to replace it. There was a decisive difference between real 'public opinion' in this sense of the phrase and the deplorable agitation into which Wedgwood and the Manchester men were being drawn. Far from serving the ends of the chamber by making manufactures a great object of policy, the latter would only turn a serious business into a party political sport. When Garbett repeated the outlines of his 'favourite object' for establishing the credentials of the General Chamber on 15 April he added a significant rider. The members of the chamber should petition on 'great national outlines to obtain a means for all the country to petition . . . and desire to be heard' not at the bar of the House of Commons but 'by council', by which he meant the Privy Council Committee for Trade and Plantations.[65]

As early as 22 March, however, Garbett had acknowledged that the manufacturers would soon have to decide whether to address themselves to Pitt or whether to approach the leaders of the opposition. He himself believed that the first alternative offered the better chance of keeping the affairs of the chamber free from damaging association with popular politics; but at the time it did not seem to hold out much hope of success. Though individuals had been examined, the chamber's own petition had been baulked by Pitt's objection to its lack of legal status, and the Ministry was avoiding any recognition of the body as a whole. On 17 April Garbett himself was complaining bitterly that even his 'favourite object' had gone astray. Pitt had refused to accommodate the manufacturers by altering the agenda of the Privy Council; instead of examining individuals face to face he was obliging them to employ legal counsel, who were bound to distort the issue; moreover he was revealing the results of the examinations. To Garbett this was adding injury to insult: 'surely' the Minister 'should have endeavoured to obtain truth without exposing it to all Europe'.[66] In these circumstances those who favoured an approach to the political opposition could be excused for thinking that theirs was likely to be the more effective course.

This conclusion is understandable, especially on the part of Wedgwood, who was already on friendly terms with Lord Sheffield and William Eden, the leading political antagonists of the Irish proposals, and the opposition at Westminster was given plenty of opportunity to attack the Ministry by pointing out inconsistencies between the evidence cited from earlier examinations before the Committee for Trade and Plantations and the testimony of witnesses to the more than sixty petitions which the manufacturers had presented to the House of Commons by the middle of May.[67] But were the manufacturers really using the political opposition to defend their own interests, or was the opposition placing the unwitting manufacturers in a false position by using them for its own purposes? Two features of the open resistance to the Irish proposals deserve attention: that it was in great measure unexpected by the Ministry, and that, contrary to the probable beliefs of many of its participants, it rested on misleading propaganda in the opposition press.

Pitt was taken by surprise in March because at that stage he had every reason to think that the manufacturers understood and accepted his intentions. The Committee for Trade and Plantations had already investigated the probable effects of the Irish proposals, and the results had been encouraging. As revealed by the evidence given to the committee between 14 January and 8 March, the attitude of the leading British manufacturers, including Wedgwood himself, was essentially what it was to be in the following year to the commercial treaty with France. With few exceptions, and with some mention of the need to offset the cheapness of Irish labour and, in Wedgwood's case, to prevent the emigration of skilled workers, they had agreed that there was nothing to fear from competition on level terms.[68] This was precisely Pitt's intention. The core of his Anglo-Irish measures was equalisation at the Irish level of the duties payable on goods passing between the two countries. To that extent the product of each country would continue to enjoy protection on its own home market, while imports from either partner would in each case still be treated more favourably than those from overseas. Each country would show 'a due preference' to the other, and thus equality would be established. In the opposition newspapers, however, 'equality' was made to convey the impression that Irish goods would enter the British market 'on equal terms' with the home product—that is, without paying any duty at all.[69] Thus 'the play of commercial opinion was turned ... by a trick'; when Pitt and George Rose tried to explain that the Irish duty of 10½ per cent would apply to both countries, this was reported as an extra imposition on home industry alone, and the impression that the manufacturers had been hoodwinked was confirmed by Pitt's inflexibility towards the General Chamber. Of Wedgwood's two friends, who were chiefly responsible for this gloss upon the facts, Lord Sheffield, whose *Observations on the Manufacture, Trade and Present State of Ireland* provided the real basis for the newspaper attack, acted from genuine conviction as the leading advocate of an advanced form of protection. The motives of William Eden, an ambitious man with considerable experience of Irish and commercial affairs who was anxious to repair the damage done to his personal career by the fall of the Fox–North coalition, were less disinterested. These two, however, had collaborated before, and they knew their business. 'The truth is at this hour & you best know it,' Eden wrote later, 'that if you & I had not worked up that Irish business, Ld. North would have slept thro the session at Bushy & Mr. Fox at St. Anne's Hill.'[70]

On this occasion at least there was some truth in Thurlow's jibe at Wedgwood in the House of Lords: 'a good potter, though but an indifferent politician'.[71] As a result of his experience with the Irish proposals, however, Wedgwood came to share much of Garbett's distaste for political entanglement. At no stage was he any less concerned than Garbett for the integrity of the General Chamber, but to begin with he had been less wary than Garbett of the dangers posed by party, and had assumed too easily that the independence of the manufacturers would be self-evident to any unbiased observer. That Wedgwood was not entirely at ease with the course which events were taking is clear from his letter to Boulton on 4 April;[72] but that letter itself had ended with a rather cavalier dismissal of the stigma of party on the grounds that 'Those who will not believe what we have already said' on the subject 'are not likely to believe anything we can say'. Wedgwood may have been right, but during the next two months actions seemed to speak louder than words, and when he next wrote to Boulton of party, late in May, his terms suggest that he had come to appreciate Garbett's views on the subject:

> I need not tell you how much we stand in need of abilities like his to strengthen & establish our infant institution & to promote the general cause of the manufacturing interests in Great Britain at this most critical & most perilous moment when open & avowed enemies are bellowing out against us stigmatizing us as sons of faction & our Chamber as a party meeting.[73]

When the General Chamber faced its second test, over the commercial treaty with France in 1786, it was assailed once more by many of the same difficulties that had beset it in the previous year. The treaty provoked a fresh set of quarrels which eventually destroyed the organisation; though they supported the treaty, many of the new manufacturers changed their opinion of the detailed terms at least once in the course of the negotiations; and in Birmingham Garbett found himself once more faced with the thankless task of enlisting the co-operation of his neighbours.[74] In other more important respects, however, circumstances had changed considerably. The divisions which this time were to prove fatal to the chamber arose not out of a disagreement on tactics, as they had done in 1785, but from fundamentally different reactions to the proposed treaty among the manufacturers themselves. The representatives of the older trades, entrenched in London behind the chartered rights of the City companies, or closely related still to the agricultural economy of the country, opposed a measure which seemed to stake the future on the unproven advantages of technical superiority and speculative finance. The leaders of the newer and more advanced industries of the Midlands and the north, confident in precisely those things which the others mistrusted, welcomed the prospect of reciprocal tariff reductions which would open the largest single market in Europe to their enterprise. Though he again ignored the General Chamber, Pitt was in close individual contact with the leading manufacturers at every stage, and it was therefore comparatively easy to overcome specific obstacles.[75] A further difference from the conditions of 1785, though it was quite unconnected with the manufacturers' relations with the Ministry, was produced by the rapid disintegration of the French bargaining position, so that the success of the negotiations exceeded even Pitt's highest expectations. Finally, of the leaders of the parliamentary opposition to the Irish proposals, Eden, his ambition now appeased, was in charge of the negotiations in Paris, while, 'on the first blush', Sheffield could not discover 'a single advantage the French have gained'.[76]

This is not to say that no attempt was made to raise a cry once more. On 10 February 1787 the representatives of the older trades met in force, wrested control of the chamber from their rivals and petitioned for delay in ratification of the French treaty. Thomas Walker, who had been Wedgwood's most active collaborator in Manchester in 1785 and still preferred Whiggism to profit, told the meeting that although the treaty 'would soon make his fortune, it would be attended with the downfall of his country'. A Mr Playfair was more theatrical. He 'believed the Commercial Treaty to be fraught with everything pernicious to English Greatness—nay perhaps if we look into the BACKGround, even RUINOUS to ENGLISH LIBERTY!' 'In future times,' he said, 'it would be accounted as great an honour to have opposed this treaty as to have fought in the Field of Agincourt.'[77] Now, however, the original leaders of the General Chamber were unanimous in their condemnation of this attempt to repeat the tactics of 1785. 'So far as it relates to the manufacturers of this place,' wrote Garbett of one opposition pamphlet, 'it is *contemptible.*' James Watt considered no conduct 'more absurd than newspaper publications on the subject', especially when they revealed information best kept secret. Wedgwood, in London trying to regain control of the chamber but doubtful of his chances 'if Mr. Walker comes there in one of his warm moods', wrote to Boulton of the disgrace to which the manufacturers had been brought

> By the weak & undigested as well as unfair reports and resolutions they fabricate from opposition pamphlets and fill the papers with them. . . . These voluminous reports, both their facts and reasoning (if I do not prostitute the term) were all assented to & gulped down at one reading by the General Meeting & ordered to be printed.[78]

Thus far had Wedgwood come since March 1785, when he himself had called the General Chamber into being to issue its first challenge to the Ministry. Now he was trying to introduce a measure of proportional representation in the chamber in order to eliminate the drawbacks of simple delegation, which had made 'the toothbrush manufacturers of London' equal to the great interests of Birmingham and Manchester.[79] Any differences which had distinguished Wedgwood's views from those of Garbett during the previous two years had been a matter of degree only. Behind them lay the same fundamental view of the General Chamber and its purposes. If there was a radical difference in outlook, it existed between Wedgwood and Garbett on one hand and Thomas Walker of Manchester on the other. Both the former thought of the chamber in eighteenth century terms as a permanent interest group which would take its rightful place alongside the older landed and commercial interests in the fabric of national politics. This was why Wedgwood had been so keen in 1786 to add something more authentic to the chamber's 'self-delegated' credentials by obtaining a charter; and though Garbett did not support the application his disapproval was based not on principle but merely on fear lest it cause dissension and distract attention from the French negotiations.[80] Thomas Walker, however, who remained closely allied to the political opposition throughout, and who suspected that Wedgwood would use his charter in collaboration with the Minister to turn the chamber into a closed and dependent corporation, thought of it as an open body more like the pressure groups of the following century.

This points to the whole ambiguity of the General Chamber. Never very effective in its own right, its members got results by lobbying individually rather than through its corporate agency. In 1785 it acted as a convenient peg for opposition harrassment of the Ministry; it collapsed early in 1787 not so much from neglect on the part of the latter as from its own contradictions. It was not really an interest group in the eighteenth century sense; yet an open movement like the Anti-Corn Law League would have been politically unacceptable at the time, even if the industrial economy of the country had been sufficiently integrated to support it. The active bases of the chamber were in the Midlands and the north; but it had to meet in London, 'the seat of government and the grand magazine of the Kingdom'.[81] The consequences were demonstrated in 1787 when their heavy concentration in the south-east of the country enabled the older trades to wrest control of the chamber from its outnumbered founders.

That the General Chamber of Manufacturers failed as a political experiment is, however, hardly surprising. Party, public opinion and pressure group were all new additions to the equipment of politics. It was to take another hundred years to learn how to bring them into effective and lasting combination; and the attempt to embody the emergent manufacturing interest in an agency which claimed to be politically impartial, yet was expressly intended to influence the political process in a situation in which party could hardly be ignored, raised the problems of doing so in an acute form. Yet the manufacturers' response to the commercial policies of the younger Pitt is significant for all that, not only as an important episode in the history of the English industrial revolution but also as an essay in extra-parliamentary political organisation at least as influential in its practical results as its more obvious contemporaries.[82] Though the intention of the General Chamber was to influence specific policies rather than to bring about comprehensive alterations in the constitution, and though its leaders, with the exception of Thomas Walker, were careful to avoid placing this limited objective in jeopardy by allowing it to become entangled with the more speculative aims of the parliamentary reformers, the difficulties encountered by the organisers of the chamber raised in a particular form the questions that attended the relationship between the House of Commons as a representative assembly, its general constituency and the particular communities of interest which the latter contained. The importance of the chamber in this respect is attested by the number of petitions, including one from Lancashire which claimed to speak for eighty thousand people, which it obtained in opposition to the Irish commercial treaty. However true it may be that these sprang from misunderstanding fostered by the guile of the political opposition, they formed one of the most extensive demonstrations of opinion that had yet been mounted for the benefit of the House of Commons; and the leading manufacturers, by their response to the problems they faced, not just in the formation of the chamber itself and in the attempt to establish its claim to be heard at

Westminster, but also in their choice between alternative courses of political action and in the mobilisation of support in their own localities, did much to widen accepted ideas of political practice.

In a wider, if less specific, sense the General Chamber was also important precisely because it collapsed. Behind its particular objectives lay a more general awareness that the manufacturing regions now had distinct concerns of their own, at least as important as those conventionally recognised by the nation's leaders, which owed little to initiative from the capital. In the West Midlands this had first shown itself in the aroused interest in local improvement which marked the later 1760s in the history of Birmingham and, more widely, in the effort devoted to the development of new communications by land and water. Activity in both these fields brought with it its own particular difficulties, and, as Samuel Garbett's relations with his local colleagues show, the same was true of the manufacturers' organisations themselves. This, however, was bound to be the case when the call for co-operation in public affairs was accompanied by the glorification of individual rivalry and emulation as the source of improvement. Perplexing though the practical reconciliation of these opposites must often have been, it was the prospect of real achievement held out by their effective combination, rather than mere unstrenuous unison, which characterised the region's ambitions. These gave new meaning to well worn notions of public spirit, liberty and independence, and their objects, which seemed so much more significant than the sophistry and manoeuvre of the Great World of Politics, fostered a powerful belief in the intrinsic superiority of provincial life. It was this which found its first broad expression in the movement for the General Chamber of Manufacturers. Had the chamber continued to meet, the Ministry would probably have continued to ignore it; somehow it would have had to find a way of coping with its own internal inconsistencies; the relationship between London and the provincial manufacturers would have remained vague, and, equally important, the same would have been true of that between interests in different parts of the country themselves. As it was, the circumstances which caused the disintegration of the chamber threw into sharp relief the differences between the industrial regions, to which the new term 'provinces' can rightly be applied, and the rest of the 'country' outside the capital. When Edmund Burke told the House of Commons that 'the opinions of two counties, however extensive and commercial, should not be taken for the sense of the people of England'[83] he said more than he knew. In future, as James Watt told Josiah Wedgwood in July 1787, the provinces must look after their own affairs, and have 'nothing to do with Londoners except on special occasions'.[84] A year earlier, in a letter to his son recalling his own difficulties in the West Midlands, Samuel Garbett had already come to the same conclusion, and his reflections were apt comment on ambitions which were characterised as much by the differences they embraced as by the aims they held in common. He was justifiably proud of the part he had played in the formation of the General Chamber, but he also knew its limitations, and he had

> escaped wonderfully . . . by being soon aware that when independent men of ability and affluent fortunes unite in any plan of importance to their country, . . . human nature doth not afford any ties that will hold them. . . . High spirits, which attend the consciousness of having no selfish views to acquire wealth, produced a competition for distinction, which created a disgust too much like

envy ... I will not say I was so free of that weakness as not to question my heart, and to give myself an excuse when I saw ill informed assured men troublesome at the meetings, and it required more skill and attention than two or three men of business could rationally give to prevent the chamber acting ridiculously, and tho' my personal character supports our Birmingham Chamber respectably, yet it is not without great caution, as our members are so perfectly independent. I need say no more ... to convince you I shall not suffer my thoughts to be diverted from the Establishment we have founded here.[85]

NOTES

1 For Wedgwood's canal activities see Eliza Meteyard, *The Life and Works of Josiah Wedgwood* (London, 2 vols, 1865–66), especially I, chapters IX, X; K. E. Farrer, ed., *The Letters of Josiah Wedgwood* (2 vols, privately printed, 1903), I, *passim*, and Anne Finer and George Savage, eds., *The Selected Letters of Josiah Wedgwood* (London, 1965), pp. 30–4, 39–40. The Liverpool edition of Thomas Bentley's *View of the Advantages of Inland Navigation* is reprinted, together with further correspondence on the Trent and Mersey canal, as an appendix to K. E. Farrer, ed., *The Correspondence of Josiah Wedgwood, 1781–94* (privately printed, 1906).

2 For Birmingham's own local network of canals see *V.C.H. Warwicks.*, VII, 33–7. For Midlands waterways in general see Charles Hadfield, *The Canals of the West Midlands* and *The Canals of the East Midlands* (both Newton Abbot, 1966).

3 *Cf.* Neil McKendrick, 'Josiah Wedgwood, an eighteenth century entrepreneur in salesmanship and marketing techniques', *Econ. Hist. Rev.*, II, xii (1959–60), 408–33.

4 Wedgwood to Darwin, 3, 15, n.d. April 1765 (*Barl.*); Wedgwood to Bentley, 27 April 1765 (*Ryl. Eng. Mss.*, 1101, p. 68).

5 Wedgwood to Darwin, 13 April, n.d. May 1765 (*Barl.*); Wedgwood to Bentley, 20 April 1765, enclosing Garbett to Wedgwood, 18 April (*Ryl. Eng. Mss.*, 1101, pp. 63–8).

6 For the drafting of the pamplet see *The Letters of Josiah Wedgwood*, I, 48–69, letters between August and November 1765, especially those of 26, 27 September, 15 October and 18 November.

7 Wedgwood to Bentley, 26 August, 15 October 1765 (*Barl.*).

8 *The Selected Letters of Josiah Wedgwood*, p. 32.

9 *The Correspondence of Josiah Wedgwood, 1781–94*, appendix, pp. 261–5, Garbett to the Secretary of the Society of Arts, n.d. October 1765, to Darwin, 16 October 1765.

10 Wedgwood to Bentley, 23 December 1765 (*Ryl. Eng. Mss.*, 1101, p. 138).

11 *Canals of the East Midlands*, pp. 18–22; *Newdigate*, CR 136/B2369, 2374, 2375, 2199: letters between Sir Roger Newdigate and Dr N. Wetherill of University College, Oxford.

12 *Canals of the East Midlands*, p. 23.

13 *Ibid*.

14 The risks involved in this were considerable. *Cf.* A. W. A. White, *Men and Mining in Warwickshire* (Coventry and North Warwickshire History Pamphlets, No. 7, Coventry branch of the Historical Association, 1970).

15 *Jopson*, 31 January, 7, 14 February 1785, letters of 'Publicola', 'A Friend to Justice' and 'A Proprietor' respectively.

16 *Canals of the East Midlands*, pp. 23–6.

17 *Aris*, 14 February 1785.

18 *Aris*, 2 January, 20 February, 22 May 1786; *Canals of the West Midlands*, pp. 74–5, 135–8; R. A. Pelham, 'The Worcester to Birmingham canal', *U.B.H.J.*, v, No. 1 (1955), 60–82. For an earlier, more localised example, in which Samuel Garbett was heavily engaged, see S. R. Broadbridge, 'Monopoly and public utility: the Birmingham canals, 1767–72', *Transport History*, v (1972), 229–42.

19 *Garbett–Lansdowne Letters*, III, Garbett to Lord Wycombe (Lansdowne's son), 12 January 1793. *Cf.* also *A.O.P.*, Garbett to Boulton, 13 January 1793, enclosing a copy of this letter.

20 For turnpike developments in general see W. A. Albert, *The Turnpike Road System in England, 1663–1840* (Cambridge, 1972).

21 Arthur Cosson, 'Warwickshire turnpikes', *T.B.A.S.*, LXIV (1941–42), 84.

22 Hutton, *History of Birmingham*, p. 264.

23 *The Selected Letters of Josiah Wedgwood*, pp. 24, 28; *Aris*, 8 July 1765, 19 June 1769.

24 See discussion in Albert, *Turnpike Road System*, ch. 5. Also *Aris*, 7 December 1767, for a letter on the standardisation of turnpike tolls, originally printed in 1754, which contained an early public appreciation of the significance of transport costs in the development of a manufacturing region, and *D.N.B.* for the career of Henry Homer, rector of Birdingbury, a small rural parish half-way between Warwick and Rugby, who became a leading authority on turnpike administration.

25 For these see Albert, *Turnpike Road System*, pp. 134, 182, and subsequent discussion of transport costs. Though the cost of broad-wheeled wagons and their draught teams was offset by toll exemptions, and was absorbed easily enough by the larger carriers, the Acts seemed to discriminate against small farmers dependent on their own transport. This was the substance of complaints in the West Midlands during the 1760s, when the cost of horse feed, the most decisive factor involved, was higher than it had been in the previous decade.

26 *Aris*, 14 February 1774.

27 *Aris*, 29 November 1762, 3 January 1763.

28 *Aris*, 6, 13, 20 June, 4 July 1768.

29 *Aris*, 25 July 1763.

30 See below, pp. 168–80.

31 Langford, *Birm. Life*, I, 224.

32 See below, pp. 61–2, 77 n. 36.

33 *Garbett–Lansdowne Letters*, I, letters between Garbett and Shelburne, October–November 1784 and enclosed copies of Garbett's correspondence with Drs Percival and Barrow of Manchester; *A.O.P.*, Garbett to James Watt and to Matthew Boulton, 13, 14 February 1786.

34 On this see Witt Bowden, *Industrial Society in England towards the End of the Eighteenth Century* (New York, 1925, 2nd edn, London, 1965), pp. 160–93; Witt Bowden, 'The English manufacturers and the commercial treaty of 1786 with France', *Amer. Hist. Rev.*, XXV (1919–20), 18–35, 'The influence of the manufacturers on some of the early policies of William Pitt', *Amer. Hist. Rev.*, XXIX (1923–24), 655–74; W. O. Henderson, 'The Anglo-French treaty of 1786', *Econ. Hist. Rev.*, II, x (1957–58), 104–12; J. M. Norris, 'Samuel Garbett and the early development of industrial lobbying in Great Britain', *Econ. Hist. Rev.*, II, x (1957–58), 450–60; Donald Read, *The English Provinces c. 1760–1960; a Study in Influence* (London, 1964), pp. 22–4.

35 Norris, 'Samuel Garbett and industrial lobbying', pp. 450–4.

36 Garbett's description, cited by Read, *The English Provinces*, p. 25.

37 Norris, 'Samuel Garbett and industrial lobbying', pp. 454–5.

38 Read, *The English Provinces*, p. 33.

39 *Aris*, 7 February 1785.

40 *Aris*, 27 April 1778; cf. T. S. Ashton, *Iron and Steel in the Industrial Revolution* (Manchester, 1924, 2nd edn, 1951), p. 166.

41 *Aris*, 9 October, 20 November 1780; 5 February, 2, 23 April, 6, 13, 27 August 1781; 18, 25 March, 15 April, 27 May, 3 June 1782; 9, 16 June, 6 October 1783.

42 *Aris*, 16 September 1782; 17 February, 9 June, 14 July, 11, 18 August 1783; *An Account of the Manner in which a Standing Commercial Committee was Established at Birmingham . . . etc.* (1784), B.R.L. 27082.

43 *Aris*, 7 February 1785.

44 *Garbett–Lansdowne Letters*, I, Garbett to Lansdowne, 11 March 1785.

45 Norris, 'Samuel Garbett and industrial lobbying', p. 456.

46 *A.O.P.*, Wedgwood to Boulton, 21 February 1785, Garbett to Boulton, 22 February 1785.

47 *A.O.P.*, Garbett to Boulton, 25 February 1785; *Garbett–Lansdowne Letters*, Garbett to Lansdowne, 11 March 1785.

48 *A.O.P.*, Garbett to Boulton, 12, 13 March 1785.

49 *A.O.P.*, Garbett to Boulton, 15 March, 16 March 7.00 p.m., 16 March 9.00 p.m., 1785. 'The wonderfull information' from Dr Pretyman, Pitt's old Cambridge tutor and

THE CHALLENGE TO THE CAPITAL

now his private secretary, probably related to Wedgwood's two unproductive interviews with the Minister on 10 and 14 March and to Pitt's intention to take up the Irish business in the House of Commons on the 16th. *Cf.* V. T. Harlow, *The Founding of the Second British Empire, 1763–93* (2 vols, London, 1952), I, 607.

50 *A.O.P.*, Garbett to Boulton, 19 March, 2, 6 April 1785.

51 *A.O.P.*, Garbett to Boulton, 19, 21 March 1785. Garbett's suggestions were Thomas Russell, Charles Lloyd, Isaac Spooner and Samuel Galton on the Birmingham petition; Mr Wilkinson, Mr Gibbons, Mr Laugher, Mr Hancock and Mr Amphlett on the West Bromwich petition.

52 *A.O.P.*, Garbett to Boulton, 20, 26, 27, 23 March 1785.

53 *A.O.P.*, Garbett to Boulton, 17 April 1785.

54 *A.O.P.*, Wedgwood to Boulton, 27, 29 April, 5, 7, 27, 31 May 1785.

55 *A.O.P.*, Wedgwood to Boulton, 28 April 1785.

56 Ashton, *Iron and Steel in the Industrial Revolution*, p. 170; *Garbett–Lansdowne Letters*, I, Garbett to Lansdowne, 1 June 1785, and enclosures.

57 Norris, 'Samuel Garbett and industrial lobbying', p. 457.

58 *Garbett–Lansdowne Letters*, I, Garbett to Lansdowne, 13, 20 May 1785; *A.O.P.*, Wedgwood to Boulton, 27 May 1785.

59 Pitt's motion for leave to bring in his reform Bill was defeated on 18 April. John Ehrman, *The Younger Pitt: the Years of Acclaim* (London, 1969), p. 227.

60 *A.O.P.*

61 *A.O.P.*, Garbett to Boulton, 3, 6 April 1785.

62 *A.O.P.*, Garbett to Boulton, 9, 11 April 1785.

63 *Garbett–Lansdowne Letters*, II, Garbett to Lansdowne, 2 October 1786.

64 *Cf. A.O.P.*, Garbett to Boulton, 25 February 1785. Pitt was 'entitled to our compassion as well as our admiration. We cannot expect to find so good a Minister among those who oppose him.'

65 *A.O.P.*, Garbett to Boulton, 15 April 1785. The Privy Council Committee for Trade and Plantations, established in March 1784, replaced the old Board of Trade, which had been abolished in 1782.

66 *A.O.P.*, Garbett to Boulton, 22 March, 17 April 1785.

67 Harlow, *Second British Empire*, I, 606–7; Witt Bowden, 'The influence of the manufacturers on the early policies of William Pitt', p. 671.

68 Harlow, *Second British Empire*, I, 593–8.

69 Harlow, *Second British Empire*, I, 598.

70 Harlow, *Second British Empire*, I, 600–8; Ehrman, *The Younger Pitt*, pp. 207 (citing Eden to Sheffield, 22 October 1785), 208.

71 Harlow, *Second British Empire*, I, 596.

72 Above, p. 40.

73 *A.O.P.*, Wedgwood to Boulton, 21 May 1785.

74 *Cf. Garbett–Lansdowne Letters*, II, Garbett to Lansdowne, 17, 21 October 1786.

75 For example, the hardware manufacturers' aversion to disclosing the intimate details of their business was overcome by agreement on a simple duty of 10 per cent on all articles.

76 Norris, 'Samuel Garbett and industrial lobbying', pp. 459–60; Ehrman, *The Younger Pitt*, pp. 488–90. Sheffield did have second thoughts later.

77 *Aris*, 26 February 1787.

78 *Garbett–Lansdowne Letters*, II, Garbett to Lansdowne, 6 February 1787; Watt to Wedgwood, 26 February 1787, cited by Ashton, *Iron and Steel in the Industrial Revolution*, p. 174, n. 1; *A.O.P.*, Wedgwood to Boulton, 23 February 1787.

79 *A.O.P.*, Wedgwood to Watt, 20 March 1787.

80 *Garbett–Lansdowne Letters*, II, copy of Garbett to Lord Hawkesbury, 14 October, enclosed in Garbett to Lansdowne, 17 October 1787.

81 Read, *The English Provinces*, p. 29.

82 In existing accounts the chamber has been treated, either in the context of economic history and the role of the manufacturers in the industrial revolution, which is, of course, its primary significance, or as one of the early episodes in the history of the younger Pitt's Ministry. In accounts of the wider political developments of the period it has received much less direct attention. In the case of John Cannon's recent *Parliamentary Reform, 1640–1832* (Cambridge, 1973) this is understandable, since the chamber falls outside the book's terms of reference. In the case of E. C. Black, *The Association: British*

Extraparliamentary Political Organization, 1769–93 (Cambridge, Mass., 1963), which deals at length with the Yorkshire Association and the movement for parliamentary reform, the Protestant Association of Lord George Gordon, the Society for Constitutional Information, the impact of the French revolution and John Reeves's Association for the Defence of Liberty and Property, the absence of any explicit account of the chamber is more serious, especially as Dr Black's passing references to it (pp. 4, 118–20, 129) suggest that he appreciates its significance.

83 Cited by Norris, 'Samuel Garbett and industrial lobbying', p. 459.

84 Watt to Wedgwood, 25 July 1787, cited by Ashton, *Iron and Steel in the Industrial Revolution*, p. 173.

85 *Garbett–Lansdowne Letters*, II, press copy of Garbett to Francis Garbett, 3 August 1786.

PART TWO

THE MEANS OF COMMUNICATION
AND THE
CREATION OF OPINION

III

THE NEWSPAPERS OF
THE WEST MIDLANDS

By 1760 the provincial newspaper had already established itself in England as a powerful instrument for the creation and guidance of public opinion.[1] It is true that neither the leading article, nor the paper deliberately committed as a matter of principle to the proposition of particular policies, made its appearance before the 1790s.[2] It is also true that, before this, most country papers felt themselves obliged to protect their circulation by professing a studious impartiality on political issues, and that a large part of their space was still divided between retailed extracts from the London papers, diplomatic and military despatches and the private advertisements which provided most of their revenue. None of this, however, meant that the provincial press was merely a register of local information and yesterday's events, or that, by consequence, provincial opinion was no more than a delayed and passive replica of attitudes in the capital.

On the contrary, the political contents of the provincial papers during the first half of the eighteenth century show that pure impartiality had already proved easier to profess than to practise, and that the retention of maximum readership was by no means always best served by jejeune neutrality. Though the partisan excitements of Queen Anne's reign had subsided for a time after reaching their climax in the Jacobite '15, the work of political education in the provinces had gone gradually on until the deliberate inflammation of common opinion in London and the publication of the *Craftsman* in 1726 signalled the opening of the great opposition to Sir Robert Walpole, and brought popular interest in politics to fever pitch once more. In the years which followed, some printers still tried to avoid controversy, but most of the more successful country papers found their advantage not in caution but in playing deliberately to a public whose prejudices were already predominantly hostile to the Minister. This they did by extracting their copy from the most sensational productions of the opposition press in the capital. Far from abstaining from the fight, they thus in part followed the lead of existing opinion and in part inflamed it still further by their own efforts. By comparison, the counter-attacks which were made in Walpole's defence were feeble affairs, and after the Excise crisis of 1733 even these were abandoned; for it was in effect the Ministerial papers that were forced to mind what they said about politics for fear of losing their readers. While the opposition press redoubled its efforts during the 1730s, the recent defenders of the Ministry affected an indifference to politics which in fact concealed a deepening disillusion with their position. The results became clear after Walpole's resignation in 1742, and particularly after the apostacy of William Pulteney, the erstwhile leader of the opposition, had made it clear that Walpole's departure was not to be followed by the fall of his political system. From then on, with the ex-Ministerial papers no longer distinguishable from their old enemies, the provincial press was virtually unanimous in its opposition to the oligarchs. Denunciations of corruption and warnings of its dire implications for the future of the constitution were never far absent now. Not even the new-found sense of unity which was inspired in the nation after 1757 by the wartime leadership of the elder Pitt could silence completely the note of criticism.[3] Under these circumstances the role of the country papers was very far from being confined to the transmission of stale news. There may as yet have been no authentically 'provincial' issues of sufficient importance to call forth much original or sustained discussion, and printers may have continued to take most of their material from the London press; but the hostile criteria by which the selection was made helped to create in the English provinces a wider political culture comparable in one of its most powerful components to that which was being formed by similar processes in the thirteen mainland colonies of North America. In English circumstances, this 'opposition version of politics'[4] was mixed with other elements. It never achieved the same dominance as it did on the other side of the Atlantic, and it could hardly have achieved the same results. But it was present nevertheless. It helped to shape provincial attitudes to the hegemony of London; and though it was eventually assimilated into other aspects of the region's outlook, so that it lost its distinctness and was turned at length to conservative rather than radical uses, it was to play a major part in the formative period of the West Midlands' political experience during the years between 1768 and 1774.[5]

Comparison of the three main newspapers which served the region[6] during the second half of the eighteenth century will show that, while the results in each individual case were now considerably more variable, the processes which had already brought the provincial press to early maturity as an agent of public opinion continued to foster its development. The paper most closely identified with the area, and that which tried most conscientiously to serve the interests of all its readers by avoiding unnecessary controversy, was *Aris's Birmingham Gazette*, founded in 1741. But even Aris could not help being edged off his preferred ground. His very discretion, coupled with his position as the printer of Birmingham's main paper, meant that on a number of occasions powerful interests used the anonymity of his columns now that the region's own development, combined with its reactions to national events, was beginning to throw up important issues within the West Midlands themselves. This was particularly the case during the opening stages of the war for America, when the *Birmingham Gazette* found itself involved in a direct confrontation with Myles Swinney's *Birmingham and Stafford Chronicle*. Since few consecutive copies of this second Birmingham paper have survived, conclusions about its character cannot be as firm as they are in the case of the *Gazette*, whose file is almost complete; but enough remains to suggest that Swinney's paper differed considerably from its older competitor. The *Birmingham and Stafford Chronicle* first appeared under that title in August 1773, though its origins can be traced under different names for four years before that. As befitted a paper which was the product of a particularly crowded and controversial period in both national and local history, its contents, political and otherwise, were from the start a good deal more adventurous than those of the *Birmingham Gazette*, so much so that in 1793 its reputation made it the object of competing designs on the part of Jacobins and loyalists alike. Before this, however, Swinney's distinctive characteristics as a journalist had already become conspicuous. Though he printed a variety of pieces on both sides of the question, the balance of his sympathies during 1775 and 1776 was unmistakably on the side of the radicals at home and the colonists abroad, and two years later he was involved in opposition journalism, not only in Birmingham but in Coventry as well, much to the disgust of *Jopson's Coventry Mercury*, the third paper which circulated extensively in the West Midlands. Founded, like the *Birmingham Gazette*, in 1741, Jopson's paper was quite unlike either of its counterparts because it was produced in entirely different circumstances. While the two Birmingham papers tried with some success to keep their differences within bounds, the *Coventry Mercury* would brook no rivals. Unlike the *Birmingham and Stafford Chronicle*, whose sympathies seem to have sprung from reasoned and disinterested conviction, its prejudices expressed the bitterness of a local political struggle in which much of the sustained passion of the early years of the century still survived. This had interesting results, particularly during the closing months of 1768, when events conspired to bring about a remarkable alteration in the *Coventry Mercury*'s political attitudes. Until then the rabid Toryism of Jopson's paper, which derived its main impetus throughout from the particular idiosyncrasies of Coventry politics, had been coupled to a critical point of view on larger questions which was a continuation of the 'opposition' traditions of the provincial press during the earlier years of the century. In keeping with this, Jopson printed a large amount of Wilkite material from 1763 onwards; but after the Coventry by-election at the end of 1768, when the corporation's Whiggish hold over the city's parliamentary representation was broken by a freeman candidate who enjoyed discreet support from the Ministry, the *Mercury*'s local loyalties parted company with its previous position on wider issues. This was now reversed, so that the paper became henceforward an indefatigable supporter of Administration, and remained so until the effect of the general election in 1784 on Coventry politics caused it to resume once more a position, if not of outright opposition, then of suspicious neutrality.

Under normal circumstances 'editorial' comment in the *Birmingham Gazette* was confined to the endorsement of accepted opinion on matters of general social concern. These evoked voluminous and often argumentative correspondence, which provides valuable evidence of the way in which opinion in the West Midlands reacted to changing patterns of life;[7] but they still remained largely outside the sphere of politics as it was conventionally understood, and since it could be assumed that all men of good will were concerned to a greater or lesser degree about such things as the price of provisions, the state of the poor and the various related problems of law, order and stability in society, editorial views could be expressed without much risk of exceeding the limits of propriety. More often than not such views were entirely banal. It is, for example, hard to imagine anybody taking exception to Aris's pleasure in January 1763 at the 'truly compassionate humane disposition' which had recently 'manifested itself in a particular manner in the City of Worcester by the large collection ... for the relief of the poor at this inclement season', or to his wish in April 1765 that others would follow the example set by the Worcester magistrates' enforcement of the laws against forestallers and regraters.[8]

Even when it did become more vehement the paper followed rather than led the majority view. In the autumn of 1765, for example, with no prospect in sight of an abatement in provision prices, its report of resolutions to enforce the old market laws in Staffordshire was accompanied not merely by another unspecific commendation of the example but by urgent emphasis on its importance 'at a time when every species of provisions seems settled by a combination of the farmers at the most exorbitant prices', and by pointed remarks about the morals of those who looked to the law for the protection of property which they had acquired through its breach.[9] By the middle of 1766 the situation had deteriorated still further, and the *Birmingham Gazette* went into italics to prophesy imminent disaster unless something was done soon to reduce prices. Now the 'middling classes of people' were beginning to be affected as well as the poor; and 'when the bulk of the people shall be in such extream want, of what import will laws be?' How could a middling tradesman support his family with butcher's meat at such exorbitant prices; and how could this be when there 'never was a greater plenty of grass'? Though Aris did not say it in so many words, something or someone must be responsible for an emergency which required government intervention far more urgently than the recent crisis in Anglo-American relations over the Stamp Act.[10] Considered from the point of view of absolute impartiality, the boldness of these comments might seem surprising, for the charges the printer preferred against the farmers and middlemen must have offended at least some of his country readers. The numerous letters on the price of provisions which he was receiving at this time offer ample confirmation, however, that the opinion of most people was set firm against those particular occupations as the supposed authors of the crisis. Aris could therefore take his cue from his correspondents when it became advisable to depart from the general rule of careful neutrality. In any case, it was only to be expected that his concern for the susceptibilities of all his readers should diminish as the situation became more serious. For the poor to go short was reasonably normal, and, within reason, perhaps no bad thing if it kept them on work and gave a chance for the exercise of a 'truly compassionate humane disposition' on the part of their betters; but when the rising cost of food began to affect the middling tradesmen who formed the greater part of the *Birmingham Gazette*'s immediate constituency, then there was real cause for alarm, and normal criteria were suspended.

On this evidence, and on that of the notices Aris issued from time to time excusing himself from publishing political contributions which might have had embarrassing consequences,[11] it would seem that the *Birmingham Gazette* did little more than lead from behind and abstain on awkward issues, and that there was therefore a good deal of truth in the later dismissal of the paper as merely 'a register of sales or a brokers' guide'.[12] This, however, dates from the early nineteenth century, and the criteria of later rivals, who judged by the partisan standards of their own day, cannot be applied retrospectively with any fairness. In the first place, it would be an obvious and fundamental mistake to regard as agents of opinion only those which sought to change it, and to ignore the contrary influence exerted by the reiteration of accepted views. Even at their most commonplace the *Birmingham Gazette*'s remarks provide useful insights into the inhibitions that governed the expression of opinion, and though the paper's more forceful comments were for the most part equally orthodox, the entrenchment of traditional attitudes which they helped to prolong was a basic characteristic of reactions to the whole range of developments taking place in the region. It bore directly on the course of events during the provision crisis of the mid-1760s, and it was a permanent component in the whole process of adjustment to social change in the Birmingham area.[13] In the second place, the care which the *Birmingham Gazette* took to remain acceptable to as many particular groups among its readers as possible probably did more than anything else to make it the paper most closely associated with the region's development. And in the third place, even though Aris's paper always regarded service to the commercial and manufacturing interests of the West Midlands as its primary *raison d'être*, it never interpreted this as meaning that it should act as nothing but an advertisement catalogue and businessman's remembrancer. It is true that on a number of occasions Aris suppressed contributions which he thought improper; it is true that during the preliminaries to the important Warwickshire election in 1774 he tried to remain all things to all men,[14] and certainly he was sometimes perhaps over-anxious about the possible reactions of his subscribers, as when he closed a lively correspondence on the Birmingham canal in January 1771 lest it prove irksome to his country readers.[15] Despite his equivocation in the final stages of the 1774 election, however, Aris had given full coverage to the popular political developments in various parts of the region which during the previous six years had prepared the ground for the contest; and for every piece which he rejected as unpublishable there was at least an equal number which he printed. On 11 September 1769, indeed, Aris deliberately omitted a number of advertisements from his paper to make room not only for letters on Wilkes and on the Militia but also for a long and detailed account of David Garrick's Shakespearean jubilee at Stratford on Avon. He was admittedly taken severely to task for this in his next issue by 'Mercator' of Shrewsbury, who had no great objection to the letters but disapproved heartily of the amount of space taken up by 'the arrival of My Lady This, and Sir That' at Stratford and warned the printer to place 'public business' before social gossip in future if he valued his own interests.[16] But in fact that was exactly what Aris had done. The Stratford jubilee brought a lot of business to Birmingham, particularly to its printers,[17] and the attention Aris paid to it was entirely in keeping with the importance attached by Matthew Boulton and others to the town's connections with the *beau-monde*:[18] far from being a piece of idle frivolity, it showed a shrewd and constructive awareness of where Birmingham's—and Aris's own— best interests lay.

The *Birmingham Gazette* thus stands revealed, not as the merely passive register which it might seem to have been at first sight, but as a newspaper which played its own intelligent and active part in the development of the area it served. However careful he may have been on other issues, Aris was always ready to stand up for the interests and self-esteem of Birmingham itself;[19] and if the limits of expression he set for himself seem unduly cautious by later standards they were well suited to the task of mediation between particular and often conflicting views which was essential to the role his paper set out to fulfil. In any case, provided it did so unobtrusively, those limits did not entirely prevent the *Birmingham Gazette* from offering its own guidance to opinion when this seemed appropriate.

This was done by an extension of the relationship between the printer and his correspondents. If the latter could be used as a cue for Aris's more vigorous proclamations of orthodoxy, they could also serve as a shield behind which he could insinuate a point of view or suggest a particular course of action without exposing his own responsibility and thereby risking the reputation of his paper with those who disagreed. Under normal circumstances letters were printed in full, and Aris himself made no direct reference to them; but this was not always the case. Quite frequently he either did draw attention to particular contributions in his local news column, to which he then printed them in close juxtaposition, or he included in the column itself a précis of letters received under some such covering formula as 'a correspondent says . . .'. Of course, this procedure may well have been nothing more than a way of giving the purport of contributions to the paper without taking up too much room. Aris's normal practice, as well as the deliberate omissions of 11 September 1769, both suggest, however, that, if it was considered worth printing at all, correspondence was given some priority in the allocation of space; and whatever its motive, the abstracting of letters in the local news column did permit a degree of editorial association with the views expressed. The uses to which this device could be put are well illustrated by 'a correspondent's' observations on 10 February 1777 on the deplorable sport of throwing at cocks on Shrove Tuesday. Correct opinion on this might seem so obvious that the *Birmingham Gazette*'s caution was superfluous. The local magistrates were currently trying to clamp down on the cruder forms of popular recreation,[20] and surely there was little risk in presuming that all who valued the honour of their country and its reputation as a Christian nation would join in supporting the authorities in 'the prevention of a custom that is altogether injurious to the character and inconsistent with the principles of a brave and generous people'. But 'middle class' manners had to make their way against traditions of popular amusement in which cruelty to animals bulked large; and though its subject was cock fighting rather than throwing at them, popular songs like John Freeth's 'Jovial Cocker',[21] which attributed to Red-blooded British Sportsmen of all ranks sentiments very different from those of the *Birmingham Gazette*'s 'brave and generous people', suggest that those traditions still had considerable support. The subject had therefore to be broached in an oblique way if the paper wished to avoid falling foul of prevalent popular sentiment.

Another issue, of a different kind, which prompted the *Birmingham Gazette* to endorse a particular course of action without appearing to take sides itself was that raised by counterfeit coining. This came to prominence at the same time as the concern over cruel sports, but while the latter raised general questions about manners and morals the problems raised by counterfeiting were of specific concern to both the interests and the reputation of the Birmingham area. In this case too, however, the issue was not as straightforward as it may seem; for, in practice, interest and reputation were opposed to each other. On one hand, the trade of the region, with its concentration of small businesses, was severely handicapped by the shortage of specie; on the other, the ease with which the unofficial remedy could be supplied by the metalworkers of the hardware district only served to perpetuate the bad name which Brummagem trades still had in some quarters. Local opinion was naturally sensitive to such undeserved detraction, and the *Birmingham Gazette* of 2 October 1775 had been quick to defend the town from the slighting remarks of the 'paragraph mongers in

London', who, 'with their usual modesty and veracity', had been publishing groundless reports of convictions for counterfeiting in Birmingham. Comments, resolutions and letters on counterfeiting had been a feature of the paper for three months previous to this rebuttal, and they continued to be so for most of the following winter.[22] Most were concerned to stop the practice by enforcing the law, and the printer could therefore take a high line against the region's detractors with some confidence; but some writers, like 'Philalethes' on 18 September 1775, had argued the opposite, and the points they made put a rather different complexion on the hardware district's attitude to the problem. As Philalethes pointed out, associations like that recently formed in Wolverhampton to outlaw the circulation of counterfeit money were ill considered because its use was inevitable under existing circumstances. For all practical purposes the counterfeits were as good as coin of the realm, and in any case, business could not go on without them—not, at least, until the government took steps to increase the amount of proper specie in circulation. This was the only permanent remedy for the situation, and in its default, resolutions about enforcing the law would be in vain: so, for the present at any rate, Wolverhampton had better make what virtue it could out of necessity by joining the other towns of the region, which were already accepting counterfeit money. Against this background it is not surprising that while the *Birmingham Gazette* was more or less bound to act in accord with its earlier defence of Birmingham's reputation, its own suggestion in September 1776 ran counter to the town's recent practice, and was offered rather more discreetly:

> A correspondent says he is greatly astonished at the imprudence of the tradesmen of this town in taking counterfeit halfpence so readily as they do at present, when it cannot but be remembered what a general injury and inconvenience attended their circulation a few months since; and thinks they would act more wisely and laudably to enter into an association to prosecute every person receiving false coin, as there is every reason to believe they are purchased at a reduced value and distributed again at the price of lawful money.[23]

The habit of sheltering behind his correspondents thus gave Aris a means of tactful intervention in the discussion of local issues; but it also had reciprocal effects on his own position. Some correspondents were more influential than others, and as national and regional affairs became more closely interrelated it became difficult for the *Birmingham Gazette* to avoid some measure of commitment to a particular point of view. This was particularly the case during the months before the outbreak of the war for America, and it is not surprising to find that during January 1775 Matthew Boulton and the Earl of Dartmouth were in consultation with each other over insertions in Aris's paper in connection with the petition in support of the Coercive Acts which Boulton was then organising in Birmingham in collaboration with Dr Roebuck of the Carron ironworks.[24] Nor is it surprising to find that though the *Birmingham Gazette* also carried news about the town's other petition, in sympathy with the colonists, which was the immediate cause of these countermeasures, its own preferences followed those of Boulton and Roebuck. This was made plain on 16 January, when a letter criticising the conciliatory activities of the London merchants trading to North America was openly supported by the printer himself, who observed in his local column that

In the present dispute with America, it may properly be asked for what end any Nation encourages and protects Colonies? Is it to erect an Independent State? Or was it for this that Great Britain sacrificed the lives of her subjects by thousands and lavished her treasures by millions, entailing thereby an enormous load of taxes on herself, and either raising up a rival to destroy her trade, or an enemy to accelerate the aera of destruction.

Such views placed the *Birmingham Gazette* in direct opposition to *Swinney's Birmingham and Stafford Chronicle,* which took the part of the conciliatory petitioners in the town, and it is to this conflict that attention must now be turned.

Even before he became the sole owner of the *Birmingham and Stafford Chronicle* in 1773 Myles Swinney had made a name for himself as a printer of considerable initiative. In 1771 eyebrows had been raised when Swinney, who was in fact in partnership with Samuel Aris at the time, printed Voltaire's *Thoughts on Religion* in the *Warwickshire Journal,*[25] one of the three precursors of the *Birmingham and Stafford Chronicle.*[26] At the same time he was also involved with a group of gentlemen sponsors in the publication of the *British Museum,* a liberal periodical venture which set out deliberately to broaden the experience and deepen the understanding of a wide range of readers, and a year later he was running one of the earliest news-room services in Birmingham.[27] Since only one number of Swinney's paper survives from the period of the American petitions, a full assessment of its reactions to them is impossible. Fortunately, however, the remaining issue,[28] for Thursday 2 February 1775, is the one which directly followed their presentation to the House of Commons, and a comparison of its contents with those of the *Birmingham Gazette* at the same time leaves little doubt where Swinney's sympathies lay. His coverage of the two petitions began with the views of 'a correspondent from Manchester', who expressed surprise at the presentation of a coercive petition from Birmingham and linked it with the activities of 'a certain Gentleman', who, after trying unsuccessfully to organise a similar demonstration on behalf of the Ministry in Manchester, had recently left for the Midland town. After this report, the subject of which was probably Dr Roebuck of the Carron iron foundry,[29] Swinney went on to an indignant refutation of 'A Letter from London', which the *Birmingham Gazette* had carried on the previous Monday. This piece had reported favourably on Boulton's loyal petition, which had been presented to the House of Commons on the 25th, and had made a number of defamatory remarks about Edmund Burke, the petition's leading parliamentary opponent. Aris had printed it alongside the text of Boulton's petition as a rebuttal of attacks on the supporters of the Ministry; Swinney now set the record straight by means of a 'Letter to the Printer' which quoted the full text of the conciliatory petition back at his rival. After this he ended his coverage with twelve questions from 'Brutus', which explored the implications of the American dispute from an opposition point of view.

Everything pointed to a further bout of replication and rejoinder in the *Birmingham Gazette's* next issue on 6 February, but instead of roundly abusing them Aris preferred to treat the American sympathisers as honest men labouring under a delusion. He reprinted the full text of Swinney's letter in support of the conciliatory petition, but disarmed it by a footnote suggesting that 'as the writer is presumed not to be a resident, his colouring ... might possibly be

found on examination much too high', and then went on to repeat the original
letter from London. This time, however, the text of the loyal petition and the
remarks on Burke were both omitted, and instead a rather righteous attempt
was made to bring the quarrel to a peaceful conclusion by stating that though
the writer stood by his original opinion of *a rebellious faction in the colonies*
and its *detestable abettors*,

> it was never meant to be applied to petitioners, who it is hoped are only mis-
> taken, and who have hitherto been treated by the author of *this letter* so truly
> as neighbours and friends, that three of their publications (by no means guarded
> against criticism) have not drawn, nor will draw, any kind of animadversion
> from him, without further provocation.

How much independent control the *Birmingham Gazette* still had over its own
political contents is difficult to say, but, for the moment at any rate, the amount
was probably not great. Certainly Matthew Boulton was heavily engaged in
the dispute,[30] and the paper's reply to Swinney was closely in accord with the
attitude expressed by the Earl of Dartmouth over a fortnight previously, before
either of the two Birmingham petitions had been presented, when he had
written to Boulton of 'the misguided and misinformed zeal of many of yr. friends
in Birmingham'.[31] In effect the *Birmingham Gazette* had been temporarily
commandeered by the authors of the coercive petition, in support of which it
continued its efforts to reunite local opinion by trying to convince the friends
of America that their opposition to the Ministry's policies was, however understandably, mistaken. The paper's main attempt to achieve this result was made
on 20 February in the form of an anonymous letter on the debate in the House
of Lords the previous week on augmentations to the navy. The writer of this
supposedly fair-minded eye-witness account congratulated the speakers on both
sides on their 'integrity and patriotism', and confessed himself agreeably surprised by the quality of the debates. He had gone with misgivings about the
direction of British policy; but though he had listened with the closest attention
to 'certain Noble Lords who are most deservedly high in the public favour',
the arguments of the opposition had not come up to his expectations. On the
other side, however, 'a most satisfactory account' had been given of the state
of the navy, on the basis of which the public could rest assured that the kingdom
was in no danger, and the case for the Ministry had been 'manly, cogent and
conclusive'. Despite personal fears for a brother who was serving with the provincial forces, the writer had therefore come away honestly convinced of the
wisdom of the measures which were in train against the colonists, and he tried
to avoid the invidious necessity of taking sides by ending with the pious hope
that 'some great, good and liberal minded man' would even now 'arise' to
bring the dispute to a conclusion compatible at once with the 'dignity and
honour of this country' and the 'liberty of our American fellow subjects'.

The contents of Swinney's paper during the following months cannot be
checked; but the absence from the *Birmingham Gazette* of further major
references to the division in local opinion suggests that the latter did manage to
turn away some of the wrath of the colonial sympathisers, and that to a corresponding degree it was able to regain the middle ground during the period of
waiting which lasted until the news of the first armed clashes in the coming
war reached England later in the summer. Thereafter both papers kept up a

rather self-conscious neutrality by printing extracts from pamphlets on both sides of the question. The abridged version of John Wesley's *Calm Address to the American Colonies* which was given as a supplement to the *Birmingham Gazette* of 16 October 1775 was thus followed a fortnight later by an answering *Letter to the Revd. John Wesley*, likewise provided by the printers at no extra cost 'to shew their impartiality does not consist in profession only'. Similarly, extracts from Richard Price's *Observations on Civil Liberty*, given on 11 March 1776, were followed on the eighteenth by *Remarks on Dr. Price's Observations*, as the printers were 'of opinion we cannot better evince our impartiality and assiduity to oblige our readers than by presenting them with a few of this judicious writer's sentiments in answer to Dr. Price'. Myles Swinney played the same game the following June, when he matched Tom Paine's *Common Sense* with answering extracts from *Plain Truth*.[32] On the other hand, however, there had been nothing neutral about the belligerent vindication of Matthew Boulton and his colleagues by 'A Boston Saint', whose railing against 'the Tinsel Orator' (Edmund Burke), his fellow 'bawlers in a certain assembly' and those who petitioned 'on behalf of the traitors in New England'[33] had been printed by the *Birmingham Gazette* in February 1775 alongside its reasonable account of proceedings in the House of Lords. And if the *Gazette* showed its *parti pris* in later months by introducing Wesley's *Calm Address* as 'sensible and dispassionate' and its reply to Dr Price as the work of a 'judicious writer', the *Birmingham and Stafford Chronicle* did so even more blatantly on 11 July 1776 by printing the 'very curious and loyal oration' given in Boston the previous April at the funeral of 'the late Worshipful Grand Master Joseph Warren' of Massachusetts by 'Percy Morton, Master Mason', and by following this call 'to seize again those rights which as men we are by nature entitled to, and which by contract we never have and never could have surrendered' with the full text of the Declaration of Independence on 22 August.

In view of the efforts made by both Birmingham papers to avoid a repetition of what had happened between them during the early weeks of 1775, however, their differences should not be overstated. During the four years before Swinney began independent publication he and Aris had been associated with each other,[34] and their subsequent political disagreements did not interfere with the complementary relationship which had developed between the two businesses in other respects. For a short time, it is true, the conflicting petitions of January 1775 had provided an issue in the town itself on which the two Birmingham papers had to take definite sides; but though several other places in the West Midlands took part the following autumn in the second round of petitioning for or against the war, Birmingham did not repeat the experiment. That opinion in the town remained divided there can be no doubt, and this had important consequences;[35] but there was not yet any permanent, institutionalised antagonism between different groups in Birmingham to which the division could attach itself and so became completely irreconcilable, as it did, for example, in Coventry, where it was fed by the running feud between freemen and corporation. The *Birmingham Gazette* therefore never felt the need to abuse its competitor as furiously as *Jopson's Coventry Mercury* did between 1778 and 1781.

Nevertheless the style and policies of Swinney's paper were quite distinctive. While the *Birmingham Gazette* still relied extensively on the official sources in

London for its American news, Swinney was more willing to give prominence to less formal reports and more speculative commentaries;[36] and if he fell foul of *Jopson's Coventry Mercury* during the later stages of the war this was because he was collaborating at the time with J. W. Piercy of the *Coventry Gazette*, a paper which not only took the wrong side in Coventry politics but also made itself available to critics of British policy in America. The signs are, moreover, that the *Birmingham and Stafford Chronicle* retained its individuality. Its surviving file is blank during the 1780s, but even in 1793, when the two Birmingham papers had drawn closer together to face the threat of revolution, the difference between their characters was still sufficiently important for John Brooke, a local magistrate and one of the chief persecutors of Birmingham's reformers, to suggest that the government acquire a controlling interest in Swinney's business.[37] The *Birmingham Gazette* was 'well affected', but since it was unwilling to jeopardise its circulation by carrying 'anything that is likely to offend the Dissenters' its usefulness as a propaganda medium was limited. The *Birmingham and Stafford Chronicle*, on the other hand, was read as an active vehicle of opinion as far afield as Lancashire and Cheshire. Swinney himself was loyal, but he was thinking of selling his paper, and had already received an offer for it from a group of 'violent supporters of Priestley and Paine' led by his own recent partner, 'a young man of the name of Walker, a rank Presbyterian Republican'.[38] Brooke had therefore secured first refusal on the paper, and urged Whitehall to act swiftly to forestall the Jacobins. The friends of Government badly needed an effective agent of their own in the West Midlands, the more so as plans were even then being formed to launch a third, and radical, paper in Birmingham. In the event nothing came of all this. The plans of the reformers did not materialise; there is no evidence that any action was taken on Brooke's suggestion;[39] Swinney found a new partner and continued to publish the *Birmingham and Stafford Chronicle* himself.[40] The fact remains, however, that by the 1790s the local representatives of Government clearly attached considerable importance to the Birmingham press, and to Swinney's paper in particular, as a means of influencing for good or ill the political disposition of a crucially important part of the country.

The particular circumstances which formed the salient characteristics of *Jopson's Coventry Mercury* were more typical of local politics in the eighteenth century than anything which yet existed in Birmingham. The Coventry paper, which remained unashamedly 'Tory' through all changes and chances from its foundation onwards, owed its bias to the prolonged struggle for control of the city's parliamentary representation which was still being fought out between the freemen and their whiggish, occasionally conforming, corporation.[41] The atmosphere of Coventry politics, both during and between elections, was still not much different from that which had prevailed in the country at large during the reign of Queen Anne. The strife of party may no longer have disrupted the affairs of the nation as a whole; but at this level old enmities lived on, and slanders more redolent of the seventeenth century than of the age of toleration were freely exchanged in a war of words, bearing little apparent relationship to larger issues, which was fought over such matters as the corporation's corrupt administration of the Coventry freemen's oath, its fraudulent use of the income from Sir Thomas White's Charity, its influence in St Michael's Vestry and the freemen's jealously guarded rights over the common land surrounding the city. In this quarrel Jopson's paper made no attempt to disguise its attachment to the freemen's side. As with the country papers in general during the heyday of opposition to Sir Robert Walpole earlier in the century, so still in Coventry, maximum readership was best served not by neutrality, nor even by any pretence of it, but by total involvement in a feud which provided a continuous excuse for virulent writing. This may diminish the value of the *Coventry Mercury* as an accurate and objective record, since the paper's political attitudes were consistent only in the light of the local quarrel. It must, however, have been a considerable asset to Jopson as a practical journalist to have on his own doorstep a permanent source of sensational copy with which he could ply his readers and play upon their prejudices, as he did, for example, on 4 April 1763 in 'A Word to the Vestry of St. Michael':

A free *toleration* in matters of religion is the glorious characteristic of Protestantism, and it is the felicity of *English Protestants* who dissent from the *Established* church to enjoy this toleration full and entire. The design of a Toleration is to preserve *Liberty of Conscience* and the *Power of the Magistrate* from mutual collisions and encroachments. All, therefore, who sincerely *desire* the continuance, or experience the *benefits* thereof should be extremely careful to confine the *plea of conscience* within its true limits, to prevent it from infringing upon *civil* rights and giving umbrage to the *Magistrate* by being made subservient to *lucrative temporal views.*

What then must be our sentiments of a certain *set of people* [identified by footnote as the Coventry Society of Friends] distinguished from their fellow subjects by *peculiar* marks of indulgence, who, notwithstanding all the *unmerited* favours they enjoy under the present happy establishment, insolently spurn its *injunctions,* and murmur at their *protectors* unless the Laws made for the support of the *Church* may be suspended in compliment to the *pretended scruples* of its most obstinate and avowed *opposers?* And should there be found a *Junto* of men whose duty leads them to pay the strictest attention to the *Church's Welfare,* capable of *conniving* through indolence or interest at so shameless a *suspension,* what softer title can be bestowed on such *Guardians of the Sanctuary* than that of notorious *betrayers of their trust?*

Perseverance in a conduct like this, after the *acquisition* of such *extraordinary* aid [a writ of *Mandamus* against the vestry] as former neglect has rendered necessary, can be construed into nothing less than a direct "joining with and strengthening such *libertines* as would stretch the Liberty of their consciences to the Prejudice of their Neighbours or to the Ruin of Human Society"

Or, more pithily, 'To the Renowned Knights of the Order of the *Elephant and Castle,* as well *Absenters* as *Dissenters* from the Church of England', on 11 April 1768:

> As Aesop's Dog in Manger lay,
> And drove the cattle from their hay,
> Which Dogs want teeth to eat,
> So our good c--p------n choose
> To keep a stir about *Church* pews,
> Where they want *grace* to sit.

During the early years of George III's reign the Coventry freemen's quarrel was associated in Jopson's paper with a more general view of politics which still reflected the preoccupations of the old 'country' opposition. During the

months before the general election of 1761, for example, pieces like the letters
of 'Britannicus', which occupied five successive issues of the paper between 25
August and 22 September 1760, or the *Hints to the Electors of Great Britain* of
the following November, repeated the familiar attack on placemen and septennial parliaments, and formed the background for other items more directly
applicable to the situation in Coventry itself, such as the letter from 'Anglicus'
which on 27 October reported the virtuous resolution of the corporation of
Bath to re-elect the borough's sitting members in recognition of their merit
alone, and contrasted it with the behaviour of other bodies 'who in their choice
of representatives pay no regard to other merit but money'. Similarly, in the
aftermath of the election a second series of letters, this time from 'Constans',
repeated the call for triennial parliaments, while numerous other contributions
consoled the Coventry freemen for the defeat of their candidate, traduced the
corporation victors and drew strength for the future from the impending publication of the Coventry poll book, the outcome of a scrutiny of the return at
Lichfield and the verdict which had been brought in for the plaintiff in a bribery
prosecution at Tamworth.[42]

In keeping with its 'independent' stance, the *Coventry Mercury* tried
ostensibly to keep its commentary on national, as opposed to local issues, above
party. In June 1762 a further letter from Britannicus urged its readers to
remain aloof from the newspaper battle over the terms of the Peace of Paris
which had recently broken out in the capital,[43] and the following month 'Simon
Neuter' asked for a fair hearing for the Earl of Bute, condemned the opposition
to him as the product of faction, not principle, and declared that

> We are not a divided, but a united people, that it is possible we may yet have a
> good peace, and that neither zeal for their country, nor a commendable industry
> is to be found in the present would-be-called party writers.[44]

Despite these concessions to neutrality, however, the general sense of the
Coventry Mercury's political copy became increasingly hostile. Extracts from
both the *North Briton* and the *Monitor*, the chief anti-Ministerial papers, were
reprinted during the latter half of 1762, not to mention pieces from other
opposition pamphlets and several more letters from Britannicus and others
attacking the Earl of Bute and criticising the peace terms.[45] During the next
five years this tendency was reinforced, both by the issues raised by John Wilkes
and by the failure of the peace to bring with it a general return to prosperity
and low prices. On 28 March 1763 the Coventry paper carried yet another
letter from Britannicus, this time on the cider tax; and on 2 May, nine days
after its first appearance and five after the author himself had been taken into
custody,[46] Jopson reprinted Wilkes's attack on the King's Speech from the
famous *North Briton* No. 45. This was followed on 6 June by extracts on the
liberty of the press, and for the next year and a half the paper carried a steady
stream of contributions on general warrants and the future of English liberties.
These culminated in the questions raised by 'T.B.' on 17 December 1764 on the
state of the national debt, the progress of corruption and the impending doom
of the constitution:

> Whether corruption and depredation can change their nature and become
> sanctified and warrantable though stampt and sealed in form by any constitution,
> either Heathen or Christian that ever existed in the world?

What community, free or enslaved, was ever duped to such a degree by another as England has been by German Connections?

Upon what did the wise man found his predictive declaration that England could never be undone but by its Parliament?

Could, or did ever any despotic monarch upon earth, by virtue of his edicts, raise half the money upon his subjects ... that the people of England have been induced to pay under Acts of Parliament?

What horrid signs will usher in the period when a Free Nation shall resign the privilege of chusing representatives, and give the preference to an absolute, but humane King?

As such ominous speculation indicates, the political issue had now been broadened into a general apprehension about the future which embraced social and economic discontents as well. 'Libertas', for example, who wrote from Uttoxeter in July 1765, began with the law for the preservation of fish, under which the most trivial and accidental trespass was punishable by seven years' transportation, and contrasted such severity with the lenient sentence recently awarded in a case involving the rape of a nine-year-old girl. He hoped this was 'not a specimen of a new system of punishments which a certain favourite, or his creatures, have a mind to introduce for daring to find fault with him'. Angling, 'a proper and natural privilege belonging to what formerly was, but what we now only call, our liberties', was now, it seemed, to fall prey to arbitrary power, along with the victims of excise, the cider tax and general warrants, while the weavers of Spitalfields starved and 'the just and miserable complaints' of working men in general were silenced by force of arms.[47] As the next general election approached, this amalgam of grievances began to assume some of the forms of a manifesto. In September 1767 readers of the *Coventry Mercury* were taught by 'Mechanicus' to sing a topical adaptation of 'Hearts of Oak' whose verses and refrain were very different in spirit from those of the original:

> Inclosing of fields and of commons I'm sure
> Can be called nothing better than robbing the poor.
> He that stops honest labour his country must wound,
> Though in Charity's deeds he may seem to abound.
>
> Honest Britons no bounty on corn will allow;
> No favour or affection,
> No brib'ry at Election.
> Let the man be opposed, who opposes the plough.
>
> A large standing army, while taxes increase,
> And Militia embody'd protect us in peace;
> True patriots no needless expenses advise,
> And all worthy statesmen set bounds to excise.
>
> Honest Britons ... &c.
>
> By luxury, extortion and National Debt,
> Alas! Poor old England, she's laid in a sweat.
> From hence arise grievances I need not name;
> The lower class suffer, but *who* bear the blame?[48]

Two months later the same general message was conveyed by 'An Obscure Parson', who repeated the usual injunctions against bribery and urged voters above all to be

> Mindful to spurn the *General Warrant Men*; the *Stamp Act Men*; the *Window Light Men*; the men who voted away their own privileges in the affair of libels. ... Never vote for a man who prosecutes on the Game or Fish Acts.

A week after this, 'T. Ireton', though less specific, was more menacing: he simply cited Cromwell's words when he expelled the rump of the Long Parliament.[49]

The refusal of Parliament to admit John Wilkes as the properly elected member for Middlesex made him once more the champion of the discontented. Even though most of the issues treated by Jopson's correspondents had no direct connection with him, it was not difficult to imagine the hero of Brentford Butts as the leader of a popular movement which would at last rid the nation of the corruption which was felt to be the root cause of its troubles. This prospect was specifically welcomed by 'Pro Patria' in the *Coventry Mercury* of 4 April 1768, and during the following months the paper continued to foster it by showing due concern over the St George's Fields massacre and printing Wilkes's address to the Middlesex freeholders on receiving sentence from Lord Mansfield for his various misdemeanours.[50] In the autumn of the year and the spring of 1769, however, Jopson's attitude was completely transformed in response to changes which took place at the same time in the course of Coventry's own political struggle. At the general election in March 1768 the corporation candidates, the Hon. Andrew Archer and the Hon. Henry Seymour-Conway, had retained their seats, but their calculations had been very nearly upset by the late appearance of Walter Waring, Esq., a Shropshire gentleman who had agreed to stand in the freemen's interest.[51] Waring stood the poll for two days, and then withdrew; but considering that he was a stranger in the city, had conducted no regular canvass and had only limited funds, he made a considerable impression. This was remembered the following November, when Archer vacated his seat to succeed his father in the House of Lords. The freemen again approached Waring, who declined standing at the by-election but recommended Sir Richard Glyn, a London banker, to their attention. The corporation interest was decaying, and it had difficulty in finding a candidate to oppose Glyn, until Thomas Nash, a linen draper, also from the capital, came forward. In view of the fact that Glyn was backed by the Ministry, that Nash enjoyed the support of the Duke of Portland and that both were London men, the claim that 'political issues did not play much part in the election'[52] will repay investigation; and this in turn will shed considerable light on the *Coventry Mercury*'s remarkable change of direction.

Previous to his appearance in Coventry Sir Richard Glyn had been severely mauled in the general election earlier in the year, when he had offered himself as a candidate for the City of London. In the course of the contest he had been attacked as a client of the Earl of Bute and ridiculed as 'a man of heavy temper, rotundity of form, vacuity of look, and therefore not a proper person to represent the City of London in Parliament'.[53] His appearance at the Coventry by-election as the candidate of the Independent Freemen was therefore the more remarkable, and the slogans used by his supporters—'High Church—Glyn and Liberty! Now or never!'[54]—made an ironic contrast with the more usual

coupling of Wilkes and liberty. The explanation of this variation on the common
theme lies, of course, in the preoccupations of Coventry politics; for the obverse
of Glyn's rallying cries was 'No Corporation Slavery! No Nash! No two
thousand pound bargains!' The by-election was certainly fought on the local
question, but this did not mean that political issues played no part in it: on the
contrary, their deliberate exclusion suggests that they played a very definite, if
unseen, part in Glyn's return.

Before the end of October, when Waring announced his decision not to stand
and recommended Glyn as his successor, the one object of the freemen's campaign had been to consolidate the gains which they had made in the spring.
When he took over the candidature Glyn continued the same tactics, and notices
throughout November called for unsworn freemen to take advantage of the
writs which their candidate had obtained for their enrolment before the poll.[55]
More important, however, are signs that Glyn was now also taking steps to
discourage the too active investigation of his own recent political past by circulating denials that he had supported general warrants and favoured the im-
portation of French silks.[56] The weaving of silk ribbons, which had been
introduced to the city at the start of the century, was the staple trade of
Coventry; Coventry silk weavers would obviously be affected by such a measure
as that alluded to, and there would also be strong sympathy in the city for the
plight of the Spitalfields weavers, whose industrial disputes had paralleled the
Wilkite disturbances in London.[57] Quite apart from the contents of Jopson's
paper up to this time, the measures taken by Glyn to scotch any reaction which
might upset his election chances therefore suggest the presence in Coventry of
considerable potential support for 'Wilkes and Liberty'. In Coventry, however,
liberty meant the overthrow of the corporation interest rather than any more
abstract ideal. With this in mind, an explanation of Glyn's success in the 1768
by-election, and of the change which came over the contents of the *Coventry
Mercury* in its aftermath, suggests itself. Waring's effort in the spring had been
sufficiently successful to draw attention to the desire of the freemen to be rid
of the corporation yoke. If he had more money available than Waring had had,
a Ministerial candidate at the by-election would stand a good chance of being
returned, especially if he was able to procure for the freemen the substance
and not the mere rhetorical shadow of liberty. Success depended very much on
keeping the election local: but once Glyn had been elected and the freemen of
Coventry had been given the prospect of the corporation's permanent downfall
in the shape of *mandamus* writs to compel the proper administration of the
freemen's oath, the work of converting the Wilkite sentiment in the city was
put in train by pointing out to the satisfied freemen the real political issues
facing the country, and by confounding the corporation and the London radicals
in joint obloquy. The result, in one of the largest urban constituencies in the
country outside the capital, was a signal triumph for the Ministry.

On 8 April 1769 Sir Richard Glyn presented the Crown with a loyal address
from his new constituents, 'The Gentlemen, Clergy, Traders, and Principal
Inhabitants' of Coventry. No mention of the corporation was made among the
authors of the address, and the *Coventry Mercury* of 10 April, which announced
the presentation, also carried a long 'Test of Patriotism' submitted to 'The
Illustrious Assembly at the London Tavern' from 'H.C., A Country Justice of
the Peace'. This began with an apparently innocent request to the Society of

the Supporters of the Bill of Rights, asking it to inspire the zeal of a sibling association 'now struggling for birth in an inland county near the middle of the kingdom' by 'declaring what British Rights and privileges have of late been cruelly invaded in violation of our most sacred Palladium, the Bill of Rights'. After this, however, the Test revealed its true purpose. The Wilkite mob had kept five hundred legitimate voters away from the hustings at Brentford: so much for the freedom of elections. In any case, Wilkes had been expelled from the House of Commons for crimes proven to its satisfaction. The ninth clause of the Bill of Rights stated that the debates and proceedings of Parliament ought not to be called in question in any court or place outside itself, yet in the recent disturbances this freedom had been infringed twice: first on the hustings at Brentford, and second in

> that private court of appeal erected by the said John Wilkes Esq. in his own chamber in the King's Bench Prison, from whence he daily publishes advertisements, or Protectorial Proclamations, not only impeaching, but flatly denying the authority of the House of Commons to exclude him.

So much for the liberties of Parliament. This brought the Test to its final peroration: by the first and second clauses of the Bill of Rights the Crown's power to suspend or dispense from the law was declared illegal:

> What the King dares not do, shall the vilest canaille, actuated by a few traitrous incendiaries, outdo, defeating all laws and insulting all authority? ... In a word, most glorious patriots, if you are true men, ... join us in a proper resentment of these public injuries, and impart to the Public any other violations of this sacred law, ... which, if you fail to do, we renounce all alliance with you.

After this the new cry was taken up by a succession of writers who vied with each other in their abuse of the radicals. 'Sir Joseph Mushroom's bristles,' wrote 'FitzNorman', were 'now up against the spirited Address from the City of Coventry.' This justly condemned the 'club of sedition' at the London Tavern; 'and yet this swineherd, this son of a vat and gin cask, with an insolence equal only to his folly and vanity, calls the Loyal Address of a respectable body of men "a false, malicious and scandalous libel"'.[58] A week later 'Poetikastos' entered the lists with an absurd attack on Junius,[59] and during the following fortnight attempts were made to discredit both the Bill of Rights Society and the corporation at one blow by means of a satirical reply to a rumour that the latter, in a fit of pique at their recent defeat, had resolved to boycott the forthcoming Godiva procession:[60]

> Notwithstanding the scandalous report industriously propagated in order to prejudice a *certain respectable body* in the opinion of the public, they are assured that they intend to support the fair, and have engaged at a very considerable expence some *capital performers* to assist in the procession.
>
> The part of Lady Godiva, by the celebrated Mrs. M'A...y
> Peeping Tom, by Sir F. B. D.....l
> St. George, by Sir J. M....y
> Bishop Blaize, by Parson H..rne, and the inferior characters of Black Guards, Morris Dancers etc., by a select detachment of *Supporters of the Bill of Rights*, from the London Tavern. Vivant Rex et Regina.[61]

For the forseeable future, at any rate, the Coventry paper had plenty to crow about. During the summer of 1769 the freemen tasted the first fruits of their recent victory when Lord Mansfield delivered judgement in the court of King's Bench against the mayor and corporation on the charges brought against them by Sir Richard Glyn.[62] At the same time the first of the two petitions from the Middlesex freeholders which followed the Commons' admission of Henry Luttrell in Wilkes's place proved to be rather less formidable than it might have been,[63] and the *Coventry Mercury* took advantage of this to redouble its attack on the so-called patriots. Doubts were cast on the spontaneity and pretensions of the Middlesex petitioners, and Wilkes himself, portrayed as a pathetic figure who had been cast aside now that 'the moon of political madness was in its wane', was advised to salvage the remnants of his public character by renouncing his past. Similarly, 'Y.Z.', who regarded the dissidents as 'the restless offspring of the cruel murderers of Charles I', advised them to 'be quiet, enjoy the Toleration and be thankful'. For three weeks during August the constitutional arguments for Wilkes's expulsion were rehearsed at length on the paper's front page, and when the corporation did raise a petition in support of Wilkes in January 1770 Jopson treated its efforts with undisguised contempt, mocking the apathy of the public meeting which the 'pretended patriots' had called at St Mary's Hall, and predicting that

> if the whole does not drop through, ... another will be adopted and ... instead of lying disregarded at the Hall, ... will be harrass'd from house to house, and very probably will make its appearance on the highways.

As 'The Ribband, an Omen' had put it the previous autumn,

> By a blue ribband's going, we may guess
> The nation have no grievance to redress;
> That factious people only do petition,
> And that complaints spring only from sedition;
> That vulgar grumblings don't affect the Great,
> And that the Minister's as fixed as fate.[64]

With the petitioning campaign of 1769–70 and 'the printers' case' of 1771 still to come, it was hardly accurate to describe the 'moon of political madness' as waning in May 1769, no matter how confident George III himself may have been that 'with firmness ... this affair will vanish into smoke';[65] and however true the description may have turned out to be in the future, the Ministry was certainly not 'as fixed as fate' while it was still under the reluctant and bewildered leadership of the Duke of Grafton.[66] With regard to national politics, the *Coventry Mercury*'s version of politics during 1769 was therefore premature, to say the least; but it was nevertheless a fitting rehearsal for the paper's attitude during the next ten years. In Coventry itself the situation went from good to better. The ascendancy of the freemen was confirmed by an Act of Parliament in 1772 which enabled all eligible applicants to obtain their freedom without obstruction and by the acquisition of a powerful new local patron in Lord Craven of Coombe Abbey.[67] When Sir Richard Glyn died in January 1773 Walter Waring succeeded unopposed to the seat which he had contested five years earlier; and at the general election in 1774, for which Waring was joined by Edward Roe Yeo, a nominee of Lord Craven, the freemen finally took both seats from the corporation, which could find no better candidate than Thomas Green, one of its own members.[68] All this was very gratifying to Jopson's paper, and it provided the continuing ground for the support which the journal gave to the North Ministry throughout the American war. Even after General Burgoyne's surrender at Saratoga, when the *Birmingham Gazette* was laying odds of four to one on a French war inside six months,[69] the Coventry paper remained as sanguine as ever;[70] and its contents during the previous three years had at times been positively bellicose, as for example in its sneering 'substance of Dr. Franklin's proposals from the American Congress to the French Court' on 3 February 1777:

> Being now to our sorrow convinced of the dastardly and cowardly behaviour of the Army of our Commonwealth, in not daring to face the troops of our once parent state; at the same time sensible of having drawn God's curse and heavy displeasure upon us for our enormous ingratitude and disobedience towards our Mother Country, we came to a resolution of applying to Your Majesty's aid in this our sad inability and disappointment in striving against such power.

The *Coventry Mercury*'s most vicious taunts were, however, still reserved for its own immediate enemies, which now included the latest of a number of attempts to establish a second newspaper in the city,[71] and to use it both in support of the opposition to the war and as an agency of the corporation. The paper first bared its teeth at the prospect of such a rival on 24 March 1777, when it announced that

> With the new year, THE COVENTRY MERCURY entered on the thirty-seventh year of its existence, during which time, it has been exposed to a combination of foes not to be paralleled in the history of English Newspapers. . . . Like the insects of a summer's day, they have buzzed and stunk [*sic*], and stunk and retired; but, like other vermin, the eggs they have deposited may, by some revolving sun of success, be hatched for the propagation of the species. Be that as it will, beings of that complexion can have no longer any effect on THE COVENTRY MERCURY, improved and strengthened as it is. . . . Assisted by BRITONS, it may fairly bid defiance to any attempts that may hereafter be made to infringe it by a YANKEE DOODLE.

Though no names were mentioned, the probable object of this scornful dismissal was J. W. Piercy's *Coventry Gazette*. This was noticed again, this time by name, on 23 February 1778, when the *Coventry Mercury* carried a violent onslaught from one of its correspondents on an address which Piercy had printed the previous Saturday, calling for the repudiation of a proposed county subscription to augment the forces of the Crown.[72] For a time after this the *Coventry Mercury* ignored its competitor; but from September 1778 until some time in 1781[73] Piercy joined forces with Myles Swinney of the *Birmingham and Stafford Chronicle*, and it was this combination which brought Jopson's fury to its climax in 1780.

The first clash of the year was provoked by the by-election in February which followed the death of Walter Waring. Waring's successor was Edward Gibbon's friend John Baker Holroyd, the future Lord Sheffield, who offered himself on instructions sent post-haste from London by Alexander Wedderburn, the Attorney General.[74] As might be expected, the *Coventry Mercury* gave full coverage to Holroyd's nomination speech, which proclaimed his loyalty to Lord North, condemned Christopher Wyvill and the Associated Counties, and called on the Coventry freemen to show themselves true 'Friends to Freedom and Government',[75] but the unopposed return which followed aroused little comment. On 14 and 21 February, however, advertisements in Jopson's paper called on the freemen to press home their latest victory by meeting at the Drapers' Hall to serve notice on the corporation under the Act of 1772 compelling it to admit their unsworn members. This provoked a reply from Swinney and Piercy. On 8 March they printed a notice of their own disputing the legality of the free-men's action and charging the *Coventry Mercury* with the deliberate sup-pression of similar warnings during the preceding weeks. This in turn was countered in Jopson's paper of 10 April by a complex rebuttal which went on to rehearse once more the freemen's case against the corporation. Here the matter rested until the general election in the autumn.

The dissolution of the 1774 Parliament on 1 September 1780, when it still had over a year to run, caught the corporation by surprise. This time, however, it put up a real fight; for it now had the local support of Lord Craven, who had changed sides since 1774, as well as powerful candidates in Sir Thomas Hallifax and Thomas Rogers, two London bankers with radical connections.[76] The corporation's tactics reflected its relationship with the Coventry electorate. While the freemen derived their strength from the position of their leading members as prominent citizens and employers, and from the steady admission of new members to the freedom of the city as they completed their apprentice-ships, the corporation relied heavily on its control of the various city charities and on its ability to use the freemen's oath to swear 'mushroom' voters at election time. In September, at the start of the unexpectedly early poll, the advantage therefore lay with the freemen, and the corporation tried every possible trick to delay the proceedings until it had brought its support up to strength. The hustings in Cross Cheaping were sited in such a way as to restrict their accessibility to voters for Holroyd and Yeo while the mushrooms had easy and private passage from the corporation headquarters in the Mayor's Parlour and the Peacock inn; Hallifax and Rogers had a brisk young clerk assigned to them as teller while their opponents had to do the best they could with a dotard, and two hundred 'constables', most of them recruited from the tenantry of Lord Craven, were brought in to control the proceedings. When the poll was closed on pretext of riot after freemen and constables had fought each other for eight days on the hustings, only ninety-seven votes had been cast, and by the time it was reopened at the end of November the corporation had sub-stantially repaired its position. This time voting went on for twenty-five more days, which were again punctuated by delaying tactics on the part of the corporation, whose candidates were still trailing. Eventually all four contestants tried to persuade their supporters to call a halt and submit the election to the arbitration of the House of Commons by making a double return, but the cor-poration persisted in polling its mushrooms until the genuine freemen took matters into their own hands and once again forced an adjournment. When the poll was eventually closed for good the corporation had at last succeeded in scraping together enough of the inmates of Bablake Hospital and other riff-raff to give their candidates some sort of a majority, and Hallifax and Rogers were accordingly returned on 29 December, nearly four months after the election had first been called. Their triumph was short-lived, however, for the return was reversed after a scrutiny, and Holroyd and Yeo were restored to their seats early the following year.[77]

At every stage in this battle the rival newspapers laid into one another with a will.[78] When Swinney and Piercy defended the sheriffs for closing the first poll in response to complaints from Hallifax and Rogers that their voters were being intimidated by the freemen the *Coventry Mercury* dismissed such 'low scurrility' as 'fraught with all that falsehood and misrepresentation that a losing cause and disappointed hopes suggest', and maintained that the freemen had acted in self-defence against the mixed band of constables and colliers let loose by the corporation to provoke a riot and enforce the closure.[79] This version was probably closer to the truth; but though the sheriffs were called to answer for their action at the bar of the House of Commons their friends continued to support them. On 20 November Jopson's paper again had to refute the false assertions of 'Swinney's Gazette',[80] and Swinney and Piercy were still charging the freemen with armed intimidation as the second poll drew to its close.[81] After this, however, the pace slackened, and it was the *Coventry Mercury* which seems to have had the last word on 15 January 1781:

> Swinney and Piercy's *Mountain*, after having been in labour for near three weeks, hath at length brought forth a *mouse!* The narrative and affidavits so long promised made their appearance on Thursday last, authenticated by the *respectable* names or marks of Thomas Collett, Edward Sanders, Richard Merry, Thomas Pickin, Will Darlison, Edward Dogatt, and Thomas Smith.... Out of five constables, a Mayor, and an Alderman, only four of the *Right Worshipful* Septemvirate have *attempted* to *write* their names. As a proper supplement to the above, we are presented with a second address, signed T. Hallifax and T. Rogers, with an anonymous advertisement from some *other respectable character*. The compilers, writers, and publishers, cannot possibly expect a *serious* answer. ... They will therefore only be treated *at present* with that contemptuous silence which is the fittest *reply* to the paltry fabricators and abettors of nonsense, lies, and perjuries.

After 1780 Coventry's internal divisions became less acute but more complex. The control of the city's franchise and the conduct of its elections were at last put on a more regular footing by the City of Coventry Elections Act of 1781;[82] the ending of the partnership between Swinney and Piercy brought the newspaper war to a close, and during the next three years the relationship between freemen and corporation with regard to the city's representation changed in response to wider political events. Of the city's two members, Holroyd remained a consistent supporter of Lord North; but Yeo, who died at the end of 1782, was replaced by William Seymour-Conway, an associate of Charles James Fox, so that during 1783–84 Coventry was represented by a replica of the Fox–North coalition. In the general election of 1784 revulsion from this infamous combination produced a realignment of political sympathies in many parts of the country.[83] In Coventry, where a new set of colours was now paraded at the hustings, the old quarrel was overlain by the broader questions raised by the election, which split the original freeman interest into an 'Old Blue' and a Pittite 'New Blue' party, to which the corporation, fighting under its personal colours of yellow and green, attached itself as *tertium gaudens*.[84] The Old Blues tried hard to keep the old struggle in the forefront of attention, but they were unable to prevent large numbers of their freemen from transferring their support to the New Blues, who stressed the overriding importance of the national issue. The Pittite and corporation candidates, Sir Sampson Gideon, another banker, and his son-in-law, John Wilmot of Berkswell, were accordingly returned. After this the division between freemen and corporation remained less clear-cut, and since the circumstances which had hitherto given the *Coventry Mercury* its distinctive bias were therefore in abeyance the paper's own contents were henceforward more restrained. During the contest it did support the effort to maintain the original position and to save Lord Sheffield's seat at least,[85] and it did continue to give sympathetic coverage to the activities of the Old Blues during the months which followed. On the other hand, however, it could not ignore the New Blues altogether, and it made no discernible effort to suppress the notices and addresses of its opponents as totally as it had done in the past; for the political changes of 1783–84 had not only modified the reason for the Coventry paper's immediate *parti-pris*, they had also disturbed the interaction between local and national affairs which had determined its alignment on the latter since 1768. In fact the election of 1784 presented the paper with the same dilemma which it posed for the freemen as a whole; and so, with the main body of its regular readership now split between New and Old Blue, the *Coventry Mercury* conformed at length to the purported first principle of provincial journalism in the eighteenth century, not so much by treading the golden mean as by subsiding into a truculent independence, still punctuated from time to time by carping at the corporation and questionable personal jokes about the city's new members.

In addition to the different parts each of them played in the formation of political opinion by its own distinctive response to the events of the day, all three of the newspapers which served the West Midlands also paid due attention to articles, extracts and letters of more general and permanent interest, which they presented either in supplements given free from time to time or in special sections within the main paper. As it had been for most of the first part of the century, except when it was supplanted by more pressing discussion of foreign affairs and war,[86] the staple material of these miscellanies was still moralistic commentary on the manners of the age. During the summer of 1760, for example, the *Coventry Mercury* gave its readers a variety of pieces which included extracts from the *Christian Magazine* and 'The Mask', an article taken from the *Universal Chronicle*, which illustrated its discussion of the rational virtue of benevolence by a story first told by Hermann Boerhaave of a French gentleman's kindness to a poor man who had robbed him to feed his starving family. At the same time, a measure of comic relief was provided by 'Amelia Single', who described her ideal husband, offered a marriage portion of £10,000 to any man who felt sufficiently qualified, and received a prompt and appropriately facetious answer from 'C.D.'. Even the lighter essays had a serious purpose behind them, however, which was well illustrated a year later by 'Some Species of Modern Vanity Exemplified'. This ended its satire with the complaint that 'we are a nation of gentry, Populus Generosorum: we have no such thing as common people among us. Between vanity and gin, the species is utterly destroyed.'[87]

In Birmingham the same themes were developed; but though they may have shared the same general purpose, the styles adopted by the town's two papers remained discernibly different. With its warning that 'it would be well if the spirit of the times would change the darling characters of fine Gentlemen and Ladies for the more rational, solid influence of sense instigated by Religion and Virtue', and its reminder that 'Children (politically speaking) do not more

properly appertain to the Father than to the Kingdom in which they are born',
the essay on education which the *Birmingham Gazette* printed on 6 July 1767
struck a note of heavy seriousness. The remaining copies of the *Birmingham and
Stafford Chronicle*, on the other hand, suggest that, while his intentions remained equally conscientious, Myles Swinney tried to avoid such overwhelming
gravity by developing the combination of instruction and diversion further than
either of the other two papers. On 18 April 1776, for example, 'Momus, or
the Laughing Philosopher' discoursed light-heartedly on the embarrassment of
riches,[88] and a month later 'Minimus' contributed 'A Sketch of Modern Female
Education' which made fun of modish frivolity, and especially of the more
ludicrous aspects of fashionable marriage.[89] A particularly good example of this
kind of writing appeared the following July, when Swinney dealt with aristocratic profligacy and the evils of prostitution not by preaching but by playing
upon the humane sensibility first created by the novels of Richardson and
Fielding. This he achieved in 'Dialogues of the Living', in which 'Lord Lovejoy', ardent for the maidenhead of his ward, Lucy, after a masquerade, was
dissuaded from his object by the manly arguments of his friend and companion,
Mr Mounteney. Admittedly Mounteney's expostulation on 'the extremity of
wretchedness of every kind to which Prostitutes are doomed', and his plea for
pity 'to those unfortunate females whose passions may be stronger than their
reason', were nothing if not earnest. But the point was not pressed to excess,
and the dialogue ended not with Lovejoy's total renunciation of the fair sex,
which would have been too good to be true, but with a realistic gentleman's
agreement to leave Lucy intact at least, and with Mounteney's promise to his
young friend that 'having gained one great point, I will give you no more
trouble at present, nor will I despair of making you in future everything which
I wish you to be'.[90]

In its balance between morality and realistic tolerance and in its appeal to
practical good sense this piece bespoke the same liberal sympathies which
prompted Swinney to publish Voltaire on religion in the *Warwickshire Journal*
during 1771,[91] or David Hume's account of his own life, to which the *Birmingham and Stafford Chronicle* devoted its 'miscellaneous Repository' on 27 March
1777. Swinney's more flexible attitude was also reflected in the greater space
which he found for the work of local authors. In this connection it would be
interesting to know what the *Birmingham and Stafford Chronicle* printed
during the later 1780s, when Swinney was also doing a good deal of work for
various members of the Lunar Society, notably Joseph Priestley and William
Withering, and for other literary and intellectual figures in the region.[92] Certainly Anna Seward of Lichfield was a regular contributor during 1792, and
in June that year the paper also carried Erasmus Darwin's lines on the steam
engine from his poetic description of natural philosophy, *The Botanic Garden*.[93]

Moral essays and *belles lettres* were not, however, the only pieces the newspapers printed in their miscellanies. They also drew on other material which
ranged from extended commentaries on current affairs to articles on humanitarian reform, accounts of foreign exploration and travel, advice on agricultural
improvements and the various aspects of political economy, and detailed reports
of important local and regional developments. The last of these categories was
most characteristic of the *Birmingham Gazette*, whose miscellany during 1772–73
followed its opening 'account of canals' with a summary of proposed extensions

to the Lamp Act and with the details of the Birmingham Assay Office Bill.[94] In addition, each of the supplements printed pamphlet extracts on major national issues which reflected the sympathies of their parent papers, but apart from this there was less to choose between them. All three gave extensive publicity to the movement for the abolition of slavery,[95] and at different times their imagination was equally caught by the interest in remote parts of the world and the ways of savage tribes still living in a state of nature which had been stimulated by the voyages of Captain Cook and his fellow explorers.[96] In other respects, too, the three papers overlapped each other. The enthusiasm for the methods and agricultural achievements of the physiocrats which was shown by Swinney on 29 August 1776 can perhaps be regarded as a new variation in the standard exercise of Anglo-French comparison, but all three papers vied with each other in their coverage of similar developments at home. In January 1764, for example, the *Coventry Mercury* was providing extracts[97] from the *Museum Rusticum*, the monthly journal published by the Society of Arts which acted as a forum for the discussion of farming improvements, and the paper was far from being overshadowed by its Birmingham counterparts with regard to the space which it devoted from then onwards to the changing social and economic state of the country. During the provision crisis of the mid-1760s articles and letters on this subject became and remained a regular characteristic of all three papers, but it is interesting to find that several of the most substantial contributions to the local debate, most notably the first abridgement of Adam Smith's ideas to reach ordinary readers in the West Midlands, which appeared on 19 August 1776 as 'Thoughts on Commerce and the Riches of a State',[98] were made not through the agency of Aris or Swinney but in the columns of the *Coventry Mercury*.

Though variations in style and approach can still be discerned, the differences in sympathy and local circumstance which distinguished the three papers with regard to their political roles thus had less effect on their more general function. Nevertheless in this respect too they served as active agents of opinion, complementing each other in the supply of 'intelligence, instruction and entertainment' to the region in which they circulated. And this leads to the consideration of different aspects of communication; for the means by which West Midlanders acquired a distinctive sense of their own identity must be sought not only in such tangible forms of expression as the newspapers themselves but also in the entire range of activities recorded within them, by which the region looked for social and cultural status as well as for political recognition. Attention must therefore now be turned to the interplay between the established round of social occasions which provided the accepted leaders of society with opportunities for the informal discussion of matters of interest, and the popular diversions which provided a medium for the beginnings of a wider articulacy among the common people.

NOTES

1 For the early history of the provincial press in England see G. A. Cranfield, *The Development of the Provincial Newspaper, 1700–60* (Oxford, 1962).

2 For these developments see Donald Read, *The English Provinces*, pp. 44–6, and *Press and People, 1790–1850* (London, 1961).

3 Cranfield, *Development of the Provincial Newspaper*, pp. 117–40.

4 See Bernard Bailyn, *The Origins of American Politics* (New York, 1968), ch. 1, especially pp. 38–9: 'For it was the opposition press as much as any single influence that shaped the political awareness of eighteenth-century Americans; it was the opposition version of politics, past and present, that became the ordinary presumption of informed Americans.'

5 See below, pp. 168–80.

6 For the geographical development of the newspapers' circulating areas see appendix 1. In addition to *Aris*, *Swinney* and *Jopson* two other papers have been referred to: *Piercy's Coventry Gazette*, which competed with *Jopson* for a short time during the later 1770s, and *Berrow's Worcester Journal*. Since the latter's area of circulation lay mainly adjacent to the region, it has not been examined in comprehensive detail for the whole period, but has been referred to specifically for corroboration of political developments in Worcester and Worcestershire between 1769 and 1774, which exerted significant influence on events in the Birmingham area (see below, pp. 104–9).

7 See below, pp. 250–5.

8 *Aris*, 24 January 1763, 1 April 1765.

9 *Aris*, 30 September 1765.

10 *Aris*, 2 June 1766

11 See, for example, *Aris*, 3, 24 April 1769, during the controversy over the Middlesex election; 16 August 1784, rejecting a piece from Shropshire which related 'too much to party matters'; 15 August 1788, refusing several contributions on 'a late Theological difference'.

12 Asa Briggs, 'Press and public opinion in early nineteenth century Birmingham', Dugdale Society, *Occasional Papers*, No. 8 (1949), p. 7.

13 See below, ch. x.

14 See below, p. 177.

15 *Aris*, 21 January 1771.

16 *Aris*, 18 September 1769.

17 See below, p. 123.

18 See below, pp. 87–91.

19 See his remarks on the Lamp Act, 20 March 1769, and his angry reaction on 1, 8 March 1773, when the London Goldsmiths' Company tried to obstruct the passage of the Birmingham Assay Office Act.

20 *V.C.H. Warwicks.*, VII, 221.

21 In the Baskerville edition of his *Political Songster* (1771), B.R.L. 81720, song XXXVII. *Cf.* R. W. Malcolmson, *Popular Recreation in English Society, 1700–1850* (Cambridge, 1973). Malcolmson notes that the Black Country was one of the areas in which the tradition of cruel sports was particularly persistent.

22 *Aris*, 10 July, 11, 18 September 1775, 29 January, 5, 12, 19 February, 4 March 1776.

23 *Aris*, 30 September 1776.

24 For this see Brian D. Bargar, 'Matthew Boulton and the Birmingham petition of 1775', *William and Mary Quarterly*, 3rd series, XIII (1956), pp. 26–30.

25 See *Voltaire's Creed Proved Insufficient for Man's Salvation, in Five Letters to Anonymous, four of which have appeared in the Warwickshire Journal, by The Objector* (Birmingham, 1771), B.R.L. 62409. The introduction to this explained that it was prompted by 'Voltaire's *Thoughts on Religion* being exhibited in a public newspaper'.

26 These were the *Birmingham and Wolverhampton Chronicle*, published by Nicholas Boden and Orion Adams, which started on Thursday 23 March 1769 and survived until 1770; a different *Birmingham Chronicle*, first issued, under the auspices of Swinney and James Sketchley, on 24 March 1769, and the *Warwickshire Journal*, launched by Samuel Aris with a free edition on 6 April following as a Thursday paper to complement the Monday *Birmingham Gazette*. Thanks probably to this association with a going concern, which gave it a ready-made system of outlets, the last of these proved the most viable. By the end of May 1769 Aris had provided it with its own extensive distribution network, concentrated towards north Worcestershire and the Severn valley, but with important offshoots north-eastwards as well; and in the autumn the *Warwickshire Journal* was effectively transferred to Swinney's management. The subtitle 'and Hereford Mercury' was added for a time in 1770, and the loose partnership with Aris continued until August 1773, after which Swinney became the independent publisher of what was thenceforward

known as *Swinney's Birmingham and Stafford Chronicle*. For these details see *V.C.H. Warwicks.*, VII, 210; Hill, *Bookmakers*, pp. 72–5; *Aris*, 10 April, 29 May, 16 November 1769, 16 August 1773. For the other printers mentioned see below, pp. 122–24.

27 See below, pp. 123–6, 141–2.
28 Among Matthew Boulton's papers: *A.O.P.*, 'America' box.
29 See below, p. 190.
30 See below, pp. 199–200.
31 *A.O.P.*, Dartmouth to Boulton, 19 January 1775.
32 *Swinney*, 7, 20 June 1776.
33 This was probably taken from the *Gazetteer*, to which 'A Boston Saint' was a regular contributor at this time. See S. Lutnick, *The American Revolution and the British Press, 1775–82* (Columbia, Mo., 1967), p. 60.
34 See above, n. 26.
35 See below, pp. 199–210.
36 See, for example, the Letter from Whitehaven which Swinney printed on 20 June 1776, giving a detailed appraisal of the political and military strengths both of Congress and of General Howe, and of the likelihood of Independence. Similarly, see the speculations on the probable consequences of American independence by M. Mignet, late of the Parlement of Paris, on 24 December 1778.
37 Public Record Office, Home Office Papers, H.O. 42/25, Brooke to Evan Nepean, 7 June 1793.
38 The partnership had begun in 1792. See Hill, *Bookmakers*, p. 78.
39 Neither in the Home Office papers nor in the record of newspaper subsidies in the Secret Service accounts; Chatham MSS, P.R.O. 30/8/229.
40 Swinney's partner from 1793 onwards was John Collins, a local song writer and music hall impresario. See Hill, *Bookmakers*, p. 78.
41 For an account of Coventry politics see *Whitley; Hist. Parl.*, I, 400–2, and *V.C.H. Warwicks.*, VIII, 251–3.
42 *Jopson*, 30 March, 6, 13 April, 11 May, 15 June–6 July, 3, 10 August 1761.
43 *Jopson*, 21 June 1762. For the London press at this time see Robert R. Rea, *The English Press and Politics, 1760–1774* (Lincoln, Neb., 1963).
44 *Jopson*, 12 July 1762.
45 *Jopson*, 19 July, 30 August, 6–27 September, 2 October 1762.
46 G. F. Rudé, *Wilkes and Liberty: a Social History of 1763–74* (Oxford, 1962), pp. 22–4.
47 *Jopson*, 1 July 1765.
48 *Jopson*, 7 September 1767.
49 *Jopson*, 2, 9, 16 November 1767.
50 *Jopson*, 27 June, 1 August 1768.
51 *Whitley*, pp. 165–8; *Hist. Parl.*, I, 401; Sir Lewis Namier, *The Structure of Politics at the Accession of George III* (2nd edn, London, 1957), pp. 102–3.
52 *Hist. Parl.*, I, 401.
53 *Hist. Parl.*, II, 506.
54 *Whitley*, p. 167.
55 *Jopson*, 7–21 November 1768.
56 *Jopson*, 28 November 1768. French silks had been excluded from the English market by an Act of 1765, which Glyn was said to have opposed.
57 Rudé, *Wilkes and Liberty*, pp. 89–104.
58 *Jopson*, 1 May 1769. 'Sir Joseph Mushroom' was Sir Joseph Mawbey, malt distiller, MP for Southwark and one of the original members of the Society of the Supporters of the Bill of Rights. (Rudé, *Wilkes and Liberty*, p. 61.)
59 *Jopson*, 8 May 1769.
60 *Jopson*, 15 May 1769: 'Verses occasioned by the report that the Corporation, being unable to set their horses together, have determined not to *riot* at the ensuing fair.'
61 *Jopson*, 22 May 1769. Lady Godiva—Catherine Macaulay; Peeping Tom—Sir Francis Blake Delaval, Bt, of Seaton Delaval, Northumberland, former MP for Andover (Rudé, *Wilkes and Liberty*, p. 179); St George—Sir Joseph Mawbey; Bishop Blaize—John Horne, parson of New Brentford vicarage, the prime mover behind the Bill of Rights Society and better known, of course, by his later style of John Horne Tooke.
62 *Jopson*, 26 June, 3 July 1769. See also *The Chronicles of the Times at Coventry*

During the Reign of Nebuchadnezzar the Third, King of Utopia (Coventry, 1776, reprinted as an appendix to *Whitley*), ch. XII, vv. 7, 8.

63 Rudé, *Wilkes and Liberty*, pp. 70–3, 200–2.

64 *Jopson*, 22 May, 24, 31 July, 7–28 August, 2 October 1769, 15 January 1770. The 'blue ribband's going' probably refers to the conferral of the Order of the Garter on the Duke of Grafton, and possibly also to rumours that the Earl of Bute had been rebuffed by the King on his recent return from the Continent: see John Brewer, 'The misfortunes of Lord Bute: a case study in eighteenth century political management and public opinion', *Historical Journal*, XVI (1973), 1–43, especially at pp. 30–1.

65 Quoted by Rudé, *Wilkes and Liberty*, p. 72.

66 Grafton did not resign until January 1770, by which time the situation of the Ministry had become critical. See *Hist. Parl.*, I, 73.

67 *V.C.H. Warwicks.*, VIII, 253; *Whitley*, p. 169; below, p. 203. Craven's support did not, however, last far beyond the 1774 election. In the autumn of 1775 his name appeared with that of Lord Archer, the corporation's leading patron, at the head of a petition against the American war, and in the 1780 election he supported the corporation.

68 Henry Seymour-Conway, hitherto the corporation's remaining member, transferred his seat to Bury St Edmunds: *V.C.H. Warwicks.*, VIII, 252.

69 *Aris*, 5 January 1778.

70 See below, p. 188.

71 The first of these was *Luckman and Sketchley's Coventry Gazette, or Weekly Country Magazine*, of 1757, which by 1761 had become *Luckman and Sketchley's Coventry Gazette and Birmingham Chronicle*, and by September 1762 the *Coventry, Birmingham and Worcester Chronicle*. See G. A. Cranfield, *Handlist of English Provincial Newspapers and Periodicals, 1700–60* (Cambridge Bibliographical Society Monographs, No. 2, 1952), p. 6. Other than this, little is known about the paper, but *Jopson* referred to it on 24 October 1763, and on 7 May 1764 cast contempt on its recent demise as a newspaper and its feeble attempt to survive by appearing as a country magazine in order to avoid advertisement duty.

72 See below, p. 188, and *Piercy's Coventry Gazette*, 2 February 1778.

73 Piercy took over Thomas Luckman's printing business in Coventry at the end of 1771 (*Jopson*, 30 December 1771). The earliest number of his paper which survives is No. 42, of 10 January 1778, which gives a conjectural starting date of 29 March 1777. During 1778, for which the file is almost complete, the paper gave extensive coverage to the affairs of the Continental Congress and to correspondence between the American leaders, and it is notable that, even before he joined forces with Swinney, Piercy's Birmingham agent was the Unitarian printer James Belcher. Piercy's first issue in conjunction with Swinney was that for 3 September 1778; the *Birmingham and Stafford Chronicle* of 24 December 1778 was also printed by Piercy and carried a special section for Coventry news, and the two printers announced the fall of Charleston in a joint *Gazette Extraordinary* (kept for some reason on the proprietor's file of *Aris*) on 17 June 1780. According to Hill, *Bookmakers*, p. 78, the partnership ended some time in 1781.

74 *Whitley*, p. 175. The Drapers' Company, which was the leading element in the freemen's party, had asked the Ministry to find them a candidate. Holroyd was in Coventry at the time as commanding officer of the troops quartered there.

75 *Jopson*, 7 February 1780.

76 For Hallifax and Rogers see *Hist. Parl.*, II, 567, III, 371. Craven's support of the corporation seems to have owed a good deal to his wife Elizabeth, the future Margravine of Anspach and one of the most celebrated beauties of the day. Cf. Epigram in *Jopson*, 4 December 1780:

> From spite and malice toward honest Yeo,
> The lovely Cr---n every length will go.
> She turns each stone for Hallifax and Rogers:
> In female breasts are such base passions lodgers.

77 *Jopson*, 25 September, 4 December 1780, 1 January 1781; *Hist. Parl.*, I, 401–2; *Whitley*, pp. 176–88.

78 The surviving evidence is all from *Jopson*, but though the reactions of Swinney's and Piercy's paper must be inferred from this, the abuse is unlikely to have been one-sided.

79 *Jopson*, 18, 25 September 1780, attacking accounts of Swinney and Piercy on 14th and 21st.

80 During the quarrel Jopson's rival was variously referred to as 'The Birmingham Chronicle', 'Swinney's Gazette' and 'Piercy's Birmingham and Coventry Gazette'.

81 *Jopson*, 18 December 1780.

82 *V.C.H. Warwicks.*, VIII, 253.

83 See M. D. George, 'Fox's martyrs and the general election of 1784', *Trans. Royal Hist. Soc.*, 4th series, XXI (1939), 133–68; also Paul Kelly, 'Radicalism and public opinion in the general election of 1784', *Bull. Inst. Hist. Res.*, XLV (1972), 73–88.

84 *Whitley*, pp. 190–9.

85 See issues for 22 March and 5 April 1784.

86 *Cf.* Cranfield, *Development of the Provincial Newspaper*, pp. 112–16.

87 *Jopson*, 16, 30 June, 7 July 1760, 29 June 1761.

88 The nearest Aris seems to have got to this sort of thing was 'The Ramblings of Mr. Frankly' on 11 January 1773.

89 *Swinney*, 23 May 1776.

90 *Swinney*, 11 July 1776.

91 See above, p. 59.

92 Hill, *Bookmakers*, p. 79.

93 *Swinney*, 5 January, 19 April, 7 June, 9, 23 August 1792.

94 *Aris*, 30 November 1772, 26 April, 21 June 1773.

95 *Aris*, 11 August, 1–29 September, 3 November 1783, 17, 22 November 1784, 24 December 1787, 7 January–18 February, 22 December 1788, 25 April, 14 November–12 December 1791. *Swinney*, 8 December 1791, 19, 26 April, 3 May 1792. *Jopson*, 27 October, 3, 10 November 1783, 14, 21, 28 November, 19 December 1785, 20 March, 5 June 1786, 2 April 1787.

96 *Aris*, 12 July 1773: an account of the South Seas; *Jopson*, 26 July 1773: 'Uncommon Notions of the Natural and Civil State of Man', from Lord Monboddo's *Treatise of the Origin and Progress of Language*. The absence of surviving copies frustrates a contemporary comparison from *Swinney*, but *cf.* 11 June 1789: the fourth letter of a series describing 'A Voyage to Botany Bay'.

97 *Jopson*, 30 January 1764.

98 See below, p. 257.

IV

SOCIAL AND CULTURAL ASPIRATIONS: MUSIC AND THE STAGE

As Samuel Pipe-Wolferstan, of Statfold, near Tamworth,[1] was to discover after the death of his first wife in 1786, the social aspirations which accompanied Birmingham's rising prosperity aroused mixed feelings in the surrounding area. Samuel, a Staffordshire gentleman of ancient lineage but progressive persuasion, was anxious to marry again. Thanks to the intellectual engagement with Unitarianism and free-thought which was his other main preoccupation at the time, the quest took longer than expected, and by 1789 had been extended not only to the eligible ladies of south Staffordshire, north Warwickshire and the western parts of Leicestershire but also to the more reputable families of Birmingham. A Birmingham match would have suited Samuel himself quite well, but when he discussed the idea with a neighbour, Mrs Rainsford, the exchange expressed succinctly the misgivings with which such an alliance was likely to be received:

> Told her I thought there must be many polished people in Birmingham. She thought but few, but however declared against recommending—(my idea was she might know some, possibly among nonconformists, as she some days ago was praising Miss Wildman, and I thought to apprize her that was no objection).[2]

County society had reservations about the acceptability of the rising town. Quite apart from the manners and the uncertain pedigrees of its people, and the still less certain notions which many of them seemed to hold on politics and religion, Birmingham was 'not a place a gentleman would choose to make his residence. Its continual noise and smoke prevent it from being desirable in that respect'.[3] But even if the better families of the West Midlands looked askance at bourgeois connections, let alone at the prospect of actually living inside the limits of the town, they came to visit it in increasing numbers, and had no objection to establishing themselves within easy reach of its attractions. Though not comparable with those of London and the more fashionable resorts, these were by no means inconsiderable. As early as 1760 Samuel Derrick, who was well qualified to judge,[4] pronounced Birmingham 'spacious and well built' and its people, who enjoyed a full round of balls, concerts, plays and assemblies, 'rich, civil and industrious'. The theatre was 'very neat'; its players were from London, and if they were not exactly a 'picked lot' Derrick did concede that they were 'greatly encouraged' during their summer visits. The concerts at Vauxhall Gardens, likewise 'small and neat, though but indifferently situated', also gave good value at a ticket price of a shilling.[5] As a result it could be claimed by the end of the century that there were 'very many families, both in the town and its vicinity, of great taste, education and refinement',[6] and William Hutton, who was confident that 'civility and humanity are ever companions of trade', could boast in 1781 that

> Even the men of inferior life among us, whose occupations one would think tend
> to produce minds as callous as the metal they work, lay a stronger claim to
> civilization than in another place with which I am acquainted.[7]

Samuel Pipe-Wolferstan's original estimate of Birmingham was therefore at least as supportable as his neighbours' distaste. If this was so, it was to a large extent the result of conscious effort on the part of the town's leaders to overcome the coolness with which Birmingham's pretensions had been received hitherto. These efforts, which were particularly concentrated on the encouragement of musical and theatrical entertainments in the town, are important because they stemmed not from a mere desire to gratify the social ambitions of new wealth —though this was no doubt an accessory motive—but from a very practical awareness that the nature of Birmingham's trades made their continuing prosperity specially dependent on the careful cultivation of an affinity at every level with the leaders, the manners and above all the taste of established society. The promotion of music and theatre, which were closely interrelated, therefore made a highly significant contribution to the town's developing character and to its political reactions. The latter was particularly the case because, despite the emphasis which was placed on high standards of respectability by the chief patrons of the two arts, neither proved entirely amenable to paternal control, and both played their part in the formation of the popular culture which was the ground for the increasing articulacy of Birmingham's ordinary people.

Whether it involved 'a band of vocal and instrumental music' at subscription assembly or pleasure garden, or excerpts from Handel's oratorios on more solemn occasions, music was the form of social diversion most readily and widely acceptable in established society. Even when the occasion was secular, performance was likely to be in the hands of gentlemen amateurs or of those who had learned their skill in the service of the Church, so that assemblies, concerts and oratorio festivals did not carry the same dubious connotations as a season of plays or other mountebank entertainment given by a travelling company of mixed origins and repute. As a result, music meetings, like that held in June 1789 in connection with the Blue Coat charity school at Bridgnorth, which included a 'grand miscellaneous concert' followed by a ball in the town hall, sacred music at St Leonard's church and a performance of *Messiah*,[8] became a regular part of the social calendar in most of the more important towns in the West Midlands. Admittedly, Bridgnorth's plans in 1789, which were consciously based on the Handel commemorations in Westminster Abbey, were more ambitious than most, but they were not unique. In 1766 the annual charity sermon at Wednesbury had likewise been marked by a performance of *Messiah*; in Coventry, where concerts and assemblies had been held since the 1740s at the Drapers' and St Mary's Halls, not to mention various other rooms in the city, a 'numerous and brilliant' audience of nobility and gentry had heard both *Messiah* and *Samson* at St Mary's Hall in 1760, and Capel Bond, the organist of St Michael's and Holy Trinity churches, who directed on this occasion, played a prominent part in the promotion of similar performances in other parts of the region, including Wolverhampton and Birmingham itself.[9]

Since he was himself an amateur cellist of some ability, Samuel Pipe-Wolferstan's diary illustrates well the part which such music meetings could play in provincial life. Quite apart from the informal evenings which he spent playing chamber music with his friends, Mr Jervis and Mr Godfrey, Samuel was a regular member of the orchestra at local concerts, and even when he was not actually playing, these occasions drew him into a widening variety of contacts and interests. In September 1777, for example, a Tamworth concert gave him a chance to discuss estate plans with a neighbour; and two months later, when he dined with Erasmus Darwin before the annual Cecilian concert in Lichfield, an acquaintance previously confined to the Doctor's frequent professional calls at Statfold was changed into something more personal, which led in due course to several more visits, including one on 9 December 1780 at which Samuel was given a demonstration of Darwin's warm-bath copying machine.[10] Nor were the fringes of the Lunar Circle the only ones to which Samuel was introduced in the cathedral city; and if he owed his contact in this instance more to the social occasion of the Cecilian concert than to shared musical interests in themselves, these probably played a larger part in his long-standing familiarity with Anna Seward and the clergy of Lichfield close. During the later 1780s, when he was in two minds whether to make a name for himself and advance his 'matrimonial imaginations' by setting his sights on the Commission of the Peace, or whether to exchange a conventional reputation for the notoriety to be gained by instituting his own Unitarian form of service at Statfold church, this relationship was an important influence on the debate which Samuel carried on with himself until his enthusiasm for eccentricity was overcome by reluctance to cut himself off from his accustomed circle and mounting alarm at the direction in which his advanced London friends seemed to be moving.[11]

The experience of Samuel Pipe-Wolferstan serves as a reminder that it was Lichfield rather than Birmingham which was the original social and cultural capital of the West Midlands.[12] Besides the fame of Dr Johnson and David Garrick, and the part the city played through Erasmus Darwin in the Lunar Society and the history of science, the Bishop's Palace, which was the home of Canon Thomas Seward and his daughter Anna,[13] was the centre of an extensive and varied circle of literati. Among this group serious music, well supplied by the resources of the cathedral, was an abiding passion, and since 1742, the annual Cecilian concert had not only been a major occasion in the Lichfield year but had also attracted envious attention from other less fortunate places. 'You revived my heart very much,' wrote the Rev. Joseph Greene, master of the Free School at Stratford on Avon, in 1754, 'by putting me in mind of Saint Cecilia's day at Lichfield: oh that Saint Cecilia would inspire as zealous devotees everywhere, especially at Stratford!'[14] Joseph went on to ask his brother, a well known Lichfield worthy, if the honorary membership of the Cecilian society which had been extended to the saint's devotees in Birmingham might be stretched yet further. This suggests not only that Stratford on Avon had little musical to offer but also that at this time Birmingham itself was looking to the older city. To judge by the frequent attention which was drawn to the participation of Lichfield musicians, particularly John Saville,[15] in Birmingham concerts later in the century, the same relationship was to prevail for some time to come.

Nevertheless by the second half of the century Birmingham was supporting a musical life of its own which probably surpassed that of Lichfield in variety, even if the older centre could still claim the advantage in standards of serious performance. As at Lichfield, it was the Church that provided the basic resources. Of Birmingham's early musical leaders, Barnabas Gunn and his successor John Eversmann were both organists at St Martin's and St Philip's; Jeremiah Clarke, perhaps the town's first fully qualified professional musician in the modern sense of the word, became organist of St Philip's in 1765 and remained so until 1803; Richard Hobbs, one of the town's earliest proponents of oratorio, served St Martin's in the same capacity, and Michael Broome, who ran a music publishing business in Lichfield Street from 1734 until his death in 1775 and was one of the founders in 1762 of the Birmingham Musical and Amicable Society, was clerk of St Philip's.[16] As Broome's example suggests, however, the interests of these men were not confined to church music, and certainly both Barnabas Gunn and John Eversmann would be better described as impresarios than as mere organists. Both were closely associated with the entertainments which were given at the Vauxhall Gardens and in Mr Sawyer's assembly room in the Square; and Gunn, who over and above his musical projects was also Birmingham's postmaster, was as much at home writing for the Moor Street and King Street theatres as he was setting psalms for the choir at St Philip's.[17] Thanks to such versatility, Birmingham people in 1760 could already take their choice from a local musical repertoire which ranged from sacred oratorio and serious opera, through comic and ballad operas like *The Dragon of Wantley* or *The Beggar's Opera* and its various imitators, to incidental music for Shakespeare and the various occasional and virtuoso pieces which made up the bulk of the programmes at the pleasure gardens.[18]

After 1760 growing demand and Birmingham's sense of its increasing importance produced rapid advances in the standard and pretensions of the town's music. Though one of the early pleasure grounds, Holte Bridgman's Apollo Gardens in Aston, had closed in 1751 when its owner returned to his original business of house painting,[19] Vauxhall continued to prosper, and in 1772 the assembly room at the Royal Hotel, built partly in response to the Duke of York's disparaging remarks some years earlier on the inadequacies of the existing facilities, replaced Mr Sawyer's older premises in the Square as the town's main setting for polite social gatherings.[20] Chief among these were the Hotel Subscription Dancing Assemblies and the concerts given by the Dilettanti Musical Society under the direction of Jeremiah Clarke. When these two were amalgamated in 1788 they were offering a regular programme throughout the year. During the winter months of the 1788–89 season six grand concerts and balls were to be interspersed with card and dancing assemblies each intervening fortnight, and a second series of monthly concerts was planned for the following summer.[21] The primary purpose of this programme was clearly social, but the Dilettanti Society nevertheless served as a valuable nursery for Birmingham's own musicians, which freed the town from its dependence on the resources of older centres. And if the serious significance of the joint evenings organised by the Dilettanti Society and the Hotel Subscription Dancing Assemblies was probably secondary, the two concerts which Mr Fletcher arranged at the hotel and St Paul's chapel on 17 and 18 May 1790 suggest that Birmingham audiences were well able to appreciate more substantial offerings, consisting as they did in the first case of overtures by Haydn and Pleyel together with songs and concerti for violin and cello performed by 'several capital players from London', and in the second of 'A grand selection of SACRED MUSIC, as intended to be performed at the ensuing meeting at Westminster Abbey:

I Overture—Esther; Recit.—"This New Creation"; Song—"Vain your triumphs"; Chorus—"He gave them hailstones"; Song—"Where'er I [*sic*] walk"; Chorus—"The Mighty Hand"; Recit.—"Rejoice Oh Judah".

II Introduction and Chorus—"Ye Sons of Israel"; Air—"Tyrants would"; Chorus—"Tyrants, ye in vain"; Song—"Angels ever"; Chorus—"The Lord"; Recit.—"For the Horse"; Chorus—"The Lord"; Recit.—"For the Horse"; Chorus—"The Lord"; Recit.—"And Miriam"; Air—"Sing Ye"; Chorus— "The Horse"; Recit.—"Ye Sacred"; Air—"Farewell"; Chorus—"From the censer".

III Overture—"Messiah"; Recit.—"Comfort Ye"; Air—"Ev'ry Valley"; Chorus —"And the"; Recit.—"For be"; Song—"The People"; Chorus—"For unto us"; Recit:—"He was"; Song—"But thou"; Chorus—"Lift up—who is— The Lord—He is"; Song—"I know"; Grand Chorus—"For the Lord".[22]

Even allowing for the truncations dictated by available newspaper space, the assumption that the average reader of the *Birmingham Gazette* would be able to pick his way through such an advertisement suggests that local audiences must have known their Handel backwards, not to mention the graphic illustration it provides of the way in which the composer's different works had become amalgamated in the English imagination into one grand national oratorio. This draws attention to the most significant development in Birmingham's musical history during the eighteenth century: the establishment of its triennial festivals. Birmingham first heard *Messiah* in 1757, and three years later the work was given again, together with *Samson* and *Judas Maccabaeus*, by a visiting orchestra from London. After this, other performances of Handel's music were given at various times by Capel Bond of Coventry, Richard Hobbs, organist of St Martin's, and Thomas Kempson, clerk of St Bartholomew's and founder in 1766 of the Oratorio Choral Society.[23] In itself, therefore, oratorio was not new to the town when the first festival was held under Capel Bond's direction in 1768, and the competitive aspects of the situation had already been hinted at the previous year in the rhetorical question

In other towns, while oratorios please,
Shall we in gloomy silence spend our days?[24]

What was new was the association of the 1768 festival with the newly founded General Hospital. In this, of course, Birmingham was following the example most obviously set by the Foundling Hospital festivals, inaugurated by Handel himself in 1749; but the association of the Birmingham festivals with the particular circumstances and motives which had led to the foundation of the General Hospital meant that they came to embody in a particularly heightened form the town's larger aspirations. As 'Crito's' lines of September 1778 'on hearing Mr. Perry perform on the Musical Glasses at Stratford' show,[25] even the most trivial musical events were apt to have their moral potential fully exploited, and the festivals came to serve as vehicles *par excellence* for solemn public ritual, at which the people of Birmingham could affirm their own high calling in the lofty themes of sacred oratorio. During the following century this process achieved physical expression in the architectural history of Birmingham's new town hall, and it reached its apotheosis in the festival of 1846, at which Felix Mendelssohn conducted the first performance of his *Elijah*. The proceedings at the start of the 1778 festival, which began with a sermon in St Philip's church 'on the necessity of a liberal and public spirited support of the objects under consideration, as tending effectually and essentially to support the interests both of religion and humanity', suggest, however, that it was consciously encouraged from the start.[26]

At a more immediate and material level, too, the festivals played an important part in Birmingham's development; for though they were always the main items on the programme the solemnity of the oratorios was set off by a judicious choice of secular offerings as well.[27] This soon established the meetings as a major rendezvous for the Quality of the West Midlands. In 1790, for example, by which time the festival had expanded until it occupied not only St Philip's but also the assembly room at the Royal Hotel and the New Street Theatre as well, the concerts were graced by the presence of the Earls of Aylesford and Warwick and enhanced by the exertions of Viscount Dudley and Ward. Lord Dudley had already served with conspicuous success as steward of the 1784 and 1787 meetings, and he had now surpassed himself by engaging the celebrated soprano Madame Mara[28] to add lustre to the performances. Among other notable members of the distinguished company was Sir Robert Lawley, and the entire gathering was attended by a ceremonial escort, provided by Henry Clay, the pupil of John Baskerville who had made a fortune out of papier-mâché toys and was now celebrating his year as High Sheriff of Warwickshire in the grand manner.[29] In addition to the obvious element of self-advertisement entailed in such extravaganzas, moreover, the festivals also served Birmingham's interests in more tangible ways. In 1785, when he was straining every nerve to rouse local opinion against William Pitt's Irish commercial proposals, Samuel Garbett discussed with Matthew Boulton the likelihood of support in high places. Though Garbett was aware that Lord Dudley's tenantry were deeply interested in the nail trade, it was the fact that 'lately he hath been not only attentive, but generous to us, by donations to our hospital, and in the handsomest manner, gave his *time* and *money* and entertainment to our music meeting,'[30] which first suggested the viscount as a potential ally. The festivals thus took their place very quickly alongside the other social occasions, such as the race meetings at Warwick and Lichfield,[31] which acted as informal channels for the complex connections which were being formed between Birmingham, the region which surrounded it and the patronage on which the prosperity of both was felt to depend.

It would, however, be wrong to leave the impression that music's part in Birmingham life was entirely confined to great occasions and genteel surroundings. At the popular level it also occupied a major place in the proceedings of the town's numerous tavern societies, whose dedication to convivial song as well as to mutual benefit and charitable works was epitomised by the motto of the Birmingham Musical and Amicable Society:

> May the Catch and the Glass go about and about,
> And another succeed to the bottle that's out.[32]

Since its leading light was Thomas Kempson and most of its original members were drawn from the choirs of St Philip's and St Bartholomew's,[33] the main affiliations of this particular group, which met at Cooke's Tavern in the Cherry Orchard, probably remained with the more formal aspects of Birmingham music. Other clubs were not so serious. The Anacreontic Society, for example, founded in 1793 'for social enjoyment' by Joseph Warden, the landlord of the Eagle and Ball in Colmore Row, included not only a predictably large proportion of local tradesmen but also a considerable number of members from outside Birmingham. Visiting actors probably accounted for the large contingent of Londoners, but Manchester, Liverpool and Sheffield were also well represented, and the membership list even named three foreigners, a Frenchman, a Pole and a German, who may have been business contacts.[34] The history of Joseph Warden and his friends belongs for the most part to the early nineteenth century, when they gave regular musical entertainments at the Eagle and Ball, but the Anacreontic Society was neither the only nor the earliest example of its kind. For at least the preceding fifty years similar groups had already acted as an equivalent among the tradesmen of Birmingham to the assemblies, concerts and festivals through which the town's more polite society had been able to extend its informal contacts with other parts of the surrounding region and the country. It was in such lesser circles that men like John Freeth, the Birmingham balladmonger, found their main material and their main audience,[35] and through them that popular music was inextricably connected with the other ways in which the town's ordinary people could take their ease. During the early winter of 1789, for example, the assembly room in the Square, now managed by Mr Cresshull and somewhat *déclassé* since its eclipse by the Royal Hotel, announced a three-day run of 'that favourite and fashionable pasticcio, Collins's Evening Brush for Rubbing off the Rust of Care', whose 'particular subjects for laughter' consisted of a comprehensive list of farcical skits and sketches followed by

> the Author's admired selection of original songs, comic, satirical and sentimental, particularly "Hark away to the Brush"; "Paddy Bull's Trip to England"; "Eloquence Upon All Fours"; "Date Obolum Belisario"; "Homer and Vergil in Doggerel"; "De Shentiments of Mordecai", and "The Golden Days We Now Possess".

Similarly, Mr Johannot, the resident clown at Swann's Amphitheatre, who celebrated his benefit night on 11 February 1788 with 'an entire new bow wow song in the character of a puppy, written by a Gentleman of Birmingham', also marked the occasion with 'Brave Admiral Benbow' and other popular songs 'as performed at the Royalty Theatre, London'; and two years later the Shakespeare Assembly Rooms in New Street made something of a hit with 'the famous Mr. Martins' and his

> most surprising vocal concert, without the assistance of any instrument whatsoever, imitating with his voice alone French Horns, Trumpets, Clarinets, Double Bass, Bassoon and Violoncello. He also sings different songs, often retaining his breath for the space of over a minute.... Mr. Martins is honoured with notice as an extraordinary phenomenon by the celebrated Dr. Burney in his History of Music.[36]

While the middle classes enjoyed their concerts, cards and dancing at Vauxhall and the Royal Hotel other establishments thus catered for different

tastes and levels of society, and the serious musical aspirations which found
expression in the triennial festivals were accompanied by the rapid growth of
a brand of popular entertainment which looked forward to the traditions of
the Victorian music hall. As the diverse interests of men like Barnabas Gunn
and John Eversmann suggest, this growth was also closely associated with the
history of the stage in Birmingham. It is in this that the interaction between
bourgeois pretensions and common culture can be most clearly observed. For
here, to an even greater extent than was the case with its musical traditions, the
town's activities became the object of conscious policy, which embodied a particular view of its character and interests. As Edmund Burke told the House of
Commons in 1777 during the first reading of the Bill to license the New Street
Theatre, the question raised by the Bill's proponents was not 'whether a man
had better be at work than go to the play'; nor whether, being idle, he should
go to the play in preference to 'some blacksmith's entertainment'; nor yet
whether the play was not 'the best place that it is probable a blacksmith's idle
moments will carry him to'. Over and above all these things, it was whether
Birmingham, 'the Great Toy Shop of Europe', was not *on that account . . . the
most proper place* in England to have a *licensed theatre*'.[37]

By 1750 Birmingham's theatrical traditions were already well established.
John Ward's Birmingham-based 'Warwickshire Company of Comedians' was
well known in the county;[38] the town had had its own permanent theatre in
Moor Street since 1740, and two others of a more temporary kind in New Street
and Smallbrook Street were in use during the next decade. In 1752 all three
of these were superseded by the King Street Theatre, a much more ambitious
venture based on London examples,[39] and eight years later, when Samuel
Derrick described the amenities of the town, this was under the direction of
Thomas Hull, later stage manager at Covent Garden.[40] Among the King Street
theatre's most regular patrons was Hull's close friend William Shenstone, one of
the West Midlands' better known literary figures during the middle years of the
century. Shenstone's chief claim to fame, however, rested not on his rather in-
sipid poetry but on the landscape garden which he created at the Leasowes,
his estate in the Clent Hills south-west of Birmingham. In Dr Johnson's words,
the Leasowes was 'a place to be visited by travellers and copied by designers',[41]
and together with Hagley, the seat of Lord Lyttleton, and Lord Stamford's
estate at Envil, it was the favourite choice for the 'party excursions' which,
according to William Hutton, were 'held in considerable esteem' in Birmingham.[42] This digression on eighteenth century sightseeing might not seem to
have much to do with the theatre, especially in a manufacturing town; but to
separate one aspect of the arts too rigidly from another would be to adopt an
artificial distinction which had little place in the outlook of contemporaries[43]
and certainly none in that of the Birmingham stage's leading sponsors. Like
Josiah Wedgwood, who spared no pains to seek out ways to develop the skill
and perception of his artists and designers,[44] these needed no telling of the vital
contribution to their interests as entrepreneurs which would be made by a
sustained improvement in the quality and acceptability of their products, or
that one of the surest ways to achieve this was to educate their workers in a
proper canon of taste. It was here that the stage, as envisaged by its chief
supporters, came into its own, and the attention which William Shenstone and
others paid to it is therefore important, not only because it illustrates yet again

how close the relationship was between the ambitions of Birmingham and the recognised leaders of society but also because, together with the reciprocal interest which Birmingham people took in the beauties of places like Hagley, Envil and the Leasowes, it formed one of the principal channels through which improved standards of artistic execution could be instilled in the town's tradesmen. It was this consideration which lay behind the enlargement of King Street in 1774 and the building in the same year of a yet more ambitious theatre in New Street, which numbered Matthew Boulton and Dr William Small,[45] the father of the Lunar Society, among its proprietors. The idea was, however, brought into its sharpest focus by the competition which developed between the New Street theatre and its older rival, and by the attempt which was made in 1777 to obtain a licence for the former.

Though Samuel Derrick described the Birmingham stage as 'greatly encouraged', it also aroused considerable opposition. In 1764 John Wesley preached against it at the old Moor Street theatre, which had by an appropriate reversal of circumstances been converted into a Methodist chapel since its eclipse by King Street;[46] and though the crowd of curious spectators which Wesley attracted on this occasion vented its disapproval on his departing congregation, the activities of visiting players were for the moment firmly controlled by the local magistrates, chief among them John Wyreley Birch of Handsworth. Birch, who was also responsible at this time for ending the Birmingham mob's habitual attacks on the Methodists,[47] was later described as 'systematically a man of pleasure', who had 'admired plays and was fond of actors and actresses',[48] but he was also well aware of the abuses to which travelling companies were tempted, particularly in a manufacturing town. While he lived, therefore, the theatre remained under close surveillance, which allowed it to exist but at the same time went some way to meet the objections of those who felt that what might be appropriate for places of fashion and leisure did not belong in Birmingham.

In 1773, however, this arrangement was challenged by a warning from the stage's opponents that they intended to prosecute any innkeeper or manager of a public room who allowed his premises to be used for dramatic performances. This threat was answered by 'A.Z.', who asked how a 'well wrote play wherein the most excellent precepts are enforced' could possibly be harmful, pointed out that since they were not given during working hours plays did not interfere with business, and left it to 'any judicious person to decide whether a workman's leisure was better spent at a reputable theatre or 'stupefying himself at an alehouse'. A.Z. concluded by hoping that the gentlemen of Birmingham would reject decisively 'the expulsion of an amusement they have so long and liberally supported for the whim, humour and caprice of one or two individuals'.[49] Had circumstances remained unchanged the town's theatre might well have continued on its existing footing. Now, however, the situation was different in a number of ways. 1773, a year of severe economic recession following the failure of the Ayr Bank, was a hard one for Birmingham's actors. Audiences and takings were small, which tempted the management to resort to underhand ways of pushing tickets and provoked quarrels among the actors themselves.[50] None of this can have recommended the players to the magistrates, especially at a time when the widening effects of the religious revival were beginning to produce a stricter attitude to social morality, and a partial ban was imposed. At first this did not affect the fortunes of the New Street theatre, which opened in June 1774 under the management of Richard Yates, an associate of David Garrick who had a solid reputation in London as a Shakespearean comic.[51] In 1775, however, John Wyreley Birch died, and his place on the Bench was not immediately filled. This meant that the local authority which had hitherto controlled the stage to the satisfaction of most people was in abeyance at precisely the time when rivalry began to develop between the King Street playhouse and its new competitor.[52] The stage's enemies in Birmingham were therefore able to point to the public nuisance which the theatrical war could be claimed to be causing in the town, and in the attempts to obtain a licence which both playhouses made during 1777 and 1778 each weakened the position of the other.

The case against Richard Yates's petition to license the New Street theatre, which was presented to the House of Commons on 10 February 1777, was made in two letters from the Rev. John Parsons of St Martin's, the organiser of the local opposition, to the evangelical Earl of Dartmouth, who was approached as the leading potential antagonist of the measure. Parsons, an evangelical himself, was confident that Dartmouth would view the matter 'in its proper light and consider it as a thing which must be productive of idleness and dissipation'. But the practical, as opposed to the moral; part of his argument turned on five points: that, as the rivalry which had plagued Birmingham intermittently since 1774 proved beyond question, two unlicensed playhouses constituted a public nuisance; that despite the claim of Yates and his supporters this would not be removed by the establishment of one licensed theatre; that, on the contrary, the latter would make abuse, particularly the forced distribution of tickets to working people in lieu of wages, permanent, by placing those responsible beyond the reach of the local authorities; that since most of those 'of fortune and credit' who had signed Yates's petition were materially interested in the New Street theatre their opinion did not represent the real wishes of the town, and that, as a poll of the ratepayers showed, the greater part of significant opinion in Birmingham was against the proposal.[53] Leaving aside the questionable accuracy of this assessment of local feeling, the crux of Parsons' case was the belief that the best way to control the stage was through the discretionary powers of the local Bench, and that to take this away would be to leave Birmingham at the mercy of whatever unscrupulous devices the manager of a licensed playhouse might choose to employ in pursuit of his own profit. It was against this that the sponsors of the New Street theatre directed their reply; for, far from denying the validity of the rest of their opponents' argument, they recognised its force and even used it themselves at some points, particularly with regard to the undesirable effects of two unlicensed houses. What Yates's backers questioned, with good reason after experiencing the effects of John Wyreley Birch's delayed replacement, was Parsons' assumption that Birmingham's 'two pimples' would 'die away of themselves, but if not, may at any time be removed by having recourse to those salutary laws, which were made for the correction of these and such like evils'. What they proposed was not the removal of local control but the replacement of the existing unreliable system by something more permanent and better suited to the town's needs. As Matthew Boulton explained in a powerfully argued letter to the Earl of Dartmouth, which is worth quoting at length because it expresses most clearly the meaning of Burke's 'Great Toyshop' metaphor, a properly licensed theatre in the town under the local but permanent supervision of a carefully chosen 'watch committee' would not only attract the time and money of fashionable tourists but would also soften the manners and refine the taste of Birmingham's tradesmen even while it entertained them.

> If we have not one house established by authority, I know we shall continue to be pestered with two, which, being more than the place can support, necessitates the losing party to have recourse to various stratagems for putting off their tickets at any rate, even at half price, and from this result many evils to apprentices and the lower class of people, . . . whereas I am convinced that one licensed house open for four months only of the year and under the direction of twenty inhabitants of respectable character in Birmingham, would produce a quite contrary effect. All well regulated states have found it expedient to indulge the people with amusements of some kind or other, and certainly those are most eligible that tend to improve the morals, the manners, or the taste of the people, and at the same time to prevent them from relapsing into the barbarous amusements which prevailed in this neighbourhood in the last century, when Birmingham was as remarkable for good forgers and filers as for their bad taste in all their works. Their diversions were bull baitings, cock fightings, boxing matches and abominable drunkenness with all its train. But now the scene is changed. The people are more polite and civilized, and the taste of their manufactures greatly improved. There is not a town of its size in Europe where mechanism is brought to such perfection, and we have also made considerable progress in some of the liberal arts, which hath been a means of extending our trade to the remotest corners of the world. I have frequently given my designers, painters and modellers tickets to the play in order to improve them in those arts by which they are to live and gain reputation, and I have found my account in it. Your Lordship I presume will allow that it is impossible for a person to paint or model an attitude or a passion which he never saw well expressed, nor can any artist arrive at any degree of elegance without advantages of this sort. Of late years, Birmingham hath been visited much in the summer by persons of fashion, and it is some inducement to prolonging their stay when their evenings can be spent in a commodious airy theatre. This is a fact that I mention from experience, and it is certainly our interest to bring company to Birmingham as it contributes much to the public good, not only from the money they leave behind them, but from their explaining their wants to the manufacturers, and giving hints for various improvements, which nothing promotes so much as an intercourse with persons from different parts of the world.[54]

In keeping with Boulton's argument, Yates had already modified his original petition by proposing to limit the New Street licence to the four months of the London off-season between June and September, and to exclude such questionable diversions as 'rope dancing, tumbling, puppet shows etc'.[55] But though Yates was thus able to win over the moderates in Birmingham, and though Edmund Burke assured the House of Commons that the town would not be exposed to the evils which abounded in Liverpool and Manchester, where the managers of licensed theatres enjoyed *carte blanche* all the year round,[56] the playhouse Bill failed. Opposition to it was particularly strong in the Birmingham Society of Friends, whose members brought pressure to bear on Burke before the second reading through their connections with his own Quaker constituents in Bristol, where a similar Bill had been defeated by the same means in 1773. Though Burke had moved the first reading of the Birmingham Bill, he now withdrew as gracefully as he could under the cover of personal compliments for Yates and the plea, somewhat specious under the circumstances, that whatever his own views he could not oppose the apparent wishes of the majority in Birmingham. After this acquiescence by the Bill's chief protagonist its second reading was easily defeated.[57]

As Boulton had predicted, the rivalry between the two unlicensed houses therefore continued, and the uncertain intervention of the local bench continued to inflame it. During the 1777 season performances were officially prohibited at both theatres, but both tried to evade the ban. Allegations of biased prosecutions were made against the town constables by the New Street party,[58] and in November George Mattocks, the manager of King Street, tried to steal a march on Yates by presenting his own licence petition. This manoeuvre, conducted with a minimum of publicity or consultation, was disowned by a public meeting at the Old Cross on 2 December, which resolved in favour of one playhouse only, preferably New Street, and suggested an amalgamation between the two companies. Mattocks, however, persisted, and in January 1778 the New Street management announced that it felt bound to protect its interests by renewing its original petition. Again the rivalry between the houses, coupled with the efforts of those who opposed them both, frustrated attempts to secure recognition for either; and meanwhile the *Birmingham Gazette* complained that

> A bill to license the Theatre in Bristol is now in the House. . . . No doubt it will pass into a law. . . . Licensed theatres are allowed at Norwich, Bath, Manchester, Liverpool, York and Hull, and yet the inhabitants of Birmingham are deprived of plays either in a licensed theatre or without. In what respect is Birmingham inferior to any of the above places?[59]

Though they could secure no official licence, however, the people of Birmingham did extend their own *de facto* recognition to the New Street theatre once experience had shown them the force of Boulton's argument. Open meetings, like that which had disowned the King Street petition and suggested an amalgamation of the companies, provided a means by which theatrical proposals could in fact be subjected to a measure of public control similar to that which Boulton had envisaged in his letter to the Earl of Dartmouth. In January 1779 the differences between the two playhouses were at length composed by the partial adoption of the suggestions first made thirteen months earlier, and the following summer a further meeting was held at the Old Cross to clarify misleading publicity for the King Street theatre and consider proposals for the coming season at New Street.[60] Within this framework the existence of the latter was now generally accepted. In 1780 it was graced by a new façade and was reckoned by many to be 'the most elegant and certainly the best theatre for summer performances of any in this kingdom'. Though its short season of plays still had to be given as free interludes in the 'concerts' which, thanks to the failure in 1777, remained its only legal source of revenue, it had been firmly established as Birmingham's principal playhouse for some time when its old rival was closed in 1786.[61]

Now that its position was secure the New Street theatre served as considerably more than a place of fashionable resort and cultural ornament. As early as 1777, when he first put his licence proposals to the town, Richard Yates had supported his bid for favour not only by modifying his plans in deference to the scruples of local opinion but also by supplementing the *Birmingham Gazette*'s résumé of the playhouse Bill on 10 March with a reminder of the 'Occasional Prologue' which had been given at New Street the previous August. Besides the usual salutes to the genius of invention, 'by whose aid industrious Art is here successful made', this had warned that

> From the pure fountain of Britannia's laws,
> Commerce her best, her sure protection draws.

and had supported the just assertion in America of

> ... that power, whose mild and legal sway
> Our brave forefathers taught us to obey.

After such a correct beginning, which was made the more necessary by the fact that at the time opinion in Birmingham was sharply divided on the American question, it is not surprising that New Street audiences were later treated to such patriotic spectacles as the 'Grand Naval Interlude' of September 1781, comprising 'The British Hearts of Oak, or True Blue ... consisting of singing and dancing, with a Naval Procession, in which Mr. Aldridge will make his entry in the Long Boat', or 'British Loyalty, or a Squeeze to St. Paul's', a re-enactment in 1790 of the procession to St Paul's cathedral on 23 April the previous year in thanksgiving for the King's recovery.[62] At least as significant as this rather blatant use of the stage to convey proper political attitudes, however, was what might in broad terms be called its educational role. Like Matthew Boulton, Thomas Hull spoke in his prologue to the coming season on 9 June 1783 of 'the Drama's useful scenes' as a reward for 'th' industrious artisan's o'er laboured day',[63] and even out of season the New Street theatre remained a focal point of attention among people excited by the promise of their own developing skills. In this sense it helped in particular to popularise the enthusiasm for scientific experiment and technical invention which was such an important cultural ingredient in the industrial revolution: both by the direct assistance which it gave to travelling lecturers like Mr Long, whose 'Astrotheatron, or large transparent Orrery improved' occupied the theatre in November 1786; and, as the correspondence shows its benefit performances provoked in 1781, when Adam Walker's astronomical lectures at the Old Assembly Rooms were the talk of the town, by the publicity it provided for exhibitions in other places.[64]

   With the New Street playhouse setting such an irreproachable example, not to mention its involvement in the oratorio festivals and such other worthy gestures as the fund-raising performance which it gave in 1787 on behalf of Birmingham's Sunday schools,[65] Matthew Boulton's apology for a properly regulated theatre would seem to have been entirely vindicated. In practice, however, the stage's universal appeal, which Boulton hoped to exploit, was as much dictated by economic necessity as it was guided by moral policy. Actors and managers had to cater for all tastes in order to survive in a town where the content and mood of audiences depended very directly on the state of trade, and this meant that the stage was not completely amenable to paternal direction. The theatre's advocates saw in it a stimulus to refinement, emulation and self-improvement within the existing social order. Once started, however, this process produced developments of its own not anticipated by its sponsors, and the programmes of establishments on the fringes of Birmingham's theatrical world show signs of a popular culture which was probably more lively than the more seemly entertainments offered by the main houses. At Cresshull's assembly rooms in December 1789, for example, the music hall farrago of 'Collins's Evening Brush' was followed a fortnight later by 'a great number of senatorial imitations', in the course of which Messrs Carey and Kean promised that 'some few real characters in life which stand very prominent in the world will be whimsically delineated'.[66] Similarly, Swann's Amphitheatre, or 'Gentleman's Private Theatre', in Livery Street, was not quite the exclusive establishment such a name might suggest. It also did duty as a riding school and circus arena, and it played a prominent part in *Saint Monday, or Scenes from Low Life,* a description of the working class week in Birmingham, which asked

> .... Why did SWANN engage
> The very dirt and sweepings of the stage?
> E'en jugglers, big with expectation, ran,
> Certain to get engagements with TOM SWANN
> How was the eye of delicacy shock'd
> And feminine decorum grossly mock'd
> By seeing women dress'd in men's attire
> Vaulting on ropes, or dancing on the wire....[67]

In the case of Birmingham's theatrical development, still more than in its musical history, it would therefore be wrong to insist on a single, definitive line of progress towards respectability. Though its development was inseparable from that of the town's music, and though it played an equally important part in Birmingham's cultural aspirations, the variety of opinions both for and against the stage persisted, and it never achieved the same degree of acceptance as the music meetings and oratorio festivals. These embodied formed and therefore safe social attitudes. Implicit in the arguments of the theatre's friends, on the other hand, was a recognition that society was not a static order but a dynamic one which was capable of spontaneous evolution. However confident the patrons of the stage may have been in their ability to direct its moral and social influence to desirable ends, their plans therefore always entailed an element of risk. In February 1788 Swann's Amphitheatre was offering a programme of spectacular circus stunts whose final tableaux illustrate well the way in which the two episodes in the history of the previous twenty years which had most involved the common people, the Middlesex election of 1768–69 and the Gordon riots, had been absorbed into the stock of vulgar comedy:

The Horsemanship to conclude with the humorous exhibition of THE TAYLOR'S JOURNEY TO BRENTFORD ELECTION, in dress and character, ... to which will be added a New Pantomime: "The Peregrinations of a Certain Great Character, or the Adventures of THE BONNY LADDIE, or HARLEQUIN JEW ... to which will be added a new Pantomime Dance called "The Drunken Dancing Jews", which has never been performed in Birmingham.... The following is the principal scenery and machinery—Newgate, in London, on fire—parts of Bethlehem [Bedlam?]—St. James's Gate—A Distant View of a Sea—Part of Dudley Street, Birmingham—The Champion of England on Horseback—A Sea Monster—etc. etc.[68]

It was through such channels as this at least as much as from the examples handed down by their betters that the ordinary people of Birmingham gained their own awareness of the times. It is to the latter—to the clubs and societies in which it took shape, to the ways in which it was expressed, to the attitudes which it embodied and to its influences on the development of Birmingham's political experience—that attention must now be turned.

NOTES

1 For Samuel Pipe-Wolferstan see the transcript of his diary, which covers the years 1776–1820, by his great-great-grandson, Henry Francis Pipe-Wolferstan. Samuel's chief factual claims to remembrance are at one time to have employed the agricultural expert William Marshall as his steward, and to have developed a broad though somewhat unfocused interest in speculative theology, humanitarian reform and radical politics during the 1780s. Samuel was educated at Pembroke College, Oxford, after which he read for the Bar at Clement's Inn. Here he came into contact with advanced ideas, and he remained for a long time a disciple of Theophilus Lindsey and the intelligentsia of the Essex Street chapel. His diary, however, shows that he found it hard to keep up his intellectual pursuits in the different surroundings of rural Staffordshire, despite periodic trips to London, involvement in several reading and discussion societies in Tamworth and attempts to build up his own library. Though he made industrious efforts to compile notes and to keep a regular commonplace book, the struggle to keep abreast of current controversies, as well as to master speculative authors like Bishop Butler, ended as often in sleep as in success. In addition to his extensive reading Samuel was actively interested in the movement for the abolition of slavery, received complimentary copies of John Howard's works on prison reform and, for a brief time in 1788, took up the cause of 'poor chimney boys'. During the following year his penchant for eccentricity was reinforced by intensive reading of controversial theology, and he thought seriously of introducing his own Unitarian form of service at Statfold church. This, however, did not last. Made nervous by what he saw at the Bastille dinner at the Crown and Anchor on 14 July 1790, when John Horne Tooke was shouted down for trying to keep the proceedings within the bounds of constitutionalism; 'pestered about Burke' by his neighbours 'till I took up the book', and disenchanted with the vain repetitions of his old theological mentors, Samuel retreated from 1792 onwards into the safer field of antiquarian research. In terms of actual results Samuel's aspirations therefore never came to very much. After reading the record of domestic comedy which attended his matrimonial plans and other local ambitions, it is indeed tempting to see him, like Mr Brooke in *Middlemarch*, simply as a country gentleman 'of acquiescent temper, miscellaneous opinions and uncertain vote' who 'took in all the new ideas', 'went into science' and was subsequently held by his neighbours to have 'contracted a too rambling habit of mind'. To do this, however, would be to miss the real value of Samuel's experience for the sake of an easy label. Though he retreated from overt to surreptitious dissent during the 1790s, he did not abandon his convictions. He kept up an active interest in the Dissenting college at Hackney; in 1801 he sent his son, Stanley, to Manchester New College, founded in 1786 as successor to the famous academy at Warrington; and when he withdrew Stanley from Manchester eighteen months later he did so not because he was dissatisfied with his son's intellectual progress but because the college seemed unable to maintain proper standards of personal discipline. (See G. M. Ditchfield, 'The early history of Manchester College', *Trans. Hist. Soc. Lancs. and Ches.*, 123, 1972, 81–104.) As set down in the extraordinary detail of his voluminous diary, the dilemmas and deliverances of Samuel Pipe-Wolferstan in fact provide an invaluable record of the multitude of influences which might have played upon a man of conventional position but open mind during nearly half a century of unprecedented social, cultural and political change.

2 *Diary*, 29 August 1789.

3 *V.C.H. Warwicks.*, VII, 209.

4 See *D.N.B.* Derrick succeeded Beau Nash as Master of Ceremonies at Bath in 1761 and held the post until his death in 1769. He also held a similar position at Tunbridge.

5 Samuel Derrick, *Letters written from Leverpoole, Chester etc.* (1767), quoted by William Bennett, *John Baskerville, the Birmingham Printer: his Press, Relations and Friends* (2 vols, Birmingham, 1937), I, 102.

6 *V.C.H. Warwicks.*, VII, 209.

7 Hutton, *History of Birmingham*, pp. 61–2.

8 *Aris*, 8 June 1789.

9 *Aris*, 25 August 1760; *V.C.H. Warwicks.*, VIII, 224; J. S. Smith, *The Story of Music in Birmingham* (Birmingham, 1945), p. 14.

10 *Pipe-Wolferstan Diary, passim*, especially summary of Samuel's activities for 1784, and more specifically 22 September, 18 November 1777, 9 December 1780. Darwin's professional services were mainly required by Mrs Pipe-Wolferstan, who had survived two normal confinements and some ten miscarriages by the time she died in 1786. For Lunar Society interest in the copying process see Schofield, *Lunar Society*, pp. 154–5.

11 For Anna Seward and her circle see Margaret Ashmun, *The Singing Swan: an account of Anna Seward and her Acquaintance with Dr Johnson, Boswell and others of their Time* (New Haven, 1931). For Samuel Pipe-Wolferstan's relations with Lichfield Close see especially *Diary*, 25, 26 August, 2 September 1785: much excitement about an exchange of dinner engagements, heightened by rumours that Samuel had been suggested for the Commission of the Peace; 26 January, 3 March 1789: his 'Statfold Church Plan', the county Bench again, 'matrimonial imaginations' and daydreams of notoriety 'on future declining oaths', which were swiftly dispelled on hearing that he might soon be pricked for sheriff; 7, 9 December 1790: his misgivings about the tendency of national events, suppressed hitherto but now brought into focus by reading Burke's *Reflections*.

12 See M. A. Hopkins, *Dr Johnson's Lichfield* (New York, 1952).

13 The Bishops of Coventry and Lichfield preferred to live outside the city at Eccleshall.

14 Levi Fox, ed., *The Correspondence of the Reverend Joseph Greene, Parson, Schoolmaster and Antiquary, 1712–90* (H.M.C. Joint Publication No. 8, with the Dugdale Society, 1965), p. 74, Joseph Greene to Richard Greene, 21 December 1754. Richard Greene was a Lichfield apothecary best remembered for the remarkable museum he kept in Market Street.

15 John Saville, an intimate friend of Anna Seward, was vicar choral of Lichfield cathedral and a tenor who was widely esteemed as an exponent of Handel.

16 Smith, *Music in Birmingham*, pp. 10–11; Hill, *Bookmakers*, p. 50.

17 Bennett, *Baskerville*, I, 104; *Music in Birmingham*, pp. 10–11.

18 For examples see Smith, *Music in Birmingham*, pp. 10–11, 17–18.

19 Smith, *Music in Birmingham*, p. 11.

20 *V.C.H. Warwicks.*, VII, 218.

21 *Aris*, 10 November 1788, and also 19 January 1789. The subscription for gentlemen, including two lady guests, was two guineas; for unaccompanied ladies, one guinea, and for strangers introduced by a subscriber, 3s 6d per concert.

22 *Aris*, 10, 17 May 1790.

23 Smith, *Music in Birmingham*, pp. 12–13, 17–18, 23.

24 *Op. cit.*, p. 12.

25 *Aris*, 14 September 1778. Crito drew a laboured analogy between musical and political harmony, which he applied to the American war.

26 *Aris*, 7 September 1778; *V.C.H. Warwicks.*, VII, 44; Smith, *Music in Birmingham*, pp. 32–4. Originally conceived in 1830 as a replica of the temple of Castor and Pollux at Rome, the town hall was in use by 1834. However, modifications, necessitated by the size of the organ stipulated by the musical committee of the General Hospital, delayed the building's completion until 1849. Reports of the first performance of *Elijah* spoke of the 'zeal and artist-like unanimity' of the participants, and of 'the addition of a fresh pleasure to the circumscribed amount of human happiness', for which there 'never was a more eager auditory, nor one more fitting'.

27 Besides *Messiah* and the overture to *Esther*, for example, the 1778 programme included a concert at the New Street theatre consisting of works by Corelli, Purcell and Arne, several songs and madrigals and a performance of Sheridan's *Duenna*. See Smith, *Music in Birmingham*, p. 25.

28 For Madame Mara, whose English reputation had been made by her singing in the Handel commemoration in 1784, see *Grove's Dictionary of Music and Musicians* (5th edn, 1954), V, 557–9.

29 *Aris*, 27 September 1790.

30 *A.O.P.*, Garbett box, Garbett to Boulton, 8 June 1785.

31 For Lichfield races see Anne J. Kettle, 'Lichfield races', *Trans. Lichfield and South*

Staffs. Arch. Soc., VI (1964–65), 39–44. For Warwick races see *Garbett–Lansdowne Letters*, II, Garbett to Lansdowne, 3 September 1787, reminding him to keep an eye open at the race meeting for Sir Robert Lawley, and for William Russell, 'which I take the liberty to mention as he is one of the most eminent Merchants in this place, and a well informed man at the head of the Presbyterians, and the patron of Dr. Priestley'.

32 Smith, *Music in Birmingham*, p. 13.

33 *Op. cit.*, p. 12.

34 Benjamin Walker, 'The Anacreontic Society', *T.B.A.S.*, LXIII (1939–40).

35 For Freeth, see below, pp. 103–4. When Freeth wrote of the experience which had shaped his style it is notable that he recalled not only his Birmingham companions but various social celebrations at Droitwich, High Wycombe, Coventry and Stratford, and personal friends in numerous other places, including Worcester, Alcester and Evesham. See preface to *The Political Songster, 1790*, B.R.L. 233171.

36 *Aris*, 11 February 1788, 30 November 1789, 18 January 1790. For Swann's Amphitheatre see below, p. 93.

37 *Aris*, 31 March 1777. Report of first reading of the Birmingham Playhouse Bill. *Parliamentary History*, XIX, includes the second reading but not the first.

38 They played in Coventry in 1752. See *V.C.H. Warwicks.*, VIII, 225.

39 *V.C.H. Warwicks.*, VII, 218–19.

40 Bennett, *Baskerville*, I, 104; *D.N.B.*

41 Quoted by *D.N.B.* on Shenstone.

42 Hutton, *History of Birmingham*, p. 130. At least two tourist guides to these attractions were published: *A Description of Hagley, Envil and the Leasowes*, which Myles Swinney put out in Birmingham in 1770, and Joseph Heely's *Letters on the Beauties of Hagley, Envil and the Leasowes, with Critical Remarks and Observations on the Modern Taste in Gardening* (London, 1777).

43 For a pertinent example of its absence see Sybil Rosenfeld, 'Landscape in eighteenth century English scenery', in Kenneth Richards and Peter Thompson, eds., *Essays on the Eighteenth Century English Stage* (London, 1972), pp. 171–7.

44 See Neil McKendrick, 'Josiah Wedgwood and factory discipline', *Historical Journal*, IV (1961), 30–55, especially 34–8.

45 *V.C.H. Warwicks.*, VII, 219; Schofield, *Lunar Society*, p. 89.

46 Nehemiah Curnock, ed., *The Journal of John Wesley* (8 vols, London, 1915, reprinted 1960), V, 48; entry for 21 March 1764; *V.C.H. Warwicks.*, VII, 219.

47 See W. C. Sheldon, 'The Birmingham magistrate who suppressed the rioters', *Proc. Wesley Hist. Soc.*, September 1903, 61–4, B.R.L. 179987.

48 Sir William Bagot's posthumous description during the second reading of the Birmingham playhouse Bill, *Parliamentary History*, XIX, 198.

49 *Aris*, 31 May 1773.

50 See William Hutton's account in *Courts of Requests*, p. 249.

51 See *D.N.B.*

52 See Sir William Bagot's account in *Parliamentary History*, XIX, 198, and *Aris*, 20 November 1775, which carried a publication notice for *The Campaign, or Birmingham Theatrical War*.

53 *H.M.C. Dartmouth* III, 232–4, Parsons to Dartmouth, 15, 24 February 1777. With his first letter Parsons sent the result of a poll of 2,449 ratepayers: 1,468 opposed; 124 in favour; 196 neuter; 665 not at home. Much obviously depended on the way the question was put, however, since Yates's opponents would include not only the stage's outright opponents but also the supporters of his King Street rival.

54 *H.M.C. Dartmouth* III, 234–5, Boulton to Dartmouth, 22 March 1777.

55 *Aris*, 17 February 1777.

56 *Aris*, 31 March 1777.

57 See P. T. Underdown, 'Religious opposition to the licensing of the Bristol and Birmingham theatres', *U.B.H.J.*, VI (1957–8), 149–60; *Parliamentary History*, XIX, 199–205; *Aris*, 5 May 1777.

58 Retrospective account in *Aris*, 16 February 1778.

59 *Aris*, 1, 8 December 1777, 12 January, 16 February 1778.

60 *Aris*, 11 January, 7, 14 June 1779.

61 *V.C.H. Warwicks.*, VII, 219, 417.

62 *Aris*, 16 September 1781, 6 September 1790

63 *Aris*, 16 June 1783.

64 *Aris*, 13, 20 November 1786 (Mr Long); 13 August, 3 September, 5 November 1781 (Adam Walker), and especially letter from 'Hoeamphelius' on 12 November 1781, occasioned by the benefit performance at New Street given for Mr William Allen, 'the contriver and maker of the best electrical machines ever constructed'. For Lunar Society contacts with Walker see Schofield, *Lunar Society*, pp. 220, 234, 248; for more on the popularisation of science see below, pp. 131–2.

65 See below, p. 100.

66 *Aris*, 14 December 1789.

67 George Davis, *Saint Monday, or Scenes from Low Life* (1790), B.R.L. 239216, pp. 13–14.

68 *Aris*, 4 February 1788. Lord George Gordon became a Jew in 1786 or 1787. He was indicted for a libel on the moral and political conduct of Marie Antoinette in August 1786, whereupon he fled, first to Amsterdam and then to Birmingham, where he hid in the town's Jewish community until he was arrested on 13 December 1787. See J. P. DeCastro, *The Gordon Riots* (Oxford, 1926), pp. 245–6.

V

TAVERNS, COFFEE HOUSES AND CLUBS: LOCAL POLITICS AND POPULAR ARTICULACY

Of all the *milieux* in which men might meet and exchange ideas in eighteenth century England, the club was the most characteristic, both of the time and the country. Whether its members met in emulation of the Royal Society or the academies of continental Europe to discuss high matters of literature and philosophy, or whether they were local politicians and tradesmen combining mutual benefit with beer, song and sociable discussion, the club provided a setting in which private friendship and formal organisation were judiciously balanced. The inhibitions imposed by the hierarchical bonds of traditional society had diminished, but though many clubs were drawn already towards wider affiliations the day of the association and the public meeting had not yet fully come. In the interval the club provided a medium through which men with something to say to each other could exchange ideas. 'Conversation, and the intercourse of mind with mind, seem to be the most fertile sources of improvement,' wrote William Godwin, for whom such 'freedom of social communication', through which knowledge might gain ground 'unaccompanied with peril in the means of its diffusion', offered the best hope for 'the promoting the best interests of mankind'.[1]

William Godwin wrote as a committed believer in the rational progress of society, and by no means every clique which met in coffee house or tavern lived up to his imagined 'spirit of comprehensive benevolence'; but his hope was not confined to a few idealists. In the West Midlands at least, the club was thought of and written about quite normally in the optimistic language of friendship.

We cherish the Arts, UNANIMITY prize,

wrote John Freeth in his *Call to the Bucks*,

> And make it our rule to be MERRY and WISE,
> From UNITY'S BANDS never seen to depart,
> For FRIENDSHIP is rooted in each jovial heart. . . .
> May FRIENDSHIP subsist and the BUCK'S noble band
> A thousand years hence flourish over the land.[2]

Nor were the women to be outdone. The annual festival of 'The Original Female Society', held at Lichfield on 29 June 1775, attracted a hundred guests, and it was hoped 'that this Society may be a precedent to others'. That the hint was taken is clear from *Midsummer Day*, dedicated to the Female Friendly Society of Yoxall, by a member.

> Long by the men's hand
> Has Friendship's fair wand
> Been carried without opposition,
> Till our sex has caught fire,
> And to Friendship aspire,
> Which is surely a noble ambition.[3]

The social virtue of friendship was thus imbued with a special significance, which was inculcated even from the pulpit. At Easter 1767, for example, the Society of Tradesmen at St Chad's, Shrewsbury, heard from the Rev. Dr Adams of 'The Advantages and Pleasures of Unity'. Similarly, in 1778 the Rev. John Adamthwaite preached on 'The Nature and Principles of Society' to 'An Amicable Society of Tradesmen' at Meriden, near Coventry.[4] If such sermons and the church services at which they were given indicate the persistence of traditional attitudes, the language of harmonious fraternity which they used expressed ideas of the rational and universal brotherhood of man which formed a secular addition to older virtues and beliefs.

The clubs of the West Midlands ranged in kind from elite groups like the Lunar Society and its direct offshoot, the Derby Literary and Philosophical Society, founded by Erasmus Darwin in 1783,[5] through country gentlemen's clubs like the Shropshire Fraternity of the True Blue, devoted to foxhunting and feasting at the Raven inn, Shrewsbury, or the Friendly Association of Worcestershire Gentlemen, which met in rotation at Stourbridge, Droitwich, Bromsgrove, Dudley and Kidderminster, to tavern coteries among the tradesmen and artisans of the region.[6] From the brief advertisements and cursory notices which have survived it is not easy to derive clear ideas of the specific purposes of many of these societies, or of the degree of permanence they attained. One feature which many of them had in common, however, was that they provided a bridge between the different ranks of society, and an outlet through which the aspirations of professional men, the ambitions of the middling tradesmen and the hopes of the skilled artisans could find expression and satisfaction. This was particularly true of the Bucks, the Freemasons, the reading clubs and the debating societies; and since the main objective here will be to trace the broadening articulacy of the common people of the West Midlands, it is these lesser clubs which will be the main concern of the two following chapters, rather than the more famous societies, which already have their memorials.

First, however, a partial exception must be made in the case of the Birmingham Bean Club. Founded soon after the Restoration as a loyalist dining club in which the gentlemen of the surrounding country districts and the principal inhabitants of the town could enjoy free and confidential discussion of matters of mutual interest,[7] the Bean Club was not exactly a common man's society; nor, though it has gone largely unnoticed by historians, was it obscure in its own day. By the later eighteenth century Bean Club members were involved in many different aspects of regional affairs. Henry Clay, the munificent sponsor of the Birmingham Oratorio Festival in 1790 and High Sheriff of Warwickshire in the same year, was elected to the club in 1775 and served as one of its town stewards in 1788–89. Samuel Aris of the *Birmingham Gazette* and his successor James Rollason were both Bean Club members. The list of Street Commissioners appointed under the terms of the Lamp Act in 1769 contained eight names which appeared in the Bean Club's membership during the next ten years, not to mention Thomas Steward, Clerk and Treasurer to the Commissioners, who was secretary of the club between 1777 and 1793.[8] The original committee of the General Hospital in 1765 likewise contained several who subsequently became Bean Club members. In addition to Henry Carver and William John Banner, who also served as Street Commissioners, these included William Dilke, Esq., Joseph Carles, Jervoise Clark, Richard Geast and Joseph Dallaway. When the building of the hospital was resumed in 1777 Bean Club members again took the lead. Lord Craven, who headed the list of subscribers to the foundation in 1779, had been county steward of the club in 1769–70.[9] His brother-in-law, Robert Augustus Johnson, of Kenilworth, who took the chair when the standing committee of the hospital first met in September 1779, had been elected to the Bean Club the previous month, and served as one of its stewards during 1780–81. Other members active in Hospital affairs were the Rev. Dr Spencer, Sir Charles Holte and Sir George Shuckburgh. Later, club members were also prominent among the subscribers to the Anglican Sunday schools in Birmingham;[10] and the vote of thanks which was accorded in October 1787 to Dr Spencer and Joseph Carles, who had arranged with Richard Yates for a benefit performance to be given at the New Street theatre in support of the schools,[11] illustrates well the way in which the club continued to embody the interrelation of different aspects of the town's life. All those involved in this collaboration were members of the Bean Club, which by the end of the century was well described as including 'representatives of the Magnates of the County, the Gentlemen and Tradesmen of the town, the Clergy and the officers from the Barracks, and the principal representative actors from the local theatre'.[12]

The Bean Club's involvement did not stop short at municipal affairs. Its members also played an influential part in the development of the organised and coherent 'Birmingham interest' which became a clearly identifiable feature of regional politics after the 1774 election.[13] Lord Craven's colleague as county steward in 1769–70 was Thomas Skipwith, elected to Parliament for Warwickshire in March 1769.[14] Skipwith acted again as steward five years later, together with Sir Charles Holte of Aston, the victor in the contested county election of 1774. In 1780–81 and 1781–82 Sir George Shuckburgh and Sir Robert Lawley, Warwickshire's two new Members, succeeded each other in the same office. It was a member and future secretary of the Bean Club, Thomas Gem,[15] who initiated the measures taken before the 1780 election to maintain and consolidate the advantages gained in 1774 in order to secure the nomination and return of Sir Robert Lawley as peculiarly 'the Member for Birmingham'.[16] Similarly, when Lawley was challenged in 1790 by Abraham Bracebridge of Atherstone it was Joseph Carles who took the chair at the town meetings which rejected this unwanted intrusion, presented a united front in favour of Sir Robert and accepted Bracebridge's subsequent withdrawal.[17] Bracebridge claimed that, as a native of Warwickshire and a kinsman of Sir Charles Holte, the original victor in 1774,[18] his right to the county seat should override that of Lawley, whose family came from Shropshire. The short shrift which this argument received is an indication of the extent to which the 'Birmingham interest' had outgrown the traditional bounds of representative politics. The same was true of the Bean Club. There was nothing incongruous about the appointment of the Hon. Edward Foley and William Lygon, Esq., the Members of Parliament for Worcestershire, as the club's county stewards in 1784. By this time the membership, which increased rapidly during the 1780s, was being drawn not from Warwickshire alone but from the whole 'county area' surrounding Birmingham. Though most of those chosen still lived in or near the town itself, others came from places as far away as Bridgnorth, Stone, Stoke (Herefordshire), Appleby (Leicestershire), Malvern, Burton on Trent and Daventry.

In its report of the Bean Club's anniversary dinner at the Swan inn on 11 August 1769 the *Birmingham Gazette* welcomed the installation of Lord Craven and Thomas Skipwith as stewards for the coming year, and hoped that under their guidance 'this society, ever devoted to the support of Liberty and Independence,' would 'flourish with as great a splendour as at any former period'. [19] In the past it may have been possible to define the meaning of such language in traditional terms without begging any serious questions. Despite the optimism of Aris's paper, however, this was not to be the case for much longer. In the history of the Bean Club the 1770s were marked by uncertainty which corresponded on a small scale to that which beset the nation at large as assumptions hitherto taken for granted became untenable in their original forms. Though the club's members played an important part in the whole formation of a 'Birmingham interest' in politics, those who actually voted in the Warwickshire contest in 1774, which marked the start of the process, showed no clear preference in their choice of candidates. The same confusion continued during the American war, and there are signs that the club was troubled more than once by disagreement over the course of British policy. [20] Underlying these symptoms of change, however, was an increasingly conservative outlook on wider events. When Matthew Boulton was organising his address in support of the Ministry's American policy early in 1775 he made a list of 'names to petition of the inhabitants of the town and neighbourhood of Birmingham to North America'. Twenty-three of the eighty-seven names which Boulton assembled appeared also in the minutes of the Bean Club before 1782, [21] and after the American war the club fast became a hotbed from which the loyalist associations of the 1790s sprang up as naturally as weeds. Edward Carver, county steward of the Bean Club in 1789, was president of the Birmingham Church and King Club, founded in November 1792; the Birmingham Association for the Preservation of Liberty and Property had at least five club members on its committee, [22] and the thoughts of Wriothesley Digby of Meriden on north Warwickshire's response to the royal proclamation of November 1792 show clearly how the long-established characteristics of the Birmingham Bean Club were transferred and adapted to the aims of the new loyal associations. Of those mentioned in Digby's letter to Sir Roger Newdigate on 5 December 1792, all except Newdigate himself were or soon became members of the Bean Club.

> I have had some conversation with Lord Aylesford, and he and other Gentlemen are of the opinion that we ought not to be the last to shew our loyalty. Sir Robert Lawley, Mr. Geast, and three or four more have promised to meet at Coleshill on Saturday at twelve o'clock. . . . We rather think it will be better to avoid large meetings, and to confine the Association (or whatsoever we may appear in) to the circle of a Hundred, or smaller district, than to make it a General County Affair. The Middle and Lower Ranks of people will be more likely to come in and sign their name, and can act more connectedly and in concert than in a larger circle where the vital parts know little of each other. [23]

This, however, does not mean that the Bean Club should be regarded merely as an agent of bigotry and intolerance. Through a society which had existed for nearly a century before 1760 the association between the established ranks of society and the men who were aspiring to leadership in the growing towns was firmly linked, in Birmingham at least, to the traditions of the eighteenth century constitution. Those traditions came under increasing strain from 1760 onwards, particularly during the American war, when the conventional formulae of Liberty and Independence, in which the Bean Club's proceedings had hitherto been enshrined, ceased to be capable of accommodating serious divergences of opinion as to the realities which lay beneath the rhetoric. Nevertheless, within the fabric of politics and society as they understood it, Bean Club members played a prominent part during the latter part of the eighteenth century in working out practical solutions to the various problems posed by the growth of Birmingham which would encourage what they considered to be the right kind of progress. Their reactions to the crisis of the 1790s may be condemned in the abstract light of Natural Justice; but they were hardly unnatural. Against the part they played in the hounding of the Dissenters and in the formation of the loyal associations must be weighed the value of their previous achievements in the adaptation of traditional attitudes to a changing situation. The Bean Club was not simply a bastion of reaction. It was a conservative institution closely associated through its membership with the whole development of Birmingham. As such it was in many respects a precursor of the attachment of the middle classes to the aristocratic constitution which was more widely achieved after 1832, and it embodied in microcosm the merits as well as the defects of that conjunction.

If the Bean Club acted as a long-established channel for the association between the merchants and manufacturers of Birmingham and the landowners of the surrounding counties, the steps taken to meet the rising demand for news of all kinds which accompanied the development of the town's physical links with a wider world acted as a powerful encouragement to the formation of newer groups in which current affairs could be discussed. Overton's coffee house in New Street, for example, advertised a news service which included all the main London papers, delivered by express messenger by two o'clock on the morrow of their publication, as well as House of Commons division lists, sessions papers, bills of entry, Lloyd's list, all the Irish and most country papers, and the *Utrecht Gazette*.[24] If these claims were genuine Overton must either have been running a considerable enterprise of his own or have been participating in a larger organisation which could afford to beat the regular posts by employing its own couriers. It is therefore not surprising that his house was soon acting as a recognised place for consultation on public business, or that William Hutton described it as 'the first in this department, which, drawing into its vortex the transactions of Europe, finds employment for the politician'.[25] In his initial advertisement in 1777, however, Overton stressed that his business was to be run 'on the London model';[26] and though he called it 'a convenience long wished for', several other houses, of more local origin, had already been open for some time. From its name 'The Navigation Coffee House' was presumably contemporary with the Birmingham canal, opened in 1769, and other local precursors of Overton's included 'Mrs. Aston's Coffee Room in the Cherry Orchard', the meeting place of the Amicable Debating Society, and 'Cooke's Coffee House' in Cherry Street, the scene of a meeting on counterfeit coinage

in December 1778.[27] Most important of all was John Freeth's Leicester Arms
tavern in Bell Street, popularly known as 'Freeth's Coffee House': indeed, the
history of popular political consciousness in Birmingham, especially during the
years of the American revolution, is in good part the history of the Leicester
Arms.

The house owned by the Freeth family at the corner of Lease Lane and Bell
Street was already known in the first half of the century as a place where
tradesmen, small businessmen, attorneys and the like met to transact business as
well as for refreshment. John Freeth, born in 1731 and originally apprenticed
to a brassfounder in Park Street, took over the property from his mother in
1768, by which time it was known as the Leicester Arms, or simply the Bell. By
that time, too, the new owner had already laid the foundation of his fame as
one of the best writers of topical ballads and election verse in the kingdom. His
first song, appropriately enough in praise of Birmingham beer, was printed by
Aris's Birmingham Gazette on 31 October 1763; by 1767 James Sketchley's
Birmingham Directory was listing him under 'Miscellaneous Tradesmen' as
'John Freeth, Poet';[28] and in the injunction of his 'Beer Drinker's Objection to
the Repeal of the Cyder Act' to 'bawl till they take off the tax on your ale'
he had already used what was obviously a favourite theme to hint at his political
views:

> No doubt some may think my design is romantic
> But sooner by far will we cross the Atlantic,
> And dwell with our friends on th'American shore,
> Ere we'll ever submit to be taxed any more.[29]

This was innocuous enough; but in the 1770s Freeth began to take the turn of
events more seriously. The interest of the Leicester Arms in current affairs was
openly avowed in 1772 by an advertisement headed POLITICS, which stated not
only that Freeth kept files of all the London papers during the past thirty-seven
years for the convenience of his customers but also that he received regular
personal reports of speeches and votes in Parliament.[30] If it was genuine this
second claim is interesting; for it means that, at precisely the time when the
freedom to report parliamentary proceedings was being established, Freeth, a
provincial publican, either had his own contacts in London or was in touch
with John Almon of the *London Evening Post* and the *Gazetteer*, which were
the only two London papers printing original reports of parliamentary debates
during 1772 and 1773. A conjectural association between Freeth and Almon,
one of the best known newspapermen of the day, a leading supporter of John
Wilkes and the only journalist not defeated after the prosecutions of 1771 by
the Commons' continued use of their power to exclude strangers during debates,[31] offers tempting ground for speculation in view of the part which Freeth
and the Leicester Arms were playing in the popular politics of the West
Midlands at this time.

The Leicester Arms was thus well equipped to act as a meeting place for
opponents of Lord North's Ministry, the more so because since at least 1758
it had been the headquarters of a book club which was closely connected with
Unitarianism in Birmingham, and which undoubtedly included political discussion among its activities.[32] In the whimsical rhyming invitations by which
John Freeth announced the dinners of the club to its members he made no

secret of his political position. His invitation on 15 June 1775, for example, ended with a joint address to the Whig opposition at home and the resistance across the Atlantic:

> And foremost for FREEDOM may EFFINGHAM stand,
> Not forgetting Lord GRANBY and SAVILLE and BURKE,
> Our good friends at BOSTON and those at NEW YORK.

and five months later, on 21 November, he underlined his preference for conciliatory measures with the wish that 'those who oppose 'em and more blood would spill' should 'be forced into service and mount BUNKER'S HILL'. The widening of the struggle in 1778 must have presented Freeth and his friends with the same problem of loyalty that baffled Josiah Wedgwood and others, but he put aside his concern for America in the name of patriotism and called on his fellow countrymen to stand united in the face of French hostility (17 June 1778). On 25 November 1778 Freeth consoled himself in adversity with the exploits of Admiral Keppel, and continued to wish for an end to the war and a change of Ministry during the two following years. His card on 13 June 1781 shows how quickly the form of Dunning's famous motion became common currency:

> . . . but still as a friend
> To my country, the war I could wish at an end,
> For Taxes we find e're the work is half finished,
> Have *increased*, are *increasing*, and should be *diminished*.
> But those who each year taste the sweets of the loan
> Undoubtedly wish the same work may go on.

Freeth's exasperation with politics and politicians reached its climax in the summer of 1783, when he called for 'The TOWER HILL STAMP public evils to cure' (18 June 1783), after which it gave way to disillusion. He joined the popular repudiation of the Fox–North coalition, but thereafter 'viewed with a smile and indifference political wranglings, being convinced that the contest of politicians is only for power and for favours'.[33]

So far as local developments were concerned the influence of the Leicester Arms as a meeting place for supporters of the opposition was at least as marked in the years before 1775 as it was during the American war itself. Freeth's invitation to the Birmingham Book Club on 29 November 1770 had made flippant reference to general warrants, and between 1768 and 1774 his tavern acted as a focal point for Birmingham's reactions to the Wilkite movement and its repercussions in local parliamentary constituencies. Acting through the group at the Leicester Arms and others like it, which assumed the traditional mantle of Liberty and Independence soon to be shed by the older Bean Club, it was these which first gave active form to the popular political consciousness of the Birmingham area. This achieved its most concrete results in the antecedents of the Warwickshire election of 1774. Before this, however, political interest in Birmingham, especially among the artisans, was particularly occupied with developments in the city and county of Worcester. It is in this respect that the significance of groups like that at the Leicester Arms becomes most clear.

The city of Worcester was a notoriously violent constituency, in which movements of popular opinion counted for much at election time.[34] Its politics were dominated by a long-standing division between Corporation, Bishop, Dean and

Chapter, Lord Lieutenant and East India Company on one side, and an Independent party, in which Dissenters were prominent, on the other. Against the formidable combination of Church, corporation, peer and nabob popular opinion placed commerce and independence. Thus to Birmingham readers the Worcester by-election of November 1773, following the death of Henry Crabb Boulton, was announced as a race between 'Mr. Kelly's horse Independency, got by Freedom upon Commerce' and ridden by Will True Blue, and 'Mr. Rous' black horse Nabob', with Tom Plassey up, 'descended from a bloody shoulder'd Arabian, full Brother to Tyranny and Corruption, back'd by Lord Jaghire and other Asiatic Sportsmen'.[35]

William Kelly, the independent candidate on this occasion, was a prosperous merchant trading with America; but though he enjoyed the freely given support of Worcester's labouring freemen, who were pledged 'to vote for no man but who shall ... use his utmost to obtain a Triennial Parliament', his purse was not deep enough to support both a by-election and a general election contest within the next two years. Kelly withdrew, much to the disgust of his supporters, who were, however, placated when he was replaced by Sir Watkin Lewes, alderman of the City of London and a founder member of the Bill of Rights Society.[36] The three campaigns at Worcester which Lewes fought during 1773 and 1774 constituted one of the major efforts made in the provinces by the Wilkite radicals.[37] On the occasion of the first poll in 1773 Sir Watkin arrived too late to arouse much interest on his own account, and merely took over Kelly's campaign. Nevertheless he managed to win 635 votes against 900 for Thomas Bates Rous. His adoption of a Wilkite stance and the success of his petition on 8 February 1774 to have the first return annulled drew attention to the contest; and at the second poll on 1 March 1774, when neither side dared to influence the result, Sir Watkin raised his share of the vote to 713 while support for Nicholas Lechmere, temporarily substituted for Rous, fell ominously to 796. At the general election later in the year Lewes again improved his overall position to 736, but once more finished third, behind Rous and John Walsh with 981 and 893 votes respectively. Although he thus failed to win a seat, Lewes continued to draw attention to himself. The hearing of his petition alleging gross bribery and corruption by the Worcester corporation dragged on until 1776, and even when it failed two further bribery suits against individuals, of whom the first was 'a reputable Birmingham Merchant', at Warwick assizes in 1776 and at Worcester in 1777, kept interest alive.[38] Sir Watkin's final campaign at Worcester in 1780 came closer to success than the polling figures— 1,106 for Rous, 847 for the Hon. William Ward, the son of Lord Dudley, and 711 for Lewes—suggest. It was only foiled by last-minute horse-trading between the corporation, Ward and the country gentlemen in order to exclude the radical intruder.

The numerical history of Sir Watkin Lewes's efforts may reveal the fundamental hopelessness of his cause; but even when due allowance has been made for simple obstinacy it is not reasonable to suppose that Lewes would have persisted for so long in challenging the formidable phalanx arrayed against him at Worcester unless his own support had remained encouragingly strong throughout. This was indeed the case, not only in Worcester and London, whence more than fifty freemen set out on foot to vote for Lewes at the second poll in March 1774, and where supporters' clubs were organised in preparation for the general election later in the year,[39] but also in Birmingham and the northern parts of Worcestershire.

Much of the strength of the Independent interest at Worcester lay with the manufacturing freemen within the city itself, and it was the corporation's effort to neutralise this by tampering with the regulations governing the freedom of the city, and particularly with the voting rights of the workers at the Worcester porcelain factory, which formed the *point d'appui* of Sir Watkin Lewes's campaigns. During the two by-election polls of November 1773 and March 1774 the local cause was elevated to become a matter of national liberty, and the association was confirmed at the general election, when the four points of the declaration adopted by the Wilkites at Mile End on 25 September 1774 were introduced directly into the Worcester contest.[40] After his defeat Sir Watkin duly protested against 'The partial decision of the presiding officer in rejecting the votes of many concerned in a very valuable branch of manufacture, who have the strongest legal title to the franchise of this city'.[41] The claims of the pottery workers were vindicated in December 1774, when a writ of *mandamus* was successfully brought against the corporation. Lord Mansfield's verdict in favour of John Steel, journeyman potter, who had been refused his freedom on the grounds that, as an apprentice, he had not fulfilled the necessary residence requirements, was greeted in Worcester with general celebrations. The china works were illuminated, bells rung, guns fired, bonfires lit, and a procession, complete with decorative streamers and band, marched from the works to a public dinner at Tom's Coffee House.[42] The verdict, which enfranchised several other workmen hitherto disqualified for the same reasons, must have done much to sustain Independent morale.

All this was eagerly followed by the people of Birmingham and northern Worcestershire. Specific aspects of the situation at Worcester—the identification of independence with freedom and commerce; the original candidature of a merchant trading with America, who, if not a Dissenter himself, bound himself to 'reverence good men of all persuasions'; the struggle of 'slow and unremitting industry'[43] against the massed forces of established interest, which was soon to find an echo in the contest with 'Lordly Power' in Warwickshire; the pottery workers' fight for their rights—all these were calculated to appeal to the people of an increasingly important though unrepresented manufacturing area, and the mood they engendered was well caught in the report of an incident during the second by-election poll which *Berrow's Worcester Journal* printed on 24 February 1774.

> A gentleman from Birmingham, dressed rather plain, coming up to the poll on Saturday last, several of Mr. Lechmere's friends called out *a pauper, a pauper*. The man polled for Sir Watkin, and told them in an indignant voice that so far from being a pauper, he was able to spare a thousand pounds towards the support of Sir Watkin without hurting his family; that he would return home immediately, and send as many Freemen to Worcester, at his own expense as he could meet with; he did so, and sent ten votes for Sir Watkin, who polled on Monday last.

Attention had been drawn to Worcester soon after the general election of 1768. During the summer of 1769 the *Birmingham Gazette* gave extensive coverage to the petitions of grievance organised by the county and city of Worcester. The county petition in particular aroused controversy, since its drafting and circulation were disputed between local supporters of the Bill of Rights Society and the associates of William Dowdeswell, Lord Rockingham's lieutenant in the House of Commons and Member of Parliament for Worcestershire. On one hand, 'A Freeholder of Forty Shillings a Year' asked in the *Worcester Journal*, whether, 'notwithstanding the proud connexions of families, the weight of overgrown estates and the wretched dependence of our boroughs, ... notwithstanding even that last breach of the Right of Election which cuts off LIBERTY from the land, we have not the POWER in our hands to do ourselves justice if we can but use it'. On the other hand, Dowdeswell, who had rejected overtures from Robert Morris, secretary of the Bill of Rights Society, was trying to steer the petition away from such extremism and confine it to the specific question of the Middlesex return. Dowdeswell had his way, but the petition went on slowly. During July and August action was successively postponed from quarter sessions to assize meeting, and from assize meeting to race week. On 4 September the *Birmingham Gazette* admitted that 'not above six gentlemen of rank' and about fifty others had signed at the freeholders' meeting in Worcester, and that the results of private circulation through the county could not be predicted. At the same time Dowdeswell was complaining that Wilkes's reputation and the excessive language of petitions from other places had deterred people of rank from signing, and that the ordinary freeholders were still waiting for a lead from their betters.[44]

Nevertheless Dowdeswell remained hopeful. Duplicates were now being circulated, and time might yet produce a creditable result. It did, and the presence among the 1,446 signatures which the petition eventually collected of names like William Russell, Thomas Russell, Thomas Rock, John and William Kettle, Thomas Gem, Henry Carver, John Banner, Edward Palmer, John Oseland and William Laugher suggests that it was sympathetically received in the Birmingham area. Indeed, the fact that many of the Birmingham signatures were closely grouped on the same part of the petition strengthens the probability that at least one of the duplicates was specifically circulated in the town. Most of the Birmingham trades were represented, from brassfounders to wire drawers, and among the professions the attorneys were particularly conspicuous, as might be expected of a group which, though comparatively small in number, was closely involved in the affairs of the region, both political and otherwise. Though John Freeth himself was not among them, those who signed included a possible third of the Birmingham Book Club's twenty-four members as first listed in 1775; and despite the absence of any sign of direct participation by the landlord of the Leicester Arms, a possible total of fourteen other Birmingham taverns and public houses were associated with the petition, including the Dog in Spiceal Street, where the assembly of subscribers to the Old Meeting House held occasional meetings from 1772 onwards.[45]

News of local demonstrations in support of John Wilkes continued to fill the Birmingham papers. On 26 February 1770 the *Birmingham Gazette* printed a circular letter from the Supporters of the Bill of Rights calling for the formation of provincial societies in correspondence with that in London. Two months later dinners were advertised for 18 April to celebrate Wilkes's release from the King's Bench prison. One was to be held at the Castle Inn; the other, organised by John Freeth, who also announced his *Ode on Wilkes' Enlargement*, was presumably held at the Leicester Arms. The following week these dinners, and the

bonfires and firework displays which followed them, were again noticed, together with similar celebrations at Bridgnorth, Worcester and 'at most other
places within the circuit of this paper'.[46] The next three years were marked by a
similar succession of incidents, all of which prevented political interest from
flagging.[47]

The Ministry's attempt to steal a march on the opposition by announcing a
sudden and premature dissolution of Parliament in the autumn of 1774 was
certainly unsuccessful in the West Midlands. Sir Watkin Lewes visited Worcester
early in August, where the ladies of the city presented his wife with a large piece
of plate. This, which was 'allowed by competent judges to exceed anything of
the kind ever seen in these kingdoms', was a product of Boulton & Fothergill's
famous works at Soho, and its iconography catalogued the popular political
causes and slogans of the previous twelve years. The whole was in the form of
a shield surrounded by a palm wreath, which enclosed the following groups:

1. In the middle, Fortitude on a rock, helmeted and leaning on a pillar, the top
   of which was lost in cloud.
2. Beneath Fortitude, Britannia with her usual emblems, Magna Carta in her
   hand.
3. Justice descending on a cloud with thunderbolts and lightning, destroying
   Bribery, 'A groveling figure, which lies struck to the earth, a bag of money
   in his hand, and money falling out."
4. 'Temperance chaining down licentiousness, represented by a satyr, in whose
   hand is a goblet inverted, the liquor pouring from it.'
5. Supporters, Eloquence and Hope.
6. Crest, Fame surrounded by a Glory.
7. On the right and left sides of the base (in clear reference to commercial considerations, opposition to the coercive acts, and the tax on cider and perry,
   which had particularly affected Worcestershire): 'A dove perched on an olive
   branch, and a cornucopia.', and 'Three pears, depending from one very slight
   thread, a sword in a hand in armour held over them in a threatening posture,
   as just ready to cut them off.'
8. The motto: 'Firm in the glorious enterprize.'

From Worcester Sir Watkin toured the northern parts of the county, and his
progress was reported in full detail by the Birmingham papers. At Kidderminster
two thousand inhabitants gave him a popular reception and he visited a constitutional club founded by Worcester freemen living in the town. Eventually
he reached Birmingham itself, where he 'met with the greatest encouragement'.[48]

Parliament was dissolved on 30 September, and the *Birmingham Gazette*,
which carried the news on 3 October, also printed a manifesto from John Freeth:

CONSTITUTIONAL SOCIETY

The sudden and unexpected dissolution of Parliament, while it plainly indicates
the deep laid system of Despotism of an arbitrary and unprincipled Administration, ought to rouse every Friend to civil and religious Liberty, to an active and
vigorous Defence of those sacred Privileges which are the glorious inheritance of
Freeborn Englishmen.—There is no time left for Hesitation and Delay; the
Designs of the Ministry are openly avowed in their late dangerous political
Manoeuvre. Every Individual is called upon by the most sacred Tie of Liberty,
to oppose, and endeavour to avert the diabolical Machinations of a Set of Men,
whose Success must inevitably terminate in the utter Subversion of Freedom and

Independence; and in the entire Extirpation of the best and noblest Privileges of Englishmen.

N.B. a Meeting of the Friends of Sir Watkin Lewes, will be held at FREE'S Coffee-House in Bell-street, Birmingham, THIS EVENING, at Seven o'Clock to consider of proper Measures to support his Election.

A week later another meeting was held, and Freeth again urged the necessity of opposition as the best means of 'restoring a distracted State to the tranquil Order and Pursuit of public Measures which may be conducive to the Prosperity and Happiness of a brave and free People'. Sir Watkin was defeated, and there is no sign that his Birmingham friends continued to meet specifically in his support after the general election. Nevertheless interest in Worcester politics was maintained by the pottery workers' successful *mandamus* case, by the fortunes of Lewes's petition against the return of Thomas Bates Rous and John Walsh and by the individual bribery suits at Warwick and Worcester assizes. Consolation was offered to Sir Watkin by the testimonial which he received from the London Court of Common Council and by the address from a public meeting of Worcester freemen which the *Birmingham Gazette* reported verbatim in its local news section on 29 July 1776. This urged Lewes to give maximum publicity to the injustice which he and the freemen had suffered, as 'a work looked for with avidity by the whole kingdom'. Though Sir Watkin failed again in 1780, his visit to the Birmingham area to canvass for votes met with great success, not only in the town itself but also in Kidderminster, Bewdley, Stourbridge and other places in the Black Country.[49]

Despite its ultimate failure, the Independent cause at Worcester had, for at least seven years, retained the political attention of the people of Birmingham and northern Worcestershire. Even if they had no voting rights in their own region, it is clear that they were neither indifferent to politics nor lacking in the sort of organisation which reflected their interest. This became particularly articulate during the period of the 1774 general election; and though it has only been relevant at this stage to construct a continuous narrative of the relations between Birmingham opinion and one particular constituency, the influence of that opinion was not confined to Worcester. In the Warwickshire election of 1774 the voters of Hemlingford Hundred—virtually Birmingham and its vicinity —outweighed the rest of the constituency and returned Sir Charles Holte against the odds as Member of Parliament for the county. This victory, which established the bridgehead from which Birmingham's claim to a pre-emptive nomination of one of the Warwickshire Members could be developed, was made possible by the fact that Birmingham opinion was already alert and organised, thanks to events at Worcester, when an Independent campaign in the county became a realistic possibility shortly before polling was due to begin.[50]

One other episode will illustrate the response of the Birmingham area to local political developments, and the way in which reaction to events in one place could produce repercussions elsewhere. Immediately after the 1774 election the death of Viscount Wentworth and subsequent elevation of Thomas Noel to the peerage created a vacancy in the representation for Leicestershire. The by-election which followed was fought between William Pochin and John Peach Hungerford, standing respectively for the 'new' and 'old' Independent interests in the county.[51] On 28 November 1774 the *Birmingham Gazette* carried an advertisement in support of Hungerford, ostensibly from Sir Charles Holte.

This asked Leicestershire freeholders living in Birmingham to give their names either to a Mr William Sadler of Castle Bromwich or to John Rickards, a Dissenting attorney who was to help in the organisation of the Birmingham petition against the Coercive Acts in January 1775,[52] so that an account could be sent on to Hungerford's own committee in Leicester. The following week a letter from Stephen Addington, Dissenting minister at Market Harborough, supported Hungerford as a well-wisher to civil and religious liberty and a man of incorruptible independence. On 12 December, however, an anonymous correspondent depicted Hungerford very differently:

> He offers his services in the OLD INDEPENDENT INTEREST, and the world knows that the interest is old—is OLDER than the Revolution; it was brooded under and fostered by the Stuarts, those Sons of Civil Liberty and Champions of the Rights of Conscience.

Hungerford was an associate of Jacobites, Roman Catholics and high-flying Tories like 'Lords D----- and W-----, and Sir Roger Newdigate, . . . and which of these voted for the Dissenters' Bill last session?'[53] The same paper also carried two notices regarding Sir Charles Holte's invitation to Leicestershire freeholders in Birmingham. In the first, William Sadler confessed that he, and not Holte, was responsible for the invitation, which now appeared highly offensive. In the second, Sir Charles himself,

> Gratefully sensible of the kindness of his friends, . . . begs leave to assure them that no consideration could have prevailed on him . . . to attempt to dictate to their Judgement, or influence their conduct, even could he flatter himself he had any *such* influence over them. In justice to himself, he is therefore obliged to declare the advertisement in his name in this paper for some weeks past relative to the Leicestershire election was absolutely without his knowledge.

Evidently Hungerford was trying to associate himself with Holte's recent victory, and was looking for votes in Birmingham, backed by Addington's letter, which, coming as it did from a man of some reputation, might be expected to carry some weight, provided too many questions were not asked.[54] Faced with this, William Pochin, himself fighting the Leicestershire election in the Dissenting interest, had Hungerford unmasked. Once this had been done, Sir Charles Holte made haste to deny any association with one whose reputation was offensive to much of his own support in the Birmingham area.

Thus once more opinion in Birmingham, which, though unrepresented itself, could participate vicariously in electoral politics through its significant concentrations of voters qualified in other places, acted as a link which was quick to transmit actions and reactions between different parliamentary constituencies, so that developments in one would be registered in the behaviour of voters and candidates elsewhere. In this process groups like that at the Leicester Arms played a central part; and once again it was John Freeth, in his invitation to the Birmingham Book Club for 24 November 1774, who produced the appropriate comment:

> Excuse all defects, 'tis a hurrying time;
> Feasting days, I confess are fond objects for rhyme;
> There hope that tomorrow your kind condescension
> Will pay to this summons the needful attention.
> As Liberty triumphs on Warwickshire plains.

You'll pass the gay moments in jocular strains.
May Leicestershire Lads the Example pursue,
Which their neighbours have set Freedom's Foes to subdue;
And since not a blot can be found on his scutcheon,
May the Toast of the Day be—Success to a POCHIN.[55]

The alertness which showed itself in the elections of 1774 embraced a wider field than politics, however; and while the Constitutional Society at Freeth's coffee house was directing attention to Worcester, debating societies were being founded in the town whose brief histories provide valuable insight into the preoccupations of Birmingham's small masters and artisans. These societies considered a surprising variety of topics, and their resolutions combined progressive self-assertion with deeply engrained conservatism. This was the background from which sprang the specifically political interests which have already been described. It was in fact from the Free Debating Society, meeting in Sam Wickens's Long Room at the Red Lion in March 1774 to decide whether 'an Opposition at the ensuing General Election for members to represent the County of Warwick' would be 'of much consequence in supporting the Freedom and Independence of the Freeholders thereof',[56] that the only sign came before October that any such action was contemplated.

Though there is no direct evidence of it, the relationship between the debating societies and the coterie at the Leicester Arms was probably close. The political sympathies of the Free Debating Society, which at the end of April 1774 upheld the right of John Wilkes to represent Middlesex and condemned the Coercive Acts,[57] were in accord with those of Freeth's Constitutional Society, and the 1771 edition of Freeth's *Political Songster* contained verses which suggest not only that an artisan's discussion club was already meeting at the Red Lion but also that it was even then paying attention to local electoral politics, particularly in Worcester.[58] The order paper of March 1774 which raised the possibility of an opposition at the next Warwickshire election was, however, the first in which the Free Debating Society drew public attention to its meetings. On 18 April its advertisement, which was now appearing every week in Aris's paper, gave the society's full title as 'The Birmingham Robin Hood Free Debating Society'. Whether this addition indicates that it had been explicitly adopted by its London namesake as a provincial offshoot is not certain, though the London Robin Hood Society did take an interest in the Birmingham club. More important at this stage was the notice on 25 April, which not only referred to attempts to suppress the society, rebutted imputations of disorderly behaviour at its meetings and referred to the respectability of its promised support, but also announced that *Swinney's Birmingham and Stafford Chronicle* on the following Thursday would contain the order papers of a similar society meeting at the Red Lion inn, Wolverhampton. On 9 May the Walsall Free Debating Society announced a meeting on the following Wednesday in the new assembly room at the Green Dragon. The two following issues of the *Birmingham Gazette* announced that the Walsall society would continue to meet every week at the Green Dragon, while, after its meeting on 26 May, the Wolverhampton club was to meet fortnightly during the summer. The Wolverhampton society evidently prospered sufficiently to announce in its notice of 18 July that its next meeting would be followed by a ball. No further details of the Walsall and Wolverhampton societies have survived, but the fact that during May announcements regarding all three debating clubs were included in single advertisements in the Birmingham papers suggests some measure of correspondence between them.

The next important development in the history of the Birmingham Robin Hood Free Debating Society came in July 1774, when it divided into two. One half retained the original name while the other called itself the Birmingham Old Robin Hood Society. The split was not immediately apparent, but the notice on 4 July was signed by a new president, Mr T. Shatford, who promised that

> Every regulation and decorum which has so long supported with the greatest reputation the Robin Hood Society in London, will be carefully preserved in the Birmingham Society.

On 18 July two advertisements were printed. The Birmingham Robin Hood Free Debating Society continued to meet at the Red Lion under the presidency of Shatford, while J. Jones, the president of the original society, announced the removal of the Old Robin Hood Society to 'the great room, late Hopkins', in Temple Row', where it was to meet on the following day to discuss questions inserted in the *Birmingham and Stafford Chronicle* the previous week. The division, which, to judge by the order papers of the two clubs, does not seem to have arisen from any fundamental difference of outlook, was possibly due to personal rivalry between Shatford and Jones, and perhaps also to local reluctance to submit to the former's introduction of the rules of the London society. After 1774 both societies disappeared almost completely from the record, but an advertisement in the *Birmingham Gazette* on 15 November 1779 for the Free Debating Society, meeting in Mr Bull's Long Room at the Red Lion, Digbeth, suggests that the parent society had reverted to its original name and had continued to meet regularly. The price of admission was still 6*d*, as it had been from the start, and according to the advertisement this could be offset by 'customary allowances'.

Only a general impression can be given of the quality of the discussion conducted in these societies. The free admission of ladies to the debates and the fact that all the societies allowed them to speak indicates a certain minimum level of decorum.[59] This may perhaps be seen as embodying a progressive and enlightened attitude, which is also reflected in the singular relevance and penetration of some of the questions considered. Some incentive to good speaking was also offered in the form of medals presented to outstanding orators,[60] and on 1 August 1774 Mr Shatford announced that the next meeting at the Red Lion would be preceded by his lecture 'on oratory and Elocution, with remarks on the Professors in the Pulpit, the Bar, and the Stage, illustrated by examples from the most celebrated authors'. However, the sheer quantity of questions proposed for discussion within the short period allotted to meetings[61] must have severely restricted the time available for single topics, so that resolutions were reached by the crudest forms of acclaim. On 11 April 1774 the Free Debating Society announced a fine of 1*s* on those who swore at its meetings, and ten weeks later the society's tumultuous proceedings exposed it to the fastidious comments of 'Alpha', who agreed that 'an institution of this nature, conducted with proper decorum, is truly rational' but confessed himself disappointed by the varying quality of the speakers. A few had been worth hearing, but in general Alpha had been shocked by the noisy disorder of the debates.

He thought it impossible that 'a poor apprentice or a mean mechanic' could possess the 'refined education' needed to be an orator; 'besides, the outward garb of many of those who spoke was rather indecent; ... the Ladies are permitted gratis, and cleanliness is a compliment due to the sex everywhere'.

These comments were summed up in a parodied couplet from *Paradise Lost*:

> Dull on their unshaved chins and dirty brows,
> Stupidity resides and vacant thought.

But though Alpha's remarks were in the main supercilious and patronising he did end on a more positive note with the hope that under proper guidance from its president the Red Lion society would attract more able speakers, and the belief that 'On such a scheme as this, Oratory will again flourish, nor can the mind of man conceive a more effectual plan for the encouragement of Elocution'.[62] Alpha's attitude to the proceedings at the Red Lion was thus very similar to that of the sponsors of the New Street theatre towards the stage, and it was probably in expression of the same outlook that a rival discussion group, pointedly called 'The Amicable Debating Society', was started. Its first notice appeared on 25 April 1774, alongside the Free Debating Society's announcement of new rules and complaint of attempted suppression.[63] From its beginning the Amicable Debating Society kept much closer control of its membership and proceedings than did its rivals. The notice spoke of the desirability of free and candid discussion, but warned that completely open membership would only lead to anarchy. A 'more liberal plan' had therefore been adopted; laws had been drawn up to which all prospective members would be obliged to subscribe. Copies of these laws had been left for public inspection at the offices of the *Birmingham Gazette* and the *Birmingham and Stafford Chronicle*, where sealed applications for membership would be received. From these, the actual members were to be chosen by ballot at a meeting arranged for the purpose at the King's Head in New Street on the following Wednesday. The prospectus thus reproduced in microcosm a more acceptable theory of politics than that implied by the rough-and-tumble at the Red Lion.

The new society further emphasised its distinction on 2 May, when it announced its first regular meeting, not in the long room of a tavern, but in Mrs Aston's Coffee Room in the Cherry Orchard. The rhetorical questions proposed for debate were commonplace enough in themselves, but they bespeak a self-righteous combativeness towards the Birmingham Robin Hood Free Debating Society:

> Is a drunkard the greater enemy to himself or to society?
> Which is most detestable in itself and most dangerous to Mankind,
> Treachery in Friendship, or Hypocrisy in Religion?
> Which are the greatest, real or imaginary evils?[64]

After this initial sally the Amicable Debating Society preferred not to advertise its proceedings regularly but posted its order papers for public inspection at the Cherry Orchard.[65] However, on 3 October it announced its removal to the King's Head during the coming winter, and continued to meet there until 27 February 1775, when it returned to the Cherry Orchard. Doubts as to the society's future were resolved in its notices of 2 and 16 October 1775 by the introduction of an admission fee of 1*s* per meeting for strangers. This involved

a departure from the original principle of named membership only, but the
high fee charged—double that of the Red Lion society—was calculated to
keep out the more unruly elements. After this there were no further notices;
but late in 1776 'mature discussion' of the General Hospital by a 'numerous
and very respectable meeting' of the 'Conversation Society' at Mrs Aston's
suggests that a descendant of the original society was still active, not only
more select than its rivals but perhaps also closer to the sources of initiative in
local development.[66]

If those recorded in the frequent advertisements of the Free Debating Society
and its derivatives are any guide, the questions debated in those societies went
far beyond the more obvious political issues of the day. They covered the whole
range from practical local topics and comment on the way in which the world
was changing to themes which touch on the basic springs of that change. Discussion of political theory included not only such well worn subjects as mixed
constitutions and their advantages but also such questions as 'Whether the Law
of Nature is not, or would not be, if more practiced, of greater advantage to the
public than the Law of the Realm?' and 'Whether Justice or Injustice depend
upon the institutions of Civil Society, or on Nature?' The club turned its attention to a fundamental moral and economic issue when it asked, 'Is Luxury
useful or detrimental to a state?' and considered the whole future of the country
in 'Is Commerce or Agriculture most to the interest of Great Britain?' Among
practical questions debated were the price of provisions; the control of auction
sales; the licensing of pawnbrokers; the comparative values of public and private
education; whether 'Holidays' were 'of bad consequence either to Servants
or Masters?'; whether it would not be better to teach foreign languages to
merchants' clerks than to go on running the risks entailed in employing
foreigners themselves, and the justice of the game laws.[67] Among the few recorded discussions of the Amicable Debating Society was one on the effects of
mechanical improvements in industry on the country at large.[68]

In the resolutions which the societies passed, traditional and novel attitudes
were evenly mixed. The Free Debating Society considered the current bastardy
laws to be destructive of virtue, but abhorred the indiscriminate use of the
death penalty, and voted in favour of 'Compelling capital offenders (except
in cases of murder and treason) to strict labour on the Public Highways, and
obliging them to wear a badge or uniform as a mark of infamy'. 'Combinations
for the prosecution of felons' were accepted as not prejudicial to the community
in general, and the power vested in Justices of the Peace was considered to be
neither 'contradictory to the constitution of our country, nor prejudicial to
individuals'. It is, perhaps, surprising to find that the society decided that the
liberty allowed to ballad singers would tend to 'corrupt the morals of the lower
Class of People'; but this precluded neither a favourable answer to the question
'Is the exhibition of Plays likely to be serviceable or detrimental to the town of
Birmingham either with respect to Temporals or to Morals?' nor the rearrange-
ment of the society's meetings in order to avoid a clash with theatrical performances during the summer season. No objections were raised to 'the custom
so much practiced (in Birmingham) of sending children to the shops to work
as soon as they are well able to walk', and the resolution 'that the want of
Religion is the Cause of the Increase of Criminal Offences, and that Prayer to
God for the Renewal of the Heart is the most likely Means to prevent them'

is an apt commentary on evangelical morality.[69] Discussion of possible remedies for 'the Distresses of the lower Class of People' produced a long letter to the president of the society from William Hutton which reviewed the points raised, so that it is possible in this one instance to get closer to the actual course of debate and to the mixture of ideas which shaped opinion. A proposal for a tax on the rich to provide an allowance for pauper families with more than five children would 'bring Child-getting into fashion; and if you will support my Children, I will not work for them, hence Manufactuaries would diminish, Exports decrease, and Poverty make larger strides amongst us.' To throw open the new enclosures so that the poor 'may graize upon the commons' would be 'bringing us towards a State of Nature, consequently distress': enclosed farms made work rather than destroyed it, 'consequently Popularity, for the more Work, the more people.' Nor would it be of any value to reduce the price of provisions by opening the ports:

> All Commercial Nations seem to have adopted this Maxim, Keep Provisions as high as you can provided they are within reach of the Poor. Lock, Gee, Postlethwayte, Griffith, and all the Authors I have seen upon Trade incline towards it .... The generality of men will do no more Work than produces a Maintenance, reduce that Maintenance to half the Price, and they will do but half the Work, here half your Comerce is distroyed at One Blow, and when a foreign Kingdom hath acquired that half you have lost, they will not be long without the other.

In sum,

> Industry and Oeconomy would answer the Purpose, the addition of another hours debate could not have fixed the argument upon a firmer Basis, I could enlarge but not improve upon it. I question if the Whole Room could have produced a Single instance of continued distress accompanied by these words.[70]

Among the more purely speculative questions, many concerned conventional morality and accepted virtues, while others considered topics like the familiar epistemological riddle 'Is it possible for a man that is born blind to have any true idea of sight?' Some, however, expressed more directly the outlook of men buoyed up by the prospect of material improvement and individual opportunity. To the question 'Has not the present age run into a greater excess of vice than any other?' the Free Debating Society, which had already asked 'Whether does curiosity or ambition lead most to the improvement of the human mind?', returned the optimistic answer that the present was 'much preferable to any former age'. This confidence in the present, and therefore, by extension, in the future as well, was in keeping with the challenge of the self-educated man to the authority of social prescription which the Free Debating Society had already issued by resolving 'that an ignorant man is a greater object of pity than a presumptuous one'.[71] The same challenge was implicit in 'Omega's' reply to 'Alpha'.

> Why, Mr. Printer, should a young Man, who has read, nay more, who has well digested what he has read, and whose Memory is retentive enough to enable him to make many pertinent observations, why I say, should he be debarred from a Society where he comes for Improvement? Is it because he pays greater Attention to that Business from whence himself, and perhaps an aged Parent derives support, than to the Length of his Beard or the Colour of his Stock?[72]

For all that, however, such a man was apt to remain sensitive about his lack of polish and eager to remedy the defect. Accordingly the Free Debating Society asked, 'Can education in a man be compleat till the conversation of the Fair has given a final polish to it?' and followed this with 'Why is Trade and Commerce in a manner become incompatible with polite literature?'[73] The questions and resolutions printed for the society on 15 November 1779 showed the same pre-occupations, concerned as they were with correct speech and manners. At the same time, however, they tolerated a certain flexibility of social discrimination, a liberty to descend 'a little below the *Ton*', which would provide stimulus and incentive for men whose acceptance of traditional forms and conventional attitudes was now tempered by their own expectations and ambitions:

> What is wit? As every man of fortune has the appellation, what are the charac-teristics of a Gentleman? Whether doth curiosity or ambition tend most to the improvement of the human mind? Whether it is better to stick to the rules of grammar or common convenience?

Of the previous week's questions,

> The second was supported with great energy on both sides till at length it seemed to turn on that of a Serjeant, with this little addition: that after the Serjeant had given him a free and open deportment, the Dancing Master should be called in to add a politer polish.

> The third . . . was kept up with great vivacity on all sides, but it passed in honour of that young woman who had prudence enough to step a little below the *Ton*.

> The fourth . . . was carried on with much opposition and some smart repartee till defined from the chair, that MY and THY should never be pronounced long, but where there was a real antithesis, or a supposed one.

Though there remains no direct evidence that debating societies continued to meet in Birmingham during the 1780s, they had by then become a familiar enough part of town life to feature in a comedy billing at the New Street theatre in 1785, when Mr Cowdroy's 'Celebrated Satyric, Humorous and Entertaining Dissertation on Faces' featured 'The faces of a learned Pedant, with his speech as President of a Debating Society' and 'The two faces of an unlearned Pedant'.[74] The wide interest in popular politics and current affairs which had shown itself in Birmingham between 1768 and 1774 was not again directly expressed in the form of political societies until the years after 1789. Nevertheless such groups as the Book Club at the Leicester Arms and its imitators, or the Liberal Society, which met at the Shakespeare tavern between 1787 and 1792,[75] kept up the habit of topical discussion, and in 1789 a new 'Society for Free Debate' was formed. Though this enjoyed the patronage of many of the Leicester Arms coterie, and though its president was James Bissett, deputy chairman of the ill starred revolution dinner in July 1791, one of Freeth's closest associates and in many ways his successor as local poet and ballad writer,[76] its proceedings were on the face of it more akin to those of the Amicable Debating Society than to those of the old club at the Red Lion. In 1790 its exclusiveness elicited sidelong comments in the *Birmingham Gazette*, and in complaining about the presence of strangers at its meetings it described itself somewhat perversely as 'The Select Society for Free Debate'.[77]

These contortions were a reflection not so much of a deliberately restrictive policy as of the difficulty of survival in increasingly repressive circumstances.

The society's exclusiveness was intended not so much to maintain internal discipline among its own members, as had been the case with the earlier Amicable Debating Society, as to defend itself from the unwelcome attentions of hecklers and provocative intruders from outside. In 1792 the society attracted the unwelcome attention of the magistrates, who tried to curtail its activities;[78] though it managed to survive this intervention, the cost was most of what remained of its supposed freedom. In October 1792 it could still ask, 'Was Brutus justified in killing Caesar?',[79] a question whose relevance to current politics was well veiled but still left scope for contemporary analogies; but the following March the society decided at its general meeting that 'questions (from which political ones are excluded) shall be debated on the first Monday of every month, instead of fortnightly, as heretofore'. This only added to the hollowness of the 'Liberal Society for Free Debate's' announcement of its next general meeting the following October.[80] By now, however, political differences in Birmingham had hardened. A virtual state of war existed between Freeth's friends at the Leicester Arms and those who drank at Joe Lyndon's Minerva tavern, which was favoured by the Tories of the town; all attempts at free discussion were under the ban of 'Job Nott's Humble Advice' to 'Hotheads, Old Maids, Gossips and Debating Boys who have kept up the ball too long', and the Society for Free Debate was under Home Office surveillance, along with other 'Associations for the relief of Pretended Grievances' elsewhere in the country.[81]

By 1793 the expression of popular opinion in Birmingham was thus being forced into the straitjacket of reaction. During the previous twenty-five years, however, it had grown extensively in both range and complexity; and there was a difference between the silence of quiescent ignorance and that of muted expression, muzzled maybe, but implicitly recognised in the attempts which were made to restrain it. The most tangible sources of this articulacy are to be found in the indirect repercussions of events elsewhere, particularly of the Wilkite movement, between 1769 and 1774. These stimulated considerable interest in Birmingham, which showed itself not only in the activities associated with the politics of surrounding parliamentary constituencies but also in the formation of debating societies in the town's taverns and coffee houses. It was these which first gave definite shape to the dawning consciousness of Birmingham's artisans. Though the histories of the debating societies reveal something of the different attitudes which were combined in the outlook of their members, their proceedings were themselves part of a larger development, based on a very much wider range of resources. Some of these have already been noticed; they must now be examined in detail if a full account is to be given of the growth and character of popular articulacy in the Birmingham area, and of the part which it played in the assimilation of the town's political experience.

NOTES

1 William Godwin, *An Enquiry Concerning Political Justice*, cited by Eric Robinson, 'The origins and life span of the Lunar Society', *U.B.H.J.*, XI, No. 1 (1967), p. 506.

2 John Freeth, *The Political Songster, 1771, Addressed to the Sons of Freedom and Lovers of Humour* (Birmingham, 1771), B.R.L. 81720, pp. 3–4.

3 *Aris*, 3 July 1775, 18 June 1781.

4 *Aris*, 25 May 1767, 13 July 1778.

5 Schofield, *Lunar Society*, pp. 236–7.

6 *Aris, passim.* Among the enormous variety of other clubs and association meetings for which notices appeared were annual reunions of the old boys of Repton, Rugby, Lichfield and Hartlebury schools; the 'Oxford Anniversary Meeting' at Vauxhall Gardens in July 1783; the Female Friendly Societies of Lichfield, Yoxall, Wolverhampton and Stafford; the Coleshill Civil Society; the club which honoured the memory of Caractacus every year at the Bowling Green House, Longnor; 'The friends and countrymen of Owen Owen under the name of Welshmen or True Ancient Britons'; the St Martin's Society at the Shakespeare tavern, Birmingham, and the Rose Inn Society of Edgbaston.

7 Sir J. B. Stone, *Annals of the Bean Club* (1904), B.R.L. 345313, p. 1. Members of the club can be identified from W. K. R. Bedford, *Notes from the Minute Book of the Bean Club, 1754–1836* (1889), B.R.L. 131399, which gives brief details of early meetings and a continuous record of membership, elections, officials and the more important resolutions from 1772 onwards. In the interests of compression, detailed references to Bedford have been omitted here unless more is to be established than simple membership.

8 Langford, *Birm. Life,* I, 190. The eight were William John Banner, Henry Carver, Esq., Thomas Faulconbridge, John Freer, Richard Goulden, Thomas Lutwyche, John Oseland and Thomas Pemberton. Thomas Steward, who signed club notices in *Aris,* 28 July 1777 and 31 July 1780, was club secretary until 13 September 1793.

9 *Aris,* 14 August 1769, 3 September 1770.

10 The Birmingham Sunday schools, founded in 1784, were originally run by a joint committee of Anglicans and Dissenters. Differences led to the independent foundation of Dissenting schools in 1787. For further details of the process, which must have contributed to the increasingly reactionary aspect of the Bean Club's membership, see below, p. 220.

11 Langford, *Birm. Life,* I, 418.

12 Stone, *Annals,* p. 7.

13 See below, pp. 210–12.

14 *Aris,* 14 August 1769; *Hist. Parl.,* III, 442–3.

15 Gem, who became secretary of the Bean Club in September 1793, was listed in Birmingham trades directories as an attorney. He took an active part in a variety of local affairs; *cf.,* for example, *Aris,* 15 February 1790, in which Gem appeared as clerk to the trustees of the Bromsgrove to Birmingham turnpike, and 17 May 1790, in which he solicited the proprietors of the Birmingham and Birmingham and Fazeley canals for the vacant appointment as clerk to the company.

16 See below, p. 211.

17 *Aris,* 22, 29 March, 5 April 1790.

18 Bracebridge, who was Sir Charles's son-in-law, had featured in election verse in 1774 as suitor to Miss Holte. *Cf.* Langford, *Birm. Life,* I, 213.

19 *Aris,* 14 August 1769.

20 For the Bean Club's uncertainties over the Warwickshire election and the American war see below, pp. 177–8, 208–10.

21 Boulton's list is in *A.O.P.,* America box. The names were Joseph Carles, Henry Clay, Richard Conquest, James Cooke, Edward Davis, William Dickenson, Thomas Faulconbridge, Samuel Ford, John Fothergill, Thomas Gem, John Gimblett, John Goodall, Richard Goulden, Joseph Green, Thomas Ingram, Thomas Lutwyche, James Male, Thomas Rock, John Meredith, Thomas Orton, Edward Palmer, Thomas Tomlinson and D. Winwood. There are three more possibles: John Simcox, John Birch and James Duker (?Dickson) Budd.

22 *V.C.H. Warwicks.,* VII, 282–3; Joseph Carles, the Rev. Dr Spencer, Sir Robert Lawley, the Rev. Charles Curtis, the Rev. George Croft.

23 *Newdigate,* CR 136/B 1632; and *cf.* Donald E. Ginter, 'The Loyalist Association movement of 1792–93 and British public opinion', *Historical Journal,* IX (1966), 179–90, especially p. 187, which emphasises the local nature and the previous social roots of the associations as the main cause of their effectiveness.

24 *Aris,* 10 November 1777. The papers listed were the *London Gazette,* the *Morning Post,* the *Morning Chronicle,* the *Public Advertiser,* the *Gazetteer, Lloyd's Evening Post,* the *London Pacquet,* the *General Evening Post,* the *St James's Chronicle,* the *London Chronicle* and the *London Evening Post.*

25 *History of Birmingham,* p. 129; and *cf. Aris,* 29 March 1780, for notice of public consultation on 'Lord Beauchamp's Debtor's Bill', a draft of which was posted for inspection at the hotel and at Overton's.

26 *Aris*, 29 September 1777.

27 Langford, *Birm. Life*, I, 255; *Aris*, 2 May 1774, 7 December 1778.

28 J. A. Langford, 'John Freeth, the Birmingham ballad maker', *Mid-England*, I (Birmingham, 1880–81), B.R.L. 63089; S. W. Light, 'Poet John Freeth', *Central Literary Magazine* (Journal of the Central Literary Association of Birmingham), December 1960; Andrew Haynes, 'A sketch of the early history of the Birmingham Book Club', among the records of the Birmingham Book Club deposited in the District Bank, Bennett's Hill, Birmingham. My thanks are due to the present librarian of the club, Eric Dinwiddie, Esq., for permission to examine these records.

29 *The Political Songster, 1766*, B.R.L. 257599.

30 *Aris*, 3 February 1772.

31 See P. D. G. Thomas, 'The beginning of parliamentary reporting in newspapers, 1768–74', *Eng. Hist. Rev.*, LXXIV (1959), 623–36. For Almon's connections with the *Gazetteer*, the *London Evening Post* and other newspapers, and for the role of his shop in Piccadilly as pamphlet factory, '*locus operandi* for political activities generally' and clearing house for American news, see Lucyle Werkmeister, *The London Daily Press, 1772–92* (Lincoln, Neb., 1963), pp. 109–18.

32 See below, pp. 142–3.

33 'Freeth's invitation cards, 1770–1801', photostat copies, B.R.L. 523407; preface to *The Political Songster*, 1790 (Birmingham, 1790), B.R.L. 233171, pp. iii, iv.

34 The following account of Worcester politics is based on *Hist. Parl.*, I, 425–7.

35 *Aris*, 8 November 1773.

36 Rudé, *Wilkes and Liberty*, p. 219; I. R. Christie, *Myth and Reality in Eighteenth Century British Politics* (London, 1970), p. 252.

37 Bernard Donoughue, *British Politics and the American Revolution; the Path to War, 1773–75* (London, 1964), p. 196. I. R. Christie, 'The Wilkites and the general election of 1774', in *Myth and Reality*, pp. 244–60.

38 *Aris*, 12 August 1776, 17 March 1777.

39 *Aris*, 14 February, 8 August 1774.

40 *Aris*, 29 November 1773, 21 February 1774; *Berrow's Worcester Journal*, 13 October 1774. The four points of the Mile End declaration were shorter Parliaments, free and equal representation of the people, freedom of elections and the repeal of the Coercive Acts.

41 *Aris*, 24 October 1774.

42 *Aris*, 12 December 1774.

43 *Aris*, 8, 22 November 1774.

44 *Aris*, 24 July, 14 August 1769; Rudé, *Wilkes and Liberty*, pp. 113–15; Lucy S. Sutherland, ed., *The Correspondence of Edmund Burke*, vol. II (Cambridge and Chicago, 1960), 53–4, 69–71: Dowdeswell to Burke, 10 August, 5 September 1769.

45 My count of signatures on the Worcestershire petition (Home Office Papers, H.O. 55/2/4) differs from that of Professor Rudé, who made it 1475 (*Wilkes and Liberty*, p. 115). The names actually quoted above were immediately recognisable after inspection of the petition. The further conclusions as to the participation of the Birmingham area are based on a comparison of the names on the petition with the contents of *Sketchley's Birmingham Directory* of 1767, the most extensive available list of the town's tradesmen and the closest in time to 1769; with the earliest membership list of the Birmingham Book Club; with those who signed notices regarding the Birmingham conciliatory petition in *Aris*, 23 January, 20 February 1775; and finally with the list of subscribers to the Old Meeting who were consulted on the possible appointment of the Rev. David Walker on 25 December 1771 (*Old Meeting House, Register of Resolutions of the General Assembly of Subscribers, 1771–91*, B.R.L. 641586, pp. 4–6). This was used, in the same way as Sketchley's *Directory*, as providing the closest and most extensive available sample of Birmingham Dissent. The detailed results of these comparisons are set out in appendix II.

46 *Aris*, 16, 23 April 1770.

47 See below, pp. 168–74.

48 *Aris*, 8, 22 August 1774.

49 *Aris*, 14 August 1780.

50 See below, pp. 174–7.

51 *Hist. Parl.*, I, 322.

52 Rickards, whose name appears frequently in the *Old Meeting Register*, signed

addresses from the organisers of the Birmingham conciliatory petition in *Aris*, 23 January
and 20 February 1775. The situation is complicated by the fact that, while Sadler had
voted for Holte only at the Warwickshire election, Rickards was recorded as one of the
very few Birmingham voters for Skipwith and Mordaunt, a lapse for which he had his
premises damaged when Holte made his triumphal entry into Birmingham after the poll.
See *Aris*, 7 November 1774, and *The Poll of the Freeholders of Warwickshire, 1774*
(Coventry City Libraries, Coventry and North Warwickshire Collection), p. 19. This
information, which came to light after the article was completed, amends the account
given in my 'Taverns, coffee houses and clubs: local politics and popular articulacy in the
Birmingham area in the age of the American revolution', *Historical Journal*, XIV (1971),
34.

53 For Sir Roger Newdigate's opposition to Dissenters' relief see above p. 2.

54 Stephen Addington had been Independent minister at Market Harborough since
1752. He ran a Dissenting academy, and was the author of several books on education, as
well as one on the effects of enclosures. That such a man should support Hungerford was
not as odd as it may seem. Addington's theological views were conservative, and he may
well have been among those ministers who had actually opposed the initiation of
Houghton's Dissenters' relief Bill in January 1773. Besides, Hungerford, who lived at
Dingley Hall, Market Harborough, was a neighbour. See *D.N.B.*; *Hist. Parl.*, III, 255;
Barlow, *Citizenship and Conscience*, p. 184.

55 This card is in a newspaper cutting book among the records of the Birmingham
Book Club.

56 *Aris*, 21 March 1774.

57 *Aris*, 25 April, 2 May 1774.

58 See 'The Red Lion Society', *The Political Songster*, 1771, B.R.L. 81720, pp. 99–100.

59 *Aris*, 2, 30 May, 6 June 1774.

60 Langford, *Birm. Life*, I, 243.

61 8.15 to 10.30 p.m.

62 *Aris*, 20 June 1774. *Cf.* Milton:
    Deep on his Front engraven
    Deliberation sat and publick care.

63 *V.C.H. Warwicks.*, VII, 217, refers to the attempted suppression of the Amicable
Debating Society. This is a misreading of Langford, *Birm. Life*, I, 241.

64 Langford, *Birm. Life*, I, 242, suggests that the questions were pointed specifically at
the rival society. The implication of the first is obvious enough, less so those of the other
two. The third was probably directed at the spurious patriotism of the political opposition;
the second may refer to occasional conformity.

65 *Aris*, 2 May 1774.

66 *Aris*, 18, 25 November 1776.

67 *Aris*, 28 March, 11 April, 23 May, 6, 20 June, 18 July, 15 August 1774.

68 *Aris*, 27 February 1775.

69 *Aris*, 23 March, 4, 11, 18 April, 2, 9, 16, 23 May, 20 June 1774.

70 Hutton–Beale MSS, 'Hutton 24', to 'the President of the Debating Society', 29 July
1774. The question was proposed for 19 July and apparently postponed to the 26th: *Aris*,
18, 25 July, 1 August 1774.

71 *Aris*, 4, 11, 25 April, 9, 16 May 1774.

72 *Aris*, 27 June 1774.

73 *Aris*, 6 June, 11 July 1774.

74 Langford, *Birm. Life*, I, 394.

75 *Aris*, 16 July 1787, 14 September 1789, 17 September, 1 October 1792.

76 *V.C.H. Warwicks.*, VII, 277. Among Freeth's own invitation cards is one from the
Society for Free Debate for 26 September 1791. For Bissett, who signed the society's
notices as president during 1792–93, see T. B. Dudley, ed., *Memoir of James Bissett,
written by himself* (Birmingham, 1904), B.R.L. 182626.

77 *Aris*, 25 January, 15 March 1790.

78 *V.C.H. Warwicks.*, VII, 217.

79 Langford, *Birm. Life*, I, 387.

80 *Aris*, 11 March, 21 October 1793.

81 S. W. Light, *Poet John Freeth*, p. 23; postscript to *Job Nott's Humble Advice*, 5th
edn (1793), B.R.L. 63934; Home Office Papers, H.O. 42/22, list dated October 1792.

VI

MASONS, BUCKS AND BOOKS: PRINTING, PUBLISHING AND POPULAR INSTRUCTION

In their entry in Charles Pye's trades directory of Birmingham for 1787, Pearson and Rollason, proprietors of the *Birmingham Gazette* and the town's leading booksellers, announced that they kept a new and second-hand sales stock of some thirty thousand volumes in various languages. By any standards the figure is a large one, surpassed only by the boast that by the latter part of the eighteenth century a hundred thousand books and pamphlets were being read in Birmingham every month.[1] Taken at its face value, and combined with an estimated population of fifty thousand in 1783, this claim produces a monthly reading average of two items per inhabitant. Such an artificial calculation clearly has no meaning save as an illustrative device, but even when due allowance has been made for exaggeration some truth can be accorded to the boast on which it is based; for if the people of Birmingham were capable of the range of discussion reflected in the records of the debating societies they must have been well supplied with books of all kinds.

Printing, publishing and bookselling were not in themselves particularly new to Birmingham. Two printers had already worked in the town at different times during the latter half of the seventeenth century; its first entirely local publication dated from 1717, and by the 1730s the town was already supporting seven booksellers, of whom the best known was Thomas Warren, proprietor of the short-lived *Birmingham Journal* and in 1733 the commissioner of Samuel Johnson's first published work.[2] In 1737 Birmingham attracted the attention of Robert Walker, a prolific promoter of cheap newspapers and the chief pioneer of inexpensive serial publication in England. When it first appeared the *Warwick and Staffordshire Journal* was merely one of several similar papers which Walker produced in London for provincial distribution as vehicles for his various serial publications.[3] It was so successful that he opened an office in Birmingham itself in 1741 and remained there until 1743, when he sold out to another newcomer from London, Thomas Aris, of the recently founded *Birmingham Gazette*, and moved on to apply the formula which had worked so well with the *Warwick and Staffordshire Journal* to the establishment of local papers in Oxford and Cambridge.[4] The easy accessibility of printed material in Birmingham can thus be dated effectively from the 1740s. Though it was a comparative latecomer in the early history of the provincial press, the success of the *Birmingham Gazette* meant that the town now had a viable newspaper of its own; Thomas Warren, who had been hiring out books since at least 1729, was soon to be joined by other circulating library promoters,[5] and the topical pieces dealing with recent

history and current affairs which were now being serialised by Robert Walker
and his imitators, in addition to proven sellers like Lawrence Clarke's *History
of the Holy Bible* and *Foxe's Book of Martyrs*, must have played an important
part in encouraging the formation of reading societies in order to catch the
latest numbers as they came from the press. The most rapid progress, however,
was to come between 1760 and 1774, when Birmingham's increasing sense of
its own importance combined with local reactions to the political turmoil of
George III's early years to produce a powerful stimulus to the nine printers[6]
who were by then working in the town.

Foremost among these, and one of Birmingham's most distinctive personalities,
was John Baskerville, who was in the process of winning a European reputation
as the leading printer of the day. An avowed deist and disciple of the third Earl
of Shaftesbury, Baskerville was in contact with many of his most famous contemporaries, including Benjamin Franklin, a close friend since 1758, and
Voltaire, whose works he may have been planning to publish in translation in
1771.[7] He was well known for the pronounced unorthodoxy of his views, especially on religion and superstition,[8] and though his social and political opinions
were more akin to the paternalism of the enlightened despot than to the
egalitarianism of the democrat[9] they did not diminish his influence on the
growth of Birmingham's common readership. Admittedly, Baskerville withheld
his own imprint when his type was used to set the edition of John Wilkes's life
and political writings which was published in Birmingham in 1769;[10] but though
he stayed aloof on this occasion he had no qualms about recognising John
Freeth, whose *Political Songster*[11] was among the fully acknowledged productions
of the Baskerville press two years later. Nor was it only through the productions
of his own press that Baskerville's influence acted in this way. Several other local
printers were either drawn to Birmingham by his reputation, like Orion Adams,
a well known figure in many parts of the country whose father had played an
important part in the origins of provincial journalism in Manchester and
Chester,[12] or actually learnt their trade in his workshops on Easy Hill, like
Robert Martin, who acted as Baskerville's general manager from 1758 onwards,
Christopher Earl, who combined printing with auctioneering and also kept the
Engine, a tavern in Dale End which must have been another Leicester Arms,
and Myles Swinney of the *Birmingham and Stafford Chronicle*.[13] Of these,
Swinney in particular inherited some of Baskerville's style and penchant for the
unorthodox. It is, for example, tempting to make a connection between
Swinney's association with Baskerville, the fact that the latter may have been
contemplating an English edition of Voltaire's works at the time and the
appearance of the French sage's *Thoughts on Religion* in the *Warwickshire
Journal* during 1771:[14] certainly Baskerville's own views on the subject support
the conjecture.

Apart from the three new local newspapers which were started with varying
degrees of success during 1769 and 1770,[15] the most significant enterprises in
the field of popular publishing which were produced by these advances in
Birmingham printing were the first local magazines. Strictly speaking, the first
of these was the short-lived *Jones's Coventry, Warwick and Birmingham
Magazine*, published by a partnership between J. Jones and Thomas Luckman
of Coventry and James Sketchley and Thomas Warren junior of Birmingham,
which ran between January and July 1764.[16] Closely associated with this, how-

ever, were the remnants of the ill starred attempt which Luckman and Sketchley had been making for the past seven years to run a newspaper based on both Birmingham and Coventry. Since 1757 this had undergone several metamorphoses in its efforts to find a permanent foothold, and by 1764 its owners had been reduced to the expedient of trying to avoid advertisement duty by issuing it from its two sources on alternate weeks and under slightly different titles as a pair of fortnightly magazines.[17] This arrangement was announced in an early issue of Jones's magazine, and on 10 and 17 May 1764 respectively appeared the first numbers of *The Birmingham Register or Entertaining Museum* and *The Coventry Museum or Universal Entertainer*, each priced at $2\frac{1}{2}d$.[18] What happened to the second of these is uncertain, but it probably fulfilled the scornful predictions of *Jopson's Coventry Mercury* by failing before many weeks had passed. *The Birmingham Register* did somewhat better, however, and survived until the end of 1765, providing local readers with a miscellany of serialised pieces which included a biographical sketch of Jonathan Swift, an attempted comparison of poetry and painting, an account of the natural humours of the English, 'Historical Memoirs of Foreign and Domestic Occurrences' and instalments of a new annotated family Bible.[19]

Nevertheless it can hardly be claimed that this modest success was of much significance. *The Birmingham Register* did reprint the *North Briton* No. 177 in October 1764, and some lines on Birmingham and its trades written originally for the King Street theatre by George Alexander Stevens, a travelling comedian best known in the Midlands for his 'celebrated Lecture on Heads', may have provided Edmund Burke with the 'Toy Shop' metaphor which he used in defence of the Birmingham playhouse Bill in 1777;[20] but apart from this there was nothing particularly startling or original about the magazine from the point of view of either its political or its local content. Four years later, however, interest in the promotion of local periodicals ran high once more, and this time the results were more remarkable. Besides the local repercussions of national politics and the quickening tempo of Birmingham's own development, David Garrick's Shakespearean jubilee at Stratford on Avon in September 1769 provoked a period of intense competition among the town's printers. This showed itself not only in the three precursors of the *Birmingham and Stafford Chronicle*, and in the fierce rivalry which developed between Robert Martin and the partnership of Nicholas Boden and Orion Adams over their respective serial editions of the Bible and Shakespeare,[21] but also in the appearance of three new magazines. The first of these, *The Birmingham Magazine or Lady's and Gentlemen's Weekly Amusement*, which Orion Adams put out in 1769, was primarily a literary venture, a compilation of short pieces, many of them culled from other sources, aimed at the newly genteel.[22] Of more interest are Adams's other venture, *The Repository or Weekly General Entertainer*, which he published in collaboration with James and Samuel Sketchley during 1770, and Myles Swinney's *British Museum, or Universal Register of Literature, Politics and Poetry* of 1771.

The *Repository*, which was in part a revival of James Sketchley's earlier *Birmingham Register*, was remarkable not because its local content had been increased but because its political comment had been considerably sharpened. It still contained the usual selection of ephemeral curiosities and *belles lettres,* but these were now accompanied by serious strictures on the vices of the age and insistent warnings of the imminent overthrow of British liberty. Luxury, the destruction of individuals and the bane of governments, was singled out as the tool of political corruption, and an 'Essay on English Liberty' concluded that the only remaining difference between Frenchmen and Englishmen was that the former had been enslaved by force, the latter by fraud. Similarly, 'Political Maxims and Prophecies lately discovered in a heap of musty old papers' warned that 'when wickedness wriggles into high station with cunning and address, the worst of fools have the best chance of preferment', and this onslaught on the politicians who were frittering away the gains of the Seven Years War was reinforced by 'Observations on the English', ostensibly from the Abbé Millot of the University of Parma, whose account of national decay since 1716 reiterated the myth of deep-laid conspiracy, gradually ripening against the spirit of the constitution, which gave urgency to the London radicals and was soon to impel the American colonists towards 'the logic of rebellion'.[23]

Sustained political commentary was also one of the features of the *British Museum*. Parliamentary proceedings, disguised as those of 'The Robin Hood Society of London', were reported in each issue, together with a regular digest of foreign and domestic news. The outcome of the Russo-Turkish war was rightly predicted to 'become very interesting to us as a commercial nation', and special attention was paid to Maupeou's struggle with the sovereign courts in France, since 'in proportion as the spirit of Liberty and Commerce prevails there, the power of our rival neighbour will become formidable and dangerous'. At home the affairs of the London radicals and their fortunes in City politics were all closely and critically followed, and the manifestoes of the Society of the Supporters of the Bill of Rights, calling for the extraction of sworn pledges from parliamentary candidates, were printed verbatim. In addition, the letters of Marcus fulminated in each issue against the iniquities of a designing Ministry, a corrupt House of Commons, a servile peerage and a King who had become the mere leader of a party. Liberty, like a woman, could not be taken by force, but during the present reign she had succumbed to the blandishments of French effeminacy. Was there a freeholder, asked Marcus, in a question which found a particular echo in the growing resentment of 'Lordly Power' in Warwickshire itself, who was so dead to reflection that he had not noticed 'this fatal change in the manners of his superiors? his Barons! his Representatives!' Had it not been for the Middlesex election, which had exposed the infamous design, Englishmen would surely by now have been enslaved as totally as ever the Romans were, even under their most despotic emperors.[24]

Marcus thus repeated the theme of conspiracy, but he tried to do more than given indiscriminate support to popular agitation. He recognised only too well the comparative insignificance of 'all overheated patriots either in Parliament, in particular societies, in taverns or in pothouses'; he was as critical of the ignorant indifference of the greater part of the nation as he was of the court and the politicians, and he sought a remedy by expounding current politics, not in isolation, but as part of a comprehensive approach to the regeneration of social life and manners. In this, he said, periodical publications had a vital part to play. They had been brought into disrepute in recent years, and it was deplorable that no magazine could 'expect to live unless it is fed by the indecent memoirs of professed debauchees and the immodest victims of their pleasure'; but nevertheless they were 'absolutely necessary as registers of the times and can only be rendered infamous by the manner in which they are presented to the world'.[25] Marcus thus emphasised the serious educational purpose of the *British Museum*, whose first number had announced that it was sponsored by 'a Society of Gentlemen' in order to provide 'Instruction and Entertainment for the Fair Sex, the Gentleman and the Mechanic', and, like a provincial *Spectator*, had opened with a didactic preface under the motto 'Let me endeavour to spend every hour of my life usefully'. Similar homilies on the virtues of a civil and active life remained a basic part of the magazine's contents, together with a section on mathematical puzzles and games, the reigns of the kings of England abridged from Hume's *History*, the lives of such exemplary figures as King Alfred, Sir Francis Bacon, Richard Baxter, Herman Boerhaave and Joseph Addison, and a section on the latest books, mostly taken from the *Critical* and *Monthly Reviews*. Even Marcus eventually put politics right behind him and dilated instead on the contemporary passion for invention in a piece which distinguished between the absurdities of dabblers in pseudo-science and the sober diligence of the tradesman, who, while he pursued 'with unabating ardour the accumulation of riches', devoted his leisure hours to the extension of his own knowledge, the instruction of others or 'the improvement of any branch of mechanicks by new discoveries, which upon every tryal answer the real purposes for which they were designed, and are crowned with the approbation and thanks of society'.[26]

Though the *Repository* was reissued in 1772, and though the *British Museum*'s closing address on 16 November 1771 raised high hopes of an early renewal, neither of them lasted for any great length of time. As in the case of the newspapers, the combination of events during the crowded years 1769–71 and competition among the different printers had thrown up more ventures than even an increasing readership could support. Besides this, it was difficult to keep up a constant supply of fresh material for very long, and though the *British Museum*'s later numbers did carry some discussion of the need for new churches in Birmingham[27] such local issues could be more effectively debated in the newspapers. It would therefore be wrong to set too much store by the direct effects of the magazines. Nevertheless their appearance remains significant. The success of the newspapers' new 'miscellany' sections, with which the magazines were in direct competition, may have contributed to the latter's failure; but it does also confirm the existence of the readership they tried to attract, and in the 'Miscellaneous Repository' which was a regular feature of the *Birmingham and Stafford Chronicle* from 1773 onwards Myles Swinney at least continued the same policies which had characterised the *British Museum*.[28] The purposes announced by the latter, and especially their specific extension to include the mechanic, are indeed the most significant feature of all. Precisely who the magazine's gentlemen sponsors were is impossible to say; but the inclusion of pieces from Voltaire and Helvetius,[29] the use of the *Monthly Review* as a main source for the section on current literature, and the prominence given in the second and third issues to Lord Mansfield's celebrated judgement in City of London *v.* Allen Evans, the case which in 1767 finally vindicated the legal rights of Protestant Dissenters under the Act of Toleration, all suggest that their outlook was liberal. A guess may be hazarded that the same group of men was involved in the promotion of the New Street theatre when it was first opened three years later,[30] but whoever they were, their sponsorship of the *British*

Museum acknowledged not only the existence of a wider reading public in Birmingham but also the need to educate it.

What Birmingham's readers did not buy they could borrow, for the town was as well served by libraries as it was by printers and booksellers. As far back as 1658 the Rev. Thomas Hall, who played a prominent part in the development of local presbyterianism during the Civil War and Interregnum, had disposed of his own very considerable collection of books by giving the best of them to 'the library at Birmingham' and by leaving the remainder, 'being ordinary books and not so fit for so publick a library', for the use of the ministers and schoolmasters of Kings Norton, Moseley and Wythall.[31] The collection in Birmingham which thus benefited from Hall's generosity was, however, dispersed after the Restoration, and the oldest existing library in the town was that founded in 1733 by the Rev. William Higgs, first rector of the new parish of St Philip's. The basis of this was Higgs's own collection, additions to which were provided for by a bequest of £200. As might be expected, the books kept were mainly theological and ecclesiastical, but the catalogue of St Philip's Parish Library which was issued in 1795 shows that besides the bound sermons of eminent churchmen, the collected tracts of the Society for the Promotion of Christian Knowledge and a large assortment of separate pieces of a similar nature, accessions during the previous twenty-five years had included many books of more secular interest. Between 1779 and 1788, for example, the library bought Lord Kames's *Essays on Natural Religion* (in 1779), his *Treatise on Education* (in 1782), his *Elements of Criticism* (in 1785) and his *Sketches of the History of Man* (in 1788). Other accessions included Dr Robertson's *History of America* (in 1788), Blackstone's *Commentaries* (in 1790), the works of John Howard (in 1791 and 1792), the *Wealth of Nations* (in 1791) and Smollett's continuation of Hume's *History* (in 1791).[32] Access to the library was, however, restricted to the clergy of the town and neighbouring parishes and to laymen with permission from the rectors of St Martin's and St Philip's. Though the accessions since 1770 made a broader range of books available to those privileged to use the library, the selection involved, and the dates at which individual items were bought, are therefore of more interest as illustrations of the process of filtration through which new works were accepted by the established ranks of society than as indicators of any real increase in their common accessibility.

The objectives of the Birmingham Library were more liberal. Founded in November 1779 by nineteen subscribers, eighteen of them Dissenters, who agreed to pay a guinea entrance and a subscription of 6s a year,[33] it was taken in hand in 1780 by Joseph Priestley, who brought to its management considerable experience of similar foundations at Warrington and Leeds. The new library was first brought to the attention of the public in June 1781, when it announced that since its books were to be bought by a committee elected from the subscribers by annual ballot it could 'never answer the purpose of any party, civil or religious, but on the contrary, may be expected to promote a spirit of liberality and friendship among all classes of men without distinction'.[34] The acquisition of permanent premises in Swan Yard did mean that in December 1781 the members were asked to approve an increase in the subscription to 8s a year;[35] but since the original agreement in 1779 had provided for a future increase of up to 10s a year, and since the entry fee remained the same, the alteration can hardly be regarded as a real restriction on the library's accessibility.

Under Dr Priestley's guidance the library's collection grew steadily, from 'near five hundred' volumes in 1782 to 'upwards of 1,600' four years later.[36] Meanwhile, in 1784, a separate section had been formed to collect scientific works, especially those in foreign languages. This was paid for by an extra annual subscription of one guinea, and its books could be taken out only by members of the section, though they were available to ordinary subscribers in the library room itself.[37] By 1786, however, the earlier predominance of Dissenters had been reversed, and the membership was embroiled in the quarrel over the admission of controversial theology which formed the first part of the prelude to the Priestley riots. The library's committee that year was dominated by an organised group of Churchmen from Deritend, who provoked the quarrel quite deliberately by voting to buy Priestley's *History of the Corruptions of Christianity* against the express wishes of the author himself and the opposition of William Russell, the only Dissenter present at the selection meeting. This manoeuvre produced predictable results. The acquisition of Priestley's work was attributed not to the cabal on the committee but to the Doctor himself and his friends, and it was followed by a series of ostentatious Anglican protests and resignations, led by the Rev. Charles Curtis of St Martin's. Up to this point Priestley had himself opposed the admission of controversial books, his own included, until the library could afford to buy publications on both sides of any question. Now that his hand had been forced, however, the Doctor understandably changed his position, supported the future acquisition of all works of controversy and practised what he preached by recommending books opposed to his own point of view. By this time the Church party, having achieved their tactical objective, were thoroughly averse to such a policy, and Priestley found his former attitude quoted against him. His initial reluctance to recommend his *History of the Corruptions of Christianity* and his subsequent change of position were put down to an unsuccessful attempt to force the work's sale by depriving would-be readers of the chance to borrow it, and during the latter part of 1787 the Church party tried to force through a motion to exclude all controversial theology. This was first proposed to the library's committee in August 1787 by a Mr Charles Cooke, who introduced it again at the general meeting in December, and supported it in the *Birmingham Gazette* by a lengthy and plausible repetition of Priestley's original arguments against the waste of money and space on ephemeral polemic. In the meantime, however, the Doctor's *Address to the Subscribers of the Birmingham Library*, a prime example of the combative righteousness which his adversaries must have found so galling, had dealt with the proposal so effectively that Cooke's motion was decisively rejected by the subscribers, despite the best efforts of the clergy, who had hastily revoked their previous resignations from the library and now tried to stave off defeat by canvassing the town for votes.

After this humiliation, which was compounded by revelations that the clergy had for some time been circulating packed lists among their supporters in order to pre-empt the committee ballot for the coming year, the Church party retired to nurse its bile. During 1788 nothing more was heard of the dispute, but the Churchmen still retained their hold on the committee. On 18 February 1789 a special meeting of the subscribers rejected by two votes a motion from Dr Priestley to reinforce the secrecy of the ballot procedure, and instead relaxed the rules in such a way that previous collusion of the kind practised by the clergy now became legitimate. This reverse marked the beginning of the end of Priestley's active participation in the library's affairs, and by the end of 1790 he had virtually broken off all connection with the institution for which he had done so much ten years before.[38] Dissatisfaction with the working of the library's committee did not end with Priestley's departure, however. It broke out afresh in 1794, when ten of the more liberal committee members, including Sampson Lloyd and Samuel Galton, lost their places for the coming year. The result, confirmed by the narrow defeat in 1795 of a second attempt to protect the freedom and secrecy of the ballot, was the establishment of the Birmingham New Library, to which most of the Dissenting subscribers transferred their support during the next two years.[39]

This setback cost the old library somewhere between thirty-nine and 178 members, but it still had 437 left in 1795, to whom a further twenty-two were added in the course of the next three years.[40] Some idea of the social range from which these were drawn can be gained from the particulars of the 158 shareholders in the tontine by which the library financed the building of its new premises in Union Street between 1792 and 1797. As might be expected, the list included several well known names, among them those of Samuel Galton the younger, Samuel Garbett, and Sampson, Charles and Samuel Lloyd. Besides these, the leading printers, booksellers and newspapermen of the town were also prominent, and the complete list contained a representative cross-section of other local occupations and social positions, running from the conventional esquire, gentleman and merchant, through the full gamut of Birmingham's manufacturers, to such esoteric, not to say bizarre, designations as 'Coffin Furniture Maker', 'Patent Brass Cock Maker' and 'Spinster and Refiner of Metals'.[41]

Such diversity suggests that the body of subscribers as a whole must have fully reflected the complexity of Birmingham society. Nevertheless the membership at the turn of the century amounted to something less than one per cent of the town's total population, and in any case, whatever was intended by its initial addresses to 'all classes of men without distinction', the library's chief purpose was to provide intensive support for specialised enquiry rather than to cater for a less discriminating general readership. The growth of its collection was sustained and impressive, but in simple rate of increase it was easily surpassed by that of the commercial enterprises which supplied most of the common demand for books. While the Birmingham Library added some 4,500 volumes to its stock in the sixteen years between 1782 and 1798, John Lowe's circulating library in the Market Place grew from 6,000 to 10,000 between 1791 and 1796, and even thirty years before this Joseph Crompton had increased the stock of his library in Colmore Row from 800 in 1763 to 3,000 in 1767.[42] Direct comparisons are, of course, unfair: while the Birmingham Library was buying expensive books for a permanent collection, the intent of the circulating libraries was to reach their most profitable size as quickly as possible, and then to adjust their stock according to current demand. Because they were run on such a basis, however, the development of these ventures and the nature of their holdings provide a better indication of the extent and character of the town's ordinary taste in books than does the Birmingham Library itself.

The foundation dates of the eight or nine commercial libraries Birmingham was supporting by 1800 clearly reflect the rate at which the town's readership was growing. The example set by Thomas Warren in 1729 was first followed by William Hutton, who began lending books soon after he came to Birmingham in 1751. Within the next two years Hutton in turn was followed by Joseph Crompton, whose business in Colmore Row was to prosper as Evans's Library for much of the following century. As the rapid increase in Crompton's stock between 1763 and 1767 shows, however, it was after 1760 that the pace really began to quicken. In the last quarter of the century Hutton and Crompton were joined by James Belcher (1775), John Lowe (*c.* 1776), M. and S. Olds (1787), Thomas Lucas (1788), Thomas Chapman (1795) and Richard Peart (*c.* 1799).[43] So far as cost alone was concerned, the difference between these ventures and the Birmingham Library lay in the admission fee charged by the latter, not in its annual subscription. This was admittedly raised for the second time in 1789, but only to 10s, and it was not increased again until 1805, when it was put up to 15s.[44] Such a rate compared favourably with the 12s annually or 4s quarterly charged by Thomas Lucas, and it made the equivalent terms at Lowe's library—16s or 5s quarterly for a two-book ticket, or a guinea a year for one worth four—seem positively expensive.[45] On a weekly basis, however, even these terms amounted to a few pence only; and while both Lucas and Lowe also lent books to casual borrowers at easy rates, a prospective member of the Birmingham Library needed enough money by him to make a substantial payment over and above his subscription. Since the beginning of the quarrel over controversial divinity the admission fee had risen sharply. In December 1786 it was put up to a guinea and a half, with provision for further increases to two guineas when the membership reached 300 and to three when another 100 had been added. In 1798, when the membership was approaching 500, the fee was raised again to four guineas, and by 1812 it stood at £10.[46] While the library remained cheap for those who were members already, it thus set itself apart by restricting its accessibility to new readers with progressive severity from the mid-1780s onwards. The major difference between the Birmingham Library and its commercial counterparts was, however, one of content. The largest class in Thomas Lucas's library was his duodecimo collection of 'History, Novels and Romances'. This accounted for approximately 34 per cent of his total holding, while plays made up another 13 per cent. In the Birmingham Library's catalogue of 1798, on the other hand, the largest classes were 'Antiquities, Biography, General History and Chronology' and 'Theology, Sermons and Ecclesiastical History'. Of the whole collection, plays accounted for a mere 3 per cent, and only a tenth was devoted to 'Novels and Romances', a proportion equalled by both 'Regulations, Politics and War' and 'Education, Language, Grammar, Rhetoric, Criticism and Polite Literature'.[47]

Nevertheless the inferiority of the circulating libraries in terms of serious content should not be overstated. In addition to his stock of popular literature Lucas also kept a collection of cheap non-fiction, listed as 'History, Adventures etc.', and a sizable quantity of more substantial octavos on 'History, Voyages and Travels'. Neither of these classifications sound especially relevant to current problems, but they were loosely defined, and the latter in particular contained a good many books which would have influenced the practical outlook of their readers.[48] The other libraries were equally well equipped. James Belcher was dispensing cheap but influential political literature as early as 1775, and was involved in the development of mechanics' education in Birmingham long before he and his sons issued the catalogue of their Artisan's Library in 1816.[49] M. and S. Olds kept a section of 'History and Voyages'[50] which was probably similar to that held by Lucas; and, as his catalogue of 1796 shows, John Lowe in particular took considerable pains to keep his library abreast of affairs. The case for the abolition of the slave trade was documented by commentaries and abstracts from the evidence presented to the House of Commons. Prison reformers could take their choice of two editions of John Howard's life and works. Those with interests in America could remind themselves of the genesis of the revolution in 'The American Farmer's Letters' (presumably John Dickinson's *Letters from a Farmer in Pennsylvania*), and brief themselves on the present state of the Union from Brissot's *Travels Through America* or from an *American Geography, Giving a Particular Account of the Climate, Trade, Constitution etc. of the United States of America*. Belsham's *Memoirs of the Reign of George III* provided an account of England's own recent political history, and, for one episode at least, Turgot's *Memoirs* as Comptroller General between 1774 and 1776 did the same for France. As might be expected, the impact of the French revolution was extensively covered, not only by Burke's *Reflections, Appeal from the New to the Old Whigs* and *Letters on a Regicide Peace* but also by Dr Moore's *View of the Causes and Progress of the French Revolution* and Mary Wollstonecraft's *Historical and Moral View of the Revolution in France and the Effects it has Caused in Europe*, which was listed together with her *Rights of Women* and her *Letters Written During a Short Residence in Sweden, Norway and Denmark*. The English repercussions of the revolution were covered by accounts of the Priestley riots and the State trials of 1794, and its military aspects by a narrative of the campaigns of 1793–95. In addition to all these, a wide selection of more general works was available, among them numerous pieces by, for or against Dr Priestley, Gibbon's *Decline and Fall*, Hume's *History*, selections from the *Encyclopaedia*, *The Wealth of Nations*, Voltaire's *Letters on Toleration, Miscellanies* and *Annals of the Empire*, Wendeborn's *View of England towards the End of the Eighteenth Century*, Witaker's history of Manchester and several French works, including *Candide* and *Rousseau Juge de Jean Jacques*. Among the new titles for 1796 were Patrick Colquhoun's *Treatise on the Police of the Metropolis, Sketches Moral, Political and Literary* by the author of *The Democrat* and Major Tench's *Letters Written during the Tyranny of Robespierre*.

Effective though it may be as a demonstration of the existence of a rapidly growing demand for books in the Birmingham area and of the ways in which this was supplied, a simple account of the available sources of printed material provides by itself only a partial explanation of the increased awareness at all levels of society on which the interest in reading was based. Nor does it say much about the ways in which the latter was communicated, not only to the town's rapidly growing 'middle class' readership but to a significant section of its artisan population as well. More revealing in this respect are two other features of Birmingham's development: first, the part played by the travelling lecturers and other showmen, and by the private schoolmasters who either visited or worked in the town; and second, the way in which these, together with the men who actually produced the books, promoted the magazines and ran the libraries, formed a recognisable element in the community.

By the 1790s Birmingham had been visited at least once, and in most cases more often than that, by a minimum of seventeen lecturers who gave extended courses of instruction in the different branches of science and its practical applications.[51] The important contribution which these men made to the technical achievements of the industrial revolution is now recognised,[52] and emphasis has therefore been justifiably placed on the activities of such lecturers as Adam Walker, Dr Henry Moyes and John Warltire, who came with the highest qualifications and recommendations. Alongside these, however, others of more dubious pedigree, such as 'The Sieur Herman Boaz', with his 'Grand Hurlophysikon',[53] exerted an equal and in many ways opposite influence by perpetuating a popular conception of science, and indeed of all knowledge, as a body of hermetic lore whose marvels might on occasion be made manifest to the admiring multitude by those who had been initiated in its secret ways. When Boaz brought his 'Grand Thaumaturgick Exhibition of Philosophical, Mathematical, Sterganographical, Sympathetical, Sciateroconatical and Magical Operations' to Birmingham in 1780, for example, the discriminating probably saved their money for John Warltire, who announced a series of lectures on metallurgy and mineralogy, specifically intended to be of use to the manufacturers of the area, just as Boaz was leaving. But whatever anybody else thought of him, Boaz at least claimed that his performances were 'more apt to improve the mind than affect the senses', and took himself sufficiently seriously to hope that 'the many and useful discoveries' which he had made by his 'unwearied application to the occult sciences' would 'suit the Learned and Virtuous as well as the Gay and Polite'. Even Warltire himself tacitly acknowledged the effect of his predecessor's exhibition, first by postponing his own lectures for a week, and then by offering to substitute a series of more entertaining, but probably less useful, experiments with a new solar apparatus for the original course if sufficient subscribers still failed to come forward.[54] In the event Warltire was able to retain his original plan, and on his subsequent visits to Birmingham during the next four years he gave courses, fully supported by chemical tables and other relevant literature, both on the parts of chemistry most applicable to the trades of the town and on the more general aspects of the subject.[55] The distinction between serious instruction and popular entertainment was still difficult to maintain, however, if only because the extensive collections of apparatus and working models which the lecturers used were remarkable in their own right. Just as Adam Walker's Eidouranion was the talk of the town in 1781, so in 1784 were Mr Pitt's whirling tables, not to mention his air gun which fired 150 yards without powder; in 1786 Mr Long's 'Astrotheatron or large transparent Orrery improved' was on display at the New Street theatre, where a band played the current musical favourites in the intervals of the lecture, and at the same time the curious were being persuaded to attend Mr Burton's lectures on centrical forces by his promise 'to experimentally prove Sir Isaac Newton's Laws of Gravitation', a feat which he had 'every reason to believe was never attempted before'.[56] Faced with such publicity, the casual spectator and the partially informed can be forgiven if they failed to differentiate between these genuine demonstrations and the less warrantable performances of people like Signor Conetti and his family, whose 'philosophical fireworks' were billed at the New Street theatre in May 1789, or Mr Breslau and Signor Pinetti, whose 'New Invented Capital Deceptions' and 'Philosophical Experiments' were combined with musical evenings at Mr Cresshull's assembly room in the same year.[57] In fact some kind of exploitation of the marvels and mysteries of science, authentic or otherwise, had become almost a *sine qua non* of any successful show. When it was put on in Dudley town hall in 1776 even George Alexander Stephens's notorious lecture on heads, a regular music hall favourite during the 1760s and 1770s, was stiffened by the addition of several 'GRAND CALCULATIONS (never done here), Mathematical Operations and Magical Card Deceptions', among them writing a lady's thoughts without asking a question and 'the famous Mr. Brest's flourishing trick with a Roasted Leg of Mutton'.[58]

Though the subject certainly engrossed a larger share of attention than any other, the common attitude to science was not the only aspect of popular consciousness which was influenced by the lecturers and travelling showmen who visited Birmingham. While the Birmingham Robin Hood Free Debating Society and its offshoots were meeting in the town, for example, would-be orators were probably able to learn something about the skills of public speaking, not only from Mr Shatford's address as president of the parent society in August 1774[59] but also from Mr Walker's lectures the following October on English pronunciation and the beauties of Shakespeare, or from the course on rhetoric and poetry, containing several figures of speech found in the best authors, which was given 'by particular desire' at 'The Academy' in Dale End during December 1775.[60] Discourses like these may have invited the ridicule of Jeremiah Sneak's 'Lecture on Lectures', or of J. Collins's 'Attic Evening's Entertainment', featuring 'the most striking instances and examples of the great use and abuse of speech',[61] but both the lectures and the satire they provoked played their part in shaping the emerging forms of popular articulacy. So also did the fairground attractions by which the town's public houses sought to amuse their customers. During the Seven Years War, for example, many of Birmingham's less educated inhabitants must have got their most vivid impressions of what was taking place in the contest between the nations not initially from books, newspapers or pamphlets but from such 'Blacksmith's entertainment' as that advertised by Mr Smallwood, the landlord of the Bird in Hand in Dale End, during March 1759:

A Dissertation on Various Subjects, particularly ANTIENT and MODERN HISTORY; which will be preceded with an ESSAY on the STANDARD OF TASTE and JUDGEMENT.

> *As nothing teaches, so nothing more delights than History: The first of these recommends it to the Study of grown Men, the latter makes me think it best for youth.*
>
> LOCKE on EDUCATION

The principal Writers consider'd are, Lord Clarendon, Bp. Burnet, Sir William Temple, Larrey, Rapin, Stow, Oldmixon, Hollingshed, and Smollet; Sir Walter Ralegh, Howell, Sallust, &c.

To these will be added, the Remarkable Occurrences and Advertisements in the London, Brussels, and Amsterdam Gazettes; Description of a certain Island; an Imaginary Contest; English and French Courage Compar'd; the Militia proved Constitutional, with some seasonable Reflections to those Defenders of their Country; Travelling Doctors; Fire Eaters; Bottle Conjurors, and Tooth Drawers, being the portraits of several originals.

To conclude with an AUCTION.

Nature with Novelty does still abound,
In every Age fresh follies may be found.

FOOTE
To begin exactly at seven.[62]

Like the less reputable stage shows, to which they were in any case closely related, such performances were one of the ways through which the events and personalities of the times were assimilated into the traditional categories of popular culture. As was the case with the common attitude to science, these were at many points incompatible with the results of more systematic knowledge; but they continued nevertheless to form an unavoidable element in the development of more sophisticated and self-conscious forms of articulacy, and, as Mr Smallwood's advertisement suggests despite the host of authors which it named, their own most powerful component was not in the first instance literary or even oral but visual. In 1760, for example, the Birmingham artisan could at least learn roughly what his rulers looked like by visiting the Seven Stars near the Old Cross, where Mrs Salmon's 'Royal Waxwork, representing the Royal Family of Great Britain richly dressed and in full proportion' could be seen for 6d admission.[63] Three years later he could satisfy his curiosity about Frederick the Great for the same price by going to the Lion and Lamb Yard in the High Street, where the Protestant hero was on show as large as life and straight from Berlin, along with a captain of the Red Hussars and various other waxworks.[64] Similarly, the apotheosis of the elder Pitt in the popular imagination was consummated in 1782 when the painting of his last speech to the House of Lords was put on show at the hotel. On this occasion, however, there was more than a hint of guidance from above, both about the place chosen for the exhibition and about the advertisement for it. When this pronounced that 'a fact so awful and interesting as the one represented in this picture cannot fail to excite the attention of the public', and therefore announced that 'every ingenious mechanic' would be admitted for the special low price of 6d, it was referring not so much to the painting's main subject as to the fact that it also showed all the peers and bishops of the realm in their full robes,[65] a spectacle which could not fail to impress the beholder with the majesty of his rulers. Those in authority thus showed that they too were well aware of the visual as an influence on the common mind. By the 1790s this was certainly so. In December 1793 the crowds who earlier in the year had gaped at the dummy executions performed in the public rooms in New Street by a working model of the guillotine were once more invited to the hotel, this time to be edified by Louis XVI's last interview with his family.[66] Meanwhile William Belcher had been prosecuted at Warwick summer assizes for selling not only the *Rights of Man* and other seditious literature but also

> a variety of caricature prints such as *The Farm House at Windsor, Farmer George and Charlotte going to Market,* and *A Voluptuary under the Horrors of Digestion,* being the Prince of Wales at a Banquett, the *Sun in his Glory* representing the side features of His Majesty on the top of a candlestick with rays darting therefrom. . . . for the wicked purpose of ridiculing the King and Royal Family . . . .[67]

If the lecturers and showmen who visited the town thus helped to shape the awareness of Birmingham people, a similar part was played by the numerous private masters who supplied the deficiencies of the town's existing school system. A distinction between these and the lecturers may seem otiose when so many of each group acted in both capacities;[68] but though many of the private schoolmasters were, to begin with, as much visitors to Birmingham as the travelling lecturers, the fact that they settled in the town, or at least stayed for some time, meant that they became more closely involved in the local community and that their influence upon it was more permanent. Of the importance of these men as an active element in the life of the area there can be no doubt, and though a full examination of the hundreds of newspaper advertisements which constitute their chief record would involve a digression too long and complex to be accep- table here, some general features of it can nevertheless be discerned which are significant in the present context.[69]

Within the West Midlands as a whole the development of private education was affected, in variable combination, by two main factors. The growing need of the manufacturing areas for a working population at least part of which was proficient, not only in a wide range of technical skills but also in such things as modern languages, book-keeping and accounts, was reflected in the large number of practical schools which were established in Birmingham itself and to a lesser extent in the Black Country towns of Dudley, Walsall, Wednesbury and Wolverhampton. Against this must be weighed the fact that several of the most interesting masters established themselves in the older towns of the region, to which they were drawn by existing circumstances and by the opportunities created by the progress of landed society rather than by the direct repercussions of industrial or urban development. In fact the situation in the West Midlands suggests that, far from being themselves the primary source of the demand for useful education, the new manufacturing areas were, in the early stages of their development, to a considerable extent the beneficiaries of practical masters from older communities who taught the wide range of skills required by society as it already existed. In addition to these considerations, however, a third factor, the social aspirations of an increasingly prosperous urban middle class, also counteracted the direct influence of the major centres, even though in large part it emanated from them. These concerns, which were increasingly reflected towards the end of the century in the tendency of schools to advertise their physical and social amenities rather than their syllabus, implied a measure of social discrimination; but it would be a mistake to regard the country schools as already the exclusive preserve of the provincial *nouveaux-riches*, eager even at this stage to lose the tradesman and manufacturer in the gentleman. Many masters confined themselves to an elementary syllabus and charged proportion- ately less than the more expensive boarding schools; some tried to grade their offerings at different prices, so as to cover a wider social bracket; others took day pupils at rates similar to those charged in the main centres; and in the case of Birmingham at least, several masters either moved freely between the board- ing schools in the neighbourhood and the day and evening classes in the town itself, or taught in both at the same time. The lines of social demarcation, though latent, were thus not yet clearly drawn. In the West Midlands at least, the development of private education, which played a substantial part in broadening the front over which the existing school system was reoriented during the later eighteenth century, was therefore able to meet the needs of economic growth by a combination of innovation and the transfer of experience already gained, which remained as yet comparatively unhampered by rigid sociological barriers.

Though the town had its fair share of boys' and girls' boarding schools by the 1780s, private education in Birmingham itself was characterised above all else by the proliferation of day and evening schools offering a wide range of subjects, most of them practical, some of them less so, to pupils of all ages and both sexes. Some masters can hardly have inspired confidence, like M. de St Raymond, who in 1774 was promising to instil as much French in a month as his pupils would get from others in six, while his wife cleaned and preserved teeth, fitted false ones and drew stumps with a hand 'lighter, if not more skilful than that of any man'.[70] Others were almost too good to be true, like the Rev. Mr Machin, whose school in Digbeth during 1767 and 1768 was offering everything from reading, writing and arithmetic to Hebrew, Chaldee, heraldry, architecture, logic, metaphysics, oratory and rhetoric, not to mention shorthand and 'most other branches of polite literature'.[71] At least as many schools, however, were kept by men with respectable credentials who offered a range of subjects amply wide enough for practical purposes without being extravagantly so; some remained in existence for appreciable lengths of time, and the prices charged by most masters—from between 3s and 5s per quarter for elementary subjects to between 10s and 15s for languages and the more advanced branches of mathematics—must have put at least some of their offerings within reach of the town's tradesmen. Their evening classes in particular, which were usually given for two hours on two or three nights a week, must have been responsible for a large part of whatever wider stock of knowledge most artisans managed to pick up outside their particular occupations. Masters like John Bogle of Worcester Street, Thomas Hanson of the Hinckleys and Samuel Porter of Suffolk Street,[72] for example, who concentrated on mathematical and scientific subjects, complemented the work of the travelling lecturers in bridging the gap between theoretical and applied science and in improving the standard of technical knowledge among the town's tradesmen. In the same way the specialised language schools, which were advertised in increasing numbers from the 1770s onwards, both reflected and helped to satisfy the needs created by Birmingham's growing interest in European markets. In a more general sense, too, establishments like Mr Wood's academy in the Cherry Orchard did provide a means by which a man could do something to remedy his lack of formal culture. Admittedly the promise in this case that those who laboured under 'the unhappiness of not understanding the meaning of various hard words, which daily occur both in reading and conversation'[73] would gain in six months an understanding of English as good for practical purposes as that of anyone brought up on the classics does seem rather excessive. As the concerns of the Free Debating Society show, however, Mr Wood was ministering to a widely felt need, and one of the features of private school notices, especially towards the end of the century, was the increasing emphasis they placed on literary subjects, which were offered not in opposition to the prevailing concentration on practical matters but as complementary to them.

Particularly important so far as the general level of articulacy in Birmingham was concerned was the extent to which these activities overlapped both socially and physically with other channels for the exchange of ideas and information. During the 1770s, for example, 'the Academy' at 89 Dale End, which served as common premises for a number of different ventures, must have acted in some ways like the Long Room at the Red Lion and other meeting places of the same kind elsewhere in the town. Moreover, whatever substance there may be in the familiar Shavian dismissal of the teaching profession in other times and places, it contained little truth in eighteenth century Birmingham. On the contrary, many of the town's private schoolmasters shared the same diversity of business interests, the same background and outlook, and even the same premises, as the tavern keepers, the newspaper and magazine journalists, the booksellers and the circulating library promoters. John Freeth, for example, tried his hand as a teacher of geography and the use of globes on at least one occasion in his varied career; and, of Freeth's particular associates, James Bissett not only gave lessons to his fellow apprentices but also kept an informal lending library, while James Sketchley maintained similar connections by letting his own rooms to various masters.[74] Quite apart from this particular group, many of Birmingham's other masters also had other interests besides their teaching. Most of the drawing schools were kept by practising designers and decorators; the language masters also worked as translators of business correspondence, and several of the more general schools were run by men who also offered their professional services in such tasks as surveying and accounting. John Lowe, for example, not only kept a school at Mr Goolden's Yard in the Bull Ring but also ran a surveying business for some years before he opened his circulating library, and the same was true of James Meer, from whom Lowe acquired his school in 1771.[75]

Last, but not least as an influence on the general awareness of Birmingham people, was the constant movement of masters which took place between schools in the town itself and those in other parts of the surrounding region, and the fact that a significant number of schools were run by immigrants from other parts of the country, especially from London. The example of M. de St Raymond and his dentist wife has already been mentioned. Other Londoners included Thomas Baker, who arrived in 1761; Charles Martin, chaser and die sinker, who in 1763 opened a drawing school on Snow Hill, where he also taught the German flute; Richard Gardiner, whose Snow Hill Drawing Academy of 1769 may have been connected with Martin's earlier venture; 'Messrs. Whites', whose school in the Cherry Orchard during 1771 paid special attention 'to the pupils' being properly instructed in Reading with propriety'; John Mayne, who in 1775 left his first post in the Birmingham area at Winson Green Academy to teach reading, writing, arithmetic, accounts and the useful branches of mathematics in a room opposite the hotel, and Mr Watson, 'professor of penmanship from an academy in London', who arrived in 1782 and offered a full range of both practical and literary subjects.[76] Such individuals as these were in a powerful position from which to influence the outlook of those with whom they came in contact. Within the community as a whole they formed a group which was not only more articulate and more mobile than most, but which was also closely connected with others of a similar nature. Under these circumstances the Masonic and other less formal connections which linked those circles together are of more than coincidental interest.

The part played by the speculative Freemasonry which took shape in England and Scotland towards the end of the seventeenth century in the diffusion of enlightenment ideas and useful knowledge during the following hundred years has been generally acknowledged, but, so far as England is concerned, little explored.[77] This state of affairs can hardly be fully remedied here, but the newspaper notices and other surviving references to the Masonic lodges of the West Midlands do give some indication of the part which the craft and its imitators played in the life of the region. The overall growth of the order, which had proceeded with only minor fluctuations since the 1720s, was particularly rapid during the 1760s. It suffered some setbacks during the years of the American revolution, and in London interest in the craft, which was disturbed by internal disputes and may also have been adversely affected by the conservative turn of City opinion following the Gordon riots, did not recover completely until the following century. In the provinces, however, the progress of the 1760s was resumed after 1780 and sustained at a still higher rate despite small and temporary reverses between 1797 and 1800 which reflected the repercussions of the Nore mutiny, the charges brought against the craft for its supposed complicity in the French revolution and its struggle for exemption from the Combination Acts of 1799 and 1800.[78] The extension of Freemasonry from London to the provinces thus kept pace with the growth of urban and industrial centres outside the capital. In the West Midlands the craft was well established in most of the more important towns by the second half of the century,[79] and its periodic festivals, such as the anniversary of St John the Baptist, which the local lodges celebrated in common each summer, must have helped to create a sense of community between people in different parts of the region. In these activities the two Birmingham lodges, which from 1784 onwards were known respectively as St Paul's and St Alban's, played a leading role, and within the lodges themselves several familiar names were prominent. This was particularly true of St Paul's, the direct descendant of the original group of Birmingham Masons who had first met at the Swan in Great Brook Street in 1733. The first master of the lodge after its reconstitution at the King's Head in 1764 was James Sketchley, the auctioneer and publisher, and among the earliest of its new members was John Freeth, the poet.[80] Of these two, Sketchley in particular was typical of the versatile middling businessmen who played such an important part in provincial town life. Besides his auctioneering business and his multifarious newspaper and magazine partnerships, which he pursued in Bristol and Bath as well as in Birmingham, he also ran the Birmingham Universal Register Office, compiled the town's first trade directory and published a wide variety of other items, including 'Sketchley's Conversation Cards'—an educational game for children —and several books on Freemasonry.[81]

For Sketchley, indeed, the craft remained an abiding passion, and he became notorious, particularly among the group at the Leicester Arms, of which he was a long-standing member, as

> A man, who, if Masonry e'er was the theme
> His bosom with Rapture would glow and expand.[82]

Sketchley and Freeth were not, however, the only Masons among that particular coterie. James Bissett, who was responsible for this verse caricature of Sketchley, was himself a member of St Alban's lodge and helped to found others at Stratford on Avon, Alcester, Henley in Arden, Sutton Coldfield, Fazeley and Tamworth. Besides Bissett, two more of Freeth's cronies—Samuel Toy, a steel toymaker who subsequently became landlord of the Mitre inn, and Jeremiah Vaux, who was well known in Birmingham as a surgeon—were members respectively of St Alban's and St Paul's lodges.[83] At least five members of 'the twelve apostles', as they were called, can thus be identified as active Freemasons, and to these can be added two more prominent local figures: James Rollason of the *Birmingham Gazette*, whose funeral in 1789 was attended by his brother Masons from St Paul's lodge,[84] and probably also Myles Swinney, who gave prominence in the *Birmingham and Stafford Chronicle* of 11 July 1776 to the Masonic oration given in Boston the previous April at the funeral of Joseph Warren, and later collaborated with Sketchley in the production of one of the latter's Masonic publications, *The Unparalleled Sufferings of John Coustos*.[85]

Connections of this kind were equally typical of the Ancient and Noble Order of Bucks, for which John Freeth wrote the song quoted at the start of the preceding chapter. The Order of Bucks was one of a number of imitators of Freemasonry which had appeared in London earlier in the century. Like the Mohocks, the Hawkabites and the notorious Hell Fire Club, the Bucks gained an unsavoury reputation during the first thirty years of their existence; but by the second half of the century, when its lodges began to appear in the provinces, the order had purged itself of this, and, according to its own profession, was devoted entirely to the promotion of 'good fellowship, freedom of conversation and innocent mirth'.[86] When they appeared in Liverpool in 1756, for example, the Bucks were known chiefly for their convivial meetings, frequent patronage of the theatre and concern for the prosperity of industry, agriculture and commerce. Much the same was true of their activities in the West Midlands, where they met regularly in Birmingham and Wolverhampton. The Birmingham lodge of the order met at the Swan inn until early in 1776, when, calling itself 'The Independent Order of Bucks', it moved to the King's Head in New Street.[87] In 1779 it moved again to Mrs Aston's coffee house in the Cherry Orchard,[88] where it remained thenceforward. Whether or not these moves and the ostentatious assumption of the style 'Independent' were in any way a reflection of the political tensions which were dividing Birmingham at the time[89] is a matter for speculation, but the lodge was entirely in keeping with the traditions of the order when it adopted the name 'Arts and Sciences' in 1777.[90] In Wolverhampton the Albion lodge of Bucks met at the Red Lion throughout,[91] and in both places familiar names appeared in lodge notices. In Birmingham both Myles Swinney and James Rollason acted as stewards at different times, and so did Thomas Gem, one of the more active members of the Bean Club; in Wolverhampton Joseph Smart, printer and bookseller, who was to produce the town's first newspaper in 1789, was named as secretary of the Albion lodge in 1780.[92]

Apart from the personal connections which they can be shown to have embodied the influence of the Freemasons and the Bucks cannot be definitively established in purely factual terms. It would, however, be as mistaken to deny any significance at all to the various lodges as it would be to regard them as the clandestine cells of a universal conspiracy. At the simplest level, the little information which is available on Masonic and quasi-Masonic activities in the West Midlands does seem to support the usual apologia for the craft: that it provided a means by which social barriers could be crossed without undermining the social order, that it served as a powerful agent in the propagation of 'middle class' values and that its activities, far from being subversive, were eminently philanthropic and patriotic. Besides the local worthies who have already been mentioned, the Freemasons included among their number such gentlemen of rank and fortune as Sir John Wrottesley and Sir Robert Lawley, and Lords Dudley and Foley both had some connection with the Bucks of the Albion lodge in Wolverhampton.[93] The public activities, particularly of the Freemasons, were entirely in keeping with such membership. In Wolverhampton in July 1779, for example, Sir John Wrottesley led his fellow members of lodge No. 58 in a patriotic response to the threat of invasion from France which earned them the unqualified praise of the *Birmingham Gazette*. In Birmingham itself[94] St Paul's lodge, which in 1780 undertook a joint subscription to the General Hospital, likewise demonstrated its zeal by contributing to the fund to buy warm clothing for the army in Flanders during November 1793.[95] Similarly, when the lodges celebrated their periodic festivals they heard a sermon appropriate to the occasion before they sat down to dine and drink their 'loyal and masonic' toasts; and if they patronised the theatre it was the regular companies that they recognised, or such improving pieces as 'British Loyalty, or a Squeeze to St. Paul's', rather than the less respectable and more frivolous performances.[96]

Nor is it necessary to accept the charges of conspiracy brought against the craft to recognise that the cabbalistic signs and ritual of Freemasonry were an important aspect of its cultural role as a transmitter of ideas, images and symbols. Despite the veil which shrouded its internal proceedings, the craft's most significant feature was not its secrecy but the openness with which it proclaimed its possession of a secret. Both the number and the character of their newspaper notices suggest that, far from shunning the light of day, the lodges positively welcomed it; for the public was constantly made aware of Masonic activity and Masonic symbolism, not only in the frequent reports of lodge meetings and festivals[97] but also in such contexts as popular songs and theatre prologues, and in the advertisements for the extensive literature which the craft produced. In July 1781, for example, readers of the *Birmingham Gazette* had their attention drawn to

> An Address to the Nobility and Gentry of both sexes on the Great and Good effects of the UNIVERSAL MEDICINE of the ANCIENT MAGI, being the Grand and Inviolable SECRET of FREEMASONRY, which was lost at the Building of Solomon's Temple, by S. FREEMAN, M.D. Ignorance is the curse of God; Knowledge the wings wherewith we fly to Heaven.[98]

Five years later James Sketchley publicised his *Freemason's Repository* by heading its publication advertisement with a sample of the 'secret way of writing used among the Brethren':[99]

〈□ ⌐ ⊔ ⌐ ⊏

and even Sketchley and Adams's *Repository or Weekly General Entertainer* of 1770 had had its title page embellished with a typographical design of lines and stars which looks as if it may have had some deeper symbolic significance.[100]

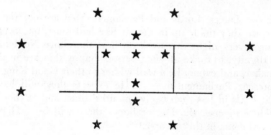

What the symbolic equipment of Freemasonry expressed was an attempt to sacramentalise the Enlightenment itself: to provide the Age of Reason with a mythical superstructure of the kind which it had itself destroyed—constructed, however, not upon the sand of superstition and error but upon the true principles of Moral Geometry and in accord with the laws of the Newtonian universe. Knowledge itself, in fact, became the Philosophers' Stone, and though this sacred vessel remained shrouded in mysteries penetrable only by the initiated the craft was by its very nature bound to proclaim its possession of such a secret. The result was an attitude closely akin to that conveyed by the 'thaumaturgic'[101] lecturers. 'The Sieur Herman Boaz', for example, probably chose his pseudonym for its Masonic connotations as one of the two pillars of Solomon's temple, and when he referred quite seriously to the utility of his discoveries in the occult sciences and described his performances, *pace* David Hume's *Essay on Miracles*, as being 'of so singular and so striking a nature as to be past all human conception, and in an Age and Country less enlightened, would have appeared supernatural'[102] he was appealing to the same set of convictions as those which inspired the Masonic ideal. This rational gnosticism, or, better, gnostic rationalism, was even more clearly personified in Boaz's rival, Gustavus Katterfelto, Freemason, quasi-scientific wonder-worker and quack, who came to England from Prussia in 1782 and rapidly became notorious as an astronomer, balloon aviator and lecturer on the 'Philosophical, Mathematical, Optical, Magnetical, Electrical, Physical, Chemical, Pneumatic, Hydraulic, Hydrostatic, Proetic, Stenographic, Blaencical and Caprimantic Arts'.[103] Katterfelto, whose usual repertoire was a shrewdly judged mixture of genuine chemical and electrical demonstrations and sensational tricks with his 'Most Wonderful Solar Microscope and Royal Patent Delineator' and other devices, was a frequent visitor to Birmingham, where he addressed himself particularly to 'all the different Clergy and Preachers, Doctors, Gentlemen, Freemasons and all Religious Persons'.[104]

The marvels and mysteries of science were not, however, the only theme he expounded. In June 1792 he used his reputation to enforce a social and political moral by prefacing the demonstrations at his lecture room in New Street with a lengthy homily in verse on enlightened benevolence, the importance of Experience in the pursuit of Knowledge and the forms of virtue appropriate to all sorts and conditions of men in their several callings.[105] The following January the people of Birmingham were astonished and gratified to hear 'the Prussian Philosopher' discoursing in fluent English on the advantages of being British. Now he was proposing a course of lectures not on the wonders of nature but on their human equivalent, the British constitution and the providential ordering of the English aristocracy:

> As Kings, Princes, Dukes, Lords and Parliament-Men are not found in the sea like fishes, nor are they made up in the air like hailstones, DR. KATTERFELTO will therefore lecture every night this week on how the above Noblemen etc. came to their great dignity, to make all such persons happy that are in despair in this town of our maker, and cannot be a well wisher to their Good King and Country, and to our present Parliament-men.... He expects they will have many different Kings at Paris in less than twelve months' time, and as there is a King to guide the whole Universe, the Doctor hopes there will be a Deputy King for many centuries to come in this country.[106]

Katterfelto thus lent his authority to the anti-Jacobin cause. And if his zeal suggests that he was well aware of the need to place the Masonic ethic above suspicion, the ease with which he not only detached it from the taint of atheism and anarchy, but also succeeded in attaching it positively to the ideals of the constitution and in imparting its mystique to the higher purposes of the nation itself, demonstrates well how, so far from being carriers of international conspiracy and subversion, the arcane rituals of the Masonic societies and their imitators could provide a way of reconciling Enlightenment aspirations to equality and fraternity with the continuing notion of hierarchy in human affairs, and therefore a way of expressing the latter which helped to preserve it through the turmoil of the revolutionary crisis.[107] Though he himself had not conceived the doctrine of prescription in quite the same terms as those used by Dr Katterfelto, Edmund Burke should have been pleased.

Like the questions which were discussed in the debating societies, the rapid growth of Birmingham's reading public reflected characteristics which, for want of a better description, may be called 'middle class'. The term is, however, unsatisfactory, because it implies a distinction, wholly out of keeping with the flexibility of Birmingham's variegated social structure, which would set these characteristics entirely apart from those of the town's common people. No doubt there was an increasingly noticeable difference between the more sophisticated awareness of the literate and the cruder forms of popular consciousness; but since Birmingham's putative 'working class' consisted in large part of skilled tradesmen, many of them small independent masters in their own right, 'middle class' aspirations to self-improvement based on literate knowledge could hardly have made their appearance without being communicated to a significant section of the town's artisan population as well. The development of this part of Birmingham's reading public owed as much to individual initiative and personal contact as it did to the simple provision of increased quantities of books. It is therefore in this respect that the importance of those involved in the Masonic lodges, and, more particularly, in the town's reading and discussion clubs, can be most readily appreciated. The experience of James Bissett provides a case in point. Bissett, who came to Birmingham from Perth in 1776 as an apprentice japanner, made a considerable contribution of his own to the local development of artisan education by lending books, prints and portfolios of drawings free of charge to his fellow apprentices, and by teaching them the elements of reading and drawing.[108] He was not himself a drinking man, but he was nevertheless fond of company, and it was this which brought him into contact with the various informal coteries that had grown up in the town. 'Convivial parties,' he recalled,

> used often to meet at "The Poet Freeth's", as also at Joe Warden's and at "The Fountains", where I very frequently attended, but my general evenings were spent at "The Union", "Shakespeare", or "Hen and Chickens Tavern", then kept by Mrs. Lloyd. I was president for many years of a debating society, and president also of Saint Andrew's Club, and in the Masonic Order, I was Provincial Grand Master for the County of Warwick.[109]

Besides those frequented by Bissett, various other groups may be mentioned. Like John Freeth, whose news-room service has already been noticed, Myles

Swinney ran a subscription club for books, pamphlets and the current London papers;[110] in 1775, when opinion in Birmingham was seriously divided in its reaction to the American situation, James Belcher used his newly opened circulating library as an outlet through which to distribute the addresses of the Continental Congress at Philadelphia at 1s 6d per dozen copies,[111] and by 1781 the Swan inn, the Red Lion in Digbeth and the Chain inn in Bull Street were all supporting reading societies similar to the Birmingham Book Club at the Leicester Arms.[112] Though the latter was thus by no means unique, however, it remains the outstanding example of its kind. Its importance as a bastion of opposition before and during the War of American Independence has already been noticed, but this was only one aspect of the long and close connection that existed between the book club and the local origins of political radicalism.

The exact origins of the Birmingham Book Club are unknown, but it was probably first formed to buy the parts of Richardson's novels and other serial publications as they came from the press during the 1740s.[113] Whatever its previous history may have been, however, it was certainly well established by 1758, when it appeared as 'The Reading Society at Mr. Freeth's Coffee House' on the subscription list for the second edition of Wellins Calcott's *Thoughts Moral and Divine*, published in Birmingham that year by Thomas Warren junior.[114] The earliest of the club's own records date from 1775, by which time its permanent affiliation with the more advanced part of the Dissenting interest in Birmingham was quite clear. Nine of its twenty-four members in 1775 were named in the same decade in the minutes of the subscribers to the Old Meeting House;[115] and since this, like the New Meeting, had been moving away from strict Trinitarian orthodoxy since the 1740s[116] it is not surprising that many of those who were invited to join the Book Club were Unitarians, among them James Belcher, whose club connections help to explain his dissemination of American propaganda in 1775, and who thereafter rapidly became known as Birmingham's most radical printer and bookseller.[117] In 1779, the Book Club was closely connected with the original subscribers to the Birmingham Library,[118] and during the years that followed it was also associated with the group which took the lead in the first permanent and systematic extension of secular education in Birmingham.

Like so many of the Book Club's members, this initiative came from the Old and New Meetings. In 1787 these seceded from the original interdenominational committee formed to manage the town's Sunday schools when they were first established in 1784.[119] In 1790 the two meetings amalgamated their own schools, and at the same time a group of younger teachers who had come under the influence of Dr Priestley started a self-supporting venture of their own. This was known as the Birmingham Sunday Society, and it set out to provide further instruction for those who had already passed through a basic Sunday school. Though the society insisted that its members attend public worship, and though moral education remained its prime concern, it taught writing, arithmetic, geography, book-keeping and drawing as well as the elements of natural and revealed religion. It thus went considerably beyond the original Sunday school rules of 1784, which had expressly forbidden the teaching of anything 'but what is suited immediately to the design of the Sabbath Day, and preserving young people from Idleness, Immorality and Ignorance',[120] and it soon went even further. An advanced class was formed, which collected its own library and apparatus for the study of mechanics, electricity, hydrostatics, pneumatics, optics and astronomy. In order to defray expenses a weekly debating club was started, whose meetings were open to the public for 6*d* admission, and free lectures on philosophy, morals, history and science were given to working men by the society's leading members.[121] Besides Thomas Wright Hill, whose son Rowland, the inventor of the penny post, was to make his father's school at Hazlewood internationally famous as one of the nineteenth century's most original and influential experiments in education,[122] these included James Lucock, Thomas Clark and Thomas Halliday, all three of whom were later to become members of the Birmingham Book Club.[123] The same was true in 1796, when the Sunday Society was expanded into the Birmingham Brotherly Society, in many ways a forerunner of the Mechanics' Institutes of George Birkbeck thirty-five years later. Once again four of the Brotherly Society's eight original managers—James Lucock, W. H. Phipson, Thomas Pemberton and Thomas Clark—can be linked with the club at the Leicester Arms.[124]

Nor was education the only aspect of Joseph Priestley's influence which this group of men kept alive in Birmingham after the Doctor had himself been driven from the town. When the local movement for parliamentary reform, severely damaged by the events of 1791, was rebuilt during the following two years the Sunday Society and the Book Club together formed one of the main sources from which it drew its new leadership, and the twelve members whom the Birmingham Society for Constitutional Information proposed for affiliation with the parent society in London in February 1793 included James Lucock, Thomas Clark and probably Thomas Wright Hill as well, though in this case the identification is not so certain.[125] Of these three, Lucock in particular deserves attention. As the real force behind the formation of the Brotherly Society in 1796, and at different times as secretary, treasurer and president of the Birmingham Book Club, he played a major part in the perpetuation of the reform movement in the town during the revolutionary and Napoleonic periods and in its open reemergence after 1815. His career in fact epitomised the 'constitutionalism', based on the ideals of individual betterment and the achievement of reform within the existing social order, which was to be the distinguishing characteristic of Birmingham radicalism in the nineteenth century. Born in 1761 and educated at Winson Green Academy, Lucock's most typical achievements were the Birmingham Unitarian Brotherly Benefit Society, started in 1798 as a sick club for members of the parent institution, and *Moral Culture*, a series of lectures to the Brotherly Society, which were published in 1817. In addition to these good works, however, Lucock was also closely involved in the drafting of the petition of protest against the prevailing distress, which was adopted by the Birmingham Hampden Club on 22 January 1817 at the first of the public meetings on Newhall Hill which culminated fifteen years later in the great rallies of the Birmingham Political Union, and his continued involvement in radical politics earned him recognition by Thomas Attwood in 1831 as 'The Father of Birmingham Reform'.[126]

The Birmingham Book Club thus acted as one of the roots of opposition and reform politics in the town from their beginnings in the 1760s until well into the following century. To what extent this and the other reading societies which have been noticed were typical of Birmingham's working population as a whole is another matter. Though social relations were not dominated by the kind of

stratification into distinct 'classes' which was beginning to cause concern in other
industrial areas, particularly in Lancashire, the finely graded scale of status
among the different trades of the town nevertheless placed a considerable distance between the highly skilled japanner at one end and the lowly pin maker
at the other. As one commentator put it in 1805,

> The manners and morals of these are as different as the employments: and it is,
> therefore, more than vague conjecture to believe that the intermediate class
> partake the like influence in a certain descending series and graduate in their
> progress accordingly: for instance, the first rank, namely the japanners, rarely
> associate in their hours of relaxation with the workers of copper, brass, iron &c.
> The latter frequent the common pot-houses; the former get into the third and
> fourth [class] inns and club-rooms with the little tradesmen, considering them-
> selves rather as artists than as artisans, dress to the character, have something
> more of a reverence for themselves, and are therefore upon the whole not only a
> more polished but also a more valuable link in the chain of society.[127]

The members of the reading societies formed an elite nearer the upper end of
this scale than the lower. This does not mean, however, that they can be isolated
from those below them. The distinctions which were maintained between the
different branches of Birmingham's trades indicate not the existence of real
barriers but the opposite. In a community characterised at all its levels by a
high degree of emulation the observance of such marks of status, far from being
an obstacle to frequent movement and contact between different groups, was the
natural corollary of its existence and of the consequent need to find ways of
maintaining the separate identity of each particular element. In any case, the
better known societies were not doing anything out of the ordinary in associat-
ing together. On the contrary, they probably represent only a fraction of the
total number of clubs of all sorts which were formed in the town. During the
later eighteenth century the formation of friendly societies among working
people was becoming a permanent and significant social tendency in the manufacturing areas of the country, and nowhere more so than in Birmingham, whose
inhabitants, according to a contributor to the *Universal Magazine* in 1802, 'are
fonder of association in clubs than those of any other place I know'.[128] The
express purposes of these associations were prudential rather than intellectual,
and even at that they were as often condemned as dens of drunkenness and
seedbeds of petty dispute as they were praised as nurseries of sobriety and
thrift.[129] In the present context, however, their significance as a forum for an
independent articulacy among working people is of more importance than their
efficiency in providing for the misfortunes of life. For a movement which was
actively, if selectively, encouraged by the higher orders[130] because it offered a
new approach to the perennial problem of the poor by encouraging the
'economic' virtues of industry, prudence and self-help could hardly avoid
admitting as well the first signs of a distinct point of view among its participants.

That this was so can be seen from the poetic description of working class life
and leisure in Birmingham given in 1790 by George Davis's *Saint Monday, or
Scenes from Low Life*. In the course of a day-by-day account of the working
week this provides a vivid impression of both aspects of the clubs' role. Workers,
paid too late on Saturday to allow them to provide properly for themselves and
their families before the market closed for the week, were still flush with cash on
Monday, which took the place of Friday night and Saturday in the modern

working week. The idleness of Monday was followed by the inevitable hang-
overs and visits to the pawnshop; and since such hardships could only be made
bearable by a hair of the dog, many, relying on credit advanced against their
contributions to a pot-house benefit club, kept their spirits up in taverns like
the Fox in Castle Street, where

> ... all the scum of the creation meet,
> For days together at the liquor stick,
> And keep SAINT MONDAY up for a whole week.

Davis's account of Monday itself culminated in a description of the drunken
uproar of a club feast dinner, and he used the remaining days of the week to
present other vignettes of low life, notably the behaviour of the gallery at the
play and the amateur theatricals of 'a 'set of *spouters* at their midnight scene'
in the same disparaging light. But the fact that these things were there to be
deprecated at all is itself an indication that some degree of awareness existed
among the common people of the town, and that some attempt was being made
to express it. While Davis deplored the debauchery of the Fox in Castle Street
and other such houses, even he was bound to remark upon

> ... the residence of peace,
> Where tradesmen club their twopences apiece
> To spend an hour like reasonable men.

And if he mocked the blundering dramatic efforts of those who

> ... with insignificance of look
> And vacant phiz, speak prologues *out o' book*.[131]

what is really remarkable is that they actually knew how to do so.

The same observer who noticed the distance which separated the japanner
from the pin maker in Birmingham's social scale also supplied his own answer
to the question which his description raised about the extent of popular consciousness in the town. 'The manufactories,' he complained,

> have their politicians and republicans as well as the barber's shop and the ale-
> house ... and it is as common to hear the downfall of states, the high and low
> church party, the indivisibility of the great nation, the imperfection of thrones and
> dominions, and the perfectibility of human nature, the bill of rights and the bill
> of wrongs discussed and determined in casting a button or pointing a pin, as at the
> Devil Tavern or the Robin Hood Society.[132]

The extent to which the club, as the main vehicle of this popular consciousness,
had been absorbed into its idiom can be seen from the cheap political tracts,
written in a faked Brummagem dialect, which were produced by Jacobins and
anti-Jacobins alike during the 1790s. On both sides great importance was
attached to the working man's newly acquired ability to get his own information
on public affairs by reading about them at his club, as if this imparted to his
opinions a special authenticity and force, and first-hand knowledge of the
printed word, even if it was only that of the newspapers, was brandished as an
invincible weapon. Thus John Nott, button burnisher, scored a point for Church
and King:

> Odzooks, I remember now reading at our club what the Parliament-men said
> about this business t'other day, when the Church was one hundred and eighty-three

ahead of you. Your friend Mr. Burke made a nation fine speech which I wrote down. . . .

and Abel Sharp, Spur Maker, retaliated in kind:

> I should as soon think of finding a pair of spurs in a butterfly as a fast friend in Mr. Burke. . . . For when I read the newspaper at our club, I thinks I see his face like a weather-cock, blown about by every wind of Church and State.[133]

Pamphleteers on both sides of the question now took a basic degree of literacy, acquired through club membership, for granted, and used it as the starting point from which to develop their particular line of argument. Beyond this, however, reactions to the working man's ability to read and write diverged sharply. Once he had learnt to read, the exemplary Job Nott, Buckle Maker, shunned any more advanced subjects and went home to teach his old mother so that she too could read the scriptures. True, he did go to evening school to learn writing and shorthand; but having got these skills 'well enough to answer *my* purpose', he would go no further, and he certainly was not going to waste his time on French.[134] In the letters of Alexander Armstrong, Whip Maker, and Abel Sharp, Spur Maker, on the other hand, can be seen many characteristics which were to become more pronounced among working men in years to come, particularly the sense of mutual dependence and solidarity against the rest of the world, the pride which a man could take in his own self-sufficiency, and the distrust of formal charity and religion as being no more than social indoctrination dispensed by the privileged.[135] 'We poor folks,' wrote Abel Sharp,

> don't extortion upon one another. . . . We Whip Makers and Button Burnishers and Spur Makers, and the whole tote on us, when anybody on us ben ailing say Well neighbour, can I lighten your burdens for you? . . . We can't like your sharping fellows who try to take people in, . . . and then we don't make believe to favour poor folks and then let 'em to know, if they don't spend all their savings to make a *to do* at making their child a Christian, we shan't church 'em again. . . .
>
> As you say, mortal right, we are all industrious, for we tug and strive ourselves to death's door to keep out of jail, for the constables won't favour us poor folks. But here's the Beauty of it John: we all eat our own gettings.

All this, moreover, was presented with a keen eye for a prospective readership which included not only the working people of Birmingham itself but also the small farmers of the neighbourhood. Like the editors of the Sheffield *Patriot*, Abel Sharp was well aware that

> An angel might exhaust his eloquence talking to *them* of the importance of *Rights, Liberties, Franchises* and *Privileges*, . . . but let the poorest d---l that ever wagged his tongue but mention *Tythes*, . . . it . . . would awaken & rivet their attention & rouse them to any measures . . . by which it might appear they wod. rid themselves of those Hay & Straw Chains in which the tenth of the produce of their Fields is bound & carried away *pro bono ecclesiae*.[136]

Accordingly he steered his subject in this direction, and, having done so, continued in the guise of a disgruntled farmer, who gave vent to a smouldering anti-clericalism by recalling his old grandfather's loathing of the 'Q rats', the two-legged vermin who stole an honest man's stock:

> Church! Church! We ha' no church *worth going to*. We are all House Protestants now. Our folks ha' got it into their heads that our rectors are *all a swarm of*

locusts. . . . As sure as you are a living man, we can't pay our way, and poor
children in our parish are just famished. As sure as my name's old honesty, I
thinks there will be a rising amongst us soon, for we are *half anotimies now.* Ay!
Ay! the Golden Days are over.[137]

Having thus brought the distress of the countryside together with the self-
consciousness which was developing in the town, Abel Sharp concluded by
damning the servile John Nott as a traitor to his kind. After this the way was
clear for Sharp's collaborator, Alexander Armstrong, to welcome, in the
teaching of Dr Priestley, the prospect of a future in which the common man
would be delivered from the hypocritical rich and their tithe-gathering toadies
and be free to speak his own mind:

> Yes, as you say, it was deadly kind of Master Priestley to give us trades-people
> a bit of advice. . . . We have long been teach'd that God a'mighty don't care for
> us, . . . that he only sent us to burnish buttons and clean stables, and that if we
> have got a soul, it's hardly worth looking a'ter: and for this reason I spose 'tis
> our parsuns don't visit us poor folks except at Christnings and Buryings. And then
> d'ye see, when do our Clergy make books for us? No—no they *know a trick worth*
> *two of that*: but as the saying is, when the belly is full, the bones will be at rest.
> Now what does Master Priestley? What does he? Why, he says, if we don't all get
> to heaven it shan't be thrown in his teeth; and then, what vastly pleases us, we
> shan't be put upon and be as tho' our eyes were pulled out and our ears cut off.
> Nothing like it. . . . As the saying is, every man for himself and God for us all. We
> may ask questions and give answers of our *own making*.[138]

'Of our own making': it was in this that the significance of the vernacular
tracts of the 1790s lay. They were the end product of the common readership
which had come into being in Birmingham during the past fifty years; and,
as the first of a long series of similar productions which were to keep pace with
the social and political history of the next half-century, they marked the
emergence of a new form of propaganda. By itself the cheapness of the tracts
was not particularly remarkable: abridged versions of major pamphlets and
other short pieces on politics had been available in Birmingham for as little
as a penny or twopence a copy since the mid-1770s at least. What was new
was the use of the first person and the simulation of direct speech in order to
create a semblance of the working man expressing his own opinions. The invention was necessary because this was precisely what he was beginning to do
for himself. It would, however, be a serious and rather elementary error to be
swept by enthusiasm for the 'artisan' cause to the assumption that the Birmingham tradesman's educational attainments and new-found political articulacy
necessarily led him to an unalloyed radicalism. Again, the literary example
of Alexander Armstrong is instructive; for immediately after his assertion that
working men should speak their own mind his admiration for 'Master Priestley'
and his anxiety to score further points off John Nott led him to strike a false
note. His veneration of the Doctor's 'fine deal of know' and membership of 'the
King's Club' (*sc.* the Royal Society) might by themselves have passed as no
more than naïve respect for book learning. But what they underscored was the
fact that Priestley *'e'ent one of us, as many parsuns be'*; and for Alexander
Armstrong to give this as a reason why the Doctor should be hearkened to by
working men squared ill with the carefully created picture of beleaguered but
self-conscious and self-sufficient solidarity previously presented by Abel Sharp.

This was tantamount to an admission that the letters of these two were in fact the skilful propaganda of an active minority, which, for all its own self-consciousness, still derived its ideas from elsewhere; and that the real purpose of the claim to represent the authentic voice of a 'working class' speaking for itself was to buttress the points of contact between the 'intellectual' radicalism of Rational Dissent and the actual movement of popular opinion in Birmingham at a time when they were under considerable strain.

The champions of Church and King were quick to fasten on this weakness in the Jacobin position, and they directed their main counter-attack towards its exposure by ridiculing the intellectual pretensions and emphasising the isolation of the reformers. 'Dr Phlogiston' himself, with his *'fine deal of know'*, his doctorate of divinity and his fellowship of the Royal Society, was of course the prime target, and his successor at the New Meeting, the Rev. John Edwards, was twitted accordingly for his lack of such qualifications:

> But meister Edwards, shoodna you ha sumthin arter your nam? Caus plane J. Edwards loks as if yow waant a mon of larnin' and ability as you say. Now I was thinkin, spoze yow was to put T.G., A.B., J.L., B.M., it whood stond for Tailors Gose Are Balon, Jock O'Lonton and Bag a Muneshine. How much honsomer this whood loke shoodna it than Meister Priestley's D.D., F.R.S.?[139]

Similarly Nicholas Noboddy emphasised that his quarrel was not with 'the Good Old Sort of Sleepy Quiet Prispitarians' who kept their mouths shut and minded their own business, but only with the 'Fresh cum up Shufflin' kind, as he called the mere 'lads or lubberdelays who have been tutored by that old Turnabout Dr. Priestley, nation saize him':

> Hees taicht you to be always shufflin about and changing your mind like himself, an old weithercock. You can't never help reeding no book as draps in your way, let it be about what it wool, and ye must always say as the book says, . . . and then you never caunt be easy but what you must always be trying to bring over everybody else to your way of thinkin.[140]

Like most other aspects of the West Midlands' reaction to the revolutionary crisis, the outcome of this propaganda contest was uncertain. It is certainly true that by the 1790s many of Birmingham's artisans had achieved a considerable degree of literate knowledge and political awareness. This, however, did not render them entirely immune from the blandishments of tradition and subordination. On the contrary, these were never rejected so decisively, even by Birmingham's avowed Jacobins, as they were by manufacturing towns elsewhere in the country, and those who did answer John Nott and his minions did so in terms which, though they expressed 'working class' attitudes clearly enough in their attempt to exploit popular grievances against established society on as broad a front as possible, also contained elements of compromise. The immediate significance of the latter was that they exposed the radical apologists to effective counter-attack. In a more permanent sense, however, they also reflected the fact that the ways in which the popular articulacy of the Birmingham area had been formed and communicated during the previous thirty years meant that it contained the alternative ethics, represented on one hand by 'working class' collectivity and on the other by the aristocratic values of self-help and individual advancement, in an inextricable mixture. As a result, the radical potential that was undoubtedly present in the developing self-consciousness of the common people was tempered by a persistent strain of practical conservatism. This balance was further sustained by the area's actual political experience during the last forty years of the century. For this too was of such a kind that the forces of reform and retention were evenly matched within it, so that, for the present at any rate, it still lent itself as plausibly to a justification of the existing situation as it did to the demand for change.

NOTES

1 *V.C.H. Warwicks.*, VII, 212.

2 *V.C.H. Warwicks.*, VII, 209–10; Hill, *Bookmakers*, pp. 14, 35, and, for the *Birmingham Journal*, G. A. Cranfield, *Handlist of English Provincial Newspapers and Periodicals*, p. 2.

3 Cranfield, *Handlist*, p. 2.

4 For Walker's career and business methods see G. A. Cranfield, *The Development of the Provincial Newspaper, 1700–60* (Oxford, 1963), pp. 51–6.

5 Hill, *Bookmakers*, p. 40, and see below, pp. 128–30.

6 *V.C.H. Warwicks.*, VII, 210.

7 Schofield, *Lunar Society*, pp. 23–4; William Bennett, *John Baskerville, the Birmingham Printer: his Press, Relations and Friends* (2 vols, Birmingham, 1937), II, 28–9.

8 For examples see Bennett, *Baskerville*, II, 71; Hill, *Bookmakers*, p. 61.

9 *Cf.* Bennett, *Baskerville*, I, 9.

10 Bennett, *Baskerville*, II, 27, and see below, p. 169. This was probably the work of Robert Martin, one of Baskerville's pupils who was managing the Baskerville press at the time while his master devoted himself to his japanning interests, and it originally appeared in serial form for distribution by James Sketchley. *Cf.* also P. Gaskell, *John Baskerville: a Bibliography* (Cambridge, 1959), p. 54.

11 B.R.L. 81720, and *cf.* Gaskell, *Baskerville Bibliography*, p. 56.

12 Hill, *Bookmakers*, pp. 72–4; Cranfield, *The Development of the Provincial Newspaper*, pp. 22, 56.

13 Hill, *Bookmakers*, pp. 61–3, 79, 82–5.

14 See above, p. 59.

15 See above, p. 76 n. 26.

16 Hill, *Bookmakers*, p. 67. Thomas Warren junior was the son of the printer of the *Birmingham Journal*, the town's first paper.

17 See above, p. 78, n. 71.

18 Hill, *Bookmakers*, pp. 67–8.

19 Hill, *Bookmakers*, pp. 68–9. The *Catalogue of the Birmingham Collection* (1918) lists the *Birmingham Register* in two volumes (I, Nos. 1–24, II, Nos. 1–15) and dates them 1765–66 rather than 1764–65. Presumably this applies to a subsequently published collected edition. If the numeration of the individual issues was accurate vol. II, No. 15, would have appeared originally about 27 November 1765.

20 Hill, *Bookmakers*, pp. 68–9.

21 See Bennett, *Baskerville*, II, 12–13, 18–22; Hill, *Bookmakers*, p. 72.

22 Hill, *Bookmakers*, p. 74.

23 *The Repository, or Weekly General Entertainer* (Birmingham, 1770, and reissued, 1772, as *The Winter's Evening Entertainer*), B.R.L. 57811, *passim*. For the importance of the idea of conspiracy see Bernard Bailyn, *The Ideological Origins of the American Revolution* (Cambridge, Mass., 1967), especially ch. 4, 'The logic of rebellion', and 'A note on conspiracy'. The extent to which British critics of the court were prepared to go in using the myth of conspiracy to justify resistance should not be overestimated, however: certainly this was not the conscious intention of the *Repository's* 'political maxims and prophecies'. However implicit in them such a remedy may have been, these avoided the implication by keeping the act of resistance firmly in the past and by seeking a remedy to the present discontents not in rebellion, which was itself condemned as a by-product of corruption, but in the *deus ex machina* of the Great Man who would condescend to give the law to prince and people alike. Their concluding hope that 'as freedom was restored

to her antient inheritance by a glorious William, . . . so in succeeding times shall atrocious rebellion fostered by m - - - l corruption be extinguished by another William . . .' is a good illustration of the way in which the fame of the elder Pitt continued to mesmerise British opinion and blind it to the true nature of the issues at stake.

24 *The British Museum, or Universal Register of Literature, Politics and Poetry, Containing Instruction and Entertainment for the Fair Sex, the Gentleman and the Mechanic* (Birmingham, 1771), B.R.L. 139847, *passim.*

25 Marcus, letters 2, 3 and 4, *The British Museum*, pp. 46–7, 81–2, 100.

26 Marcus, letter 7, *The British Museum*, p. 184.

27 *The British Museum*, pp. 219–20.

28 See above, p. 74.

29 'Dialogue between Solitaire and Mundoso', and 'The most criminal not always the most unhappy, a moral tale by the celebrated Helvetius', *The British Museum*, pp. 203–5, 335.

30 See above, pp. 88–91. If such a connection did exist it would help to explain why the *British Museum* also devoted a good deal of space to the memoirs of famous actors and actresses. No doubt these were included to lighten the heavy diet provided by the rest of the contents and to attract a wider readership. Nevertheless they seem a little incongruous next to the serious professions of intent made elsewhere, and the editors themselves felt constrained to point out that they were intended simply to satisfy natural curiosity and provide innocent diversion in rather the same way that Matthew Boulton explained his support of the New Street theatre to the Earl of Dartmouth in 1777.

31 For Hall see *V.C.H. Warwicks.*, VII, 411; *D.N.B.*; *Correspondence, Newspaper Cuttings, etc, relating to Kings Norton Parish Library*, B.R.L. 142706, and *An Eighteenth Century Shelf List of the Parochial Library at Kings Norton*, B.R.L. 662017.

32 *Catalogue of St Philip's Parish Library* (Birmingham, 1795), B.R.L. 60380.

33 Charles Parish, *History of the Birmingham Library* (London, for the Library Association, 1966), pp. 11–12.

34 *Aris*, 11 June 1781.

35 Parish, *Birmingham Library*, pp. 13–14.

36 *Aris*, 9 December 1782, 11 December 1786.

37 *Aris*, 31 May, 14 June 1784. In 1790 a second special section, devoted to medicine, was started by Dr Withering. See S. Timmins, *Centenary of the Birmingham Library, 1779–1879*, B.R.L. 210166, p. 19, and *Aris*, 20 June 1791.

38 The preceding account of the quarrel among the members of the library between 1786 and 1790 is based on the material provided by Parish, *Birmingham Library*, pp. 16 ff and appendix C, pp. 90–7.

39 Parish, *Birmingham Library*, pp. 34–5, 60–3.

40 Parish, *Birmingham Library*, pp. 61–2, 89. The size of the secession to the New Library is estimated from the number present at its first meeting (thirty-nine) and from the total number of subscribers listed in its treasurer's account for 1796 (178).

41 The library's tontine deed is printed in full by Parish, *Birmingham Library*, appendix F, pp. 105–31.

42 Figures given in the Birmingham Library's notices of its annual meetings, combined with information from the catalogues of 1795 and 1798 provided by Parish (*Birmingham Library*, pp. 48–9), enable its growth to be followed closely during the first twenty years of its existence:

Aris,		Annual rate:
9 December 1782:	'Near 500'	1782–84, 200
8 December 1783:	'Near 700'	1784–85, 300
6 December 1784:	'Near 900'	1785–86, 400
12 December 1785:	'Near 1,200'	1786–87, 600
11 December 1786:	'Upwards of 1,600'	1787–88, 800
10 December 1787:	'Near 2,200'	1788–89, 400
8 December 1788:	'Near 3,000'	1789–95, 133
7 December 1789:	'Near 3,400'	1795–98, 165
Catalogue, 1795:	4,200	
Catalogue, 1798:	4,696	

The figures quoted (from *V.C.H. Warwicks.*, VII, 211) for Crompton's and Lowe's circulating libraries give averages of 550 and 800 per year respectively, rates of increase which the Birmingham Library only equalled between 1786 and 1788. It is particularly noticeable that the growth of Lowe's library occurred during the years when the Birmingham Library's increase had slowed considerably, when it was affected by the Dissenters' secession and when it was raising its admission fees (see below). The considerable number of serious works listed in Lowe's catalogue of 1796 (see below) suggests that he was catering for a readership which might well have used the Birmingham Library under different circumstances.

43 *Cf. V.C.H. Warwicks.*, vii, 210–11, and Hill, *Bookmakers*, pp. 45, 80, 90–103. This list differs somewhat from that given by *V.C.H.*, which does not mention Belcher until 1816, though he was advertising in 1775 (see below), and omits Lucas altogether, though he issued his first catalogue in 1788 (B.R.L. 239816).

44 Parish, *Birmingham Library*, pp. 23, 64.

45 *Catalogue of Lucas's Circulating Library* (1788), B.R.L. 239816; *Catalogue of Lowe's Circulating Library* (1796), B.R.L. 60769.

46 Parish, *Birmingham Library*, pp. 19, 37, 64.

47 *Cf.* Lucas's catalogue (1788), listing a total of 1,382 works in 2,343 volumes, and analysis of Birmingham Library catalogue provided by Parish, *Birmingham Library*, pp. 49–50. The percentages of holdings in both cases are of the total number of volumes, not of the total of works.

48 These two classes formed respectively $31\frac{1}{2}$ per cent and $9\frac{1}{2}$ per cent of Lucas's total. Among the octavos, as listed, were the following: *A Historical Dissertation Concerning the Antiquity of the English Constitution; An Appeal to Common Sense*; Andrews's *History of the Late War, 1775–83; Britannia Triumphant*, an account of British naval history; *Pilgrim's Progress; Civil and Ecclesiastical History from the Creation to 1781*; Cartwright's *Legislative Rights*; an anthology of extracts from John Locke; a life of Cromwell; *Essays on the Spirit of Legislation in the Encouragement of Agriculture, Population, Manufacture and Commerce; History of America* (presumably William Robertson's); *History of the Late War*; William Hutton's *History of Birmingham* and *Courts of Requests; History of the Seven Years' War; History of Magna Carta*; a life of John Wilkes; Murray's *History of the American War; The Political State of Great Britain*, and Priestley's *Disquisitions on Matter and Spirit*. If the serious reader could not satisfy himself from these he could always turn to Lucas's shelf on 'Physic, Agriculture, Gardening, Botany, Cookery, Art, Trade etc.', or to his selection of popular divinity, which included John Bunyan's *Law and Grace Unfolded* and his *Holy War*, the *Christian*, and *Gospel* magazines, two editions of George Whitefield's sermons and, a recent addition, *The Beauties of John Wesley*.

49 See below, p. 142, and *V.C.H. Warwicks.*, vii, 210–11.

50 *V.C.H. Warwicks.*, vii, 211.

51 *Aris, passim*: Thomas Yeoman (1746–47), Benjamin Martin (1747), John Taylor (1748), William Griffiths (1755), Joseph Hornblower (1757), James Ferguson (1761, 1771), John Arden (1765, 1767, 1771), John Warltire (1776, 1778, 1779, 1780, 1781, 1782, 1784, 1789), Mr Pitt (1778, 1784), Benjamin Donn (1779), Adam Walker (1781, 1783), Henry Moyes (1782), James Booth (1785, 1788, 1789), Mr Long (1786), Mr Burton (1786, 1791), John Banks (1791), Mr Malton (1793). In addition to these, exhibitions of optical instruments designed on Newtonian principles, and of 'the microcosm, or world in miniature' (probably a transparent orrery), had been advertised as early as 1742, and Erasmus Darwin gave a course of anatomy lectures in 1762 on the cadaver of a recently executed criminal. A similar course, this time on a fresh human foetus with arteries injected, was given in 1768, and Mr Tomlinson of the General Hospital was lecturing on anatomy and surgery in the autumn of 1779. Nor were such courses confined to Birmingham. 'An elegant collection of experiments on the Air Pump' was demonstrated at the Sun in Wolverhampton in October 1762; John Arden lectured in Newcastle under Lyme and Shrewsbury the following year; Mr Pitt did so in Coventry in 1778, and Mr Burton's proposed itinerary in 1786 included 'the principal towns of Worcestershire and Warwickshire'. John Warltire was particularly assiduous in this respect. In 1779 he gave a special course on agricultural chemistry at Tamworth, and entries in Samuel Pipe-Wolferstan's diary indicate that both he and Booth also lectured there in 1781 and 1784 respectively. Warltire also visited Wolverhampton at least twice: in 1784, when his itinerary included Stourbridge, Stourport, Dudley and Walsall as well, and in 1789, when he also lectured at Bromwich Heath.

52 See A. E. Musson and Eric Robinson, 'Science and industry in the late eighteenth century', *Econ. Hist. Rev.*, 2nd series, xiii (1960–61), 222–44, and their major expansion

of this article in *Science and Technology in the Industrial Revolution* (Manchester, 1969), ch. 3.

53 *Aris*, 28 January, 11 March 1793.

54 *Aris*, 3, 10 April 1780.

55 *Aris*, 30 July 1781, 20 May, 24 June 1782, 27 September 1784.

56 For Walker see above, pp. 92, 97 n. 64; for Pitt, *Aris*, 15 November 1784; for Long and Burton, *Aris*, 13, 20 November 1786.

57 *Aris*, 9 February, 25 May 1789. The attitude of the average amateur emerges very clearly from Samuel Pipe-Wolferstan's diary. In January 1779 Samuel subscribed to a course on agricultural chemistry which John Warltire was giving in Tamworth, and he did attend some of the lectures, both then and on Warltire's second visit in 1781, though he took his womenfolk along as well and combined the expeditions with an evening at the local card assembly as well. Warltire's lecture on telescopes in 1781 seems to have brought on one of Samuel's fits of enthusiasm, because he spent the next year dabbling in astronomy with one of his neighbours, went to Birmingham to see Adam Walker's Eidouranion in 1783, bought his own telescope in 1784 and went gallivanting over his own and other people's rooftops making observations of the planets. The difference between the amateur and the professional is revealed by Samuel's petulant reaction to William Marshall, the agricultural expert, whom he had retained as his estate manager: 'Pestered by Marshall with his Linnaeus and did nothing all evening' (12 April 1784). When James Booth visited Tamworth later in the year Samuel went with Marshall to Booth's opening discourse, and though he found it 'very bad' he changed his mind three days later, when Booth's lecture on pneumatics struck him as 'not ill entertainment', after which he paid his subscription and seems to have attended most of the remainder of the course.

58 *Aris*, 12 August 1776. The conjunction raises questions about the nature of the lecture on heads. On the face of it, the lecture was nothing more than a piece of popular burlesque in which various standard character types and personalities were mimicked and mocked on the stage. It is possible, however, that in some of its versions it became an early essay in popular phrenology as well.

59 See above, p. 000.

60 *Aris*, 23 October 1774, 4 December 1775.

61 *Aris*, 2 May 1774, 30 October 1775.

62 *Aris*, 26 March 1759.

63 *Aris*, 28 January 1760.

64 *Aris*, 31 January 1763.

65 *Aris*, 18 February 1782.

66 *Aris*, 22 April, 16, 23 December 1793.

67 Public Record Office, Treasury Solicitor's Papers, TS 11/578/1893, bundle 1: indictments and prosecution briefs in Rex *v.* Belcher, Warwick summer assizes, 27 July 1793.

68 For examples among the scientific lecturers see Musson and Robinson, *Science and Technology*, pp. 102, 104, 145. Among non-scientific lecturers who visited Birmingham, Mr Wratislavia, who gave courses in French during 1774, also kept a language school in the town; Mr Groombridge both taught and lectured in geography and the use of globes in 1786, and M. Gerard, another French lecturer, was taking private pupils in 1787. (*Aris*, 17 October 1774, 8 May 1786, 2 July 1787.)

69 For a more detailed account, on which the following paragraphs are based, see my article 'The schoolmasters of Birmingham and the West Midlands, 1750–90: private education and cultural change in the English provinces during the early industrial revolution', *Social History/Histoire Sociale* (Ottawa), x, No. 1 (Spring 1976), 129–53.

70 *Aris*, 2 May 1774.

71 *Aris*, 13 July 1767, 19 December 1768.

72 *Aris*, 25 October 1756, 29 December 1760, 10 November 1788.

73 *Aris*, 26 November 1764.

74 *Aris*, 20 September 1762, 9 May 1764; below, p. 141.

75 *Aris*, 8 August 1768, 6 May 1771.

76 *Aris*, 3 August 1761, 14 February 1763, 23 January 1769, 21 January 1771, 9 October 1775, 16 September 1782.

77 *Cf.* J. M. Roberts, 'Freemasonry: possibilities of a neglected topic', *Eng. Hist. Rev.*, LXXXIV (April 1969), 323–35. For the origins of speculative Masonry see D. Knoop and

G. P. Jones, *The Genesis of Freemasonry* (Manchester, 1947), and for the importance of the craft in the development of secular education during the eighteenth century, N. Hans, *New Trends in Education in the Eighteenth Century* (London, 1951), pp. 137–40, 165–72.

78 See S. Pope, 'The development of Freemasonry in England and Wales, as depicted by graphs from particulars in Lane's *Masonic Records*, second edition', *A.Q.C.*, 68–70 (1956–58), 129–31; R. F. Gould, *History of Freemasonry* (rev. edn, 1936), pp. 71–2, 77–8. Pope's account must, however, be treated with caution, especially as regards the situation in London after 1780. The fact that an internal dispute caused many lodges to be struck from the Grand Lodge register between 1783 and 1800 did not mean that the disowned societies ceased to meet.

79 See details in John Lane, *Masonic Records, 1717–1894* (2nd edn, Torquay, 1895).

80 *Early Records of St Paul's Lodge, No. 43*, B.R.L. 184100.

81 For Sketchley's career see Benjamin Walker, 'Birmingham directories', *T.B.A.S.*, LVIII (1934), 1–36, especially pp. 1–13.

82 Walker, 'Birmingham directories', p. 13.

83 For Bissett see T. B. Dudley, ed., *Memoir of James Bissett*; for Toy, T. M. Carter, 'St John's lodge in Henley in Arden, 1791–1811', *A.Q.C.*, xxxix (1928), 4–60, p. 7; for Vaux, who signed notices for St Paul's lodge in 1785, see *Aris*, 14 June 1785. For all three see also the biographical sketches and identifying notes to the group portrait of Freeth's circle in 1791 in Birmingham Book Club records.

84 *Aris*, 20 April 1789.

85 See above, p. 61, and Walker, 'Birmingham directories', p. 11. The *Sufferings of John Coustos* was a translation from a French account of atrocities allegedly committed against Freemasons by the Portuguese Inquisition. The work was originally published in London in 1746.

86 For a general history of the order see W. H. Rylands, 'A forgotten rival of Masonry: the Noble Order of Bucks', *A.Q.C.*, III (1890), 140–62.

87 *Aris*, 21 February 1776.

88 *Aris*, 9 August 1779.

89 See below, pp. 199–210.

90 *Aris*, 11 August 1777.

91 *Aris*, 14 August 1775, 22 July 1776, 9 June, 14 July 1777, 7 August 1780, 5 August 1782, 18 August 1783.

92 *Aris*, 11 August 1777, 7 August 1780, 5 August 1782, 4 August 1783, 6 August 1792. Smart's *Wolverhampton Chronicle and Staffordshire Advertiser* was announced in *Aris*, 17 August 1789.

93 For Wrottesley see *Aris*, 26 December 1774, which named him as Master of lodge No. 58 at the Swan inn, Wolverhampton; for Lawley, whose particular affiliations were admittedly with one of the more fashionable London lodges, the Cross Keys in Henrietta Street, rather than with a local lodge, see W. G. Fisher, 'A cavalcade of Freemasons in 1731 as recorded in the *Gentleman's Magazine*', *A.Q.C.*, 74 (1961), 32–49. Dudley and Foley were named as stewards of the Albion lodge of Bucks in *Aris*, 14 July 1777.

94 *Aris*, 12 July 1779.

95 *Early Records of St Paul's Lodge*, pp. 20, 30.

96 *Cf.* reports of Masonic celebrations in *Aris*, 26 June 1780, 23 August 1784, 14 June 1785, 3 July 1786, and playbill for 'A squeeze to St Paul's', *Aris*, 6 September 1790.

97 See, for example, not only the writings of John Freeth but also such pieces as the Epilogue in the Character of a Mason's Wife spoken by Mrs Newton after a performance at the 'Histrionic Academy' in Wolverhampton given under Masonic sponsorship in 1765 (*Aris*, 24 June 1765), Brother Rowswell's Eulogium of Freemasonry, which was advertised to precede the 'Squeeze to St. Paul's' or verse 4 of 'A New Song in Praise of the Loom', written and sung by Mr Young in the character of a Coventry weaver at the theatre in Coventry: '... The Sword and the Scales of strict Justice we bear/And like good *Free Masons* will act on the *Square*' (*Jopson*, 12 February 1781).

98 *Aris*, 2 July 1781.

99 *Aris*, 20 June 1786.

100 Hill, *Bookmakers*, p. 72.

101 The description was used by the lecturers themselves, and it is valuable because it distinguishes their purpose from traditional 'magic' on the one hand and from 'science'

in the modern sense of the word on the other. The popularity of the thaumaturgic lecturers is one indication that though the rise of science may have been hostile to the traditional magic of the past it was quite capable of replacing it by a substitute of its own creation. Similarly, the popularity of Freemasonry among the middling tradesmen of towns like Birmingham emphasises Mr K. V. Thomas's warning against 'too facile an equation between agriculture and magic, industry and rationalism' (K. V. Thomas, *Religion and the Decline of Magic*, London, 1971, p. 665, and review by Margaret Bowker in the *Historical Journal*, 15, No. 2, June 1972, 363–6). For another recent treatment of the same theme, though in a different mode, see Robert Darnton, *Mesmerism and the End of the Enlightenment in France* (Cambridge, Mass., 1968).

102 *Aris*, 10 April 1780.

103 For Katterfelto see *D.N.B.*, and A. Stuart Brown, 'Gustavus Katterfelto, Mason and magician', *A.Q.C.*, LXIX (1957), 136–8.

104 See advertisements in *Aris*, 30 January, 9 April, 4 June, 20 August 1792, 14 January, 4 February 1793.

105 *Aris*, 11 June 1792.

106 *Aris*, 21, 28 January 1792.

107 For this point see 'The lodges and their legend', review of J. M. Roberts, *The Mythology of the Secret Societies* (London, 1972), in *Times Literary Supplement*, 15 December 1972.

108 T. B. Dudley, ed., *Memoir of James Bissett*, introduction, p. 33.

109 *Memoir of James Bissett*, p. 76.

110 *Aris*, 10 February 1772.

111 *Aris*, 16 January 1775.

112 Subscription list to first edition of William Hutton's *History of Birmingham* (1781), B.R.L. 5835.

113 Andrew Haynes, 'A brief sketch of the early history of the Birmingham Book Club', in Birmingham Book Club records.

114 B.R.L. 259403.

115 See Birmingham Book Club records, which contain names of members in 1775, 1786, 1796 and 1806, as well as an intermediate list of no specific date, and *Old Meeting House, Register of Resolutions ... 1771–91*, signatures to invitations to the Rev. Mr Walker, 1771, and to the Rev. Mr Nicholls, 1780: Joseph Chantry, Joseph Price, Samuel Pemberton, Samuel Chantry, William Medley, James Benton, Joseph Bosworth and Joseph Wright. Unfortunately no equivalent comparison with the New Meeting is possible, but it seems likely that this would account for many of the remaining members of the Book Club.

116 *V.C.H. Warwicks.*, VII, 416.

117 For Belcher, who was included in the Birmingham Book Club's membership lists for 1775, 1786 and 1796, see Hill, *Bookmakers*, pp. 94–5.

118 *A Brief Sketch of the History of the Birmingham Book Club* (1864), B.R.L. 123505, p. 2.

119 For details of the secession see below, p. 220.

120 *Aris*, 12 July 1784.

121 *V.C.H. Warwicks.*, VII, 215–6; James Lucock, 'Narrative of the proceedings relative to the erection of the Old Meeting Sunday schools, Birmingham, and of various occurrences therewith connected' (MS, *c.* 1832), B.R.L. 390807, pp. 78–9.

122 See W. H. G. Armytage, *Four Hundred Years of English Education* (2nd edn, Cambridge, 1970), pp. 82–5; W. A. C. Stewart and W. B. McCann, *The Educational Innovators, 1750–1880* (London, 1967), pp. 98–123.

123 See Lucock, 'Narrative', p. 78, and Birmingham Book Club records, 1806, and intermediate membership lists.

124 *V.C.H. Warwicks.*, VII, 216; Birmingham Book Club records, 1806 and intermediate membership lists; Rules and Declaration of the Birmingham Brotherly Society, in vol. 1 of the minute books of the Birmingham Unitarian Brotherly Benefit Society, B.R.L. 391175.

125 See Public Record Office, Treasury Solicitor's Papers, TS 11/962, Minute book of the Society for Constitutional Information, 1792–94, entry for 15 February 1793.

126 See Lucock, 'Narrative', pp. 85 ff; Thomas Clark junior, *Biographical Tribute to the Memory of James Lucock, Father of Sunday School Instruction in Birmingham* (Birmingham, 1835), B.R.L. 64750; *Remarks on the Character of the Late James Lucock* (Birmingham, 1835), B.R.L. 61802, and *V.C.H. Warwicks.*, VII, 286–97.

127 *Supplementary Gleanings collected in the Years 1782 and 1783 on the Warwick-shire Station, including the Communications of J. Morfitt, Esq.* (London, 1805), p. 385.

128 Quoted in C. Gill, *History of Birmingham*, I, 127. For the formation of friendly societies see P. H. J. H. Godsden, *The Friendly Societies in England, 1815–75* (Manchester, 1962).

129 *Cf.* William Hutton, *Courts of Requests*, pp. 154–5, 161.

130 See J. R. Poynter, *Society and Pauperism: English Ideas on Poor Relief*, 1795–1834 (London and Toronto, 1969), pp. 35–9.

131 George Davis, *Saint Monday, or Scenes from Low Life* (Birmingham, 1790), B.R.L. 239216, *passim*. For other examples of the same genre see E. P. Thompson, 'Time, work discipline and industrial capitalism', *Past and Present*, 38 (1967), 57–97, especially pp. 72 ff.

132 *Supplementary Gleanings*, p. 417.

133 John Nott, Button Burnisher, *Very Familiar Letters to Dr. Priestley in Answer to his Familiar Letters to the Inhabitants of Birmingham* (Birmingham, 1790), B.R.L. 66723. p. 21; Alexander Armstrong, Whip Maker, and Abel Sharp, Spur Maker, *Very Familiar Letters to John Nott, Button Burnisher, in Reply to his Very Familiar Letters to Dr. Priestley* (Birmingham, 1790), B.R.L. 4415, p. 23. Birmingham, however, produced no example of this obsession with literacy and the printed word quite as graphic as the sample tobacco paper, as distributed to guests at the Horns, Kennington, which was sent to John Reeves of the A.P.L.P. on 11 December 1792:

j am p. uzz. led ho?

w. Tolivew hil: ek inG.C.R.

aft mA. Ya bus E my.

R - - i G - - ht

SAND TAX! the. JOY, - - so. F!

DAY.

This apparently meaningless jumble of different type faces, irregular spacing and random punctuation would have presented no problem to a newly literate artisan spelling out the letters one by one with the help of his finger: 'I am puzzled how to live while kingcraft may abuse my rights and tax the joys of day' (British Museum, Add. mss. 16922, f. 13).

134 *The Life and Adventures of Job Nott Bucklemaker of Birmingham, First Cousin to the Celebrated Button Burnisher* (Birmingham, 1793), B.R.L. 63937, p. 4.

135 *Cf.* E. P. Thompson, *The Making of the English Working Class* (London, 1963), pp. 418 ff, 'The rituals of mutuality'.

136 Public Record Office, Treasury Solicitor's Papers, TS 11/952/3496 (2), editors of the *Patriot* to Daniel Adams of the Society for Constitutional Information, 11 June 1792.

137 Alexander Armstrong and Abel Sharp, *Very Familiar Letters*, letter v, pp. 6–11.

138 *Op. cit.*, letter VI, pp. 12–13.

139 John *Not* Button Burnisher, *A Letter of Advice to the Reverend J. Edwards, with Remarks on his late Productions* (Birmingham, 1792), B.R.L. 65027, p. 13.

140 *A Wurd or 2 of Good Counsil to abowt Hafe a Duzzen Diffrunt Sorts o Fokes, by Nicholas Noboddy, Brass Candlestick Maker (First Cousin to Job Nott the Buckel Maker, and sum kin of John Nott the Button Burnisher)*, 'sold at the Printer's Shap in the Bool-Ring for tup punse' (Birmingham, 1792), B.R.L. 589744, pp. 6, 8–9.

PART THREE

'WHAT IS CALLED POLITICS'

VII

THE WARWICKSHIRE ELECTION OF 1774 AND ITS ANTECEDENTS: THE WEST MIDLANDS IN THE 1760s

It has been suggested that George Eliot's description of the English Midlands in the 1820s would have been equally appropriate, in its broadest essentials, to the preceding fifty years. Nevertheless one major change seems to be necessary. 'Politics' for the novelist meant something urban and popular, a matter of 'riots and trades union meetings' quite distinct from the affairs of the traditional order of society. She associated politics almost wholly with the more recent of her 'phases of English life' and very little with the other, 'where men with a considerable banking account were accustomed to say that "they never meddled with politics themselves".' In this respect at least, George Eliot described a world very different from that of the preceding century, in which politics were still largely a matter of relationships between members of an established order, conducted with little or no direct regard for a wider public. It may be, however, that historians have accepted this stereotype too easily and have applied it too broadly. As he admitted to Lord Rawdon in May 1784, Samuel Garbett and his fellow manufacturers had little patience with 'what is called politics by those who guide the affairs of this country',[1] and the experience of West Midlanders during Garbett's lifetime provides ample evidence that those who lived in this part of England were being led through a multitude of channels to a general notion of politics which was a good deal more comprehensive than that which the term conventionally implied.

From this point of view the history of the region reveals once more an intricate counterpoint between what was new and the older forms which continued to contain it. On one hand, it is possible to point to the manufacturers' response to the commercial policies of the younger Pitt as a clear manifestation, both of the widening scope of political concern and of provincial dissatisfaction with the capital. Similarly, it is possible to cite the opinions of Josiah Wedgwood, whose thoughts in 1780 on 'General and Particular Representation' endorsed the theories of Dr John Jebb of the Society for Constitutional Information and at the same time reflected his own practical experience of delegated responsibility in turnpike and navigation business.[2] On the other hand, it can be objected that these examples relate to particular interests rather than to any general consciousness; that the activities of the Society for Constitutional Information were a matter of the converted preaching to the converted, and that the real state of political opinion in the West Midlands is best shown by the region's apparent lack of interest in the County Association movement between 1779 and 1785. There were, however, reasons for this.

Though Joseph Priestley was obliged to admit to Christopher Wyvill in 1782 that 'What you call a *pause of astonishment* is in this part of the country a *pause of indifference*',[3] the aims of the Associated Counties were discussed in Birmingham, and so was the prospect of a petition in support of William Pitt's parliamentary reform Bill in 1785.[4] If the town's leaders decided not to act, they did so not so much because they were indifferent to the idea of reform in principle but partly because they were generally unimpressed by the specific proposals of Wyvill and Pitt, partly because they were more occupied with the effects of Pitt's commercial policies and anxious to keep their activities on this score free from extraneous entanglement, and particularly because the reformers failed to offer a more attractive alternative to the very satisfactory accommodation which had recently been worked out between Birmingham and the parliamentary representation of Warwickshire. The opportunity to develop this arrangement, which by 1785 was allowing the leaders of the Birmingham interest to assume a degree of accountability on the part of both Warwickshire Members indistinguishable for practical purposes from that advocated in principle by Josiah Wedgwood five years earlier,[5] had been provided by Sir Charles Holte's defeat of John Mordaunt in the contested county election of 1774. It was this victory and its consequences, rather than the direct impact of any larger event or movement in the nation's history, which exerted the most powerful single influence on the formation of the region's own political experience. It is therefore important to begin by examining the nature and origins of the movement of opinion which gave Holte his seat, as well as the way in which his success was turned to account in Birmingham.

Even if the results of the victory in 1774 are left out of account, the political influence which Birmingham could exert in the counties and boroughs of the West Midlands was considerable. The interest of Matthew Boulton was a valuable electoral asset both at Lichfield and at Bridgnorth,[6] and Birmingham's leaders could muster an impressive lobby of Members from Midlands constituencies when the occasion demanded it.[7] Though connections of this kind were much more seriously cultivated during the later eighteenth century, they were no new thing. It was Sir Richard Newdigate, Member of Parliament for Warwickshire, who in 1692 secured for the gunsmiths of Birmingham a major contract from His Majesty's Board of Ordnance,[8] and the example of the Bean Club serves as a reminder of the social relationships that had long existed between the town's more prominent inhabitants and the gentlemen of the surrounding country districts. After about 1760, however, new connections of a different kind began to appear between Birmingham and its surrounding region alongside those which already existed. It was these which provided the essential foundation for Holte's success.

The immigrants from the surrounding counties[9] who swelled the population of Birmingham represented in themselves the divided sympathies of the West Midlands, drawn as they were by the opportunities offered by the town, yet leaving behind them interests and loyalties in their original homes. Not least among the consequences of this was its effect on the political awareness of the town. Though Birmingham itself sent no representatives to Westminster, it acted as a reservoir of potential votes which were wooed by candidates in other places. The sustained interest in Worcester politics and the repercussions in Birmingham of the Leicestershire by-election during December 1774, which have already been discussed, are only the most conspicuous examples of this. In May 1790 any freeman of Lincoln living in Birmingham was invited to dine with Mr Rice Lewis at the George inn in Bull Street, and the following month Leicester freemen were similarly treated at the Garrick's Head in Lower Temple Street by S. Smith and Brassey Halhed.[10] The account of John Massey, who handled a complicated political struggle at Newcastle under Lyme on behalf of the Marquess of Stafford between 1790 and 1793, included in its grand total of £6,939 10s 7½d several charges for travel to Birmingham to secure voters and for money advanced to them via Massey's contact in the town, one Moses Snape.[11] Josiah Wedgwood's recipe for successful electioneering in 1765, recommended to friends of Sir William Meredith, who was facing a by-election at Liverpool, with the hope that it would prove 'as successful as it hath lately been at a burrough in our county', included not only roasted bullocks, cannon to be fired when votes were won from the enemy, a fighting captain to rally the faint-hearted and a sharp election lawyer but also a poet, who was 'absolutely necessary, & may be heard of at Birmm.'[12] Wedgwood may well have been thinking of John Freeth, and 'The Birmingham Bard', written for the contest at Lichfield in 1799 between Sir Nigel Gresley and Sir John Wrottesley, suggests that the town kept up its dubious reputation for such versifiers:

> When the Baronet's cause was declining
> And his friends at his fate were repining,
> The delusion was o'er, his schemes were all marred,
> So he sent an express for the Birmingham Bard.
> Birmingham Bard,
> Niggy's drove hard,
> And the cause now depends on a Birmingham Bard.
>
> Tho' this Bard now invokes all the Muses,
> Their Birmingham cause he confuses,
> 'Twere better for him if he never had come,
> Lest by chance he may meet with a kick o' the bum.
> Birmingham Bum,
> He shouldn't have come,
> For by chance he may meet with a kick o' the bum.[13]

In such ways were Birmingham people drawn into the affairs of surrounding parliamentary constituencies, and the process had a reciprocal effect on the town's own political consciousness. Because so many of its inhabitants were new-comers who retained interests in their old homes, Birmingham's attention was fixed not on its own affairs alone but on those of surrounding centres as well. The considerations which shaped the reactions of its people were therefore far more diverse than was the case in any one of those separate localities. Moreover, because it was itself unrepresented in Parliament and unincorporate, discussion of Birmingham's own affairs was not yet continuously distorted by any single local feud of the kind which tended to predetermine the political responses of other places. The reporting of news in the Birmingham papers, for example, was not consistently coloured by the violent partisanship which characterised *Jopson's Coventry Mercury*, even though Aris and Swinney often offered different points of view. Birmingham was thus a point of confluence, where popular opinions originating from a wide area could affect each other, as well as a rising centre of influence in its own right. In the absence of any continuous predisposing condition until the latent tension between Church and Dissent became visible and provided a polarising issue within the town itself, the immediate response of the inhabitants was therefore more important in determining Birmingham's political reactions than was the case elsewhere. This was particularly true during the years before the 1774 election.

Apart from an assortment of epigrams late in 1762 and a report which deplored in rather ambiguous terms the 'indecencies' to which Londoners were 'now hurried by the spirit of party',[14] the *Birmingham Gazette* contained little in the way of local political reaction before 1763. During the summer of that year, however, opposition to the cider tax in Worcestershire, Gloucestershire and Herefordshire attracted a good deal of attention,[15] and the paper also printed a number of local contributions in support of John Wilkes. On 6 June he was seen by 'Truth and Justice' as the champion of 'poor authors, poor printers and poor publishers'. A fortnight later Samuel Aris himself ventured beyond his customary caution so far as to say that the freedom of the press was not only the 'Birthright of Englishmen, but also of use to those in power, ... since it gives them notice of the causes of discontent before they can be united into opposition, and it will discover opposition before it becomes disaffection', and on 18 July his paper printed 'Wilkes and Liberty', a song 'written in Birmingham upon a late verdict'. Despite these stirrings, however, there was as yet no real foreshadowing of the sustained and extensive interest in politics which was to develop in the West Midlands five years later. For the moment 'The Moderator, or Advice to Mechanical Patriots', which urged its readers on 18 June 1764 to leave politics to the experts, since ordinary people could neither affect the outcome of the political struggle nor improve their own lot by trying to do so, was probably better attuned to reactions in the Birmingham area than other more enthusiastic contributions.

During the next three years, however, the situation changed decisively. Between the summer of 1765 and the following spring attention in the West Midlands was divided between the commercial crisis precipitated by American resistance to the Stamp Act and the campaign, which has already been described,[16] for the Trent and Mersey canal. So far as the visible demonstration of public opinion was concerned, the second of these developments worked against the first; but in their different ways both served to enhance the region's self-awareness, the first by demonstrating its sensitivity to the course of national policy, the second by emphasising the mutual interests shared by its different parts. At the same time the Black Country in particular began to feel the effects of more fundamental changes, which brought with them the first indications of wider claims to political participation. Alterations in the scale and structure of industry and commerce produced in September 1763 the first signs of organised correspondence among the common manufacturers of Birmingham, Wolverhampton, Walsall and Bilston, and strains affecting the normal course of relations between masters and men were again noticed in 1767.[17] As was the case in London, these developments ran parallel with response to John Wilkes, and the two do not seem to have impinged directly on each other to any great extent.[18] Nevertheless they shared the same social base in the taverns and clubs of Birmingham and the other hardware towns, and this common context may have been more marked in the West Midlands than it was in the capital, for the region was among those most severely affected by the sharp rise in provision prices between 1765 and 1768.

Local attention was first drawn to the rising tide of American resistance to the Stamp Act during October 1765. On the 14th the *Birmingham Gazette* carried an account of demonstrations in Boston the previous August, and a week later it reprinted a letter from Connecticut which warned that

> If the North Americans are stopt from making use of those lawful means to get money to discharge their debts which is justly due to their correspondents in London, what can be expected but that England must suffer by them?

That 'time' seemed indeed about to 'evidence these obvious truths' was confirmed on 28 October when readers of the Birmingham paper learnt that the value of American orders had fallen by £600,000 during the past eighteen months. Several further demonstrations were reported on 4 November, when Aris also printed a letter from a gentleman in Philadelphia to his friend in Bristol. This stated the Americans' objections to the stamp duty while continuing to emphasise both their willingness in principle to share the burden of imperial debt and their anxiety as honourable men to satisfy their commercial creditors in England. Though some interest was shown in the larger political implications of the American position the following week, when the paper noticed the receipt in London of the *Constitutional Courant,* the news sheet of the American Sons of Liberty,[19] the good faith of the colonial merchants and the serious commercial consequences that would follow any attempt to persevere with an unwise and impracticable policy were thus established as the dominant terms in which the crisis was presented to opinion in the West Midlands.

The region's reactions reached their climax at the turn of the year. Besides adding a further note of urgency by reprinting the New York non-importation agreement on 16 December, the *Birmingham Gazette* also kept its readers informed during the first part of the month of the meetings which were taking place in London between members of the Rockingham Ministry and Barlow Trecothick's committee of London merchants trading to North America.[20] When the latter, acting in collaboration with the Ministry, issued its circular appeal to the out-ports and manufacturing towns for their assistance in the agitation against the Stamp Act, Samuel Garbett joined Joseph Wilkinson and eighteen others to organise local support. At a meeting of Birmingham merchants trading to America on 23 December a committee was appointed to draft a petition to the House of Commons, together with a letter soliciting the help of members of the nobility and gentry likely to favour repeal.[21] During the following week a second request for action was received, this time from the Bristol Company of Merchant Venturers,[22] and on 6 January 1766 the *Birmingham Gazette* gave up a large part of its front page to a letter from 'A.B.' which warned that non-importation would affect everyone, minimised the seriousness of political disaffection in America and exonerated the commercial interest in England from any responsibility for the crisis. If this letter's special appeal to 'those who are of the first rank in our happy constitution' is any guide, it was either a public version of the appeal to the peerage prepared by Garbett and his colleagues on the Birmingham committee or was at least intended to support it. Orders, said the letter, had been falling since 1764, but the worst had come during the past year, when many of the colonists had taken advantage of the deterioration of relations to withhold payments to their British creditors. Loss of remittances had damaged the financial basis of the American market, and this in turn had affected the manufacturers, who were now left with surplus stocks of no value elsewhere. The Americans, having no specie, could not remit their debts, and they refused to open their ports to British goods. Those most seriously affected would be the labouring poor, who were threatened with reduced wages and unemployment at a time when provision prices were rising. Yet in spite of all this many still attributed the protests to selfish motives, while

> others will object to us the indecent behaviour of our colonists. But has this been universal? and has not the greater part of this perhaps been owing to a mistake of principles than to a general and avowed disobedience to Government? Besides, have we either encouraged or vindicated their extravagances? Shall this be of sufficient weight to exclude our remonstrances?

These seemed petty resentments when weighed against a situation which threatened the entire community, and self-preservation at the very least dictated united action to end the emergency by securing the repeal of the offending legislation.

Trecothick's appeal produced convincing results. Thirty copies were sent out, and between 17 and 29 January 1766 twenty-four out of a final total of twenty-six petitions for relief were received by the House of Commons, the majority of them in two large groups.[23] The first of these, presented on the 17th, consisted of ten petitions, led by that from London but otherwise coming predominantly from Lancashire, the West Riding and the Bristol area. In the second, presented on the 20th, the degree of concentration was even greater, for apart from two petitions from Frome and Macclesfield, which look like stragglers from the first collection, this group consisted of five petitions from Birmingham, Coventry, Wolverhampton, Stourbridge and Dudley. Though this suggests a considerable degree of local co-ordination in the West Midlands,[24] however, there are few surviving signs of any concerted action in the region; and while Garbett and his colleagues acted effectively enough so far as Birmingham itself was concerned, the town's reactions in fact leave a mixed impression. Over a fortnight elapsed, between 6 and 21 December, before the London committee's circular was answered. Admittedly the delay is easily explained: since the appeal was addressed not to anyone in particular but simply to the 'Chief Magistrate' of Birmingham, it was delivered first to a local Justice with no business connections, and did not reach Samuel Garbett and his colleagues until the 20th. The very fact that the delay can be explained in such terms suggests, however, that nobody in Birmingham had thought seriously of petitioning, let alone made any preparations to do so, before the letter from Trecothick's committee arrived. In this sense the town followed the lead given by the capital; but though Trecothick's committee was anxious to summon up provincial support it had to be very careful to avoid any hint that it was suggesting specific measures to the recipients of its circular letter, least of all that they should use a given form to petition outright for the repeal of the Stamp Act, since this would have made the whole demonstration of mercantile opinion seem far too blatantly artificial.[25] Assessment of the situation in the Birmingham area is therefore plagued by uncertainty. On one hand, there is no evidence of moves to petition before the London circular arrived; on the other hand, the lead from London itself did no more than solicit applications for relief in general terms, and left each locality free to follow its own line in producing them. Besides this, there are two other considerations to be taken into account: Birmingham was not among the centres which remained in regular contact with the London committee, and despite its heavy dependence on the American market the Birmingham area as a whole sent no witnesses to be examined during February 1766, when the House of Commons investigated the American disturbances and their effects.[26]

At least in the case of Birmingham itself, the answer to these questions lies in the very full extent to which the town took advantage of the freedom left to it by the terms of the London circular. Once the appeal from Trecothick's committee had prompted the initial move to petition, the Birmingham committee preferred to act through its own connections, particularly with the Earl of Dartmouth, who had the double recommendation of having a considerable personal interest in the West Midland iron industry and of being President of the Board of Trade in the Rockingham Ministry. Samuel Garbett had in fact had previous dealings with Dartmouth's department over other aspects of the iron industry,[27] and his main line of recourse when he assumed the leadership of the Birmingham merchants was therefore already established. When he answered Trecothick on 21 December he described the situation in the West Midlands and promised to provide information which would help the effort to relieve the crisis. Garbett did this, however, by forwarding the appeal to Dartmouth, together with a copy of his reply and a covering note, outlining facts to be presented to the forthcoming meeting in Birmingham and urging the necessity of repealing the Act. Four days later Dartmouth learned the result of the meeting through the same channel, and on 4 January 1766 the Birmingham merchants as a body sent their proposed petition for his approval, at the same time asking him to use the information which they had collected to avert the imminent danger of large-scale unemployment in the West Midlands.[28]

The value of this close contact was clear from the start. In correspondence with Dartmouth, Garbett and his colleagues felt free to go beyond the more cautious application for relief solicited by Trecothick's committee; and since their patron was present on 27 and 31 December at the two dinners given by Rockingham at which the first tentative outlines of the Ministry's eventual policy began to emerge,[29] the information which the Birmingham merchants provided was probably put to use even before their petition had been drafted or sent up. Certainly Dartmouth's statement in the House of Lords a few days later that 'not less than fifty thousand men in this kingdom were at this time ripe for rebellion for want of work from the uneasy situation in the colonies'[30] suggests that he amply fulfilled the expectations of his clients. Given these advantages, given also the fact that its principal spokesman was at precisely this time forming his own ideas on the techniques of industrial lobbying, it is not surprising that the Birmingham committee preferred such avenues of approach to the more exposed procedure of corresponding with Trecothick's committee and sending witnesses to be examined by the House of Commons. In fact, considered from the point of view of developing attitudes in the West Midlands, the most remarkable aspect of Birmingham's response to the Stamp

Act crisis is the extent to which it foreshadowed the town's reactions nineteen years later, during April and May 1785. This is apparent not only in the close contact which was established with Dartmouth, and in the decision of Garbett's committee to seek further support from the aristocracy, but also in the second series of appeals to the nobility and gentry which occupied Garbett personally during the first half of February. In these he again briefed Dartmouth with calculations designed to show the total effect of non-importation on the British economy. Despite this, however, he demurred at the suggestion that he or his colleagues should testify to the House of Commons, on the grounds that disclosures there would at best be abused by faction and at worst find their way to unfriendly ears on the Continent. Finally, in all his letters he tried to retain the good opinion of his landed patrons by balancing his warnings against further delay in relieving the crisis with strenuous denials of seditious intent in urging concession to the American position.[31]

The same characteristics were also reflected in the attitude of the *Birmingham Gazette*, whose reporting priorities at the time draw attention to another powerful reason why interests in the West Midlands remained comparatively reticent in their public reactions to the crisis, and preferred to keep their dealings with Westminster as confidential as possible. Though it reprinted a good deal of news from the London press and supplemented this with items from the out-ports, Aris's paper carried surprisingly little information on reactions within its own area of circulation. By the standards of later years, for example, the *Gazette* might at least have been expected to draw attention to the meetings of the Birmingham merchants' committee by an appropriate comment in its local news section. The only references to the meetings which the paper carried were two-line notices of their time and place on 23 and 30 December 1765. After the first week of the new year the same apparent neglect continued. Apart from a set of 'political questions' vindicating the Rockingham Ministry, which it reprinted from the London press on 13 January, and a letter from the capital on 3 February pointing out once more the dire consequences of persisting with the Stamp Act, the *Birmingham Gazette* took little further notice of the crisis. The presentation of the Birmingham petition went unreported, and so did that of the other applications from the West Midlands, until 17 February, when the paper remarked in general on the petitions which had been sent up from Birmingham, Sheffield and the other hardware towns. None of the latter were mentioned by name until the celebrations which greeted the news of repeal in Birmingham, Wolverhampton, Walsall and Stourbridge were reported on 24 March. Admittedly, 'A.B.'s' letter had been given pride of place on 6 January 1766, which suggests that Garbett and his colleagues were quite prepared to give their measures the degree of publicity they thought necessary; but once again the local news section had had no supporting comment to make. It did, on the other hand, spend several lines on the important meeting held at Wolseley Bridge in Staffordshire on 30 December 1765 under the leadership of Lord Gower, at which the promoters of the Trent and Mersey canal resolved to apply to the House of Commons during the next session for a Bill to put their plans into effect. The result of the application was, of course, a matter of crucial importance, and the measures taken to promote the canal reached their peak between 15 January 1766, when the original petition was presented, and 14 May, when the necessary Act of Parliament was passed. In the interval it was navigation business, concerned not only with the Trent and Mersey but also with other schemes dependent on the latter's success, especially the Staffordshire and Worcestershire canal, which filled the local columns of the *Birmingham Gazette*. The many petitions which were sent up from groups whose interests were affected also claimed a good deal of attention at Westminster,[32] and this during the weeks when American policy was being debated. Under these circumstances, and considering the political connections of Lord Gower, the Trent and Mersey's most powerful backer, Josiah Wedgwood's warning the previous November against offending supporters of the late Grenville administration, 'on some of whom we chiefly depend',[33] assumes an added force: West Midlanders had very material motives of their own for keeping their public reactions to the Stamp Act crisis within bounds.

The visible effects of the emergency on the political awareness of the region were thus comparatively restrained. The threat of disruption was severe while it lasted, but repeal brought relief, at least for the time being. The restoration of normal conditions after the constrictions of the previous year produced a rebound effect on trade as merchants and manufacturers alike worked to satisfy a backlog of orders from America, and now that their most material fears had been calmed few retained much interest in the less tangible aspects of the colonial problem. Of more immediate significance was the general rise in food prices after 1764.

On the evidence of the local minimum and maximum prices of a bushel of wheat quoted each week in the *Birmingham Gazette*, the scarcity of provisions was more serious and prolonged in the West Midlands than it was in London. In the capital the quarter of wheat, which had cost between 32s and 32s 6d during 1763–64, rose sharply during the autumn of 1766. After this it reached peaks of 50s in July and October 1767, fell slightly during the following winter, then rose again to 50s 6d in May 1768, and eventually resumed its former level by January 1769.[34] In Birmingham a rising trend was noticeable a good deal earlier than it seems to have been in London. During 1764 the bushel rose from a minimum of 4s (32s per quarter) on 16 January to between 5s 9d and 6s 6d (46s–52s per quarter) in early October, and remained at nearly the same figures for the rest of the year. Prices eased for the first three months of 1765, but rose sharply again to 6s 8d by 22 April, and reached 6s 10d (54s 8d per quarter) in late September before dropping by about a shilling for the remaining months. The first half of 1766 was easier as the bushel fell to between 4s 10d and 5s 4d in mid-June; but though this must have contributed to the sense of relief in the Birmingham area at the passing of the Stamp Act crisis, the recovery was short-lived. After July prices rose again until weekly maxima exceeded 7s at the end of September and reached a peak of 7s 6d (60s per quarter) on 22 December. The climax came in 1767, when minima as well as maxima stayed above 7s during the winter, and the bushel reached its overall summit of 9s 6d (76s per quarter) during the third week in March. Prices remained at nearly the same level for the next month, fell back a few pence during the summer and again eased slightly to between 7s and 8s during October and November. At the end of December they were still between 6s and 6s 8d, a high enough level but at least better than it had been. The worst was now over, but only by comparison with what had gone before, for minima and maxima were again above 7s between late February and early May 1768. After this they eased gradually to between 5*s* 6*d* and 6*s* by the end of the year. Only in 1769 did prices recover their overall stability through the year, and then only at a level between 1*s* and 2*s* higher per bushel than that of 1764.

Because its size made it an obvious place to be watched in case of trouble, Birmingham was less affected by the most direct consequences of scarcity than other smaller centres in the West Midlands. Thanks to prompt intervention by John Wyreley Birch, Esq., JP, the one resort to violence which did threaten the town, during the week of 29 September to 6 October 1766, was averted. A relief subscription was started; steps were taken to distribute provisions at reduced prices; on 8 October two troops of General Elliot's Light Horse were moved to Birmingham from Shrewsbury, and an armed force remained available for the rest of the winter. Emergency supplies were brought in from London at the end of March 1767, and these were followed in June and August by shipments of rice, which the *Birmingham Gazette* recommended as 'a good substitute for bread and meat', especially if boiled for three hours 'with half a pound of meat of any sort, salt or fresh'.[35] Other places were less fortunate. During the week when Birmingham faced its single real threat of violence riots were reported not only at Coventry and Wolverhampton but also at Halesowen and Alveley in Shropshire, and at Kidderminster, Stourbridge, Bewdley, Bromsgrove, Worcester, Gloucester and Cirencester. At the end of October supplies intended for the London market were threatened by interception in the Midlands; and though the deep snow and severe flooding which isolated many places during January and February 1767 may have discouraged further concerted intervention they must also have increased the hardship which the region had to bear. During the following April barges were held up on the Severn near Worcester, whence the dragoons had to be called out in November 1767 to defend the mills at Stourbridge and Kidderminster. Though the worst was over by 1768, the misfortunes of Worcestershire were not yet at an end. Blight, which had severely damaged the fruit and hop crops in 1767, was again reported during the following May, and the destruction was taken a stage further in June when the hay harvest was ruined by continual rain and a freak storm which produced hailstones three and a half inches in diameter.[36]

In assessing the way in which these events affected political and social attitudes in the West Midlands, both their place in the perspective of long-term developments and the more immediate reactions they provoked must be considered; for though these two aspects were obviously related to each other, the second did not point directly towards the first. Taken as a whole, the disturbances of the mid-1760s can perhaps be regarded as marking the first major stage in the closing of ranks against the threat of disruption from below which thenceforward characterised the social reactions of the established orders.[37] Certainly, levelling threats like that from 'Kidderminster and Stourbridge', which was pinned to the Gold Cross on Snow Hill in 1766,[38] gave some substance to talk of 'the spirit of insurrection' and lent urgency to such panicky insistences on legality as the *Birmingham Gazette*'s account of the riots at Alveley, which ended by saying that

> Instead of encouraging these poor unhappy wretches, a practice much too common in many towns, they and their encouragers should endeavour to use the most effectual methods, which *must* be *legal*, of reducing the Price of Provisions, and never can be done by tumult and violence.[39]

As this report more than half admitted, however, public reaction to the riots was characterised as much by sympathy as by calls for repression. The very terms in which Aris insisted on obedience to the law betrayed a consciousness that he was begging questions about who, in moral terms, was breaking it, and about what 'the most effectual methods' actually were. Two weeks earlier he had been noticeably more at ease with the example of *taxation populaire* set by several hundred Stourbridge colliers, who had helped to supervise proceedings at Kidderminster while grain was shared out at reduced prices.[40] In fact, though the Kidderminster millers exonerated themselves on this occasion by a prudent undertaking to 'set aside their own business in general to serve the poor', the general impression left by accounts of the riots is of a community of sentiment between magistrates and poor in placing the blame for scarcity on those who supplied the markets.

The context of this sentiment was of course the traditional code of paternal responsibility enshrined in the old Edwardian statutes against forestalling, re-grating and engrossing. Since these failed conspicuously when they were invoked in 1766,[41] it is not surprising that the old framework of interventionist regulation began thereafter to be seriously questioned. Just as the disturbances can be seen in retrospect to have marked the beginning of social reaction, so, therefore, it was at this time that the coverings of traditional sentiment began to be stripped once and for all from the dichotomy between the economics of *laisser-faire* and the 'moral economy' of the poor.[42] Though the final destination can once again be clearly discerned, however, the way towards it was not as direct as it may seem. Traditional concerns persisted, and the immediate call was not for the rejection of the policy of intervention but for it to be brought up to date and made effective. Criticism of local middlemen was now joined to demands for more extensive action. On 26 May 1766 the *Birmingham Gazette* told its readers that 'the midling sort may find that it is now high time to instruct their representatives to make a law to encourage the plow and to prevent depopulating pasturage'. The following September 'Y.Z.' attacked the corn bounty, urged Birmingham to lead a joint petition to Parliament from the manufacturing towns on the price of provisions and suggested that this should be the central issue at the next election. In November a petition was in fact sent up from Dudley, and the example was commended in the expectation that it would 'soon be productive of the most salutary results'. Six years later, when provision prices were again high, the same reactions followed. In April 1772 a meeting at Tom's Coffee House in Worcester resolved to address the city's Members of Parliament on the need for remedial measures, and in October 1773 William Kelly tried to exploit the vein of opinion represented by such 'useful instructions' by basing his by-election campaign at Worcester in part on his expert knowledge of the benefits to be gained from importing wheat from America.[43] In the long term these demonstrations of localised dissatisfaction at the apparent gulf between real problems and the indifference of the great may not have amounted to much. But they did help to produce the movement in defence of independence and freeholders' rights which developed in the West Midlands after 1768, and which expressed itself first in the regional repercussions of the Wilkite movement and after that in the popular antecedents of the Warwickshire election of 1774.

Sympathy and support for John Wilkes came from many places in the West

Midlands after 1768. In the cider counties, which overlapped with the south-western parts of the region, the response had already gone deep, giving as it did new and more pointed expression to an accumulation of local grievances.[44] In Worcestershire opponents of the cider tax in 1763 had used language already familiar to the small farmers and freeholders who had met only a few months earlier to condemn the Broad Wheel Acts. After five years of hardship, and with their crops ruined by blight, storm damage and floods, it is not surprising to find that in June and July 1768 the same resentment was showing itself among the farmers of Warwickshire and Staffordshire.[45] In November an address, signed by Henry Coles and Thomas Hayes of Wolverhampton, urged the freeholders of Middlesex to set aside any defamation of Wilkes's private character and, mindful of republican Rome, whose 'citizens voted as their soldiers fought', to 'vote at the next election for the County of Middlesex so that they may remain free . . . to preserve the Grand Charter of England in its pristine vigour and force'. Early in 1769 the gentlemen of Broseley presented Wilkes with forty-five gross of clay pipes, and in March the independent gentlemen of Shropshire met in Shrewsbury at the Raven to toast the survival of Wilkes and liberty.[46] During July a serial edition of Wilkes's life and political writings, set in Baskerville's type, and available from the agents of James Sketchley,[47] was widely advertised in the region, which marked the author's release from the King's Bench prison with appropriate festivities during April 1771.

Events in Worcester and Worcestershire have already been described, but this was only the most conspicuous example of the way in which the Wilkite movement affected local constituencies. On 26 June 1769 the *Birmingham Gazette* welcomed and recommended 'the spirited conduct of the Burgesses of Wenlock in scrutinizing into, and either censuring or approving the measures of their representatives'. In April 1771 an address from the burgesses of Stafford was presented to Brass Crosby, Lord Mayor of London and a staunch Wilkite, who had been committed to the Tower for obstructing the messenger sent by the House of Commons to arrest John Miller of the *London Evening Post*. Like the Wenlock enquiry, this too was recommended to readers of the *Birmingham Gazette* as an example to be followed, and doubts cast on the authenticity of the address, which was signed by neither mayor, aldermen nor principal burgesses, gave the paper an excuse to deliver a lecture on the rights of electors:

> We are desired from authority to inform the author of that most illiberal para-graph . . . that the address was signed by more than a majority of the resident electors. . . . If the author had not been as ignorant as he was illiberal, he would have seen that the address was not that . . . of the Mayor and Aldermen, but the address of the Burgesses. Every elector that has a vote and is a Freeman (and there was not a man who signed that had not), let his fortune or employment be what it will, has an equal title to a share in the community, and as such, is entitled to approve or disapprove of the conduct of the representatives in Parliament, or of any branch of the legislative power.[48]

Three months later, rumours reached Birmingham from Bridgnorth, then preparing for a by-election, that 'there will be an opposition, . . . and Mr. Sheriff Bull is talked of as a candidate'. Like Crosby, Frederick Bull, Sheriff of London and future Lord Mayor, was a leading supporter of Wilkes. In the event nothing materialised and the seat at Bridgnorth stayed in the Whitmore family, where it had been for all but three years since 1660 and where it would remain until 1870; but the mention of Bull's name and the possibility of a contest was enough to provoke a heated discussion of the Whitmores' title to represent the borough in the weeks before the election.[49]

These reactions do not, of course, indicate the existence in the towns affected of undiluted metropolitan radicalism. In each place the simple response to Wilkes was modified by long-standing local circumstances, which means that there were two sides to every incident. These can be seen tolerably well in the situation at Bridgnorth, but the clearest example is provided by the Wenlock enquiry of June 1769. At this the borough's representatives were given detailed instructions on matters ranging from the rights of electors, the defence of civil liberties, the punishment of corruption and the redress of American grievances (but 'in such a manner as to preserve in its full force the unquestionable controul of the British Legislature over them'), to the preservation of trade and industry by reducing the price of provisions and reducing the malt tax. After one of them had been given the chance to explain his parliamentary conduct, the enquiry ended with a vote of thanks to both the Wenlock Members. On the face of it this looked like a welcome subordination of representatives to their constituents, and this was how it was presented to the public. In fact the meeting was an example not so much of the electorate exacting obedience from its delegates as of an equal co-operation between two parties to a single mutually convenient compact, and the instructions 'probably expressed the Members' views as much as those of their constituents'.[50] The same kind of double image was produced five years later at Droitwich, the pocket borough of the Foley family, where the franchise was confined to the members of the corporation. When, on 7 April 1774, Andrew Foley succeeded to the seat which he was to occupy until his death in 1818, the *Birmingham Gazette* announced that 'to the honour of the burgesses of that borough (in conformity with the laudable example of the Independent Freemen of Worcester), be it remembered that to shew the freedom of their choice, they all strenuously insisted on defraying their own expenses'. Perhaps Aris remembered that in 1769 Thomas Foley, the head of the family and Member for Herefordshire, had raised a petition from the county against the Middlesex return, and perhaps this explains his enthusiasm; but even so, it hardly seems consistent in retrospect to speak of the 'strenuous' conduct of the only fourteen men privileged to vote at Droitwich in the same breath as the fight of the independent freemen in the populous franchise of Worcester.[51]

In its own place, each side of these reactions was more significant than the other. Bridgnorth, Wenlock and Droitwich were all constituencies where family patronage was a freely accepted part of the political scene. In Bridgnorth itself the most important aspect of the by-election controversy in 1771 was that the attack launched under the stimulus of 'Mr. Sheriff Bull's' possible candidature came to nothing, and that the Whitmore interest survived, even if it did look a little precarious for a time.[52] To the people of Birmingham, who were told that 'the out-burgesses of that borough, which are very numerous' had 'long time waited for the opportunity to pay their respects to the *Corporation*',[53] the rumour was more important than the eventual reality. In Wenlock, where one of the seats was filled by thirteen members of the same family, not counting relatives, between 1529 and 1885,[54] 'the free, safe, and peacable exercise of their rights' meant the burgesses' freedom to go on returning Foresters as they had done time out of mind. The readers of the *Birmingham Gazette*, however, were told that 'the spirited conduct of the Burgesses of Wenlock ... would ... convince the elected that they are the ministers, and not the masters of the electors'. As was the case with Sir Watkin Lewes's campaigns at Worcester, it was not so much the actual outcome of these reactions that was important so far as the political awareness of Birmingham people were concerned as the noise they made. Within this frame of reference Aris's enthusiasm for the 'independence' of the Droitwich corporation causes less surprise.

'Will you now submit to that yoke etc. etc.,' wrote 'Another Freeholder' in Aris's paper on the eve of the 1768 general election,

> is so bandied a phrase, and has ever been accompanied with such interested views (regardless of the discord which it may produce, and however much it may inthral you), that it would be insulting your judgement to suppose that your conduct could in any wise be influenced thereby, much less that it should produce an ungrateful return to those worthies whose easiness of access, and assiduity has been equally remarkable to their honour, in the event of every instance which they have undertaken for the service of their constituents. . . .[55]

The immediate effect of popular agitation on Birmingham opinion was thus not to create dissatisfaction with the Warwickshire representation but to confirm the town's confidence in the sitting Members, Sir Charles Mordaunt and William Bromley, Esq., who were returned without opposition on 30 March. Birmingham people did not need the scribblings of a London hack to tell them about liberty and independence; they had lived with the real thing:

> If the advertisement signed "A Freeholder" in the St. James's Chronicle of 24th instant has any other foundation than meaning to fill the Public Houses at Warwick on an approaching occasion, you may rely on the numerous appearance there from hence of many of the real Friends to Liberty, in support of those whose predecessors as well as themselves we have so long experienced to be exempt from any dangerous influence whatever, the importance indeed of which is so well known to every sect in these parts that it would be a matter of no small amazement should one individual amongst them (who has a regard to his character) be weak enough to show himself ignorant thereof.[56]

Twelve months later, however, at the by-election which followed the death of William Bromley, Birmingham was called on to show a more militant aspect of its unanimity than satisfied acquiescence in a settled arrangement. Warwickshire elections had been uncontested since the early years of the century; but though the *modus vivendi* which had been reached between gentry and aristocracy had hitherto remained undisturbed it was the latter, specifically the Barons Craven and the Earls of Warwick, Aylesford and Hertford, whose influence had been paramount in county politics.[57] Now the first signs of discontent began to appear as notions of independence among the freeholders, especially those of the Birmingham area, began to diverge from those held by their betters. On 13 March 1769 the *Birmingham Gazette* listed three other possible competitors for the vacant county seat besides Thomas Skipwith, the successful candidate. One of these, a Mr Partereche of Stratford on Avon, remained in obscurity. As sons of peers the other two, Lord Beauchamp and the Hon. Mr

Craven, were more remarkable, and the latter may indeed have thought that
he had some prescriptive claim to the seat which his father had held for
eighteen years before succeeding to the family title in 1764.[58] Birmingham
opinion, however, was unimpressed, and remained solidly committed to Skipwith, who was returned without a contest on 29 March 1769.

Since the town was involved at the time in a heated internal debate over
the final details of the Lamp Act, there was some justification for the special
credit which the *Birmingham Gazette* accorded to such 'unanimous zeal' on
the part of 'freeholders and inhabitants of every sect or denomination'. More
to the point, however, was John Freeth's 'Epigram on the Bill now Depending
for Removing Public Nuisances'.

> The Greatest nuisances we want
> Fairly from the land to shove,
> Are worse than any town complaint,
> And every day are seen above.[59]

In June 1770 Freeth again caught the mood of local opinion with his 'Extem-
pore on hearing that Mr. Skipwith was remarkably active in preventing the
exportation of wheat by opposing the motion in the House of Commons',
which plainly defied the old basis of Warwickshire politics:

> Strange! that the sons of Warwickshire,
> Whose ancestors on trial were
> For English Courage noted,
> Should so degenerate have grown
> As out of six to have but one
> On Freedom's side that voted.
>
> But though we of no more can boast,
> His name shall honest Britons toast
> And faithfully adore,
> And when the House dissolv'd shall be,
> SKIPWITH again shall chosen be,
> In spite of Lordly power.[60]

Added reasons for this defiance had been given by the events of the previous
autumn, when 'Lordly power' had prevented the Warwickshire freeholders
from petitioning against the Middlesex return.

During the summer of 1769 attention had been occupied by the various
activities and demonstrations in support of Wilkes which have already been
described. The progress of the Worcestershire petition was watched particularly
closely, and from the end of September onwards several writers in the *Birmingham Gazette* urged Warwickshire to follow suit. Most of these followed the lead
of the 'Several Independent Freeholders' who began by offering congratu-
lations on the impartial return of Skipwith earlier in the year, urged the county
to apply not to a manifestly corrupt House of Commons but to the Crown,
and advised the freeholders of Warwickshire to rely not so much on the
leadership of rank and quality as on their own numbers, 'for the lowest are
as much interested as the greatest whenever National Rights are invaded'.
More general advice came from 'Considerations for the Freeholders of Yorkshire and other electors of Great Britain' which were recommended to the

attention of the Warwickshire freeholders on 9 October. Like the 'Several Independent Freeholders', this pressed for a dissolution of Parliament; but as might be expected, coming as it did from the Marquess of Rockingham's county, it tried to avoid the hint of democracy implicit in pure numbers by stressing that the remedy sought was within the existing fabric of the constitution. The prerogative of dissolution had been left to the Crown specifically

> to be used for the benefit of the people, and in gracious compliance with their just desires whenever the representatives of the people appear to entertain a greater regard for their own power than for the rights of those who have chosen them. It is provided in order that the electors may have an opportunity by a new election of committing their affairs into Hands more worthy of their trust.

Thus 'the wisdom of the constitution has not left us without a remedy'; for the right to petition for a dissolution under such circumstances, which was declared by the Act of Settlement, was one of the first fruits of the Glorious Revolution. In this way the argument was elevated to the high plane of Whig constitutionalism, whence a week later it was swung towards that of classical republicanism by 'Tiberius Gracchus', who, true to his pseudonym, called for a dissolution and placed his final trust in the *virtù* of the people as the only sure remedy for political evils. Finally, on 23 October, 'Aemilius' brought the discussion back to home ground again:

> As Birmingham is a commercial town, whose very being depends upon the encouragement and success of trade, which can never prosper unless the General Liberties and Rights of the People are preserved inviolate, it is incumbent upon us to oppose with vigour any invasion of the Constitution. In this just cause, it is hoped the landed interest will join, and indeed, all parties concur.[61]

The landed interest was not so keen, however, and on 30 October the *Birmingham Gazette* reported 'several *important* visits among the Great', calculated 'to stem the torrent of petitioners in this extensive county and loyal town'. In particular 'a certain respectable Colonel of Militia', probably Lord Beauchamp, had spent several hours at Combe Abbey, the seat of Lord Craven; 'but we have not authority to say whether the virtue of the much admired young Lord resident there, or his esteem for the Rights and Prerogatives of his country and native county have in the least abated'.[62] These measures among the great were successful, and though it came close enough to doing so to be thanked for its efforts by the *Independent Chronicle* on 13 January 1770[63] Warwickshire was not after all among the petitioning counties in 1769.

The cause of Independence was nevertheless kept alive in Warwickshire by the diversity of political news from other parts of the West Midlands. In February 1772 'A Shropshire Freeholder' supported the nomination of Sir Watkin Williams-Wynn to succeed Sir John Astley as Member for the county in language which must have won applause from the men of Warwickshire, especially when he hoped 'that you will never suffer a union of Lords to elect your representatives'.[64] In Staffordshire, too, opposition, though restrained, was not entirely muzzled. Although Ministerial influence was expected to prevent a petition in 1769, the freeholders showed signs of forsaking their usual subservience and of presuming to instruct their Members, 'a right', said Aris, 'the immediate exertion of which, though perhaps not altogether consistent with good manners, is however highly necessary'.[65] Though no meeting was held, the possibility was not forgotten, at least not by the *Birmingham Gazette*, which was still harping on the same theme in its report of Lichfield races a year later:

> Notwithstanding the *state of dissension has not been seen in the County of Stafford for some time past, and the freeholders have return'd to their good manners*, we cannot help remarking that an inauspicious omen appeared at the races; viz, on Wednesday evening, forty five ladies dined at the ornary' and Junius won the plate.[66]

Latent opposition in Staffordshire, which was doubtless maintained by Richard Whitworth's exploits in the county town on behalf of Brass Crosby, showed itself again in April 1773 in an address which brought the time-honoured attack on placemen and septennial Parliaments into harness with the cause of Dissenters' rights. As 'Friends to the Civil and Religious Liberties of Mankind' the freeholders of the county were urged to think ahead to the next general election, and to join the rest of the nation in 'nobly endeavouring to extirpate from the senate those tools of corruption and slaves of power, who on matters of public importance only watch the signal of the minister to give their voices'.[67] As it revealed by alluding to 'men whose actions betray a spirit of bigotry utterly repugnant to the cause of Christian Liberty', this address was particularly provoked by the recent rejection of Sir Henry Houghton's second Dissenters' relief Bill, in which Sir William Bagot, one of the Staffordshire Members, had played a prominent part.[68] Bagot's 'faithful steady endeavours . . . to vindicate the most essential doctrines of the scriptures agreeably both to the Declaration of the Church of England and to the Toleration Act' were defended the following week, and at the Staffordshire election in 1774 he was returned unopposed together with Sir John Wrottesley: but not before 'many freeholders in Wolverhampton' had promised their votes to any two 'whom their constituents may depend upon as friends of the fundamental principles of the Constitution' and had pledged themselves to do their utmost to prevent the return of 'those implicit tools of despotism whose detested names stand recorded in Miller's black catalogue'.[69]

Though it was only in the Hemlingford Hundred of Warwickshire that it achieved sufficient concentration to exert decisive influence, the movement of opinion which was to carry Sir Charles Holte to victory in 1774 was thus very far from being confined to this area alone. During the preceding six years it had, to a greater or lesser extent, affected all four of the counties adjacent to Birmingham as well as most places of any significance within them. Nevertheless it is not surprising that the cumulative effects of events and rumours of events elsewhere should have been most marked in the region's largest centre of population, especially when the means through which the latter could discuss and assimilate the increasing volume and variety of news had expanded so much since 1768. Already the first order paper of the Free Debating Society on 21 March 1774 had hinted that, given the chance, the freeholders of Warwickshire would try to avenge the repression of 1769.[70] At this stage, however, as much could equally well be said with regard to southern Staffordshire: there too the freeholders had showed signs of restlessness at intervals since 1769. But their potential opposition was never given the opportunity to develop further, and the 'many freeholders in Wolverhampton' were still looking in vain for suitable candidates on the eve of the general election. A successful attack on the established pattern of Warwickshire politics would need more behind it than the Free Debating Society. It would need a leader behind whom the voting power of the independent freeholders could be rallied. More important, it would need the right opportunity; for, despite everything that had happened since the last election, any opposition would have to overcome the profound inertia of an electorate whose first concern was still likely to be the peace of the county. As yet the date of the general election was unknown; no suitable candidate had declared himself, and the right opportunity neither existed nor looked like doing so. Preparatory organisation was thus out of the question, and although political interest in Birmingham did not flag during the summer of 1774 the town was occupied with the affairs of Worcester rather than with those of the home county.

The general election was not in fact due until 1775, and by dissolving early the Ministry imposed a tight schedule on the entire proceedings. So far as Warwickshire was concerned, however, the most important piece of news was not the dissolution itself, proclaimed in London on 1 October 1774 and probably not common knowledge in the Birmingham area until Aris printed it on the 3rd, but Sir Charles Mordaunt's decision not to seek re-election. It was this that made the prospect of a contest real and gave the independents their opportunity; for only in the event of a vacancy could they avoid the odium which would have damned any attempt to oust a sitting Member in a county undisturbed in living memory. Mordaunt's retirement was not announced until 4 October, which meant that, unless the *Birmingham and Stafford Chronicle* printed it on the 6th,[71] the news had to wait until the *Birmingham Gazette* carried it on the 10th before it reached the county at large. By that time only three days remained before the nomination meeting at Warwick, and another week after that before the poll began.[72] Thus, if the chronology of announcements in the local papers is any guide to the rate at which news reached the people of the Birmingham area, they had a possible thirteen days, and probably only ten, in which to organise support for a candidate of their own choosing to replace Mordaunt.

For different reasons the other side also had to make, or rather remake, its plans in a hurry. Mordaunt's retirement probably came as less of a surprise to his friends than it did to the county at large, and there must already have been some speculation among those from whom, in the normal course of events, his successor could expect to be chosen. Among these the favourite was Lord Guernsey, the eldest son of the Earl of Aylesford, and steps were taken to smooth the way towards his unopposed succession to the county seat. Besides the influence of his own family, Guernsey had the support of Lord Craven at least among the other magnates of the county. In order to secure as much interest as possible in the Birmingham area, his mother wrote on his behalf to Matthew Boulton, and he was the subject of an anonymous newspaper puff which reported that 'it seems to be the prevailing sense of the freeholders ... that they cannot place the sacred deposits of their interests in better hands than those of Lord Guernsey.'[73] There seems little doubt that it was from Guernsey, as the original choice to replace Mordaunt, that the freeholders of Hemlingford Hundred first recoiled, and thus broke a record for uncontested general elections in the county which stretched back to 1705. Lord Craven met with such rebuffs from the freeholders that he instructed his friends and tenants to abstain at the election and departed for Berkshire in high dudgeon, leaving behind him a letter to Sir William Wheeler which was to be read to the nomination meeting. Having stated his preference for Lord Guernsey and his refusal to support 'ANY OTHER NOMINATION', Craven went on to 'flatter myself' that 'had it been my inclination to have disturbed the peace of the county, ... THE MEANS WERE IN MY POWER'. Nevertheless, he said, he would not

> depart from those principles I have always acted on, which have ever been, to promote the Peace and Tranquillity, as well as the prosperity of those counties where I have any property, to act with Independence myself, and to support those only WHO GIVE ME THE FULLEST ASSURANCES of holding the like conduct.

It was probably just as well that this rather futile piece of foot stamping was not in fact read out at Warwick on the 13th,[74] and Craven showed more petulance than sense by having it printed, complete with capitals and italics, in the *Birmingham Gazette* on 17 October, where it can only have added to the stigma which hung about the 'Lordly' interest. No doubt his pride had been injured, but it is hard to imagine how Craven could have done more to ruin whatever chances the interest had. His departure deprived Guernsey of one of his chief backers, and by instructing his friends and tenants to abstain he placed valuable votes beyond the command of any other candidate. Faced with the prospect of a close and unexpected contest, and with his position weakened by Craven's defection, Guernsey kept quiet at the nomination meeting. Instead of standing as a candidate himself he supported John Mordaunt, who by all accounts had had no previous intention of offering himself in his father's place.

As candidates for the vacant Warwickshire seat Holte and Mordaunt were thus both last-minute choices. In this respect they started equal, but otherwise the advantage lay with the former. Any edge which Mordaunt might have gained from his more influential backers was more than neutralised by the confusion in which he had replaced Lord Guernsey. On the other hand, while it would have been impossible in the time available to have drummed up enough votes for Holte *ex nihilo*, this was not necessary, because there already existed in the Birmingham area a large body of potential support, alert and at least partly organised thanks to events elsewhere, which could be transferred to the home county with little extra effort once the prospect of a contest became a reality. It was this that first threw the 'Lordly' interest into disarray by provoking the hot-headed reaction from Lord Craven which destroyed Lord Guernsey as a candidate, and then overwhelmed Mordaunt at the election. John Freeth's Constitutional Society, with its Worcester connections, may have disappeared from the record, but even as it did so the Independent Constitutional Society of the Freeholders of Warwickshire was meeting at the Swan inn to celebrate Holte's victory. By 1775 the title of this body had become simply the Independent Constitutional Society.[75] Probably it was little more than a loose confederation of the different groups whose interests had coincided in Holte's candidature, and there is no sign, in the newspapers at least, that it continued to meet after 1775. Nevertheless the reason given in that year for the postponement of the society's anniversary meeting—that the early meeting of Parliament 'will prevent the attendance of several of the members'[76]—suggests that it had attracted a fair amount of attention. In particular the presence of Robert Lawley's name on the Independent Constitutional Society's first notices in 1774 suggests that the future 'member for Birmingham' was already cultivating his prospective constituency.

All this, however, happened after Holte's election, not before it. In the first instance the independent freeholders owed their victory not to organisation but to the fact that when the unexpected turn of events in October 1774 gave them their chance to fight they were in a position to take advantage of their good luck. Both the newspaper discussion which accompanied the contest and the evidence of the poll book which was published soon after it ended show that, while Holte's support in the Birmingham area was almost unanimous, it was not very highly co-ordinated. The attitude of the *Birmingham Gazette* was ambiguous. The paper is supposed to have 'stood firmly by Mr. Mordaunt'[77] throughout the contest, and this is certainly the impression left by its report on 17 October of the nomination meeting at Warwick. This recommended Mordaunt as a man of '*sense and sound judgement, diligence* and application to business', and referred to his 'sensible, eloquent and manly speech', in which he promised ('putting his hand upon his breast') that he would 'discharge his duty in Parliament... with honour and independency'. On the other hand, Aris, whose reporting of the various 'opposition' incidents during the previous six years had been sympathetic, used much the same language on the same page to describe Isaac Hawkins-Brown's popular but unsuccessful challenge at Tamworth to Thomas de Grey and Edward Thurlow.[78] Also, again in the same issue, Aris printed a letter which, without actually mentioning any names, gave voters respectable and cogent reasons for placing public duty above private loyalty and for supporting Holte in preference to Mordaunt as

> the man who, from known *abilities and integrity* is more likely to serve the county at large, but particularly this populous and commercial town, which at the present aera requires in our representatives the utmost vigilance, activity and ability to promote (perhaps to preserve) its consequence.

Thus, whatever its original intentions may have been, the *Birmingham Gazette* tried in fact to remain as impartial as possible, and in the event Samuel Aris himself, far from supporting Mordaunt, followed the advice of his own correspondent and voted for Holte and Skipwith.[79]

Aris may be forgiven his equivocation. Common prudence normally required that he avoid offending his readers by avoiding excessive commitment to any single point of view. In its reporting of regional politics during the past six years the *Birmingham Gazette* had accordingly run the gamut of phrases and words connected with the notion of Independence, applying them without much discrimination to each incident in turn. By so doing the paper helped to foster the generalised movement of opinion which produced the upset in October 1774. This demonstration that the people of the Birmingham area preferred the independence of Sir Charles Holte to that professed with equal fervour by John Mordaunt caught the *Gazette* by surprise, and it had hurriedly to discard any lingering loyalty it may have felt to the traditional arrangement of county politics in order to recognise the changed disposition of the greater part of its readers. Besides, Aris was not alone in his confusion. If anyone might have been expected to show a concerted preference one way or the other it was the merchants and gentlemen of the Bean Club. Yet if the club's records are compared with the Warwickshire poll book the most striking feature which emerges is that, out of a total of sixty-three members listed in the minutes up to the time of the election, only a third actually voted at Warwick. Granted, some of the remainder may well not have been qualified to do so, or may have voted in other constituencies; but the Bean Club was precisely the sort of body whose members were interested in politics and likely to own the freeholds which would enable them to express their interest at the county hustings. How many of them took their lead from Lord Craven, himself a club member, is impossible to say, but it seems likely that a good part of the Bean Club's membership abstained at the election. Of those who did vote, and whose votes can be confidently attributed, nine chose Mordaunt and Skipwith; nine, possibly thirteen, preferred Holte and Skipwith, and a possible two more plumped for Holte. The Bean Club was in two minds, and the election to its membership of Lord Guernsey and his younger brother, the Hon. Charles Finch, only two months before the county contest must have made confusion worse confounded, especially as the stewards at the time were, of all people, Thomas Skipwith and Sir Charles Holte.[80]

It is true that of the twenty-four members of the Birmingham Book Club in 1775 the ten who voted all supported Holte rather than Mordaunt, and that of the twenty-seven subscribers to the Old Meeting recorded in the poll book all save two did likewise; but neither of these examples amounts to very much when the numbers involved were so small, and when the vote of nine-tenths of the Birmingham area went the same way in any case. In fact the concentration of Holte's support in the townships of Hemlingford Hundred, which produced 1,175 of his 1,845 votes, conceals almost as much as it reveals. Though the daily totals of votes cast for Holte were highest on the first four days of the poll, they did not equal those cast for Mordaunt, who remained comfortably in the lead at that stage. It was not until the eighth of the ten days that Holte overhauled his opponent, largely because his own support did not tail off so fast, which suggests that it took time for Holte's friends to make up for their late start. The size of the Hemlingford Hundred vote also hides the fact that Holte picked up useful majorities in townships elsewhere in the county, and conversely that he suffered some reverses on his home ground. Thus in Barlichway Hundred Bidford and Lapworth both returned strong majorities for Holte, and so did five smaller places. In Kington Hundred, Holte was conspicuously successful at Stourton, Tanworth and Whichford, while in Knightlow Hundred he was strongly favoured at Flecknow and Napton on the Hill. In addition sizable Holte minorities were polled for Henley in Arden, Stratford on Avon and Warwick. On the other hand, in Hemlingford Hundred itself Berkswell, Bickenhill, Chilvers Coton, Coleshill, Hampton in Arden, Meriden, Polesworth and Nether Whitacre all preferred Mordaunt.[81] Whatever the truth of rumours that he was acting under orders from Lord North, Sir Roger Newdigate's steward was certainly busy recruiting for the 'Lordly' party in the area north of Coventry,[82] which explains why Holte was in the minority at Chilvers Coton, and why he had to contend with a respectable showing for Mordaunt from Nuneaton, even though he had a majority there.

These variations in the dominant pattern mean that, though the return of Sir Charles Holte showed social differences between the Birmingham area and the rest of Warwickshire,[83] and demonstrated for the first time the crude voting strength of the north-western part of the county, the sources of the independent freeholders' strength were rather more diffuse, even if they were most conspicuous in Hemlingford Hundred. The most basic of them was the feeling that in recent years, and particularly since the suppression of the movement to petition in 1769, the aristocracy of Warwickshire had betrayed the spirit of the arrangements which had served the county for so long. In addition to this, some part was played by Protestant Dissent. Though the voting of the few Old Meeting subscribers who went to the poll proved little itself, Holte showed himself very sensitive to the implications of the situation in the Leicestershire by-election in December 1774,[84] and there was also a rough relationship between the distribution of Dissent in the county and that of Sir Charles's support. Of the places in Hemlingford Hundred, other than those immediately adjacent to Birmingham, which gave him their votes, Atherstone and Tamworth at least contained well established Dissenting communities. The reverse was also true, at least at Berkswell and Meriden. Here Dissent was weak, and so was Holte's support.[85] In the absence of comprehensive information it is impossible to say how consistent this relationship was, but it may explain the presence of sizable Holte minorities in such towns as Stratford on Avon and Henley in Arden.[86] Beyond this the search is more difficult. Juggling with groups, samples and poll book comparisons leads to the temptation to speculate on the results as if they contained the kind of objective 'pro' or 'con' information which is claimed for modern opinion surveys. But little enough is understood about voting behaviour today, and if the eighteenth century electorate was smaller, its behaviour was influenced by a very different and equally complex set of variables. The most that can be done to explain the presence of enclaves of Holte support far removed from Birmingham in the agricultural south of the county is to invoke a combination of possible factors. Thus, for example, Napton on the Hill, described in 1772 as an open field parish containing four families of 'anabaptists' and a licensed meeting house,[87] may have been less amenable to 'Lordly' patronage than other places in the area. At Bidford voting was probably influenced by Sir Francis Skipwith, patron of the living, father of the continuing Warwickshire Member and himself a supporter of Holte at the election. At Tanworth, in Kington Hundred, several of whose freeholders actually lived in or near Birmingham anyway, the same role was played by Lord Archer, whose own political connections were with the Whig corporation of Coventry and who was to act as one of the stewards of the Independent Constitutional Society in 1775.[88]

One thing is certain, however: whatever else he may have been, Sir Charles Holte was not in any real sense 'the nominee of the Birmingham Manufacturing Gentry',[89] a description which implies a degree of premeditation which did not yet exist. During the years before 1774 attention was drawn on a number of occasions to Birmingham's special need for some kind of representation, and this certainly played its part in Holte's return. But whatever the connections between them, the political discussion which filled the newspapers was conducted in the language of ancient Whiggery and freeholders' rights, not that of commercial and industrial ambition. Holte, past middle age and not very fit,[90] was hardly the best qualified of men to 'take the lead in considering our commerce as a matter of politics',[91] and there was little in common between the attitude of the independent freeholders of Warwickshire and that revealed by Samuel Garbett in 1772 when he told Matthew Boulton that 'nothing but real and well known landed property joined with Ministerial Connections can make a Bank at Birmingham so lucrative as to be worth your or my notice as principals'.[92] Two years later, with the crucial decision about to be made on the renewal of James Watt's patents, Boulton had added reasons of his own for sharing Garbett's general point of view. Before the election Lady Aylesford asked for his help on her son's behalf, and after it John Mordaunt thanked him, together with 'the rest of my friends at Birmingham', for his 'zealous endeavours to serve me'. It comes as no surprise, therefore, to discover that though Boulton himself did not vote at Warwick, John Fothergill, his partner in the toy trade, did: for Skipwith and Mordaunt.[93] Without Garbett, Boulton and Fothergill, three of its most prominent leaders, a formed 'Birmingham interest' can hardly be said to have existed, let alone be claimed in support of Sir Charles Holte.

It could indeed be argued that if anyone was originally intended to be 'the nominee of the Birmingham manufacturing gentry' it was Lord Guernsey. Birmingham's manufacturers attached considerable importance to the patronage of the fashionable world—witness the attempts which were made to attract aristocratic tourists to the town; Guernsey's family lived in the area;[94] he had just been elected to the Bean Club; his chief backer, Lord Craven, was already a club member, and was soon to add to his own Birmingham connections by giving his patronage to the General Hospital. The logical way to construct a 'Birmingham interest' would have been to base it on the influence of the two leading families in the northern half of Warwickshire, and to hold it together by means of the Bean Club. This may have been the original intention. Had it succeeded it would have produced a situation much closer to that which did in fact develop in the 1780s, when Guernsey, by then Earl of Aylesford, played a prominent part in Birmingham affairs, than that which immediately followed Holte's return. For the present, however, two obstacles stood in the way of any such plans. The first was the popular revulsion against 'Lordly power' which had destroyed Guernsey's prospects. The second was the disagreement which now divided Birmingham's own leaders; for the truth was that the merchants and manufacturers of the town, who had been united in their reaction to the Stamp Act nine years previously, were soon to show themselves fiercely at odds with each other in their reactions to the coming crisis in relations with the Thirteen Colonies. Within three months of Holte's election the extent of their differences was made quite plain. By the end of January 1775 the House of Commons had received two petitions from Birmingham, one asking for conciliation, the other urging the enforcement of the Coercive Acts. Not until the causes of these two diametrically opposed expressions of opinion from the same place had been removed, or until changed circumstances had deprived them of their importance, would Birmingham's leaders be able to make deliberate use of the potential advantages won for the town in October 1774.

NOTES

1 *Garbett–Lansdowne Letters*, I, Garbett to Lord Rawdon, n.d., May 1784.

2 Wedgwood to Bentley, 20 May 1780, *The Selected Letters of Josiah Wedgwood*, pp. 250–1.

3 Christopher Wyvill, *Political Papers* (York, 1794–1808), IV, 157: Priestley to Wyvill, 14 February 1782.

4 *Cf.* E. C. Black, *The Association*, p. 50, for plans suggested in 1780 by Gamaliel Lloyd of Leeds for correspondence with Birmingham and other manufacturing centres; *Aris*, 13 January 1783, 31 January, 21 February 1785; Wyvill, *Political Papers*, loc. cit., and IV, 458: Wyvill to Boulton, 31 January 1785, 'having understood from several friends how much you are disposed to give every important assistance in the cause of Political Reformation', and especially *A.O.P.*, P. Deane of Broseley to Boulton, 28 January 1785. Deane's letter expressed serious doubts about the efficacy of the proposals of Wyvill and Pitt, and enclosed a much more extensive plan of reform, which Boulton was urged to publish. Since this plan corresponded exactly with that of 'A Real Reformer' in *Aris*, 31 January 1785; and since Boulton's papers also contain several broadsheet copies of this address, still in mint condition, it seems probable that the Birmingham leader acted on Deane's suggestion.

5 See below, pp. 212–13.

6 *A.O.P.*: request from Thomas Anson and Thomas Gilbert for Boulton's vote and interest at Lichfield, n.d., 1768; request from Anson and Sir John Wrottesley, 1 July 1802, for Boulton's presence during their forthcoming canvass of Lichfield, and several papers concerning the Bridgnorth election of 1802, when Boulton and Watt helped to mobilise Birmingham voters at short notice on behalf of Isaac Hawkins-Brown and J. Whitmore.

7 *V.C.H. Warwicks.*, VII, 275–6, lists them. *Cf.* also J. M. Norris, 'Samuel Garbett and the early development of industrial lobbying in Great Britain', and Eric Robinson, 'Matthew Boulton and the art of parliamentary lobbying', *Historical Journal*, VII (1964), 209–29.

8 *V.C.H. Warwicks.*, VII, 85, 273.

9 For the pattern of immigration into Birmingham, *cf.* W. H. B. Court, *The Rise of the Midlands Industries*, pp. 47–50, and R. A. Pelham, 'The immigrant population of Birmingham, 1688–1726', *T.B.A.S.*, LXI (1937), 45–80. A full-scale study of this pattern and its implications along the lines established by E. A. Wrigley in 'A simple model of London's importance in changing English society and economy, 1650–1750', *Past and Present*, 37 (1967), 44–70, would be of great value.

10 *Aris*, 10 May, 14 June 1790.

11 Stafford, County Record Office, Leveson-Gower MSS, D 593 S/16/10/5.

12 *The Letters of Josiah Wedgwood*, I, 57–8, Wedgwood to Bentley, 27 September 1765. The 'burrough in our county' was probably Stafford, where a by-election was held on 4 March 1765 (*Hist. Parl.*, I, 375–6).

13 Stafford, County Record Office, Dyott MSS, D 661/19/2.

14 *Aris*, 8, 15 November, 6 December 1762.

15 *Aris*, 16, 30 May, 6 June, 25 July, 8 August 1763.

16 See above, pp. 24–7.

17 See below, p. 260, and *Aris*, 15 June 1767.

18 Rudé, *Wilkes and Liberty*, p. 194.

19 For the Sons of Liberty and the *Constitutional Courant* see Edmund S. and Helen M. Morgan, *The Stamp Act Crisis: Prologue to Revolution* (Chapel Hill, N.C., 1953, rev. edn, New York, 1963), p. 257.

20 For Trecothick's committee, its role in the mobilisation of commercial opinion during the Stamp Act crisis and its relationship to the Rockingham Ministry see Lucy S. Sutherland, 'Edmund Burke and the first Rockingham Ministry', *Eng. Hist. Rev.*, XLVII (1932), 46–72, especially pp. 59–68, and, more recently and extensively, two unpublished theses in the University of Sheffield by D. H. Watson, 'Barlow Trecothick and other associates of Lord Rockingham during the Stamp Act crisis, 1765–66' (M.A., 1958), and 'The Duke of Newcastle, the Marquis of Rockingham and mercantile interests in the provinces, 1761–68' (Ph.D., 1968). For the politics of the crisis in general see P. Langford, *The First Rockingham Administration* (Oxford, 1973), and P. D. G. Thomas, *British Politics and*

the Stamp Act Crisis: the First Phase of the American Revolution, 1763–67 (Oxford, 1975).

21 For the steps taken by the Birmingham committee see Staffordshire Record Office, Dartmouth MSS, D(W) 1778/America/130, 132, 147: Garbett to Dartmouth, 21, 24 December 1765, 4 January 1766. The other eighteen who joined Garbett and Wilkinson were William Russell, Samuel Galton, Samuel Richards, John Startin, John Twigg jr., William Welch, Sampson Freeth & Son, John Russell, Samuel Walford, Joseph Smith, Thomas Bedford, Thomas Fletcher, John Gold, John Lane, Thomas Westley, Thomas Ward, James Dallaway, George Dallaway. From these a working committee was struck, which on 4 January 1766 sought the additional support of Earls Huntingdon, Denbigh and Gower, Lord Craven and the two Warwickshire Members, Sir Charles Mordaunt and William Bromley.

22 Watson, 'The Duke of Newcastle, the Marquis of Rockingham and mercantile interests', p. 352 and n. 154.

23 For details see *Commons Journals*, xxx, 462 ff.

24 This point is made by Watson, *op. cit.*, p. 353.

25 Watson, *op. cit.*, pp. 351, 353–4.

26 See *Commons Journals*, xxx, 513 ff. The witnesses are thoroughly analysed in Watson, *op. cit.*, pp. 367–74.

27 See his correspondence with William Burke in Public Record Office, State Papers, Domestic, George III, SP 37/4, and with Dartmouth, *H.M.C. Dartmouth*, III, 180.

28 Dartmouth MSS, as cited, n. 21.

29 Watson, *op. cit.*, pp. 355–7; Langford, *First Rockingham Administration*, pp. 131–2.

30 Cited by C. R. Ritcheson, *British Politics and the American Revolution* (Norman, Okl., 1954), p. 42, n. 7.

31 Northants Record Office, Fitzwilliam (Milton) Burke papers, A xxvi 18: copies of Garbett to Colonel Isaac Barré, Sir Roger Newdigate, John Mordaunt, Esq., Earl of Denbigh, Earl of Shelburne, Sir Charles Mordaunt, Earl of Dartmouth, 5–13 February 1766.

32 For details see *Commons Journals*, xxx, 451 ff. The Staffordshire and Worcestershire canal received its enabling act on the same day as the Trent and Mersey.

33 See above, p. 26. This interpretation is again corroborated by the behaviour of Samuel Garbett, who told Shelburne on 6 February 1766 that he had instructed Aris 'not to insert an article' on the Stamp Act 'but what he may copy from the London papers', and whose reluctance to appear on the American question did not deter him from planning to show himself in London on navigation business within the next fortnight. Cf. Fitzwilliam (Milton) Burke papers, A xxvi 18: Garbett to Sir Roger Newdigate, 5 February, to Shelburne, 6 February 1766.

34 Rudé, *Wilkes and Liberty*, pp. 188–9.

35 *Aris*, 6, 13 October, 22 December 1766, 30 March, 6 April, 8 June, 10 August 1767.

36 *Aris*, 22, 29 September, 13 October 1766, 20 April, 16 November 1767, 30 May, 13, 20 June 1768; *Calendar of Home Office Papers, George III*, II, 90–1: circular to the High Sheriffs of Warwickshire, Nottinghamshire, Leicestershire, Staffordshire and Derbyshire re. interception of provisions.

37 For a full account of the disturbances see W. J. Shelton, *English Hunger and Industrial Disorders: a Study of Social Conflict during the First Decade of George III's Reign* (London, 1973).

38 '... there is a small Army of us upwards of three thousand all ready to fight
& I'll be dam'd if we don't make the King's Army to shite
If so be the King & Parliment don't order better
we will turn England into a Litter
& if so be as things don't get cheaper
I'll be damd if we don't burn down the Parliment House & make all better ...'
Cited by E. P. Thompson, 'The moral economy of the English crowd in the eighteenth century', *Past and Present*, 50 (1971), 76–136, at p. 127.

39 *Aris*, 13 October 1766.

40 *Aris*, 29 September 1766.

41 For the particular reasons for the failure see Shelton, *op. cit.*, the argument of which is summarised below, pp. 246–9.

42 For this see Thompson, *op. cit.*

43 *Aris*, 22 September, 10 November 1766, 27 April 1772; *H.M.C. Dartmouth*, II, 179: Kelly to Dartmouth, 30 October 1773, asking permission to print a paper on the import of grain and the price of provisions, which he had sent to Dartmouth the previous May, in the hope that its circulation would help his chances at Worcester.

44 Rudé, *Wilkes and Liberty*, pp. 175, 187–8.

45 See above, pp. 31–2.

46 *Aris*, 7 November 1768, 9 January, 6, 13 March 1769.

47 See above, pp. 122, 149 n. 10.

48 *Aris*, 29 April, 13 May 1771; Rudé, *Wilkes and Liberty*, pp. 158–64.

49 *Aris*, 19 August, 2, 16 September 1771; Rudé, *Wilkes and Liberty*, pp. 166, n. 1, 170, 195; *Hist. Parl.*, III, 631.

50 *Hist. Parl.*, II, 450.

51 *Aris*, 11 April 1774; *Hist. Parl.*, I, 423–4; II, 444–5; Rudé, *Wilkes and Liberty*, pp. 122–4.

52 Evidence of popular opposition to the established pattern came not only in 1771 but also in 1774, when Richard Asprey tried to raise support on the grounds that the town had been too long represented by strangers. Asprey was unsuccessful; but in 1784, when Isaac Hawkins-Brown was invited to stand by the resident burgesses, Whitmore lost his customary place at the head of the poll, and held on to his seat only by maintaining a judicious neutrality between Brown and Hugh Pigot, the third candidate. *Cf. Hist. Parl.*, I, 362–3, 376, II, 123, III, 279, 281, 631; *Aris*, 13 June, 17 October 1774.

53 *Aris*, 2 September 1771.

54 *Hist. Parl.*, II, 451.

55 *Aris*, 30 March 1768.

56 *Ibid.*

57 *Hist. Parl.*, I, 399–400.

58 Lord Beauchamp was the eldest son of the Earl of Hertford. The Hon. Mr Craven's father, William, fifth Baron Craven of Combe Abbey, near Coventry, represented Warwickshire between 1746 and 1764. (*Hist. Parl.*, II, 275.)

59 *Aris*, 20 March 1769.

60 *Aris*, 4 June 1770.

61 *Aris*, 25 September, 9, 16, 23 October 1769.

62 *Aris*, 30 October 1769. The young Lord Craven, who had only recently succeeded his father, found himself in a quandary. Being so nearly related to an ex-county Member, the freeholders looked to him for sympathy and leadership. This, however, Craven was not disposed to give. He was in fact devoting his political energies to the courtship of the Coventry freemen, whose triumph over their corporation and simultaneous conversion to the support of the Ministry have been described above, pp. 66–9.

63 Rudé, *Wilkes and Liberty*, p. 133, n. 3.

64 *Aris*, 24 February 1772.

65 *Aris*, 13 November 1769.

66 *Aris*, 1 October 1770.

67 *Aris*, 19 April 1773.

68 Barlow, *Citizenship and Conscience*, pp. 186–7.

69 *Aris*, 26 April 1773, 10 October 1774.

70 See above, p. 111.

71 Unfortunately, this copy of *Swinney* has not survived, so the presence or absence of any reference to Mordaunt cannot be checked.

72 The nomination meeting was arranged for the 13th; the poll began on the 20th: *Aris*, 10 October 1774.

73 For Craven's support, see his letter to Sir William Wheeler in *Aris*, 17 October 1774, quoted below; for the approach to Boulton see *A.O.P.*, undated note from Lady Aylesford. The newspaper puff is quoted by *Hist. Parl.*, I, 400, but no source is given.

74 See the note which preceded the letter when it was printed in *Aris*.

75 *Aris*, 7, 14, 21, 28 November 1774, 16 October 1775.

76 *Aris*, 23 October 1775.

77 Langford, *Birm. Life*, I, 212.

78 Aris commiserated with Brown on his defeat. Had he started his canvass at the same time as his opponents, he would have won handsomely. Even so, considering that he did not offer himself as a candidate until three days before the election, the result did him

honour. 'After returning thanks in person to the one hundred and eighteen that polled for him totally uninfluenced', Brown 'left the town most deservedly beloved. In short, to point out all Mr. Brown's virtues would be endless; let it suffice to say that he is truly good, generous and just.'

79 *The Poll of the Freeholders of Warwickshire*, 1774, p. 24.

80 For details of Bean Club voting see appendix III. Guernsey and his brother were elected to the club on 10 August, when Holte and Skipwith were chosen as its county stewards for the year. See Bedford, *Minutes*.

81 For details see appendix III.

82 *Newdigate*, CR 136/box 17, unnumbered fragment addressed to Sir Roger Newdigate, dated Arbury, 13 October 1774. Rumours that Newdigate's steward was acting on instructions from Lord North were denied in *Aris*, 24 October 1774, repeated on 21 November, and denied again, by affidavit, on the 28th.

83 *Hist. Parl.*, I, 400, notes that 134 'Esquires' and seventy-seven 'Reverends' voted for Mordaunt, compared with ninety-nine and thirty-three respectively for Holte.

84 See above, pp. 109–11.

85 See descriptions of Atherstone, Tamworth, Berkswell and Meriden in Lichfield Joint Record Office, B/V/5, Visitation returns, Diocese of Coventry and Lichfield, 1772.

86 The explanation of the appreciable minority of freeholders at Warwick itself who voted for Holte is, however, more complicated. Here the division between Church and Dissent did not become important until the late 1780s; but in 1774 the Castle interest, which had increasingly dominated Warwick politics since the death of Henry Archer in 1768, was strongly challenged in the borough election by Robert Ladbroke, a London banker with an estate at Idlicote. Ladbroke stood on behalf of the independent 'Gentlemen's party', and his defiance of 'Lordly power' in the borough may have had local repercussions on the county contest. Cf. *V.C.H. Warwicks.*, VIII, 502.

87 Lichfield Joint Record Office, B/V/5.

88 For Bidford and Tanworth see Mary Ransome, ed., *The State of the Bishopric of Worcester, 1782–1808* (Worcestershire Historical Society Publications, new series, 6, 1968), pp. 191–2, 208–9. For Lord Archer, who sat for Coventry in the corporation interest from 1761 to 1768, and was recorder of the city from 1769 until his death in 1777, see *Hist. Parl.*, II, 26 and *Aris*, 16 October 1775.

89 *Hist. Parl.*, I, 400.

90 *Hist. Parl.*, II, 634. Sir Charles, born in 1721, was only sporadic in his attendance at Westminster. Ill health forced his retirement in 1780, and he died two years later.

91 Garbett's phrase in his letter to William Burke, 4 May 1766 (State Papers, Domestic, George III, SP 37/5/78), 'someone is sorely needed, who is not only intelligent but hath enlarged views, to take the lead . . . etc').

92 *A.O.P.*, Garbett to Boulton, 5 January 1772.

93 *A.O.P.*, John Mordaunt to Boulton, 11 November 1774; *The Poll of the Freeholders of Warwickshire*, p. 10. Fothergill voted as a freeholder at Moreton Bagot. For Boulton's political connections and motives at this time, especially with regard to Watt's patents, see B. D. Bargar, 'Matthew Boulton and the Birmingham petition of 1775', and Eric Robinson, 'Matthew Boulton and the art of parliamentary lobbying'.

94 At Great Packington, near Meriden, which is half way between Birmingham and Coventry.

VIII

THE WAR FOR AMERICA

Though the Warwickshire election of 1774 provided a means of achieving political expression for the uneasiness among the independent freeholders which had affected most parts of the West Midlands during the preceding years, the apparent decisiveness of the result concealed real uncertainty. Even within the limits imposed by the absence at this stage of a concerted 'Birmingham interest', by the improbability that Sir Charles Holte would have been its first choice as a representative if such an interest had existed and by the absence of any clear intent in the voting of the Bean Club, the division of opinion revealed by the contest did not follow predictable lines. Given, for example, the nature of Holte's support and the rumoured connections between the 'Lordly' interest and the Ministry; given also the part played by Matthew Boulton, both in the election and in the Birmingham loyal address three months later, it is tempting to assume that a vote for Holte in 1774 was a vote against the Coercive Acts, and that support for Mordaunt implied the opposite. In many cases this may have been true—Boulton was subsequently attacked on such lines—but it was not necessarily so. Of the eighty-seven listed by Boulton in January 1775 as likely supporters of the loyal address, only twenty-three had voted the previous October, fifteen of them for Holte and a mere eight for Mordaunt.[1] The pattern is the same as that produced by examination of the Bean Club: a large majority who either could not or did not vote, and confusion among those who did.

This confusion was one instance of the general uncertainty produced by the continuing dispute with the thirteen colonies, now about to reach its climax in the War of American Independence. This posed problems of peculiar difficulty, not only for British statesmen and commanders, but also for British opinion. Pitted against adversaries who could not be regarded as full belligerents, since it was claimed that they always had been and should continue to be members of the same polity, yet adversaries who for all that could hardly be treated as common traitors, the imperial government sought an absolute objective, the overthrow of the revolutionary regime. This, however, could not be achieved by total war, even if such a thing had been logistically and strategically feasible, since such a solution to the military difficulties would destroy any chance of solving the problems of political reconciliation which would have to be faced when the fighting ended.[2] It was the indeterminate nature imposed on the war by these limitations on policy which carried the most serious implications for British opinion. As the uncertain conflict wore on, perceptions of its nature changed, until what had started from the point of view of the mother country as the punishment of a dissident minority, the logical conclusion of the disciplinary legislation enacted during 1774, ended by raising fundamental questions of political obligation. It was in these larger problems that the particular divisions that affected the political experience of the West Midlands had their ground.

The American struggle has recently been described in successive sentences as 'the last great war of the *Ancien Regime*', and then as that in which 'there first appeared the fearful spectacle of a nation in arms; and the *odium theologicum* which had been banished from warfare for a century returned to distress the nations'.[3] Given the complexity of the struggle—part embittered strife among the colonists themselves, part regular engagement between British arms and the forces of the Congressional government, part limited war between Britain and France, fought for high but conventional stakes—there is no contradiction implicit in this. It is not, however, entirely true that the *odium theologicum* was confined to the other side of the Atlantic while the European participants, their leaders reluctant to run the risks to social stability entailed in the popular participation which was the price of total war, remained unaffected by the conflict's deeper implications.

At one level this may have seemed the case. Despite its manifest inadequacies the Ministry of Lord North did not fall until the independents in the House of Commons finally withdrew their support after Yorktown.[4] In this respect it could be argued that despite everything which had happened the working of British politics did not, in its essentials, deviate very far from its usual pattern. But this did not mean that the country at large remained undisturbed. Though the movement for reform led by the Yorkshire Association aroused as much misgiving as enthusiasm from a political nation made apprehensive by the violence of the Gordon riots, the very breadth of the spectrum covered by the political views of the reformers is evidence enough of this, even if diversity did prevent the opposition from commanding sufficient parliamentary support to bring the Ministry down before Cornwallis surrendered. Similarly, it may be true that, as belligerents, Britain and France 'were not divided by fanaticism', and that they 'observed the rules'.[5] Nevertheless it was the French intervention in 1778, coming on top of the arrival the previous December of news of General Burgoyne's surrender at Saratoga, that changed the nature of the war in the eyes of most Englishmen and immeasurably deepened the issues it raised. 'It is not the question whether we shall assert the right of taxing the Americans,' wrote 'a Citizen of Coventry' in January 1778, 'but whether we shall exist as a nation.'[6] At this stage war with France was still only a threat, but it is only necessary to read John Wesley's *Journal* at this time to be aware that the *Coventry Mercury*'s correspondent was not alone.[7] Granted, Wesley's point of view was a special one, and his impressions were coloured accordingly; but he was in a unique position not only to observe the reactions of the nation at large but also to influence the basic attitudes of a growing body of opinion within it. Eighteen months later the Channel was commanded by an enemy fleet for the first time in ninety years. The real danger of invasion in August 1779 may have been exaggerated, but the panic was real enough. Like 'most of those who have the fullest intercourse with God', Wesley remained confident that 'our enemies will never be permitted to land in England'.[8] Others, however, were not so sure, either about this or about what they should do to prevent it. 'Patriotism' may have been 'as evident as in other crises',[9] but patriotism in the circumstances of 1779 raised baffling questions. Josiah Tucker was probably right to reassure the faint-hearted that an invasion could not succeed unless it was joined by republican risings in England and Ireland, but Josiah Wedgwood at least found the tendency of Tucker's argument obnoxious, especially when it seemed to imply that England's safety lay in the prejudices of priests and papists.[10] Patriotism and the problems of conscience which it raised when its demands conflicted with political conviction; evangelical fervour; signs that anti-gallican chauvinism threatened to overstep 'the rules'—during the Gordon riots M. Potet, the paroled prisoner of war engaged as French tutor to the Wedgwood children, went in fear of his life;[11] 'the fearful spectacle of a nation in arms'—the American example was specifically held up to the people of Birmingham for emulation in June 1782 when Lord Shelburne was trying to raise volunteer corps for national defence:[12] despite Nathaniel Wraxall's assertion that 'no fears of subversion, extinction, and subjugation to foreign violence, or to revolutionary arts, interrupted the general tranquillity of society',[13] much that was to be characteristic of the greater crisis of the following decade can be found foreshadowed in the British response to the war for America.

The initial policies of Lord North and his colleagues commanded wide approval and wider acquiescence. In the 1774 election the American question was raised as an overt issue only in a handful of constituencies. The friends of America in Parliament were weak in numbers, divided among themselves and bereft now of the support withoutdoors which had enabled them to secure the repeal of the Stamp Act in 1766. The appeal to public opinion against the Coercive Acts early in 1775 produced no clear response, and the several conciliatory petitions presented to the House of Commons were balanced by a similar number asking for the opposite. Burke, already disappointed by the London petition's reluctance to express 'any preference for one system of American Government over another', had to suffer the mortification of seeing every request for conciliation manoeuvred into the hands of what he rightly called a committee of oblivion. When the Rockingham Whigs again tried to salvage the remnants of the old alliance out of doors later in the year they did so not with any real confidence but rather as a last attempt to regain some sort of footing from which to continue what was left of their opposition. They found the merchants 'gone from us, and from themselves'. In 1774 the treaty of Kutchuk-Kainardji between Russia and Turkey had opened large alternative outlets for British trade in eastern Europe, and these, together with the heavy demand produced by the war effort across the Atlantic, had cushioned the effects of the closure of the American market. The best the Whigs could do was to try to separate 'the sound from the rotten contract hunting part of the Mercantile Interest' and to 'revive the importance of the City of London'. This, however, meant that they had to steer their support down a virtually non-existent path between the court on one side, and 'the hands of the Wilkeses, Olivers, Hornes, Mascalls and Joels' on the other. In late September 1775 the Marquess of Rockingham was complaining bitterly to Burke at the rash of loyal addresses provoked by the activities of the London radicals, whose sympathy with the American extremists was as abhorrent as the attitude of the Ministers themselves. Despite the efforts of the Whigs, the greater part of British opinion was convinced that American resistance ought to be broken, and, during 1775–77, was confident that it would be.[14]

Nevertheless the coming of war created new divisions and aggravated old ones, both of which deepened as the years passed. One of the most characteristic British responses to the rebellion, and one peculiarly calculated to inflame domestic prejudice, was to take refuge in the belief that it sprang not from the

Americans' own deluded will but from a conspiracy between a few colonial
dissidents and a band of levelling fanatics at home. It was in places where older
quarrels still smouldered that the divisive effects of this belief in subversive
collusion were most conspicuous. Such was the case in Coventry, where, from
first to last, *Jopson's Coventry Mercury* kept up a stream of scurrilous invective
against corporation dissenters, patriots and anyone who presumed to criticise
British policy. It was not hard for the paper to shift its attention from the
'*Brethren* and *Friends*' of Mr Joseph Craner, the 'ANABAPTIST currier', who had
inaugurated his second term as mayor of Coventry in October 1771 by toasting
'the immortal memory of OLIVER CROMWELL', to the 'Devil's Emissaries on
earth to spread abroad the seeds of sedition and rebellion', whose 'infamous
libel under the title of the "Fall of Britain"' was summarily burnt on a public
bonfire in Coventry market place in December 1776: both sets of men were
'impelled by the fanatical leaven of the last century'. In August 1777, scornful
of 'any attempt that may be made hereafter to infringe it by a YANKEE DOODLE',
the *Coventry Mercury* repaid rebel fanaticism in kind by reproducing an advertisement from the *Boston Gazette* calling for the extirpation of the loyalists
as an 'example of American Government' derived directly from the regicide tyranny of the New Model Army.[15] After Saratoga the ability to whistle in the
dark which enabled the paper to belittle its correspondents' fears of French intervention, and to present General Burgoyne's march as a military exploit sur-
passing that of Xenophon and the Ten Thousand, was sustained by further
attacks on the patriots at home. On 23 February 1778 an address in *Piercy's
Coventry Gazette* calling for the dismissal of a 'wicked and sinful Ministry,
notoriously incapable of anything but reducing this once happy country to
infamy and ruin', was denounced by 'Portius' as a 'fanatical popgun' and its
author apostrophised as 'endeavouring to annihilate the monarchic part of the
constitution, and to reduce the rest to a factious democracy'. Such a one 'ought
to be excluded from the indulgence of his CIVIL AND RELIGIOUS LIBERTY and the
NATURAL RIGHTS of mankind. But such are the glories reserved for MODERN
PATRIOTISM.' In 1780 'the instigators of the pernicious associations', as they were
called by Colonel Holroyd in his election address to the freemen of Coventry,
were accused of deliberately undermining the unity of the nation in order to fulfil
their own prophecies of disaster, and the General Meeting of Deputies from the
Associated Counties was denounced as a seditious convention intended to coerce
Parliament itself. A year later the chairing song, with which the *Coventry
Mercury* celebrated the return for the city of Holroyd and Yeo after one of the
longest, bloodiest and most corrupt elections of the century, again coupled the
vices of the corporation to the supposed friends of America, and sounded its
own note of chauvinism.

> Of the Charities too may we never lose sight;
> May all deeds of darkness be soon brought to light;
> Our vile Corporation far hence may we drive,
> And honesty then shall by honesty thrive.

> 'Tis but right boys, that they who *New* England prefer
> Should be banished the *Old* and transported to her.
> Let them *there* cant and lie, utter treason and pray
> While we truth and loyalty's dictates obey.[16]

Much of this, it is true, was mere rant on the part of a paper whose politics had long been a notoriously apoplectic shade of blue, written for a particular audience whose reactions would have been dominated by the old animus between Church and Dissent even if there had been no American question to inflame them. The prejudice shown by the *Coventry Mercury* was not, however, confined to partisan journalism in the provinces. In his sermon to the Society for the Propagation of the Gospel on 21 February 1777 Archbishop Markham of York warned of the dangers of faction and the limits of toleration, attacked the Whigs for their support of the American cause and threatened the Dissenters for their share in it. So effective were these cathedral thunders that nine months later Edmund Burke told Charles James Fox that the Dissenters, 'the main effective part of Whig strength', were still 'rather intimidated than provoked at the denunciations of the court'. It was in these circumstances that Burke tried to account for the ineffectiveness of Whig politics and the uncritical public acceptance of the Ministry's American measures by postulating a 'resurrection of the Tory Party', in which the clergy were 'astonishingly warm'.[17]

According to Burke, the Tories, who 'universally think their power and consequence involved in the success of this American business',

> no longer criticise, as all disengaged people in the world will, on the acts of Government, but they are silent under every evil, and hide and cover up every ministerial blunder and misfortune with the officious zeal of men, who think they have a party of their own to support in power.

This reveals more about the state of Whiggism than it does about the revival of the Tories. Burke was writing before Saratoga; after it, far from being so integral to 'their power and consequence' that it inspired each and every putative Tory with party spirit and drove them to cover up for the Ministry, 'this American business' left many of them just as bewildered and confused as the members of Burke's own party had been before news arrived of Burgoyne's surrender. In Staffordshire, for example, Josiah Wedgwood found at the end of December 1777 that 'our Anti-Americans now think that the war would be ended in the best manner we could wish, by granting the Americans all they have hitherto ask'd us for, but acknowledge this is rather to be hoped for than expected'.[18] Though North's Ministry did not fall until 1782, the resurrection of the Tories as a specific party to be supported in power was a figment of Burke's Whig imagination. Nevertheless the fact that the old terms were again being applied to the political scene is an indication that, though their effectiveness and precision are dubious, those who used them were aware once more of a genuine polarity in the country. This may be difficult to trace through the kaleidoscope of faction groups and personal followings which was the immediate reality of English politics, and Burke may have been mistaken in taking abstention from criticism for positive commitment to a revived Tory party. But he was right to notice signs of change in the outlook of the nation, signs which showed most clearly in the two things to which he drew particular attention: in the predicament of Dissent and, if not in the warmth of the clergy as a whole, then at least in a different temper among a significant part of their number.

The years before 1775 had seen the culmination of the Dissenters' first attempt to recover their full civil and religious liberties. Effectively begun in

1767 following Lord Mansfield's judgement in City of London *v.* Allen Evans, Esq., this had based its hopes partly on the Dissenters' proven loyalty to the Hanoverian succession, partly on its coincidence with the movement within the Anglican Church led by Archdeacon Blackburne for a relaxation of the requirements relating to subscription to the thirty-nine articles, and partly on the belief that, since one section of the established Church itself was thus seeking accommodation for scruples of intellect and conscience, the time was ripe for an appeal to the candour of an enlightened legislature.[19] These movements, which at this stage were brought to an end by the defeat of Sir Henry Houghton's Dissenters' relief Bills and the rejection of the Feathers Tavern petition during 1772 and 1773, produced two immediate results. On one hand, the close connections which had been formed between the leading Dissenters, the instigators of the Feathers petition and the radical supporters of the American cause, accelerated the tendency of the Dissenters to transfer the emphasis of their arguments for civil and religious liberty from the reiteration of historic justification to the claiming of natural rights. On the other hand, the same connections provoked the first signs of the division between the *avant-garde* and the more traditional members of the Dissenting interest which was to leave the so-called Rational Dissenters so isolated after 1790. Already support for Houghton's Bills had been offset by a declaration against them from Dissenting ministers, mainly in the lesser centres outside London, who were uneasy at the position which was being imposed on them by their self-appointed leaders.[20] The hostility the interest encountered during the war widened the division and increased the reluctance of many Dissenters to become involved in opposition to the Ministry. No doubt simple commercial prudence had as much to do with it as anything else, but in February 1775 Josiah Wedgwood found that Ministerial propaganda, distributed in Manchester and other manufacturing towns by Dr Roebuck of the Carron iron foundry in order to prevent and counteract conciliatory petitions, was having 'a very considerable effect amongst many, Dissenters and others'.[21] Whatever it was, the effect must have lasted, for in May 1779, when the affairs of the nation were approaching their worst, Wedgwood learned from a Mr Godwin of Gatacre that the Dissenters in the north-west were still quiet: so quiet, indeed, that, despite a rather reluctant readiness to grant the Americans their independence if that would bring the war to an end, their politics seemed almost 'Tory':

> ... Mr. G. is a very good and loyal subject: indeed I may say, a very thorough friend of the King and his ministers, & he is persuaded that a majority of the dissenters in Liverpool, Lancashire and Cheshire are the same; but he should continue so not a moment longer than his conviction of any serious attempt against the liberties of the people, either civil or religious. At present, he is perswaded all is well; at least that the ministry would have done no worse things than another ministry would have done in the same situation, and therefore we ought to be quiet. . . .
>
> I was pleased to find that Mr. G. was for Peace with America, even upon the plan of independence: but then it seems we must not acknowledge, or give it up to them—No, that would be too mortifying for our high stomachs. We must sulkily clear the ground & let them take it. As much as to say—Go to the D--l in your own way. I well know this plan was not of my friends own projecting, & could not help grieving that any good man would stoop to pick up so mean & worthless a fardel. . . .

So much for politicks. In religion we did not *dispute*. I believe Mr. G. knew my
sentiments on those matters, we therefore only *conversed* & that upon such points
as we were not likely to differ in. We agreed . . . that the dissenting interest was
on the decline & something should be done if possible, even upon political
principles, to support it. Here I reverted a little gently to the dissenters having,
many of them, deserted the good old cause of Whigism & Liberty & become
advocates of prerogative & toryism. We went farther upon this subject than I can
follow in writing, but the best argument for the dissenters *changing their position*
I found was, that the popular part of our government was grown too strong in the
last reign, witness the Jew Bill & some others being given up to the clamors of the
populace. It was therefore thought requisite to assist the crown a little in the
present, to bring the political scale to an equilibrium again!!!22

Much of the difficulty of understanding what lay behind both Wedgwood's
perplexity at the vagaries of Dissenting opinion in 1779 and Burke's assessment
of politics two years earlier lies in the language which both men used. They
expressed the problem in terms of an antithesis between Whig and Tory; but
though the two words were both alike used as political labels their content was
not really similar. Though Burke admitted that the Whigs had 'not yet learnd
the application of their principles to the present state of things', Whiggism still
signified a fairly specific body of consciously held political traditions and
attitudes. A revived Toryism, if such a thing existed in any sense of the
word, sprang from something less definite: from the deeply engrained social
reflexes which accompanied a profound belief in the principle of subordination.
From this point of view the simple antithesis between Whig and Tory dis-
appears, and most Englishmen in the 1770s would have claimed to be both:
Whig in their acknowledgement of the Revolution of 1688, in their loyalty to
the Hanoverian succession and in their belief in the conventions of mixed
government as the only guarantees of real liberty; Tory in their attachment to
a Crown which, though it no longer wielded the prerogatives of its predecessors,
remained an essential part of a society of whose hierarchical order it was both
symbol and head. So far the inconsistencies of this combination had been
successfully subsumed in the aspirations of a nation conscious of its strength,
eager to play a leading part in the world and convinced of its right to do so, since
it alone had achieved the reconciliation of true liberty with necessary authority.

The War of American Independence exposed once more the anomalies which
underlay this hybrid confidence. For all the success of its oligarchic exponents
during the preceding half-century Whiggism still retained from its seventeenth
century origins an element of anti-authoritarianism which could no more be
fully squared with aristocratic connections than its ideal of liberty could be
contained indefinitely within the framework of the British nation and its
imperial destiny. The results can be seen not only in the difficulties which beset
English Whiggism at the start of the war, but also in the problem of patriotism.
The very word was ambivalent, used equally to abuse factious rebels who were
endangering the nation by their republican politics and to appeal to national
virtue in time of danger. In peacetime the complexities of patriotism could
remain undefined. In previous wars, fought against recognisable enemies for
ends generally approved, this undefined but powerful sentiment had helped to
fuse together the disparate elements in the nation's consciousness. In the war
for America it divided those elements once more because doubts about the

justice of the struggle, and therefore about the precise meaning of patriotism, were at the centre of British reactions. Josiah Wedgwood found that these impinged even on his manufacturing plans. Because the cameo medallions of prominent personalities which he was making might be construed as reflecting political preferences, which might in turn be detrimental to a business that depended to a great extent on sensitivity to the foibles of its customers, Wedgwood had to be careful in his choice of subjects. In July 1777 he discussed with Thomas Bentley the advisability of making casts for medals of Gustavus III of Sweden, who 'had just enslav'd a kingdom', and an unnamed American, probably either Franklin or Washington. 'It cannot be right,' Wedgwood wrote, 'to celebrate them both. Perhaps neither. I may think one of them worthily employed, but many circumstances may make it highly improper *for me & at this season* to strike medals to his honor.' From these thoughts Wedgwood was led in his next letter to a general consideration of the problem:

> My objections to striking medals from the Bronze you sent me rather increase. It would be doing no service to the cause of *Liberty in general*, at least so it appears to me & might hurt us very much *individually*. Nay the personage is himself at this time more absolute than any Despot in Europe, how then can he be celebrated in such circumstances as the Patron of Liberty?—Besides, if France should declare herself openly an ally & c & c I am from that moment an enemy to both, & the case being very probable I would not bring myself into so whimsical a situation as you may easily conceive, by throwing these circumstances together a little in your mind. I might add, that as the two Powers may be said to act really as Allies against us, though for political reasons without the form of a public declaration, the event of this conceal'd warfare may be more fatal to us than an open rupture & I may as a subject of the British Empire declare myself an enemy to all its enemies & their allies though I may curse most bitterly those who have brought us to this dilemma of calling those our enemies who were & might have continued to be, our best friends.[23]

Despite this rationalisation Wedgwood was obviously uncomfortable especially when he had to equivocate again later in the year by insisting that his subscription to the relief fund for American prisoners of war be kept secret, 'for reasons I can give you in plenty'. Two years later, during the national emergency of August 1779, when Wedgwood's resolution that 'I may as a subject of the British Empire declare myself an enemy to all its enemies' was put to the test, it was no easier to keep than it had been to make. At the meeting held to decide what steps the county of Stafford should take to help the raising of extra forces, several voices were raised against any idea of subscription whatever and Wedgwood was caught halting between two opinions. He could not but approve of Mr Eld, who 'in these days of our humiliation and despondency which should be a time for learning wisdom' wished the county to address the King 'and humbly beseech him to grant such terms to his late subjects in America as free men may expect'. Equally to the point was Mr Anson's attack on a Ministry which allowed Parliament to remain in recess at such a time and expected voluntary subscriptions of doubtful legality to tide it over the emergency, when a proper vote of supply was the only fair and constitutional way of raising the necessary money. On the other hand, the danger of invasion seemed to be very real and very near; and, unconvinced by those who believed it 'better to fall a prey to a foreign enemy rather than defend ourselves under the present ministry', Wedgwood was ready to 'defend the land of my nativity, my family and friends against a foreign foe, where conquest and slavery were inseparable, under any leaders—the best I could get for the moment, and wait for better times to displace an obnoxious minister, and settle domestic affairs'.[24] Nevertheless it was not an easy decision, and he must have been secretly relieved when the passing of the immediate threat of invasion enabled him to distinguish between necessary help in time of trouble and 'my free will offerings', which 'I shall keep back ... till measures are pursued more agreeable to my political creed'.[25] For men who believed that the nation's only true justification lay in service to a cause wider and more ideal than the prerogatives of Englishmen the moral demands of patriotic duty posed problems to which there were no easy answers.

Those for whom the righteousness of the British cause was self-evident may have been spared such heart-searching, but the war as it progressed sat no easier with the 'Tory' element in the nation's consciousness. With this the enforcement of imperial authority may have been more consistent; but to it, as Burke maintained, the success of the attempt was also more essential, and the plain fact was that this was unattainable. Even *Jopson's Coventry Mercury* admitted this when, in April 1778, it devoted its 'Miscellaneous Repository' in successive issues to an apologia for the Carlisle Peace Commission, sent to negotiate with Congress after Saratoga, which acknowledged that

> We were at war with a country, not with a particular set of men. . . . In vain were battles fought and victories gained in a country itself containing nothing to reward the victors, and whose extent, by affording back retreats, secured the vanquished from the consequences of defeat.[26]

What Burke and Wedgwood both saw, as the truth of this became increasingly apparent, was not the Toryism of positive party commitment, nor yet that of full grown reaction, but rather what might be called the Toryism of Doubt which preceded it: the essentially apolitical response of those who, faced with a situation beyond their powers of understanding or influence, gave up the conscious effort to grasp what was happening and retreated into the conventions and attitudes of their own familiar world. So frustrated and disillusioned were the Tories of Staffordshire in the early months of 1778 that Wedgwood found them sharing much of his own disgust at the apparent nonchalance with which Lord North had tried to avoid a frank recognition of necessity in his speech to the House of Commons on the Carlisle Peace Commission:

> I have not seen a paper in the public prints, nor a speech in the House that has handled this recantation at all to my satisfaction, nor made that use of it to expose the absurdity, folly and wickedness of our whole proceedings with America, which the Minister's confessions and concessions have given ample room for. You will perhaps say that the Minister has done all this so fully and effectually himself that he has left no room for his friends in the minority to assist him. Something of this kind may be the case, but some of the most violent Tories here abuse him most heartily and kindly offer me their assistance in that line to any extent I please.—D--n him, they say, could not he resign like a man without exposing himself so shabbily, and meanly filching Lord Chatham's plan in order to continue himself in place under the next administration? These people are quite chop-fallen and dismayed, and nothing but half a score of Highland, Manchestrian and Liverpool regiments amongst us will raise their malignant

spirits again, or enable them to look any man who has not been as mad as themselves in the face.[27]

The following autumn the state of the nation was no longer a thing the Staffordshire gentry cared to talk about. At dinner after a meeting in September on the enclosure of Needwood Forest, 'we had a few words on politics and but a few, for everyone seem'd very guarded'. Perhaps the presence of a Crown agent inhibited discussion on this occasion, but though this was not the case a month later, when Wedgwood entertained his neighbours at Etruria, the same constraint prevailed after dinner, when 'we had but little discussion upon politicks, the company being so much divided upon that subject, it might have broke in upon our harmony'. The following summer even Josiah himself, who was about as close to political Toryism as George III was to American republicanism, found 'a wonderful propensity, with the Ostridge and our wise governors, to thrust my head into a bush, and seeing no danger, believe there is none'. There seemed to be only one sensible thing to do: to leave politics to other people and get on with his business—assuming, of course, that the two could be separated.[28]

To some extent, uncertainty was overridden by the intervention of the Bourbon powers, which, by creating an immediate threat from the nation's traditional enemies, gave the doubters a situation in which their duty was clear. However, confidence so severely shaken as that of most Englishmen had been by the accumulation of reverses which had befallen their country since 1763 required an internal restorative as well as an external stimulus. The country did not lack energy; it was the assumptions on which it was to be exerted and the direction which the exertion should take that were in doubt. England's predicament therefore called for a response which was both comprehensive explanation and remedy; which, instead of shattering, would knit up the ravelled threads in the nation's consciousness. This was sought in the notion of divine punishment. In this way failure itself could be presented as a sign that God still watched over His Englishmen, and fast-day jeremiads which bewailed the sickness of the nation, its pride, luxury and godless vanity, looked also for the fruits of contrition. 'And he said, I will not destroy the city for ten's sake': it was Jehovah's answer to Abraham's intercession for Gomorrah that gave John Wesley his text for the National Fast on 10 February 1779; but though this awful example remained as a warning to heedless sinners it was to the fortunes of another biblical city that Wesley turned during the months which followed. 'Now is the time, at this awful crisis,' he wrote in July, 'for the inhabitants of the land to learn righteousness—who knoweth but God may be entreated of us as He was for Nineveh?' By the end of August the evangelist had been vindicated by events. As he told his congregation at Bristol on 5 September, 'the Lord sitteth above the water-flood; and the Lord remaineth a King for ever'. Ahithophel had retreated in confusion from Plymouth Sound, and if any further proof was needed of God's hearing prayer it could be found 'in the malignant fever which has broken out in their fleet and already destroyed several thousands of men'. Once the danger was past the lesson could be enforced and its future retention made doubly sure by such threepenny tracts as *An Estimate of the Manners of the Present Times* and *Hymns for the Nation* (omitting, however, specific items 'for the loyal Americans' and 'for the conversion of the French'), large numbers of which were sent on Wesley's instructions to the Methodists of Leeds, Sheffield and Newcastle during April 1782.[29]

The call to humiliation and repentance *in angustiis* thus provided the nation's sense of its own destiny with a future vehicle of formidable power. It would be wrong to attribute entirely to the American crisis a process which achieved its full momentum only in response to the French revolution; but nevertheless the years between 1775 and 1782 did mark a major stage in the acceptance of the religious revival, not only as a potential agent of social conservation but also as an element in the nation's awareness of its common purposes and in the identification of its presumed enemies. The invocation of collective sin, whose guilt could nevertheless be laid primarily at the Dissenters' door; the call to repentance, carrying with it, even if only unintentionally, the implication that sin might best be expiated by the chastisement of those peculiarly responsible; the call for evangelical zeal in 'impressing forcibly on the minds of our hearers the great practical doctrines of Christianity which are no less beneficial to society than necessary to salvation': as early as the war's first year all these had already been drawn together and applied specifically to the American crisis in a way peculiarly calculated to attract attention by the Rev. John Riland, M.A., of St Mary's Chapel in Birmingham, later Rector of Sutton Coldfield, and one of the most influential clergymen in the area.[30] In two discourses from his pulpit on *The Sinful State of the Nation; and the Expectation of God's Judgement upon it, with the Way to Save Us from Ruin,*[31] Riland maintained 'that there has been no change for the better in our nation in consequence of the *national fasts* during the last war'. On the contrary, the nation had 'kept the fasts and also kept their sins'. Deistic arguments were openly discussed in the newspapers; the Feathers petition was flaunted before the public; Arianism, no longer secret, was allowed to walk abroad in the noon of the day—witness Dr Priestley's *Free Address to Protestant Dissenters on the Lord's Supper*—and 'the enemies of the Cross of Christ call everyone that lives Godly in Christ a Methodist without letting them know what the term means'. London in particular was 'a mart of infidelity', its inhabitants given over wholly to pleasure and luxury, lewdness and profanation of the Sabbath. 'If you would save the nation from Ruin', advised Riland,

> labour to keep from those particular, gross, GOD provoking sins which have set GOD against us and caused him to permit the present state of affairs in this land and in America. You may, in tracing to the bottom to find out the cause of the present commotion, talk of the Stamp Act and other Acts of Parliament; but you are not got to the bottom yet; you are wide of the mark. *Sin* is the cause: repeal this Act of the nation and all will be well. A reconciliation will take place between the colonies and us.

And for the accomplishment of this vital task one method alone would answer. The present style of preaching was useless, 'so merely moral' was it, 'so devoid of evangelical truth and so destitute of application and use'. Only 'a due regard to the word of GOD and the preaching of it . . . will be followed with the return of his favour'. Riland therefore concluded that 'if ever a reformation is produced, . . . it must, under the influence of the eternal spirit, be produced by the doctrines of free grace and justification through a redeemer's righteousness', exhorted his hearers and readers to intercession for the nation in their prayers and to mutual love and harmony in their lives, and consoled them as long as they were 'marching through this howling wilderness to the heavenly Canaan' with the reflection that 'though the present are evil days, there are better days to come'.

Before he reached this sublimation of present trouble, however, Riland had surely sown the earthly seeds of wrath to come; for his discourses had not been all of Gospel charity and the unworldly consolations of a future state. The nation as a whole had gone astray in more ways than one; but it was above all the sin of infidelity that lay at the root of error, and, for this, guilt could be more precisely assigned. Prime among the infidels were 'the Gentlemen at the Feathers Tavern' and their dissenting coadjutors, whose religion was as tainted with atheism as their politics were with fanatic republicanism. Infidelity was accompanied by 'a spirit of *Faction*', which in turn brought with it 'a strange licentiousness both of sentiment and conduct, a spirit of disrespect to superiors and contempt of lawful authority'. Like the Root and Branch petition, that from the Feathers tavern was aimed at the very foundation of the Church, and this too at a time 'when a spirit of licentiousness seems to be prevailing, and a contempt of all government which threatens a subversion of our happy government both in Church and State'.

> In the last century this was the very event of the rebellious spirit which then raged in the land.... We all talk of liberty and some of us as if we had lost, or were losing it; I think we have too much of it. By an excess or by an abuse of our civil and religious liberty we are become licentious. Would any of us, hating monarchy (and *our*, our *limited* monarchy too), have it fall and a republican government rise up in its stead? By this stroke we shall lose our liberty and procure slavery.... The Americans are thus infatuated.... If there be amongst us those who are taking no short strides this road, and are advancing apace upon us, I would ask what sort of Englishmen are these? What sort of friends to their country? And if they profess themselves of the establishment, what sort of Church-of-England-men are these? ... Particularly fix your eyes if you do not your hearts, upon the whole services for January 30th, May 28th and November 5th ... are you not good subjects at Church and rebels at home? .... In this manner do such people stand condemned out of their own mouths and prove themselves hypocrites by their own prayers, who are indulging and furthering the factious spirit of the present day and yet call themselves Church-of-England-men. And if those indulge and further the same spirit, who are not of the establishment but dissent from it, to such persons what shall I say? If these gentlemen, ... enjoying all the civil liberties and all the religious toleration that men of any reason could possibly wish to be indulged with yet allow themselves to appear as inimical to our constitution in Church and State, their spirit and behaviour, in all the malignity of it, exceeds the reach of any pencil, much more mine, to paint in its proper colours. I therefore leave them ... only with this remark, that if GOD for the transgression of our land, ... thus permits the overthrow of our Church and State, we shall have in this century, in a very considerable degree, to thank the deistical and factious dissenters for this great evil, as in the last, to thank their forefathers, the puritans, for the very same.

The divisions of the previous century had not been forgotten. Five years still remained before Joseph Priestley came to live in Birmingham, and some six more would pass before the first open blows were struck in the local quarrels which formed the prelude to the Priestley riots, but already the fires that burned in July 1791 had been partly laid.

For most of the period that followed the repeal of the Stamp Act the greater part of opinion in the West Midlands continued to be more concerned with questions of immediate expediency than with the deeper implications of the American dispute. In July 1768 the *Birmingham Gazette* did print an early warning of the risks involved in trying to tie the development of the mainland colonies too closely to the concepts of European power politics and the economic requirements of mercantilism. Two months later, when reports began to arrive of mounting colonial resistance to the Townshend duties, the forebodings of 'Philo Patriae' did compete for prominence with a reprinting of Lord Chatham's famous speech of 1766 welcoming American resistance.[32] But though the larger questions were thus not ignored it remained possible at this stage for those who believed that American grievances were legitimate to shelter behind the Declaratory Act and to hope that an accommodation could still be reached within the existing structure of the empire.[33] This was particularly important with regard to the movement among the independent freeholders which affected so many parts of the region. It may have contained a nucleus which had been affected through events at Worcester and elsewhere by the ideas and attitudes of the London radicals, but the wider support which it enjoyed came from men whose dissatisfaction was less systematic in nature. While sympathy with the Americans remained compatible with a wider range of opinion than would have been the case had positions on either side of the dispute already hardened, this amalgam remained intact. The confusion which underlay the relationship between the Warwickshire election of 1774 and the Birmingham petitions of January 1775[34] suggests, however, that so far as America was concerned many of the 'Independents' had second thoughts about their position as the probability diminished of conciliation within the bounds of existing relationships.

It was among the merchants and manufacturers that signs of change were most marked. Though the *Birmingham Gazette* welcomed the prospect of conciliation following the partial repeal of the Townshend duties and paid close attention to the gradual reopening of colonial ports to British goods,[35] the West Midlands were much less uniformly affected by non-importation during 1768–70 than they had been in 1765–66.[36] Commercial support for American complaints had always been based on economic expedience rather than constitutional principle; and economic expedience could just as easily cut the other way, especially when helped to do so by considerations of policy and self-interest of the kind to which the *Birmingham Gazette* drew attention on 17 October 1768, when it devoted a large part of its 'editorial' column to 'a correspondent's' warnings of the 'fatal consequences' which would arise from allowing the emigration of skilled artisans to the mainland colonies. This article, whose preoccupation with the problems of protective tariffs for the iron industry as well as with the dangers of unrestricted emigration suggests that it may well have come originally from Samuel Garbett, ended by hoping that 'the several towns so interested in checking the growing manufactures in New England will petition this next sessions for such remedy as the House of Commons in their wisdom shall see fitting'. Whatever their immediate sympathy with American grievances, the merchants and manufacturers of the West Midlands had long been keeping a jealous eye on the development of industries in the colonies which might challenge them for control of their largest single export market. Their reactions to the dispute with the colonies therefore became increasingly mixed as the years passed. The process is well illustrated by the local correspondence of the Earl of Dartmouth between 1773 and 1775.

In their suggestions for adjustments to the relationship between Britain and the colonies several of Dartmouth's correspondents went some way towards recognition of the Americans' constitutional grievances. None of them, however, showed any real appreciation of the full implication of the American position. Their discussion still revolved primarily about economic expedience, and belated pleas for lenience in the interests of trade were balanced by frank suspicion of colonial manufacturers as potential rivals whose challenge ought to be nipped in the bud. John Willday of Atherstone, who had already sent the Earl his views in August 1772, considered in March 1774 that it would be better to give up the right of taxing the colonies, and to substitute a series of requisitions from the colonial assemblies. Though they were to have no vote on matters relating to domestic taxation, Willday wished the Americans to be given seats in Parliament so that they could help in the process of imperial legislation. Arguments for conciliation also came from James Perry of Wolverhampton, who wrote on 15 March 1775 of the damage done to trade with America by the Prohibitory Act, and six months later predicted the ruin of both countries if the confrontation continued.[37] Others, however, took a harder line. On 10 February 1773 Isaac Spooner of Birmingham had written to oppose the application of Mr Quincey for permission to make steel in New England, which was then before the House of Commons, on the grounds that

> If they are permitted to make steel and draw it with tilt hammers, they will soon manufacture it, that being the next step, and though the beginning may be small, yet manufacturers will soon increase with them to the great prejudice of England, on which I am sure I need not enlarge to your Ldship, nor need I mention to you how greatly any progress in the Iron and Steel Manufactures will tend to promote the favourite scheme of America: Independence on this Kingdom.

The attitude of John Florry of Cleobury, near Bewdley, was equally hostile, not to say bloodthirsty. Florry advocated the use of mercantile pressure, not to persuade the government to yield to Colonial demands in the hope of restoring prosperity to the American trade, but as the most effective source of sanctions against the rebels. On 29 December 1774 he let Dartmouth know that he and his friends in Birmingham were preparing a printed reply to American propaganda, and suggested that a conference of merchants in the seaports be called to agree on a method of taxing the colonies and regulating their trade, particularly with regard to the recovery of debts. This, he thought, would be the quickest way of bringing them to heel. Florry had already sent Dartmouth his own thoughts on American taxation a fortnight earlier, when he had reminded the Earl of his investments in production for the American market, and had drawn attention to his newly improved line in cannon balls and muskets. Dartmouth, himself a man of peace and a rather reluctant party to the Coercive Acts, must have been severely shaken the following June when

Florry wrote again to say that he thought his special bullets would be of great service in America, and that he had thought of a new way to take prisoners, which he would divulge for a reasonable consideration.[38]

By 1775 the broad sharing of sympathy with colonial grievances, within which precise attitudes could remain undefined, had broken down, leaving behind it sharp disagreement between those who still joined support for the Americans with agitation for the eradication of political abuse at home, and those who now felt, regardless of any complaints they may still have had about other matters, that a firm stand by Government was the best way both to maintain the integrity of the empire and to cure the ills of domestic politics. Typical of the latter was the Rev. John Birch of Handsworth, a collaborator of Matthew Boulton and Dr Roebuck in the work of inspiring support for Government, who was

> ready to acknowledge Mr. W[ilkes'] merit with regard to General Warrants etc., but ever since the time of Lord B[ute's] refusing to employ him, he set himself to pour out the most unexampled abuse not only upon Lord B but on the whole Scottish Nation, and defaming a person of high rank and avowing a purpose of being a thorn in the King's side; from that time, I thought it my duty to fling a squib occasionally at him. My two last squibs were sent to Dr. Roe. I enclose another squib; if you think it worth while, you may send it to your correspondent.... There seems to be a fine opening in America. Should Lord N. reduce them to submit to ye authority of a British Parliament without bloodshed, I think Faction would be struck dumb, and I am sure Posterity will honour him as a most consummate statesman.[39]

On the other hand, the complaints of the colonists had been discussed at various times and from various points of view by all three of Birmingham's debating societies, and in two of them they had been linked with the grievances of the Wilkite radicals at home. By the time John Riland's two Fast Sermons were printed in 1776 the American cause had been the subject of heated and divisive argument in Birmingham for the best part of two years, and the availability through the agency of men like John Freeth, Myles Swinney and James Belcher, the Unitarian bookseller, of political literature and cheap tracts of the kind more usually associated with the years after 1790[40] must have helped to convince the Chaplain of St Mary's that he had good cause to sound the alarm.

The extent to which opinion was now divided in the Birmingham area was made plain by the petitions of January 1775. On the 2nd of the month the *Birmingham Gazette* carried extracts from a letter from Philadelphia, and reported that six hundred casks of nails and assorted hardware intended for America had been landed again at Bristol as a result of the resolutions of Congress. In its next two issues the paper printed a full report of the meeting of North American merchants at the King's Head tavern, Cornhill, together with the notices of meetings to be held in Birmingham, Dudley and Wolverhampton in support of the Londoners. Petitions for conciliation with the colonies were presented to the House of Commons from Dudley and Birmingham on 25 and 27 January respectively. Meanwhile, however, Matthew Boulton had been in correspondence with the Earl of Dartmouth. Despite the help of Dr Roebuck, Boulton had been unable to prevent or divert the Birmingham petition when it was discussed and drafted on the 11th and 17th, but he had published twelve 'Queries on the Propriety of Petitioning Parliament on the

Present Interruption of American Commerce' in the *Birmingham Gazette*, and had raised his own counter-petition. This beat its rival to the House of Commons by two days, being presented by Thomas Skipwith on 25 January.[41]

With the *Birmingham Gazette* being used to put the coercive argument and *Swinney's Birmingham and Stafford Chronicle* supporting the opposite sense, the stage was set for the controversy of the following months. Some attempt was made to conceal the most visible manifestations of this, but the transparent charade of impartiality which the Birmingham papers acted out during 1775–76[42] itself suggests that opinion in the West Midlands was more sharply divided than either of them found it prudent or profitable to admit. Boulton was not only threatened with commercial reprisals by the American merchants but also warned that if the worst came to the worst, and the unemployed nailers of the Black Country villages turned violent, his own factory would be 'one of their first objects of plunder'.[43] The execration which was heaped on the master of Soho, and repaid by him with interest,[44] is significant not only from the point of view of Boulton's own career and reputation but also from that of local politics. Coming so soon after his involvement in the Warwickshire election on behalf of John Mordaunt, Boulton's exertions left him doubly open to the kind of attack exemplified in the letter from 'Veritas' which was published in the *London Evening Post* of 7–9 February 1775:

> Birmingham, like other large towns, is not without those toad-eating sycophants, who, from a prospect of self emolument, would lick the hands of a bloodthirsty minister, and rejoice at the sufferings of their fellow creatures. But to convince the world that the major part do not espouse the odious doctrine of passive obedience and non-resistance, in the late struggle for Knight of the Shire, as the contest lay between an Independant Gentleman and a placeman, ... of six hundred Birmingham freeholders, only forty voted for the latter, out of which despicable, dimunative [sic] junto, are formed the leaders of the counter-petition; nor should it be forgot, that the effigy of their boasted champion, for his strenuous efforts against the freedom and independence of that county, was carried thro' the public streets and treated in the same manner as a Scotch W--ne in North America. This assuming *Gentleman*, who attempts to sway the town with a rod of iron, and whose matchless effrontery has caused him to be much better known than respected, in colleague with a noted mechanick, who closely treads upon ye heels of the celebrated Pinchey, and who is equally fond of exhibiting his glittering baubles at St. James's, are the two who are endeavouring to load the town with that ignominy and disgrace which far the greater part of the inhabitants utterly abhor. ...
>
> P.S. It should not be forgot, that amongst the emissaries employ'd by government to poison the minds of the people, an apostate from the C-- Company in Scotland, who was a strenuous adviser of the repeal of the Stamp Act, and who was lately introduced to Lord S--k, has in his circuit to procure counterpetitions, visited Birmingham, Manchester, Sheffield and Leeds. ... By this person was the contemptible epistle handed to Mr. Skipwith, sign'd by a group of druggists, grocers, barbers, shoemakers, taylors, butchers & c. But to the credit of the town, we are inform'd, that not ten mechanicks are upon the infamous list.[45]

The suspected source of this was the Birmingham firm of Welch Wilkinson & Startin, who were among the leaders of the pro-American group in the town. Its insults were answered a month later by 'Detector', and the formally polite but acid correspondence which the exchange provoked between Boulton and his assailants can hardly have helped to sweeten relationships among 'the Birmingham Manufacturing Gentry'.[46]

In the early months of 1775 there was still some ground, small but genuine, for hoping that war might be averted. Up to the end of February the government's extension of the policies of coercion was accompanied by an offer to give up the right to tax the colonies 'except for commercial purposes only' in return for a promise to pay for the Boston Tea Party and a system of requisitions through which the colonists themselves would pay for their own defence and civil government. On this basis the Earl of Dartmouth remained in contact with Benjamin Franklin, through the Quakers David Barclay and Dr John Fothergill, until the negotiations were brought to an end on 1 March by the Americans' refusal to consider the British offer unless the Coercive Acts themselves were first repealed.[47] Seven weeks later the skirmishes at Lexington and Concord on 18 and 19 April, soon to be followed by the seizure of Crown Point and Ticonderoga and then by Bunker Hill on 19 June, put the matter beyond redemption. The breadth of the Atlantic meant that some seven or eight weeks of continuing uncertainty passed in each case before news of these first blows began to affect British opinion, but by the late summer they were all common knowledge. Despite the finality of the news from America, however, there were many even now who were ready to snatch at any faint chance, however unreal, that events might take another course, and the autumn was marked by a second wave of petitions. Proposals for conciliation, which eventually took concrete form in the abortive Howe Peace Commission of 1776, were once again in the air.[48] In November Josiah Wedgwood asked to be 'unriddled' of a newspaper report 'that the idea of taxing the colonies is given up *on all sides*',[49] and rumours of this kind may have helped to encourage some of the requests for concession which were again sent to Westminster. In Birmingham even the Amicable Debating Society, while casting aspersions on the motives of the political opposition and its supporters, wondered in its order paper of 16 October whether lenience would not bring reconciliation with the colonists sooner than force. However, though the autumn petitions testified to the country's continuing uncertainty, they were now forlorn gestures rather than part of a campaign which had any hope of success, and the contrary protestations of loyalty they provoked merely consolidated acceptance of the situation. The newspapers had raised Wedgwood's hopes of a 'mighty Revolution' in British policy; but when it came, with Dartmouth's replacement at the head of the American Department by Lord George Germain, the 'change in our Ministerial system' was not in the direction of peace.

After the two petitions at the start of the year, Birmingham itself gave no further explicit expression during 1775 to its feelings on either side of the American question. However, several other places in the surrounding region were among those which made their views known in the autumn, and they did so in terms noticeably different from those which had been used earlier by Boulton and his opponents. Though their aftermath showed that the attempt was unsuccessful, the Birmingham petitions in the spring had tried to avoid political animus by concentrating on the commercial aspects of the dispute, and both had been moderately worded. Like the London merchants, whose caution so annoyed Edmund Burke,[50] the organisers of the conciliatory petition had practically conceded their position in advance by going no further than the expression of a reluctant but necessary duty to remind the House of Commons of the West Midlands' dependence on the American market and a request for 'such relief as in Your Great Wisdom shall be judged necessary'.[51] Boulton had thus been able to follow the Earl of Dartmouth's advice to confine his counter-petition to a 'prayer in general terms' for 'the support of the Authority of the laws of the Kingdom over all the dominions of the Crown' in order to safeguard the region's commercial interests.[52] The only loyal address from the West Midlands which took this form later in the year was that from the corporation of Bewdley, whose members stressed their anxiety as 'men whose welfare is more immediately dependent on trade' to see the colonies brought back to a proper obedience. Several of the other addresses did include this point and professed the readiness of their authors to tolerate short-term hardship in the interests of a permanent solution to the problem; but what distinguished them was the brevity of their attention to the Americans and the length at which they hastened to disavow any sympathy with the opposition at home. The pattern was set by the Gentlemen, Clergy, Traders and Principal Inhabitants of Coventry, who affirmed at great length that the 'patrons of sedition' at home were entirely responsible for a rebellion 'the most unnatural, because excited and fomented by the false representations and encouragement of a desperate domestic faction'; deplored the 'continued series of ill treatment' to which the King and 'the Ministry you have so judiciously made choice of' had been subjected, and prayed for

> the prosecution of such measures, as, in your Royal Wisdom, you shall think proper to adopt for the suppression of the present outrageous commotions abroad, for the Restoration of peace and good order at Home, for the maintaining of due regard for the authority of the legislature, and for the support of our admirable Constitution both in Church and State.

None of the other addresses were quite so explicit, but the Mayor, Recorder, Aldermen, Burgesses and Inhabitants of Warwick abhorred 'the cloak of mock patriotism' which concealed the 'misrepresentations of artfull, designing and seditious men, both at home and abroad'; the Mayor, Aldermen and Burgesses of Shrewsbury deplored the American rebellion but looked 'with equal grief, but not without indignation . . . upon a discontented faction at home promoting and encouraging these unhappy disturbances', and the Mayor, Aldermen and Citizens of Worcester, in an address almost as vehement as that from Coventry, condemned

> those seditious principles which, under the mask of patriotism, have been industriously propagated by artful and evil designing men through all ranks of Your Majesty's subjects in these kingdoms, and have excited a most atrocious and unnatural rebellion in many of your American Colonies, which we implore Your Majesty to suppress by an exertion of the powers with which you are invested.[53]

These variations on a common theme were typical of the dominant British attitude at the time, and they no doubt gained extra colour by reaction from the activities of the Middlesex freeholders, whose petition of grievance, covering everything from the Middlesex election to the Coercive Acts, was noticed, together with their circular letter to the Freeholders of Great Britain,[54] in the *Birmingham Gazette* on 2 October. But there was more behind the loyal addresses than the mere parroting of conventional formulae in generalised abomination of the opposition to the war. The particular nuances of each address, through which a succinct summary of opinion at its source could be conveyed to the perceptive reader, were just as important as the overall sentiments expressed. In at least three of the examples given, the language used bespoke not mere searching for a suitably pompous form of words but a specific sensitivity to local tension. Thus the drafters of the Warwick address, mindful of the internal quarrels in which the borough's politics were even then embroiled,[55] set out its authors in carefully graded order of precedence and, having done so, went out of their way to emphasise that they were 'unbias'd by party'. If the Worcester address spoke of 'seditious principles . . . industriously propagated . . . through all ranks of Your Majesty's subjects' it did so with good reason: on 25 October, the very day of its presentation to the King, 'several inhabitants' of Worcester met with Sir Watkin Lewes at Tom's Coffee House to draw up a petition in the reverse sense.[56] Similarly, the mayor and corporation of Coventry were conspicuous by their absence from the listed authors of that city's address, whose anxiety for Church and State was heightened by the presence of opposition in Coventry itself. True, the *Birmingham Gazette* on 16 October did notice that six days previously Councillor Green had spoken to 'a numerous and respectable meeting of the inhabitants of Coventry' at the King's Head, and that the assembled company, headed by Lords Archer and Craven, had approved an address and petition 'on the present awful and distressed state of this Kingdom and the American Colonies'.[57] The Birmingham paper spoke of this as 'spirited, manly and loyal'. The first two it may have been, depending on the meaning of the words; much to the alarm of the Earl of Denbigh at Newnham Paddox, near Rugby, however, it was hardly 'loyal'. His lordship, already disturbed both by the absence of any encouraging news from America and by the country's backwardness in attesting its support for the King and his Ministers, was disgusted to see the names of Archer and Craven at the head of what he called 'a very extraordinary counter-address to that presented by the members for the City of Coventry'. And, of the latter, Edward Roe Yeo refused to have anything to do with the presentation of this second address.[58]

It was, however, in Staffordshire that the balance of opinion was most clearly visible. Lichfield was jolted into a rather hasty loyal address after the mayor of the city had been approached on behalf of 'many sincere Friends to Liberty' by Thomas Joel of London, who asked for help in the formation of a conciliatory association.[59] In addition, the patriots made a particular effort to recruit further support by doing their best to counteract the loyal address from the county. Preparation for the address did not prove quite as straightforward as its organisers had expected. A county meeting had to be held, and in their notices for this the sheriff and justices tried to preempt its conclusions by calling it to consider not the American situation *per se* but a previously prepared address on 'the rebellious state of the Colonies against the legislative authority of this country'. [60] For proposing this 'courtly race to St. James's' the organisers of the meeting were taken to task by 'a Freeholder of Staffordshire' in the *Birmingham Gazette* of 16 October 1775. The Americans might be deluded and prejudiced, 'as we will for a moment allow'; but they were 'fighting like men—like ENGLISHMEN, for law and liberty supposed to be violated',

If we must be politicians, and interpose our advice on public affairs, let us, and our representatives with us, set out for St. James's with Truth as well as loyalty in our mouths, and honestly tell the King that his ministers are not capable of making either war or peace: not peace because the Americans will not trust them for Faith which they have so often broken—and their genius for war appears by this woeful specimen.

When the county met on 20 October it heard not one address but three. Apart from that which was eventually presented, confirming Staffordshire's support for the policies of Government, the meeting considered two conciliatory proposals. The first of these was introduced by Sir Thomas Boughton, Bt, one of the county gentry. The baronet's views, however, were obviously not strong enough to induce him to risk the opprobrium of his neighbours; for, much to the wonder of Josiah Wedgwood, 'he told the Gentn., if they did not adopt his petition, he should agree to their address!' The sponsor of the second was a Mr Woolridge. Though a native of Staffordshire and a landowner in the county, Woolridge had considerable commercial interests in London. He had been a member of the Committee of London Merchants Trading to America which had petitioned Parliament the previous January; he was 'a deputy chairman in one of the Patriotic Societies', and he was not so easily deterred into conformity as his predecessor. 'The Gentlemen were *cut down* & could not answer him', and though the meeting safeguarded its rejection of his views by a prudent adjournment, Woolridge took independent steps to circulate his own petition. In the fortnight after the county had met, this was made available for signature at the Bull's Head in Walsall until 31 October, and then on successive days until 6 November at the Red Lion in Wolverhampton, the Hen and Chickens in Birmingham, the George at Lichfield, the Castle at Tamworth, and lastly—which pleased Wedgwood greatly—at the Swan in Handley Green.[61]

It was probably as a result of this opposition that two days before Woolridge's petition was due at the Swan Wedgwood found himself the surprised recipient of a parcel sent by special messenger 'from the House of a noble Lord in our neighbourhood'. Inside, without so much as a word of explanation, were half a dozen copies of John Wesley's *Calm Address*. Steps were obviously being taken by the supporters of the Ministry to gauge and guide opinion in the county; and Wedgwood's astonishment at being singled out as a prospective distributor for the one piece of propaganda which above all others he was anxious to see refuted was surpassed only when he was asked how he thought the people of Staffordshire would react to the embodiment of the militia. Why ask him of all people? Why not someone 'whose devotion is unquestionable'? The choice showed shrewdness and sensitivity on the part of the county leaders, for Wedgwood was in a better position than most to assess the feelings of the common people. But it pitched him already on to the horns of the dilemma which he faced most acutely four years later: could he, consistent with his principles as a supporter of the American cause, recommend any course of action which might assist the attempt to destroy it? In his answer the conclusion which he reached in 1779 was already foreshadowed. Raising the militia was the least of three evils, the other two being the use of foreign troops or being left defenceless: 'One of them, thanks to our wise and upright rulers, I believe we must submit to.'[62]

Great care was taken to present the Staffordshire conciliatory petition to the

public in the most acceptable way possible. Those who might doubt its respectability were reassured that the petition, which was described as 'loyal and
dutiful', would be accompanied at each of its resting places by 'a Gentleman
of Character', and its attendant publicity was addressed not merely to the
gentlemen, clergy and freeholders of the county, as the conventional formula
went, but specifically to the traders and manufacturers as well.[63] It is therefore
all the more surprising to find that Wedgwood himself did not sign the petition
after all. However, as he explained to Thomas Bentley in a phrase which he
was to use more than once during the next four years, Wedgwood had 'several
reasons' for abstaining, chief among them that

> we had very lately petition'd *in a body* as the *Staffordshire Potters*, & I think as
> we have in that & in other respects distinguish'd ourselves as a particular Body of
> Men (though not Corporate), it will be right to continue our applications, when
> they are proper to be made at all, in the same mode.[64]

Wedgwood's scruples about the Staffordshire conciliatory petition, in spite of
the pains which had been taken to include such men as himself within its
scope, were, in an obverse sense, of a piece with the careful enunciation of
authors which was characteristic of the loyal addresses. Like the latter, they
show that the mixed reactions of the country at large to the start of the war for
America produced, in the concern for the legitimate and effective representation
of different points of view, an enhanced awareness of the distinct elements which
together constituted public opinion. So far as the political experience of the
West Midlands was concerned it was this, rather than any influence they may
have exerted on the actual course of events, which was the most important
result of the petitions and addresses of 1775. In the importance Wedgwood
attached to the identity of his fellow manufacturers as a particular body of
men, even if they had no charter to prove it, many of the procedural problems
of the General Chamber of Manufacturers were foreshadowed.[65] Wedgwood's
concern for the political distinctness of the potters followed naturally from his
industrial plans, both for his own works and for the development of the Staffordshire potteries as a whole. A similar relationship existed between Birmingham's
reactions to the American war and the wider aspirations to distinct significance
which matched the town's physical growth.

It is not surprising that neither conciliatory petition nor loyal address came
from Birmingham in the autumn of 1775. A second set of gestures would have
been bound to carry heavy political overtones, would have added nothing of
any substance to the commercial views expressed in the January petitions, and
would have served only to stir up once more the ill feeling which the latter had
provoked. Nevertheless the later petitions and addresses from other parts of the
West Midlands did not leave Birmingham unaffected; for they gave rise to
discussion, not only of British policy in general but also of the particular rights
and wrongs of petitioning as a constitutional means of representing the opinions
of different sections of the community. The implications of this can be seen in
the letter from 'A Mechanic' in *Swinney's Birmingham and Stafford Chronicle*
of 4 April 1776. A large part of this was devoted to a defence of Richard Price's
Observations on Civil Liberty and a refutation of Wesley's *Calm Address*; but
before he dealt with these larger themes the writer also upheld the right to
petition the Crown as the sole and specific constitutional privilege of the

unrepresented tradesman. Much had changed since this privilege was first accorded its place in the Anglo-Saxon constitution. 'Commerce is now at its height of perfection, money is the wealth of the Kingdom ... merchants, tradesmen, etc. are the producers of it, and our landed men must come at their wealth through their means'; yet

> though they are the bulk and strength of the kingdom and the procurers of all its wealth, yet our constitution makes no provision for them, whereby to secure their interests, ... but supposes them (as in its primitive state) as cyphers or servants, who have no real property either to secure or lose.

Faced as they now were with a war which endangered commerce, the tradesmen had seized their 'only privilege by petitioning His Majesty for reconciliation with his American subjects', and the rejection of those petitions, so the writer claimed was due entirely to counter-petitions from landed men who 'in THIS act of petitioning have encroached on our right'. The address to the Crown debated and passed by both Houses of Parliament between 2 and 8 February 1775 had in fact made any further expression of opinion from the landed interest both superfluous and constitutionally inadmissible:

> As every landed man is represented in Parliament and as their representatives had thus done according to their minds, what need had they, nay, what right had they to petition at all? was it not superfluous? was it not invading the tradesman's right, who is NOT represented in Parliament, and encroaching on his privilege who did NOT acquiesce in the Parliamentary address?

None of this was very original, and it contained conspicuous flaws. The indiscriminate use of the words 'commerce', 'trade', 'merchant' and 'tradesman' without any precise definition in each case squared ill with the attempt to confine the right to petition to a single section of the community. The stress on the imbalance in the constitution was little more than commonplace; and to later readers the concern for Anglo-Saxon precedents must seem perverse when the writer should surely have been exploring the idea of representative reform itself, not using antique arguments to dress up the right to petition as an alternative to it. Most readers, however, probably found an argument still couched in the familiar terms of the Ancient Constitution better attuned to their own ways of thinking than one which advanced the case for full-scale representative reform. And though the fact that many merchants and manufacturers now supported coercion made nonsense of the claim that war with America had been foisted on the nation by landed men alone in open disregard of the rights of tradesmen, it was still possible to meet this objection by adopting Edmund Burke's distinction between the sound and 'the rotten, contract-hunting part of the Mercantile Interest'. In retrospect, the eventual inadequacy of such a position may be plain; but it was tenable enough at the time, especially in a town where the traditions of the Ancient Constitution had recently won a famous victory, in which only a contemptible minority had made common cause with the minions of 'Lordly power'. Arguments like those advanced by 'A Mechanic', which were in close accord with local circumstances and perceptions, must have helped considerably to emphasise the singularity of Birmingham's position as the rising centre of one of the country's most important manufacturing areas, even though they did not in themselves contain any significant challenge to existing political arrangements.

Such arguments, however, also tended to prolong the disagreements which had divided the people of Birmingham itself during the previous two years, and these still hampered the town's desire to realise its own distinctness within the special relationship which was now felt to exist between itself and the county of Warwick. This showed itself very clearly in Birmingham's response in 1778 to the call for subscriptions to augment the forces of the Crown. To begin with, the course of local events was not unlike that of January 1775. As early as 15 December 1777, when the news of Burgoyne's surrender at Saratoga was still less than a fortnight old, the *Birmingham Gazette* tried to put its readers on their mettle by drawing attention to 'the seasonable and spirited conduct' of Manchester, whose declared intention to raise enough money to support 1,600 infantrymen must, it thought, 'strike dumb every incendiary of sedition and every tool of party'. No immediate action was taken, but on 27 December the Earl of Dartmouth suggested to Matthew Boulton that support from Birmingham would be particularly welcome, since 'it is feared there are some who are not much dispos'd to lend a helping hand to a cause in which they are all materially interested'.[66] In Warwickshire a county meeting was called for 14 January 1778, and it was probably the combination of this example and Dartmouth's prompting which led to the first meeting of Birmingham's leaders at the Cherry Orchard on 8 January. By most standards this was a great success. The organiser went out of his way to urge 'this opulent town' to distinguish itself by keeping its own donation separate from those of the nobility and gentry, who could be expected to dominate the county subscription. So effective was this argument that £2,200 was put up on the spot, even though public contributions were not sought until four days later.[67] Gratifying though this must have been, however, there were also signs of opposition. One of the suggested advantages of a separate Birmingham subscription was that it would give the well disposed part of the town a chance to identify itself and rebut any suspicion of disaffection. In particular the organiser explained that the subscription had first been discussed in private because to have called a public meeting at once would have been an open invitation for the disaffected to come and disrupt the proceedings. On 19 January the *Birmingham Gazette* betrayed the same rather unwilling awareness of opposition in the town by the very vehemence of its hope that the subscription would be

> prosecuted with such vigour and cordial unanimity by the inhabitants at large, as will totally annihilate every idea of division, and stamp indelibly that reputation upon the place to which it hath hitherto been so justly entitled.

In addition to this, the paper announced that it had suppressed a contribution received from 'A real friend to his King and Country' on the grounds that 'though in every way worthy of insertion, ... its appearance might be productive of a controversy the printers hereof are studious to avoid'. Disagreement could not, however, be kept entirely out of the newspapers, especially when the decision was taken after all to incorporate the troops raised by the town's own efforts into the regiment which was to be supported by the county, and to distinguish them as 'the Birmingham Companies'.[68] By embroiling the town subscription in the complexities of county politics[69] this gave its enemies plausible grounds for their opposition. 'A well wisher to his country' was thus able to concede that 'we all wish well to our country, and would readily give any LEGAL assistance', but advised his readers to

> have nothing to do with the ambition or private interest of others. You shewed yourselves men of spirit and independency in the last general election; abide by the same: what is it to you my Friends and Neighbours, whether Lord Warwick is a Lord of the Bedchamber, his brother Charles a Lord of Trade, or his brother Robert Colonel of a Regiment.... Keep clear of all parties: whilst you are at liberty, you have the balance in your hands, and will be respectable for it.... Give me leave to say a word to the Manufacturers of Birmingham and Coventry. Times have been good to you, I sincerely hope they may continue; but whilst you are in trade, mind that; set not yourselves up above your rank and condition; think not of raising regiments and encouraging warfare. Peace is for your interests, and a prosperous, successful trade will make you of more weight than any connections or acquaintance with Lords.... Your consequence will arise more from your art and assiduity as manufacturers than as politicians and subscribers to regiments.[70]

The people of Birmingham were thus urged on the one hand to prove their loyalty in a manner befitting the consequence of the town, and on the other to maintain the independence which they had shown in 1774 by having nothing to do with subscription. From both sides, Birmingham was expected to decide and to act its own part; but, equally, the differences of opinion which produced these opposing points of view still precluded any really cohesive response.

The same was true of the attempts which had so far been made to develop a 'Birmingham interest' in county politics. There is no sign that the Independent Constitutional Society of the Freeholders of Warwickshire, which in any case was a rather amorphous body, continued to meet after 1775; and what evidence there is on the subject suggests that the Bean Club, the one body which might have provided a nucleus of leadership for the town's political ambitions, was itself seriously affected by disagreement among its members. That the club was divided in October 1774 has already been seen,[71] but the confusion did not end there. The attitude of a large part of the membership to the American question can be gauged from Boulton's 'list of names to petition' of 1775;[72] yet Boulton had been active on behalf of the minority in the Warwickshire election, and it was from that 'despicable dimunative junto' that the leaders of his counter-petition were reputed to have been drawn. Though a vote for Holte and Skipwith in the previous October was by no means incompatible with support for coercion in 1775,[73] both the latter and the association with Boulton ran counter to the Bean Club's links with the Warwickshire Members. Of these, who were serving together as the club's county stewards at the time, Sir Charles Holte was an independent whose sympathies were Whig if anything; while Thomas Skipwith was very definitely in the Rockingham camp, despite his presentation of Boulton's counter-petition, and voted consistently against the Ministry for the duration of the war.[74] As a result of this situation the Bean Club was virtually split in two for most of the war's first three years. Of the two authorities on its early history, Sir J. B. Stone claims that the club was in abeyance between 11 August 1775 and 22 August 1777, while W. K. R. Bedford's transcript of its minutes not only records meetings during the interval but also notes the blackballing of John Gough of Perry Hall on 22 August 1778 for arranging rival dinners to clash with Bean Club meetings.[75] The suspicion that part of the membership may have seceded for a time so that the rest of the club became more than usually sensitive about its proceedings is reinforced by the resolution, which accompanied Gough's blackballing, to make the attendance of town members at the Bean Club's anniversary dinners compulsory on pain of expulsion.

On the basis of Bedford's transcript of its minutes, few of the members who had voted for the minority in the Warwickshire election seem to have played much part in the Bean Club during the years that followed. On the other hand, those who had supported Holte and Skipwith attended the club regularly and increased their strength within it as new members were elected.[76] To assume that this group now formed a faction of opposition adherents which sought to dominate the Bean Club would, however, be unwarrantable on two counts. In the first place, by far the largest part of the club's active membership after 1774 had taken no part in the Warwickshire election and therefore cannot be allocated to either side in that contest. In the second place, despite its association with Holte and Skipwith, and despite the political sympathies of these two, it is unlikely that the club would have allowed itself to be drawn very far away from its own traditions. Hitherto these had been quite consistent with the kind of non-partisan resistance to the encroachment of authority enshrined in the language of Bean Club anniversaries;[77] but as the issues raised by the American war seemed to change the nature of opposition, so they also altered the connotation of independence. As the former came to imply attachment to a specific group of men for the sake of specific political objectives, so the latter came to involve acquiescence in what seemed to be unavoidable policies, suspension of political judgement, except on local affairs, and avoidance of anything which might be construed as faction. That the divisions in the Bean Club eventually resolved themselves in this way is suggested by the one clue which its records provide to the attitude of the membership during the years after 1775: the fact that while Samuel Aris and Thomas Pearson of the *Birmingham Gazette* were both members, the nomination of Myles Swinney of the more partisan *Birmingham and Stafford Chronicle* was turned down on 22 August 1777.[78] Such a resolution, however, was bound to affect the Bean Club's relations with Warwickshire's Members of Parliament. In the case of Sir Charles Holte no great problem was raised. Holte's age and health made his attendance at Westminster sporadic, and his occasional votes against the Ministry were no more than might still be expected from a country gentleman who took little sustained interest and no active part in national politics: certainly they were hardly enough to label him as a regular supporter of the opposition. In any case, he was unlikely to seek re-election in 1780, and a more acceptable successor was already emerging in the person of Robert Lawley. As a regular supporter of the Rockingham Whigs, however, Skipwith was a different proposition; and the contrast between the reputation he enjoyed before 1775 and the circumstances of his unexpected departure in 1780 illustrates well how the changing implications of opposition affected the accepted meaning of independence. Between 1769 and 1774 Skipwith earned wide popularity as Warwickshire's only genuinely independent Member of Parliament, popularity which was overwhelmingly vindicated in the contest of the latter year; yet in 1780 he complained to the Duke of Portland that it was impossible for him to stand again for Warwickshire after the treatment he had received, and was transferred to a safe Rockingham seat at Steyning. According to the *Independent Chronicle*, Skipwith's resignation was regarded by the people of Warwickshire as 'in the number of the most paradoxical things that may have happened among them'.[79] Despite appearances, however, the probable truth of the matter was that Skipwith had parted company with at least one important group among his constituents, and if this was so the Bean Club may well have been involved.

The first sign of preparation in Birmingham for the next general election came in June 1780, when attention was drawn to recently passed legislation which made freeholders' qualification for the county franchise dependent on the proper inclusion of their names in the land tax records. In view of this the freeholders of Birmingham were advised to waste no time in securing their right to vote by registering immediately with the town constables, Jonathan Wigley and John Geast, at the Chain in Bull Street.[80] The urgency of the notice was explained by 'the General Election coming near'. The election was in fact held only three months later, and the constables seem in retrospect to have acted only just in time. When they issued their notice, however, the existing Parliament had still nearly eighteen months to run, for the decision to dissolve it well over a year early was not taken until August. No doubt the early dissolution in 1774 and the possibility that the same experiment might be repeated put them on their guard; but to begin with, at any rate, those in Birmingham who were preparing for the election were working on a longer time scale than that which eventually confronted them.

They were able to do so because by 1780 the obstacles which had hitherto prevented concerted action had begun to diminish. Events across the Atlantic no longer attracted the same attention or produced the same reaction as they had done earlier. During 1779 Birmingham's demonstrations of anti-gallican patriotism barely mentioned the war in America, and bore no sign of the conflict of opinion which had accompanied the subscription proposals of the previous year.[81] Thanks to the continued diversification of the town's trade, preoccupation with the problems of the American market was no longer the divisive issue it had been five years earlier. The merchants and manufacturers were being drawn together once more by the shared concerns which led to the foundation of the Birmingham Commercial Committee in 1783. If it did anything, therefore, the disruption of the erstwhile colonial trade and the consequent search for other markets now emphasised the common need to secure the town's means of influencing the government's commercial policies. In addition, the promotion of the General Hospital and its attendant oratorio festivals had provided Birmingham with a new outlet for its aspirations, one which reunited the leadership dispersed by disagreement in 1774 and linked it once more to the nobility and gentry of the county. Finally, the reunion of Birmingham's more prominent inhabitants was probably helped by defensive reaction to the danger that the Gordon riots might spread to the town during June 1780. This actually came to nothing beyond the burning of an effigy of Dr Dodd by a crowd of some 1,500 people, but inflammatory papers had been distributed, and a Roman Catholic chapel at Edgbaston was threatened. A party of rioters from the town was also reported to be on its way to London, and the High Bailiff, Thomas Faulconbridge, was sufficiently disturbed to offer to lead an association to keep the peace in Birmingham in case the situation got out of control.[82]

The early dissolution of Parliament, which was announced on 1 September 1780 after the government's intentions had been successfully concealed until the last possible minute,[83] reduced the time available in which Birmingham could take steps to shape the course of Warwickshire politics to its liking, especially when the resignations of Holte and Skipwith on 3 and 8 September[84] respectively meant that both county seats were now vacant. Nevertheless the town was in a better position to exert deliberate influence than it had been in 1774. The resignation of Sir Charles Holte at least was probably no real surprise, and everything suggests that Sir Robert Lawley, newly succeeded to his own family inheritance, had been regarded as Holte's political heir for some time. It was a member of the Bean Club, Thomas Gem, who initiated the measures which secured Lawley's nomination and return by informing the Earl of Dartmouth on 14 September of the importance Birmingham attached to the choice of properly qualified successors to the retiring members.[85] Gem was confident that the local gentry would support Sir Robert. He was willing to be nominated at the county meeting, and the freeholders of Birmingham were 'almost unanimous' in his favour. In securing the last point the leaders in Birmingham had already been active. The *Birmingham Gazette* of 11 September, which announced the nomination meeting at Warwick on the 15th, also carried an 'Address to the Gentlemen, Clergy, and Inhabitants of Warwickshire, especially to those resident in or near the town and neighbourhood of Birmingham' which warned that two strangers would probably be nominated to the county seats if nothing was done. A meeting of the leading freeholders in the Birmingham area had therefore decided to form 'an Association of the Independent Freeholders in this Town and County, and particularly to invite all the friends of our late worthy members to concur in the attempt to return two Gentlemen who may be likely to pursue the same line of Parliamentary conduct'. A public meeting would be held shortly, and in the meantime 'every friend to commerce and freedom' was urged to remain ready to support the association by making it as general as possible, 'since it is unanimity alone that will preserve the importance of this town and ensure success in this meritorious cause'.

By thus forming their own organisation and virtually conducting their own nomination before the county met at Warwick, Birmingham's leaders were able to maintain and consolidate the advantages won in 1774. And if the attempt to strengthen the sense of continuity with the earlier victory raised any misgivings in the light of Skipwith's recent political record, these were set to rest by his particular successor, Sir George Shuckburgh, who, in his nomination speech at Warwick, bound himself to support

> the Laws and Liberties of this Country upon the solid principles of our most excellent Constitution, by preventing so far as in me lies so admirable a frame of government from every inroad to innovation and abuse which designing or visionary men propose, and ... by promoting the commercial interests of this extended Empire in which this County claims so considerable a share.[86]

This pledge expressed the attitude which was to be typical of Birmingham's political leaders in the years ahead. With the divisions of the previous five years now behind them, their objective was to develop the position gained by Sir Charles Holte and retained by Sir Robert Lawley in such a way that the Birmingham interest would be permanently integrated into the established structure of Warwickshire politics. This, however, meant that only one aspect of the original achievement would be willingly perpetuated, while memories of the other would be discouraged or at least shaped to fit the new order. Far from being the result of previous arrangement between Birmingham and the magnates of Warwickshire, Holte had owed his victory in 1774 primarily to the simple voting strength of an electorate roused by repercussions of the Wilkite movement to defend its independence in opposition to the county hierarchy. The defeat of 'Lordly power' had involved a considerable degree of popular participation, and though the outcome on this occasion had been in Birmingham's favour, memories of the episode might well be used to justify the same kind of participation in the future with less convenient results. The recollection of Holte's triumph had therefore to be adapted to the new situation. Suitably controlled and associated with Birmingham's own rising pride, it could be used to foster a sense of achievement shared between the common people and their betters which would help the town to meet the political and social strains of the next two decades.[87] But now that they were in a position to adapt the gains of 1774 to their own advantage by themselves assuming a permanent position in the county hierarchy, Birmingham's leaders were not anxious to see such things bulk too large in the formation of the town's political traditions.

Four years later the situation was well in hand. Birmingham now had a permanent forum for its own special concerns in the Commercial Committee, founded the previous year, and since any distinction there may ever have been between the political and commercial aspects of the Birmingham interest was rapidly disappearing it is not surprising to find that during the months before the 1784 election the Commercial Committee extended its activities to lead the town's political response. On 23 December 1783, at the height of the India Bill crisis, the High Bailiff called a meeting at the hotel to confirm Birmingham's support for Lawley and Shuckburgh now that Parliament was expected to be dissolved at any moment.[88] Apart from this, the older authorities stood rather pointedly aloof. Samuel Garbett, on the other hand, called a meeting of the Commercial Committee for 10 February 1784 at which an address to the Crown was drafted and approved by ninety-eight votes to nine before being left at the hotel for public signature and sent up for presentation by the Warwickshire members.[89] On 1 April the Commercial Committee discussed Birmingham's preparations for the coming election. Though the meeting was unanimous in its support for Lawley and Shuckburgh, it adjourned without passing a formal resolution, in deference to the county nomination meeting, due to be held at Warwick on 5 April. In addition, a formal declaration from Sir Robert Lawley was published, denying that he had entered into 'certain engagements respecting his future political conduct inconsistent with the character of an independent representative of the County of Warwick'.[90] Unnecessary friction between town and county was thus avoided; but though correct protocol was observed and some play made to the old shibboleths at the same time, the Commercial Committee had in effect conducted once more what amounted to Birmingham's pre-emptive nomination to the Warwickshire seats. A year later Samuel Garbett was writing of Sir George Shuckburgh, who was not usually regarded as particularly beholden to Birmingham, in terms which suggest that the town was now presuming to proprietary rights over both the county's representatives. On 8 June 1785 he sent Boulton a memorandum from the Commercial Committee to William Pitt on industrial espionage. Since Sir Robert Lawley was unable to take charge of it, Boulton was asked to pass the paper on to Pitt himself:

> And if Mr. Pitt should intimate that Sir George Shuckburgh had not yet left town, it would give you an opportunity of saying we were dissatisfied with the disregard he has shown us, and therefore do not apply to him, ... and perhaps that may obtain us favour, as a compliment to Sir George, who will otherwise certainly lose his seat in consequence of the slight we have had from him.[91]

With so much of the apparent substance of Particular Representation already in their possession, it is hardly surprising that men like Garbett and Boulton saw no point in pursuing the theory by giving their countenance to the early movement for parliamentary reform.[92]

In the 1790 election Abraham Bracebridge, of Atherstone, tried to revive the original forces which had returned Sir Charles Holte by offering himself in place of Lawley as a native son of the county who would 'support our present excellent administration so long as it preserves the limits assigned to its sphere in our constitutional system'. Since he also pledged himself to 'preserve his own freedom and independence' by resigning the moment his own views differed from those of his constituents, Bracebridge can hardly have expected much sympathy when his promise was at once taken up by the Birmingham interest, 'as few events of a public nature could be more injurious to this town than a contested election for the county'. The manufacturers were more than satisfied with Sir Robert Lawley, 'who hath with truth been considered particularly the Representative of Birmingham' and 'has often declared that he was ready at an hour's notice to leave his home and go to London (whether Parliament was sitting or not) whenever it was thought he could be of use to the trade of the town'. So far from embodying a welcome return to the independence of 1774, a contested election would call forth 'the same spirit which hath of late years been shewn by Birmingham upon the election of *one* member for the County', and this would be 'instantly exerted to prevent the peace of the town being unnecessarily disturbed'.[93] By the time of Lawley's death, indeed, events had apparently turned full circle, for in March 1793 he was succeeded by the man whom Holte had beaten in 1774, and even an old Tory like Sir Roger Newdigate was satisfied:

> Our loss in our late respectable Representative, to whose attentions we were much obliged, is very great, ... but ... I am happy ... to find that our ancient method of preserving the peace of the county is likely to be restored, and that a general meeting will again be permitted to recommend a knight to the free-holders as formerly, when he whom they favoured was chosen unanimously and without expense. For, in contradiction to modern opinions, I must hold that the County or Borough that is honestly and independently represented is more obliged to their member than he to them. I am happy to find Sir John Mordaunt is first in every mouth, and heartily wish he may be prevailed upon to accept a preference so truly honourable.[94]

Birmingham, it seemed, had been entirely assimilated into the county once more; but 'modern opinions' could not be gainsaid. The previous December Matthew Boulton had told the Marquess of Stafford that the public meeting in support of the town's newly formed Association for the Protection of Liberty and Property had been 'the most numerous I ever witnessed in Birmingham'. He had taken previous steps 'to reconcile some of the leading Dissenters to the principles of the meeting', and he had been distributing counter-revolutionary papers among the common people. 'On the whole,' he thought, 'we have put a check to republican principles, and . . . all will go on tranquil and well at Birmingham.' Nevertheless Boulton could not 'conceil [sic] . . . that there seems to be an earnest wish among all ranks for a reform of Parliament, in some shape or other, and without something of that kind is done, I fear there will exist a pretence for disquiet'.[95] Three months later Boulton's misgivings were justified; for while Sir Roger Newdigate was welcoming the return of 'our ancient method', and the county was proceeding to the nomination of Sir John Mordaunt, the Birmingham Society for Constitutional Information, founded on 20 November 1792, was seeking affiliation with its London namesake, and was urging the artisans of the town to

> be determined to think, to speak, and to act for yourselves; and . . . to lend this Society your aid and assistance, by signing your names to a Petition to be sent to the Honourable House of Commons, praying for an equal representation of the people, whereby you may regain your long lost rights, and restore to yourselves and posterity the ancient privilege of constantly, uniformly, and uninterruptedly, speaking their sentiments.[96]

NOTES

1 See appendix III.

2 For an elaboration on these difficulties see Piers Mackesy, *The War for America, 1775–83* (London, 1964), pp. 32–7.

3 Mackesy, *War for America*, p. 4.

4 See Ian R. Christie, *The End of North's Ministry, 1780–82* (London, 1958).

5 Mackesy, *War for America*, p. 4.

6 *Jopson*, 12 January 1778.

7 See Nehemiah Curnock, ed., *The Journal of John Wesley* (8 vols, London, 1915, repr. 1960), VI, 181, 182; entries for 4, 21 March 1778, at Bristol and Manchester respectively. The situation, Wesley felt, could be compared only with 'the alarm, which spread through the nation in King William's time, that on that very night the Irish Papists were to cut the throats of all the Protestants in England'.

8 John Telford, ed., *The Letters of the Revd. John Wesley* (8 vols, London, 1931, repr. 1960), VI, 358, Wesley to Samuel Bradburn, 10 October 1779.

9 Mackesy, *War for America*, p. 291.

10 See Wedgwood's views on Tucker's 'Thoughts on the Present Posture of Affairs' in his letter to Bentley of 12 August 1779 (Barl.). With respect to Ireland in particular, 'our protestant Dean builds his security principally upon the bulk of the . . . people . . . being roman catholics & consequently not tainted with republican, i.e. whigish principles'. According to Tucker, in other words, any risk to England came from the fact that 'the bulk of the people here are not roman catholics as they happily are in Ireland'. The logical conclusion of this was that the catholics should be entrusted with the defence of the nation against 'the Protestant & patriotic part of the Community'. 'Seriously,' Wedgwood concluded, 'if I could perswade myself that the bulk of the good people of England were of this red hot churchman's opinion I would not stir out of my seat to save them all from their beloved popery slavery & wooden shoes, but I cannot yet think so meanly of my *lay brothers* – The clergy ever had a separate interest from the body of the people; they have acted accordingly & preserve their character to the present hour.'

11 *The Selected Letters of Josiah Wedgwood*, p. 253, Wedgwood to Bentley, 13 June 1780.

12 See the appendix addressed 'to the inhabitants of the Central Counties in general, and to those of the town of Birmingham in particular', given with *Aris*, 10, 17 June 1872. The country was 'impoverished by chimerical projects of subduing America', but if it were 'once truly inspired with a martial and patriotic ardour, I should then consider the French invaders, however numerous, as so many victims to the genius of our Island. Think of the fate of Burgoyne and Cornwallis and you will know what might be expected! Have not the Americans shown that a nation in arms fighting in their own cause are superior to all the supposed advantages of discipline and professional military skill?'

13 Quoted by Mackesy, *War for America*, p. 5.

14 For the disintegration of the original Whig position see in general Bernard Donoughue, *British Politics and the American Revolution*, chs VI, VIII, IX, and in particular G. H. Guttridge, ed., *The Correspondence of Edmund Burke*, III, 97–8, 191, 216, 224: Burke to Rockingham, 12 January, 22–3 August, 1 October 1775, Rockingham to Burke, 24 September 1775.

15 *Jopson*, 4 November 1771, 2 December 1776, 24 March, 11 August 1777.

16 *Jopson*, 5 January 1778, 3 January, 7 February 1780, 16 April 1781.

17 *The Correspondence of Edmund Burke*, III, 383: Burke to Fox, 8 October 1777.

18 Wedgwood to Bentley, 29 December 1777 (*Barl.*).

19 See A. H. Lincoln, *Some Social and Political Ideas of English Dissent, 1763–1800* (Cambridge, 1938), and R. B. Barlow, *Citizenship and Conscience*.

20 R. B. Barlow, *Citizenship and Conscience*, pp. 182–4.

21 Wedgwood to Bentley, 6 February 1775 (*Barl.*).

22 Wedgwood to Bentley, 9 May 1779 (*Barl.*).

23 Wedgwood to Bentley, 17, 19 July 1777, *The Letters of Josiah Wedgwood*, II, 254, 259.

24 Wedgwood to Bentley, 7 August 1779, (*Barl.*).

25 Wedgwood to Bentley, 12 August 1779 (*Barl.*).

26 *Jopson*, 20, 27 April 1778.

27 Wedgwood to Bentley, 3 March 1778 (*Barl.*). For a précis of Lord North's speech on the Carlisle Peace Commission see Charles R. Ritcheson, *British Politics and the American Revolution* (Norman, Okl., 1954), pp. 261–3.

28 Wedgwood to Bentley, 10 September, 6 October 1768 (*Ryl. Eng.* MSS., 1107, pp. 1078–9, 1088), 20 June 1779, *The Letters of Josiah Wedgwood*, II, 383.

29 Wesley's *Journal*, VI, 222, 253: entries for 10 February, 5, 6 September 1779; *Letters*, VI, 348, 358, VII, 117–18; Wesley to Samuel Bradburn, 10 July, 10 October 1779, and to John Atlay, 4 April 1782.

30 Built in 1774 under a private Act of Parliament of 1772, and endowed by subscription from Birmingham's leading inhabitants, St Mary's Chapel, like its sister foundation of St Paul's, built between 1777 and 1779, was the result of the same kind of initiative for local improvement which had produced the Lamp Act. The first incumbent of St Mary's was in a particularly advantageous position from which to influence opinion, and it is some measure of the extent to which the religious revival was accepted and supported in Birmingham that both the Rev. John Riland and his assistant, the Rev. Edward Burn, should have been zealous evangelicals. Riland, who had been successively curate to Henry Venn of Huddersfield and curate at Sutton Coldfield before coming to Birmingham, was one of the group of clergy to whom John Wesley had proposed the formation of an evangelical preaching union in April 1764, and he remained an active ally of the Methodists, both during his years at St Mary's and after he returned to Sutton Coldfield as rector in 1790. Edward Burn, Riland's curate and successor at St Mary's, came to Birmingham from Trevecca, the college established for the ministers of her connection by the Countess of Huntingdon. Thought he subsequently repented of it, Burn was one of the chief local railers against Dr Priestley. *Cf.* Langford, *Birm. Life*, I, 165, 205–9; *V.C.H. Warwicks.*, VII, 368, 371; Wesley's *Journal*, V, 60–63, VII, 149, n. 1.

31 B.R.L. 66448.

32 *Aris*, 25 July, 12, 19, 26 September 1768.

33 See, for example, the Wenlock instructions of June 1769, above, p. 170.

34 See above, p. 185.

35 *Aris*, 5 March, 25 June, 16, 23 July, 27 August, 3 September 1770.

36 See D. M. Clark, *British Opinion and the American Revolution* (Yale, 1930, repr. 1966), pp. 52–65.

37 *H.M.C. Dartmouth*, II, 89, 204, 280, 378, 389: letters from John Willday, 22 August 1772, 19 March 1774, and from James Perry, 15 March, 10 September, 2 October 1775.

38 *H.M.C. Dartmouth*, II, 137, 239, 244, 318: letters of Isaac Spooner, 10 February 1773, and of John Florry, 14, 29 December 1774, 22 June 1775.

39 *A.O.P.*, the Rev. John Birch to Boulton, n.d. (? 1774). The names 'Roe' and 'Roebuck' seem to have been interchangeable. They were also used thus by Wedgwood in his letter to Bentley of 6 February 1775, cited above, p. 190.

40 See above, pp. 141–2.

41 *Aris*, 2, 9, 16, 23, 30 January 1775; *Parliamentary History*, XVIII (1774–77), 182; Brian D. Bargar, 'Matthew Boulton and the Birmingham petition of 1775'.

42 See above, pp. 60–61.

43 Bargar, *op. cit.*, p. 34.

44 See *A.O.P.*, America box, for an undated draft by Boulton of a trenchant reply to his critics.

45 MS copy in *A.O.P.*

46 See letters between February and April 1775, in *A.O.P.*

47 For details of the negotiations with Franklin, their breakdown and the opening stages of the war, see Bernard Donoughue, *British Politics and the American Revolution: the Path to War, 1773–75*, pp. 214–15, 221–5, 244–6, 266–79.

48 Donoughue, *op. cit.*, p. 222; C. R. Ritcheson, *British Politics and the American Revolution*, pp. 200 ff.

49 Wedgwood to Bentley, 14 November 1775 (*Barl.*).

50 See above, p. 187.

51 Text as in *Aris*, 6 February 1775.

52 *A.O.P.*, Dartmouth to Boulton, 19 January 1775. The text of Boulton's petition is cited by Bargar, 'Matthew Boulton and the Birmingham petition of 1775', p. 28.

53 Public Record Office, Home Office Papers, H.O. 55/7/23 (Bewdley), 55/11/6 (Coventry), 55/9/1 (Warwick), 55/11/3 (Shrewsbury), 55/7/10 (Worcester).

54 It was probably this that disturbed Lord Rockingham. See above, p. 187.

55 See *V.C.H. Warwicks.*, VIII, 502.

56 *Aris*, 30 October 1775.

57 The signatures to this, but no text, are in H.O. 55/7/6.

58 *H.M.C. Denbigh*, v, 298: Denbigh to Dr Rochford, 19 October 1775; *Whitley*, pp. 162, 172–3. The signature of Lord Archer, a staunch Whig and a patron of the corporation, was to be expected; not so that of Lord Craven, who had supported Waring and Yeo against the corporation in the 1774 election. Craven's unexpected apostacy, which provoked a quarrel with Yeo, must have added to Denbigh's surprise, and have helped to confirm him in his opinion that 'sending a Duke, or any peer or two, to the Tower, if they continue to hold the same language in Parliament will . . . go further towards settling matters in America than winning a battle'.

59 *H.M.C. Dartmouth*, II, 376–7, 393: Charles Simpson, town clerk of Lichfield, to Dartmouth, 9 September (enclosing letter of 4 September from Thomas Joel to the mayor of Lichfield), 23 October 1775. The Lichfield address is in H.O. 55/7/9.

60 *Aris*, 9 October 1775.

61 *Correspondence of Edmund Burke*, III, 106; Wedgwood to Bentley, 5 November 1775, (*Barl.*); *Aris*, 30 October 1775.

62 Wedgwood to Bentley, 27 November 1775 (*Barl.*).

63 See the advertisement in *Aris*, 30 October 1775, from which Wedgwood undoubtedly took the phrase 'A Gentn. of Character is to attend', which he quoted when writing to Bentley on 5 November.

64 Wedgwood to Bentley, 14 November 1775 (*Barl.*).

65 See above, pp. 33–46.

66 *A.O.P.*

67 *Aris*, 12 January 1778, especially 'The Speech of a Gentleman who attended the first meeting of the Inhabitants of Birmingham'. This may well have been Boulton, considering the prompting he had received from Dartmouth the previous month.

68 *Aris*, 2 February 1778.

69 Details of these are in *Aris*, issues from 19 January to 16 February 1778, supplemented by *Newdigate*, CR 136/1707, Thomas Payne of Coventry to Sir Roger Newdigate,

n.d. (? 6 or 7 January 1778). To begin with, the Sheriff refused to call the county together without the previous agreement both of its Members of Parliament and of the Earl of Hertford, its Lord Lieutenant. The meeting at Warwick on 14 January was therefore called by the Earl of Warwick, acting on his own initiative. Reactions in the county seem to have divided along lines comparable to those of 1774. Strong support for the 'truly patriotic principle' came from the Church interest in Coventry, from the magistrates of north-eastern Warwickshire, who met at Nuneaton on 8 January, and in general from Knightlow and East Hemlingford hundreds, where Thomas Payne distributed several thousand handbills advertising the Warwick meeting. Hertford, however, withheld his consent, apparently on the grounds that the King disapproved, and continued to regard Warwick's action as an infringement on his own prerogative as Lord Lieutenant. The meeting on 14 January was told by a Major Gregory of royal displeasure at the measures proposed to raise recruits; but Gregory subsequently admitted that he himself had had the rumour from Hertford, and the objection was waived by the Earl of Warwick, who read a letter to the meeting, ostensibly from Hertford, which approved of the plan and offered to subscribe. On 26 January, the *Birmingham Gazette* reported that an express letter had reached Warwick assuring the county of the King's approval; on 2 February Hertford was said to have agreed to call the county together after all, and the following week the Birmingham paper printed a letter from the Secretary at War informing the Earl of Warwick that the 6th Regiment of Foot was under orders to start recruiting in Warwickshire. On 16 February, however, Hertford announced that he would not under any circumstances call a meeting of the county. Readers of the *Birmingham Gazette* were thus kept guessing as to the true state of affairs for the best part of two months, during which opponents of the Birmingham subscription had ample opportunity to advise the town to stay well clear of the whole business.

70 *Aris*, 9 February 1778.

71 See above, p. 178.

72 See above, p. 101.

73 See above, p. 185.

74 *Hist. Parl.*, II, 634, III, 442–3; *Parliamentary History*, XVIII (1774–77), 182.

75 Stone, *Annals*, p. 8; Bedford, *Minutes*, *passim*. Meetings were also advertised in *Aris*, 3 June and 5 August 1776.

76 See appendix III.

77 See above, pp. 101–2.

78 Together, incidentally, with that of Dr Withering of the Lunar Society.

79 *Hist. Parl.*, III, 442–3.

80 *Aris*, 12 June 1780.

81 See *Aris*, 5, 12, 26 July, 2, 9, 30 August, 13 September 1779. The Birmingham loyal address, drawn up during July, concentrated on the Bourbon powers and hardly mentioned America. It was presented to the King by Lord Hertford, who in August gave his blessing as Lord Lieutenant to 'the Constitutional Purpose of increasing the Militia by volunteer companies' within the county. Captain Carver's company of Birmingham Volunteers, recruiting at the White Horse and the Death of General Wolfe in Digbeth, filled its ranks in five days, and in September recruits were still flocking to join the British Volunteers, 'notwithstanding the astonishing success that hath attended the recruiting service in general in this town – as well in raising volunteers as for the regulars'.

82 *H.M.C. Dartmouth*, III, 250–1: Thomas Faulconbridge to Dartmouth, 8, 14 June 1780. For Dr Dodd – the Rev. William Dodd, LL.D., the fashionable preacher and sometime Chaplain to the King who was hanged for forgery in 1777, see *D.N.B.* and Gerald Howson, *The Macaroni Parson* (London, 1973).

83 I. R. Christie, *The End of North's Ministry*, pp. 41–5.

84 *Aris*, 11 September 1780.

85 *H.M.C. Dartmouth*, III, 252–3.

86 *Aris*, 18 September 1780.

87 See below, pp. 265–6.

88 *Aris*, 22 December 1783.

89 *Aris*, 9, 16, 23 February 1784. In contrast to the activity of the Commercial Committee, the constables had declared on 9 February that they had 'no concern in calling a meeting of the town to address His Majesty, presuming such a measure incompatible with the harmony and interest of the town, which they ever wish to see preserved. '

90 *Aris*, 29 March, 5 April 1784. Charles Bowyer Adderley, who offered himself briefly as a prospective alternative to Lawley, faced a similar test. Having boasted that he was 'supported by certain Lords in the county', Adderley was challenged by 'A Freeholder' to 'inform the Freeholders assembled at Warwick how many of these Lords belong in the Bedchamber, or have posts about the Court'.

91 *A.O.P.*

92 See above, pp. 159, 181 n. 4.

93 *Aris*, 22, 29 March 1790. By this time Shuckburgh was back in favour as well—at any rate, he was included in the testimonial which Birmingham presented to the Warwickshire Members following their uncontested return, when they each received a ceremonial sword of first-quality Birmingham make in recognition of their services to the town. See *Aris*, 21 June 1790.

94 *Newdigate*, CR 136/B1399: Sir Robert's draft 'answer to Mr. Digby'. Lawley died on 11 March, and since Mordaunt at first declined the vacancy Charles Bowyer Adderley and Wriothesley Digby offered themselves as candidates. Digby had asked Newdigate for his support on 14 March, but at the county meeting at Warwick Mordaunt agreed to stand in order to avoid a contest, and the other two men deferred to this solution to the problem. See *Aris*, 18, 25 March, 1 April 1793.

95 *A.O.P.*, Boulton to the Marquess of Stafford, 11 December 1792.

96 Public Record Office, Treasury Solicitor's Papers, TS 11/962, Minute book of the Society for Constitutional Information, 15 February 1793; TS 11/953/3497, Address of the Birmingham Society for Constitutional Information, 4 March 1793.

IX

AN UNCERTAIN ANSWER:
THE WEST MIDLANDS AND THE
FRENCH REVOLUTION

Some four years before Sir John Mordaunt succeeded Lawley the centenary of the Glorious Revolution had provided Birmingham with a fitting opportunity to combine self-congratulation on its newly achieved solidarity and political influence with a more general celebration of the glories of the constitution. A commemoration banquet was given at the hotel by the High and Low Bailiffs. The guests, who included prominent local figures 'of every persuasion' as well as the High Sheriff of Warwickshire and the county Members, wore orange capes decorated with silver emblematic buttons. To mark the occasion they were presented with silver medals, and similar mementos 'of a different metal' were handed out to the crowd which gathered to watch the proceedings.[1] Despite the express wish that the unanimity of the commemoration might 'seal the extinction of parties', however, the lingering repercussions of old differences were soon to be caught up in more destructive divisions. In 1788 local leaders of all denominations were working together in Birmingham to support Thomas Clarkson's campaign for the abolition of slavery;[2] but though the diners at the hotel drank to 'the universal propagation of liberty and benevolence' this example of philanthropic harmony marked only a temporary respite in the worsening of relations between Churchmen and Dissenters.[3]

During the previous three years this had become an uncomfortably conspicuous feature of local life. In 1785 the first signs had appeared of the quarrel over the admission of controversial theology to the Birmingham Library;[4] and it was on the anniversary of the Revolution that year, in the sermon which he afterwards published as *The Importance and Extent of Free Enquiry in Matters of Religion*, that Joseph Priestley had laid the foundation for the later misconstruction of his intentions by describing the activities of Rational Dissent as gunpowder, laid 'grain by grain, under the old building of error and superstition, which a single spark may hereafter inflame, so as to produce an instantanious explosion'. Priestley went on to qualify this notorious metaphor with the warning that 'until things are ripe for such a revolution, it would be absurd to expect it, and in vain to attempt it', but the very terms of this qualification invited the attention of the Doctor's enemies. Chief among these was Samuel Horsley, the violent opponent of the repeal of the Test and Corporation Acts who led the orthodox attack on Priestley's theology. That Horsley made blatant use of his position as Bishop of St David's to influence the voting of his clergy in the 1790 election is well enough known.[5] Four years earlier, however, he had already taken advantage of an oversight in the licensing of the Birmingham

New Meeting House to reply in kind to Priestley's talk of ripening revolution, by encouraging his readers to

> trust ... for the present ... to the trade of the good town of Birmingham, and to the wise connivance of the magistrate, (who watches, no doubt while he deems it politic to wink,) to nip Dr. Priestley's goodly projects in the bud; which nothing would be so likely to ripen to a dangerous effect as constraint excessively or unseasonably used.[6]

Horsley's reliance on the balance of opinion and the discretion of the local authorities to achieve what could not be done by direct intervention was vindicated in 1786, when, by threatening to withdraw their support, the subscribers to the Birmingham Sunday schools frustrated the Dissenters' attempt to alter the rules of the original joint committee of 1784 so that they could run their own schools.[7] The Dissenters were thus baulked while at the same time the liaison between the different denominations involved in the Sunday schools remained as yet free from explicit damage. In 1787, however, the original combined organisation broke down completely. A second attempt was made to alter the rules, this time so that children in the schools might at least be allowed to worship with their parents' own congregations. When this was rejected, the Old and New Meetings seceded and established schools of their own.[8] In one of the most influential aspects of their relationship with the community Church and Dissent were now divided against each other, and much of their pastoral work henceforward assumed the form of a mutual battle for the minds of the younger generation. When the Anglican clergy handed out free copies of *A Preservative against Socinianism* in July 1787 to all those in Birmingham recently confirmed by the Bishop of Worcester, Dr Priestley countered by producing a penny abridgement of his *Appeal to the Serious and Candid Professors of Christianity*, and by advertising cheap editions of the full pamphlet, price 2d or 6d, depending on the quality of the paper.[9]

With the beginning of the movement for the repeal of the Test and Corporation Acts, the mixture of personal spite and *odium theologicum* produced by these quarrels was caught up in a national political issue of the first magnitude.[10] Led by Priestley and his friend William Russell, who as early as February 1787 was an active associate of the committee of London Dissenters formed by Thomas Jefferys to conduct the repeal campaign, the Birmingham Unitarians were prominent from the start in the agitation against the two Acts. This reached its climax in 1789–90. At their second attempt, in May 1789, the repealers were able to reduce the majority against them in the House of Commons to a mere twenty votes.[11] After this near-success they looked confidently for victory at the third time of asking. Preparations for this far exceeded anything which had preceded the two previous attempts. For the only time during the century Dissenters in the country at large were broadly united behind their leaders in London,[12] and plans for a national convention of the interest were enthusiastically supported by large meetings in the provinces. On 14 October 1789 William Russell and his fellow Unitarians persuaded representatives of all the Dissenting congregations in Birmingham, Presbyterian, Baptist and Independent alike, to meet at the hotel, where they established the 'Committee of the Seven Congregations of the Three Denominations'.[13] The announced purpose of this was to consult Protestant Dissenters elsewhere in order to plan the systematic division of the country into districts, each of which was to send delegates to a general meeting of Dissenters in London. Within three months the Birmingham committee had become one of the prime movers behind the largest and most significant of the provincial associations, which was formed on 13 January 1790 at a meeting in Leicester of 'Deputies of Protestant Dissenters of the Three Denominations within the Midland District'.[14] 'District' was indeed barely an adequate description of an organisation which embraced the counties of Derby, Nottingham, Lincoln, Warwick, Worcester, Salop, Leicester and Rutland.

At least in the comprehensiveness of its declarations and the extent of its plans the Midland District Association was running ahead of all but the most advanced opinion in the rest of the country, London included.[15] Taking its stand on the principles of natural right, the meeting at Leicester issued a sweeping condemnation, not only of the Test and Corporation Acts but of all penal legislation of any kind whatsoever. To achieve this, it asked for the formation of

a permanent mode of collecting the sense and uniting the efforts of the whole body of Dissenters of every denomination, so that they may have their Representatives to meet in London or elsewhere and make proper applications to the legislature as circumstances require.

Delegates were accordingly nominated to 'the National Meeting now in contemplation', and the deputies at Leicester set up their own organisation to bring this forward by appointing William Russell as secretary and treasurer of an executive committee, which was instructed to establish regular contact with similar bodies in other parts of the country in order to co-ordinate their activities with the coming parliamentary campaign.[16] The techniques of extra-parliamentary organisation first developed by Christopher Wyvill's Yorkshire Association were thus applied to a cause whose supporters, inspired now by the news from France, were convinced that their coming liberation from civil bondage was as certain as the overthrow of despotism itself. Not even the size of the majority in the House of Commons, which on 2 March 1790 overwhelmed the third application for repeal by 294 votes to 105, deterred them. In its manifesto of 19 May the Jefferys committee spurned the charges of republicanism and disloyalty which were being levelled at it, and announced its intention to persevere until 'a generous nation that of late has been misled by false alarms... shall return to calmer feelings'.[17] In *The Dissenter's Plea*, published in Birmingham for the Midland District Association a month later, George Walker of Nottingham, one of the ablest advocates of the Dissenters' case, again denounced all penal legislation in the uncompromising language of natural right, and exposed the time-honoured alliance between Church and State as 'the substituting convenience for morality and accommodating the unalterable rules of justice to the notions of speculative utility'.[18]

By the middle of 1790, however, the Unitarian *avant-garde* was losing touch with the more orthodox Trinitarians who formed the greater part of the Dissenting interest, and was basing its confidence on the example of France rather than the reality of England. John Hurford Stone of Hackney, who saw a surer portent in the Assemblée Nationale's secularisation of the property of the French Church than in the House of Commons' continuing attachment to the Test and Corporation Acts, congratulated Priestley 'on what must inevitably come to pass'. For such men it required

> no uncommon marks of sagacity to foresee that an idiot King, a slavish Hierarchy and the delusion of the People must melt away like snow before the Sun of Truth.[19]

What exhilarated Priestley and his friends, however, filled the rest of the nation with alarm. After the comparative improvement of 1788, sectarian relationships in Birmingham had started to deteriorate again several months before Priestley's sermon of 5 November 1789 to the Old and New Meetings on *The Conduct to be Observed by Dissenters, in order to Procure the Repeal of the Corporation and Test Acts* brought the local quarrel between Church and Dissent fully into the open. The response to Priestley from the local clergy was embittered. On 3 January 1790 the Rev. George Croft accused the Dissenters of abusing their existing privileges by their efforts to secure political commitments from Members of Parliament as the price of their electoral support, reviewed their history from the time of Charles I in order to demonstrate the moroseness, the inherent bigotry and the destructiveness of their principles, and warned that 'while their meeting houses are open, they are weakening, and almost demolishing the whole fabric of Christianity'. Six weeks later Spencer Madan, the Rector of St Philip's, again warned that 'Presbyterian principles are unquestionably republican', and reminded his congregation that 'these abettors of a republican system' had 'been already tried upon this point, to the great sorrow and distress of the nation'.[20] Meanwhile, as befitted an ex-pupil of Samuel Horsley, the Earl of Aylesford had presided over a county meeting at Warwick on 2 February at which the friends of the Church considered 'proper measures for the Defence of the Constitution'.[21] By the beginning of March, when the debate on the Test and Corporation Acts came on in Parliament, Priestley was already anticipating reprisals from the mob if, as was now generally expected, the vote at Westminster went against the Dissenters.[22]

For the moment the mob was restrained;[23] but the exchange of pamphlets and tracts continued unabated, and other factors now began to influence the situation. During 1790 the dispute between Church and Dissent over the civil liberties of the latter became embroiled in the quarrel which had recently developed over the rating of small houses in Birmingham. The exchanges which this produced between William Hutton, the Vestry and the Overseers gave particular plausibility to rumours that the Dissenters were intent on giving an immediate demonstration of the most sinister consequences of weakening the alliance between Church and State by conspiring to take over the government of the town.[24] At the same time the state of the buckle and button trades, which in their various branches were probably the largest employers in Birmingham, took a decided turn for the worse.[25] The combined effect of these developments was that the uproar now involved a much wider range of local interests than it had done hitherto, and that it was now deliberately extended to the common people. Priestley's *Familiar Letters to the Inhabitants of Birmingham*, originally intended to answer the charges made by the clergy of the town, called forth a mass of vernacular replies, most of them bogus—which adds to the charge of incitement which has been brought against the local authorities for what happened the following year—some of them possibly genuine. Particularly significant was the first production of the Nott family, 'John Nott, Button Burnisher's' *Very Familiar Letters*, which used every cheap device to ridicule the Dissenters' position and to impugn their motives in local affairs. In crude but menacing imitation of Sheridan's Mrs Malaprop, Priestley was thanked for his letters to 'us townsmen and malefactors of Birmingham', which Honest John, who reckoned himself an expert on the subject, had nevertheless found funnier than the Doctor's other books. No clearer proof could be wanting that Mr Madan and Mr Croft were right about the disturbing mental effects of Presbyterianism than all this raving about gunpowder, not to mention the 'unsettled' principles of these lunatic philosophers and their obsessive tendency to 'write and print so plaguy fast' in their own defence. If only the Dissenters would hearken, if not to Mr Madan, then at least to St Paul, they would surely realise

> how wicked it was for 'em to be brawling here and crawling there, and to go brawling to Leicester and brawling all over the Kingdom about Corporations and Sacraments and such sort of things.

In any case, John could not understand 'what the plague you bother us so much about corporation and testy acts' for—unless, of course, what they were saying was true, and 'you and Mr. Russell won't be easy ... till you've made Birmingham a corporation town, and then it will be no bigger than Sutton. ...'[26] If this was indeed the case, all the assurances that repeal would not harm the Church might as well have come from Little Red Riding Hood's granny. Mr Burke had seen the light, and the sooner Priestley and his friends followed their erstwhile friend's example the sooner the people of Birmingham would cease to repent 'as we do now that you ever came among us'.[27]

Tension continued to grow during the closing months of 1790, when Birmingham again faced the possibility of sectarian rioting. It received new impetus the following spring, when the Unitarians turned their attention from the comparatively specific question of the Test and Corporation Acts to the more general one of political reform; and it reached its climax in the week of rioting that followed Dr Priestley's attempt to recruit support for a Warwickshire Constitutional Society, the circulation of inflammatory handbills in the town and the dinner held at the hotel on the anniversary of the capture of the Bastille. The actual course of the Priestley riots needs little rehearsal here;[28] what does require consideration is their effect on the development of democratic clubs in the Birmingham area. There can be no doubt that the expulsion of the Dissenters from the prominent position they had hitherto occupied in Birmingham's affairs severely damaged the reform movement in the town. Nor can it be denied that the riots demonstrated with brutal clarity the extent to which Priestley and his colleagues had isolated themselves from those to whom they looked for ultimate vindication. On the other hand, the development of the reform movement was not brought to a complete stand; whatever their social differences, the men who led and sustained its revival after 1792 were not entirely unconnected with those who had suffered during the previous year. In the immediate aftermath of the riots the Rational Dissenters may have seemed little more than an eccentric minority, a self-constituted, self-absorbed elite of 'middle class' intellectuals, the arrogance of whose theoretical claims made a ludicrous contrast to their real ignorance of the popular mind. To accept this view is, however, to forget the

attention Priestley had himself paid to the instruction of the younger members
of his congregation, and to overlook the leading part played by the Unitarians in
fostering the reading societies and book clubs which had been the principal
agents in the extension of popular articulacy in Birmingham during the previous
two decades. From this point of view the continued existence of the Birmingham
Book Club and of the group of teachers who were responsible first for the
Sunday Society and then for the Brotherly Society is of more significance than
the burning of the New Meeting. It was through these links that a connection
was preserved between the original leaders of the reform movement in the
town and those who followed them.[29] By 1796, when its warden, Edward Corn,
was among those who worked closely with John Binns and John Gale Jones
during their visit to Birmingham as delegates of the London Corresponding
Society,[30] the New Meeting itself was again involved in the cause, even though
it was still in temporary accommodation in Livery Street at the time.[31]

The difficulties involved in assessing the effect of the riots are part of the
larger ambiguity which characterised the relationship between the West Midlands as a whole and the political developments of the early 1790s.[32] Before the
closing months of 1792, and apart from the part played by its Dissenters in the
agitation against the Test and Corporation Acts, the region's contribution to
those developments was comparatively insignificant. William Russell had been a
member of the Society for Constitutional Information since January 1783,[33] but
Priestley never joined it, despite his plans to start a Warwickshire Constitutional
Society in 1791. In fact, as far as the West Midlands were concerned, the
London society seems to have relied chiefly on Mr Hall of Shrewsbury for the
distribution of its literature during the 1780s; and though Hall was assisted in
Worcestershire and Gloucestershire by a Mr Martin, who may have based his
activities on Birmingham,[34] there is no sign that the town was particularly
prominent among the Society for Constitutional Information's early points of
contact outside the capital. This was in accord with the general political disposition of the region at the time; but even in June 1792, when the society did
supply Birmingham with 600 copies of a letter from Tom Paine to Henry
Dundas defending his cheap edition of the *Rights of Man*, this must be seen in
relation to the very much larger quantities sent elsewhere. Of the 9,000 copies in
the first printing, by far the largest consignments, 1,200 in each case, went to
Sheffield, Norwich and Manchester. The same was true of the society's resolutions on the royal proclamation, 1,000 copies of which were sent to each of the
latter centres, while Birmingham received only 100. And when a further 12,000
copies of Paine's letter were distributed, the total allocation for the entire Midlands came once more to a mere 850, shared out between the Rev. Mr Rowe of
Shrewsbury; Mr Fox of Derby; the editor of the *Leicester Herald*; the Rev.
John Edwards, who succeeded Priestley at the Birmingham New Meeting; Mr
Thomas Francis and the Rev. Mr Martin, also of Birmingham, and the Rev. Mr
Corrie of Bromsgrove.[35]

At this stage there was no sign in the West Midlands of the kind of democratic
political association which already existed in Sheffield, Manchester and Norwich. What contact there was with the movement for reform was being maintained through the Society for Constitutional Information's links with what
remained of the original local leadership. This was drawn predominantly from
the Dissenting ministers of the region and their congregations. At Bromsgrove,

for example, it consisted of two ministers, Corrie and Wells, of whom the former had been a pupil of Priestley at Hackney New College; a Quaker who sold seditious pamphlets; two Dissenting laymen, of whom one was further identified as a grocer, and a third 'of no religion'.[36] Such a description gives an impression of small-town obscurity, but connections of this kind were not negligible. They did mean that when the West Midlands responded to the popular political excitement of the closing months of 1792 the region was not without existing points of activity to which new developments could be joined; and if the group at Bromsgrove remains of minor significance, that at Shrewsbury demands more respect. Led by William Tayleur, a wealthy merchant, and by the Rev. John Rowe, its minister from 1787 to 1798, the congregation at the High Street chapel had been a centre for the dissemination of advanced opinions for at least the past ten years.[37] In addition a society at Shrewsbury 'headed by Tayleur, a Dissenter; Mr. Darwin, and other Dissenters' was noticed by the Home Office's list of 'Associations for the Relief of Pretended Grievances' in October 1792.[38] 'Mr. Darwin' was Robert Waring Darwin, son of Erasmus and father of Charles. He had been established in medical practice in Shrewsbury since 1788,[39] and the appearance of so famous a name serves as a reminder of the part played in the broadcasting of radical ideas by many of those, particularly of the younger generation, who were connected with such groups as the Lunar Society and other provincial literary and philosophical societies. In this connection, indeed, interesting ground for speculation is offered by the relationship which may have existed between Robert Darwin's group at Shrewsbury and members of his father's Derby Philosophical Society,[40] and between the latter and the political society which the Home Office listed as forming in Derby in October 1792 under the auspices of Mr Fox. Developments at Derby hardly qualify for inclusion in the West Midlands on their own account, but they do seem to have had some effect on the spread of radical politics in Shropshire, where a Dr Beddowes who lived near Derby was reported to be distributing seditious propaganda in the Shifnal area during the autumn of 1792.[41]

By this time the Jacobins of Lancashire and the West Riding had extended their range southwards to cover the whole of the Midlands, reviving the old and creating new centres of activity as they came. In December the townships in the Wem district of Shropshire, which had also 'become clamorous for reform and revolution principals [sic]', were said to be in touch both with Mr Cooper of the Manchester Constitutional Society and with 'others in Birmingham, forming a sort of Committee of Correspondence between these places of a most dangerous tendency'.[42] From Birmingham itself John Reeve's newly formed Association for the Preservation of Liberty and Property was challenged in November 1792 by a 'Patriot' who asked how it hoped to 'quench the ardour of investigation which now fires the breasts of Englishmen and mankind at large'. When William Belcher was indicted at Warwick assizes in July 1793 for selling the *Rights of Man* in Birmingham the previous December he was able to defend himself by pointing out that the work was on sale at every bookseller's in town. By the following July the Sheffield *Patriot* was circulating at least as far south as Tewkesbury, where there was 'scarcely an old woman but is talking politics'.[43] In the Potteries, where a prolonged and riotous election dispute at Newcastle under Lyme[44] contributed its share of particular vehemence to the general excitement, republican feeling had become particularly conspicuous since the *sans-culottes*' victory at Jemappes. Paine's works, supplied by Joseph Straphan of Hanley and circulated by 'many notorious Leaders', were in the hands of most people, especially the journeymen potters. So far there had been no public meetings, but the common people, entranced by the prospective end to taxation which Paine promised, were calling openly for revolution, while the local magistrates sought in vain for the courage to act vigorously against them. So bad was the situation that John Massey of Newcastle feared an early end to the constitution if the rest of the country were no better.[45]

The major expansion of Jacobin activity in the Midlands after the summer of 1792 meant that Birmingham came to play a crucial part in the calculations both of the reformers and of their opponents. As the centre of one of the principal manufacturing areas of the country, whose independent small masters and skilled artisans shared many of the characteristics which had already made the men of Sheffield so formidable, its immediate importance to the Jacobins was obvious. Even more significant, however, was Birmingham's value as a centre of communications situated half way between London and the north, and with access to the middle west. Admittedly the recent behaviour of the town had not been encouraging, but there were already signs that its disposition was beginning to change. In any case, from the point of view of strategy, Birmingham's printing presses and bookshops, several of which were already in sympathetic hands, were more important than its mob. If the partial damage caused by the Priestley riots could be restored and the incident itself be forgotten, the kind of association among working men which Birmingham and its trades had long nurtured would still be capable of producing a local leadership which was articulate, self reliant, ready to take its own decisions, to write and circulate its own propaganda and to fight its own battles. If this could be brought about, Birmingham, like Sheffield, might be established as a major Jacobin stronghold from which the word might be spread yet farther. The correspondence which was thought to exist with the townships in the Wem district of Shropshire and with the Manchester Constitutional Society in December 1792 is some indication of Birmingham's importance in this respect. So are the apparent plans for *Swinney's Birmingham and Stafford Chronicle* which so disturbed John Brooke in June 1793 that he urged the government to take immediate action lest the paper fall into Jacobin hands.[46] The clearest example, however, is the connection established by John Harrison between Sheffield, Birmingham, Coventry and the London Corresponding Society. It was Harrison, a Sheffield razor maker,[47] who played the main part in forming the Birmingham Society for Constitutional Information in November 1792, and he continued to guide its activities until the following August, when he moved on to Coventry. Here attempts had already been made to found a society during the previous winter, when Thomas Prosser, its eventual chairman, had asked the Society for Constitutional Information for details of the organisation of the Sheffield societies; but the venture had been scotched for the time being by the city's corporation, which was only too glad of the chance to rid itself of the persistent taint of its own Dissenting past by taking prompt and vigorous action against the reformers.[48] Nevertheless, when Harrison himself arrived in Coventry *en route* for London, he believed that with help and encouragement from the London Corresponding Society he could start something even 'in this despotic town'. Despite fierce opposition his confidence was justified, and he was able to leave Prosser in charge of a viable society whose membership showed encouraging signs of growth, in good contact with other parts of the country and well supplied with printed propaganda, not only from the London Corresponding Society but also from Birmingham.[49] The rapid politicisation of a trade dispute among the shag weavers in the area south of the city towards Banbury during August 1793 suggests that the Coventry society lost little time in putting these assets to work on its own account.[50]

That Whitehall was also well aware of Birmingham's importance had already been demonstrated by the swiftness of its reaction to the Priestley riots. If this stood in marked contrast to the complaisance of the Warwickshire magistrates, it did so not out of any love for the Dissenters or concern for their violated rights but because the violence in Birmingham was recognised for what it was: a serious threat, not merely to the good order of one particular area but to the government's capacity to control a large part of the entire country. In the past the only place of sufficient size to pose this kind of threat had been London itself. As the first major outbreak of large-scale urban rioting outside the capital, the Priestley riots demonstrated that by the end of the eighteenth century this was no longer the case; and if the new manufacturing towns of the Midlands and the north were none of them individually as large as London, their diversity, the weakness in many cases of their existing civil authorities and their geographical dispersion meant that, collectively, they raised problems of control which had never been met before. From this point of view, the fact that the riots actually occurred where they did in 1791 was comparatively incidental. On one hand, the breakdown of authority in Birmingham soon attracted elements from other places. Colliers from the Black Country moved in to loot; several of the mob's ringleaders were thought to have come from Coventry, where a large party stood by throughout the riots ready to maul the city's own Dissenters if it was given half a chance, and by 19 July, five days after the ill fated dinner at the hotel, hard-core criminals from London were on the road to the Midlands.[51] On the other hand, the disturbance itself threatened to spread, and not simply to the surrounding district. In Sheffield, which was already being troubled by sporadic resistance to the enclosure of the town commons, the authorities were seriously worried lest 'the rioters from Birmingham ... flock here in numbers from the similarity of the manufactures and take the chance of committing further depredations'. Manchester also looked dangerous for a time; so did Leicester and Wolverhampton; and the mayor of Bristol was warned that

> We are coming Near two 2,000 Good harty hail strong Rufins which will Pull Down your fine Manchin house and your fine Baptis Meating and not your Meating only But Presperterines Likewise and Romands and all your Decenters houses shall share the same fate as them at Burmingham ...[52]

In these circumstances the movement of troops to quell the riots in Birmingham meant that the government had to take a succession of calculated risks with the security of other places which would be left temporarily vulnerable. Before order was restored the disposition of forces over the entire country had become involved,[53] and it was therefore just as well that Nottingham, whence came both the first troops to reach Birmingham and a large part of those sent to Sheffield,[54] showed no disposition to riot on its own account. As it was, according to one eye-witness, the nearest troops to Birmingham, a small detachment at Coventry which might have arrived before the mob got completely out of hand, was persuaded not to leave its base by the mayor, who feared for the safety of his own city.[55] Similarly, the orders sent to the Ist Dragoons at Manchester on 17 July were hastily cancelled following an alarmed letter from the magistrates there warning the Home Office of the serious danger of trouble, particularly from the Irish, if the military presence in the area was weakened—a warning which was repeated a week later when the Dragoons were again placed in readiness, this time to march to Sheffield.[56]

The crisis passed, but the danger of disturbance remained very real. If the Jacobins regarded Birmingham as one of the keys to their future strength, the government was equally determined to deny them any such advantage. Though the diners of 1791 had recently abandoned their plans to meet again the following July, the renewed possibility of rioting at Whitsun in 1792, when troops from Bromsgrove and Kidderminster were called up to reinforce those already in Birmingham, served as a reminder that, given the chance, the mob would be on the streets again, pretext or no pretext.[57] At the same time Samuel Ashton of Sheffield was already discussing the prospect of future operations in the provinces with the secretary of the Society for Constitutional Information, and emphasising that

> Birmingham in particular claims all the assistance from established societies which can possibly be administered; there are great numbers in that place Friendly to the cause of the people, and we hope (notwithstanding the late tragical transactions) if prudent methods are adopted & pursued, the people's attention may be turned to their own interest and the mouths of ranting bigots stopped, which is & must be the sincere wish of every real Friend to the peace & welfare of Mankind.[58]

As Colonel De Lancey, who had commanded the forces sent to Birmingham the previous year, pointed out in his report of June 1792 on the disposition and morale of the troops deployed in the provinces, the situation in the town remained in the balance. Conditions were not as bad as they were in Sheffield, and though they were ready to harrass the Dissenters at every available opportunity, most people were still very loyal. Nevertheless both parties were 'carrying on a literary war, no day passing without some publication or other, each tending to inflame the animosity that exists between them'. To some extent this had been checked by the royal proclamation against treason and sedition, which produced the appropriate loyal address from Birmingham.[59] The circulation of seditious tracts had been inhibited, and one man in particular, who had received a large quantity of the cheap edition of the *Rights of Man*, had been frightened into holding on to the entire consignment. The tension in the town was not, however, confined to the mutual execration of Church and Dissent. The presence of the Blues was resented by everyone; brawls involving soldiers and civilians were almost an everyday occurrence, and the position of the former was far from pleasant. Billeted out in taverns and public houses, they were exposed constantly to 'the licentious conduct of the manufacturers, who in this town are particularly dissipated'. Not only was this obviously bad for morale, but De Lancey feared that it could render the troops ineffective in an emergency, since the mob would be able to prevent them from mustering to take concerted action. In sum, the situation in Birmingham was typical of the entire country. For the moment most people were well disposed, but there was a spirit of mischief abroad which would have to be checked, and checked at once, before it was too late.[60]

As the insurrection of 10 August, the September massacres and the victories at Valmy and Jemappes brought the *sans-culottes* to the central position in the French revolution and the revolution to its climax, the possibility of rebellion at home and Birmingham's reputation as a major producer of arms gave the government a new and urgent reason to keep close watch on the town. On 21 September Dr William Maxwell, a member of the Society for Constitutional Information who had undertaken to raise money to buy arms for the French, was said to be ordering pikes and poniards in Birmingham at the rate of two thousand a week to a total of some twenty-four thousand. These figures were probably exaggerated, but some weapons at least were not only delivered but also shipped from Dover, much to the chagrin of the government, which as yet lacked a legal way of stopping them. Samples of the daggers—in John Brooke's lurid description 'ye most dangerous assassinating weapons I ever saw'—were hastily procured, and it was one of these which Edmund Burke obtained and flourished melodramatically in the House of Commons on 28 December during the second reading of the aliens Bill. In the House itself the incident fell rather flat; but despite the opportunity it gave the caricaturists it was probably more effective out of doors. From Birmingham Burke received a copy of one of John Nott's tracts, together with a sample brass button stamped 'Liberté' and 'Egalité', three thousand of which were supposed to have been ordered for Manchester and Sheffield in readiness for 'a bloody day' on Queen Charlotte's birthday the following January, and rumours of impending massacre were further fed by other portents of the same kind. Suspicious-looking Frenchmen were supposed to be landing at Dover, and a coincidence of sorts was discovered between the total reached by Maxwell's French subscription and multiples of the prices recently paid to London arms dealers by unidentified foreign customers.

Nor were these doings the only source of anxiety. Quite apart from Maxwell's daggers, Birmingham's gunsmith's and sword cutlers were reported to be working at full stretch on massive orders for every kind of weapon from bayonets and boarding spikes to blunderbusses. So pressing was the demand that large quantities of used Tower muskets which had recently been auctioned off by the War Office were being reconditioned to supply the deficiency of new stock. Ostensibly most of this extra production, which was estimated at a thousand per week above the usual run of business, was destined for the Continent, and several foreign agents, mainly from France, had been noticed in Birmingham trying to place orders. Besides the fact that the capacity of her own armouries seemed to make it unlikely that all the town's output was going to France, however, what particularly attracted attention was the production of a weapon lighter and cheaper than the standard design, remarkably similar to that which had been used by the Irish Volunteers ten years previously. Several of the leading makers in Birmingham and Wolverhampton, notably Galton and Whateley, were said to be working on this, and reports that arms shipments from Birmingham were reaching Dublin seemed to confirm the fear that this gun was intended for use nearer home than the battlefields of Flanders.

How much truth there was in all this is difficult to tell: the makers themselves, who were 'generally speaking more occupied in seducing each other's workmen than in considering the purpose for which the arms they were making are intended', probably had no clear idea where their goods were going. Certainly old Samuel Galton proved 'very ingenuous in his declarations' when he was pressed on the subject in November. He denied any knowledge of Irish orders, whether placed with his own firm or with other businesses, disclaimed responsibility for the improved blunderbuss which he was supposed to be sending by the thousand to Liverpool every week and said that he had repeatedly turned down orders for cheap arms from a French merchant, M. Le Coint. Galton's account was corroborated by confidential examination of the books of the Trent and Mersey Canal Company, the waggons which plied between Birmingham and Liverpool and the customs records at the port, none of which produced any evidence of suspicious packages; but the government's fears were not allayed. Its spies remained convinced that 'considerable quantities of arms have been sent by one means or another to Ireland and . . . to Scotland also'. David Blair, another gunsmith and 'a violent leveller', who had acted for Dr Maxwell and was soon to be one of the twelve members of the Birmingham Society for Constitutional Information proposed for affiliation with the parent society, was said to have given up his usual trade in fowling pieces in order to concentrate on refitting muskets, apparently for a buyer in Scotland. And whatever the reputation of the elder Galton, that of the son was no better than Blair's, so that when reports reached London in December that the two Galtons were again busy, this time on a large quantity of reconditioned muskets whose destination they were trying to conceal from their workmen, serious doubt was cast on the father's candour of the previous month.[61]

The spies, employed by the Home Office and controlled locally by John Brooke, who investigated the arms trade were also used to keep watch on the activities of Birmingham's Jacobins. The Society for Free Debate was infiltrated on instructions from Evan Nepean early in November,[62] but the most fruitful source of information at this stage was the house of Mr Moore at the sign of the Bell in Colmore Row, where, on 5 October, Mr Hill, an attorney's clerk,[63] had provoked a heated argument by referring to kings in general as 'a set of useless beings set up for fools to worship' and to George III as 'a mere *Thing, a Tool*, of no use, as he had no power or will of his own'. On being threatened with eviction Hill had claimed that there were plenty of others who shared his views, and that

> It was very hard he should be turned out for saying so in a Room where there were but 16 people & he had spoke ten times as much in another House where there were near 50 in company, & no-one found the least Fault with him.

Hill was supported by a Mr Hesketh, who denied the existence of the constitution and drank reformation to Church and King; and it was therefore probably as well for the reputation of the house that their abuse was answered the following day by a barrister, Mr Moffat, who spoke very favourably of the constitution. Nevertheless Hill and Hesketh continued to frequent the Bell, together with an Italian language teacher, Mr Vergani, who was said to be a Jacobin agent. In mid-November, when slogans proclaiming NO KING NO CHURCH appeared in several parts of the town, the three of them were again making trouble, boasting that they were going to establish 'a *Rights of Man* club in Birmingham, which was to consist of the lower classes of people only', and ridiculing the Church and King Club as a drunken bout, the very idea of which was 'enough to make a Dog Laugh'.[64]

By this time several emissaries from Sheffield and Manchester were also spreading the word, and it was these whom John Harrison brought together to form the nucleus of the Birmingham Society for Constitutional Information.[65] Like the Sheffield societies and the London Corresponding Society, the Birmingham reformers organised themselves in separate divisions, each of which was represented on a central committee, and the only restriction placed on membership was that all should read and subscribe to the address which the reformers issued on 20 November. This managed to express the ideals of traditional constitutionalism in almost Rousseauistic terms. On one hand, it explicitly denied any revolutionary intention, recalled the objectives of the Yorkshire Association and the early professions of William Pitt, and declared that the Birmingham society was 'anxious for the restoration of our CONSTITUTION to its primitive simplicity'. On the other hand, it inveighed against public ignorance, the handmaid of priestcraft and statecraft; and if it pledged its subscribers to work for a peaceable reform of Parliament rather than for revolution it did so in order to 'obtain a real representation of the *national will*', and called to mind

> the sentiments which nature has engraved in the heart of every citizen and which take a new force when solemnly recognized by all.... For a nation to love liberty, it is sufficient that she knows it; and to be free, it is sufficient that she wills it.[66]

Though its address was thus an exercise in studied ambiguity, however, the reports which reached the Home Office showed that the Birmingham society was well versed in the prospective mechanics of democratic government as set out in part two of the *Rights of Man*. Besides 'the very powerful argument held out to our workmen in this place, that they shall have ale at 2*d* a quart', there was to be 'no King, no taxes, & they have gone so far in their calculations as to fix that a Man with 3 children will have £50 a year'.[67] On this evidence at least, there seemed to be little doubt which way the uncertainties in the proclaimed intentions of the Birmingham Jacobins were likely to be resolved, especially when it was accompanied by intercepted correspondence which spoke of pistols by the thousand and boasted that Liberty was 'on the march for Birmingham', where five thousand converts had been made in the past two months.[68]

It would, of course, be wrong to take at their face value either the enthusiastic claims of partisans or the testimony of spies eager to earn their reward in the government's service. As John Hurd, one of the Home Office's more reliable informers, wrote at the time, it is

> extremely difficult to come at matters of fact, at the same time Ministers cannot have too early intelligence, even of rumours, but care should be taken not to cry out the Wolf the Wolf too often.

Hurd's own judgement was that Birmingham had nothing to fear for the moment, since the loyalists outnumbered their opponents by at least six to one. This was corroborated by the support given to the town's loyal associations.

Though it earned the scorn of the company at the Bell in Colmore Row, the Church and King Club, formed by Edward Carver and John Brooke, had been advertising since 12 November and was recruiting at Hobson's Tavern in Worcester Street on the 20th.[69] The Loyal True Blues, in which Brooke also had a hand, opened its books at the Union tavern in Cherry Street on 3 December, and four days later the Birmingham Association for the Protection (sic) of Liberty and Property held its first meeting at the hotel.[70] At this, according to Matthew Boulton, 'there was not one dissenting voice, and in every question the answer ay seemed to come from one gyant with 800 voices, for there were that number'.[71] But numbers were not everything: however loyal the greater part of the town, it might easily be rendered powerless by a determined and organised minority. Despite his confidence in the present safety of the situation John Hurd therefore also passed on an anonymous warning that 'on the first stroke of a riot commencing here' parties would be sent by the Jacobins to raid the armouries of the Warwickshire, Staffordshire, Worcestershire and Derbyshire militias, and continued to emphasise the need for active measures against the constitutional societies as the essential means to retain control, both of Birmingham itself and of the Black Country towns.[72]

It was, however, one thing to draw attention to the problem and quite another to find ways of solving it. The campaign of prosecutions launched by the government against the retailers of seditious literature was less successful at this stage in Birmingham than it was in other places.[73] Depite Hurd's wishes to the contrary, no sufficient pretext yet existed for taking the leaders of the Constitutional Society into custody, and both Harrison and John Kilmister, its secretary, were still at large. The only remaining course of action seemed to be that adopted by the Loyal True Blues: to challenge the Jacobins at their own game by organising the loyalists at the same social level, and in a similar way. This, however, was to court the very danger of riot whose avoidance was crucial to the security of the entire region. After the Loyal True Blues' first meeting on 3 December bands of hooligans bawling the national anthem took to the streets and mobbed the houses of William Hutton and William Humphreys in what looked disconcertingly like the start of a re-enactment of the Priestley riots.[74] The result of such tactics, as John Brooke learned from one of his contacts in the Loyal True Blues, was that Birmingham was reduced to a state of gang warfare which made the control of the local magistrates look pretty precarious, and the True Blues had to be hastily called off:

This town swarms with Jacobins & our Society is forbid to meet because they are afraid we whod. be numerous & riot—I went home last night & the night before to oblige Mr. Carles & some or. gentn. & a Party of Loyal True Blues were fairly beat out of the Church [Tavern] in Church St. by the Jacobins—The Loyal True Blues request yr. opinion whether they shod. not be kept embodied & meet abt. 20 at a time or the society shod. be dissolved.—But they are determined to support the King & Constitution & will not give it up—As for me I leave it to your better Judgt. to advise us, we are above 400 & all young & hearty in the Cause & I am certain there is great need of us in the Country— Mr. Ward says orders were given to take Harrison into confinement but he is still at large. Above 150 of the Loyal True Blues have been sworn to be faithful to the King & Constn., amongst whom are Crutchloe, Ward, Chater & myself as secy. —I have told the Society if they will meet in companys of abot. 20 or so at

the Union or Mrs. Hobsons (who has offered her Rooms) I have no objection but
that I will not hold any meetings at the Church & they are agreeable.[75]

Under these circumstances it is not surprising that, however impressive the
Association at the hotel was in its affirmation of loyalty, it was less successful
in its second and in many ways more important objective: to bring to an end
the division between Church and Dissent which had beset Birmingham's
leadership for the past five years. Though the Dissenters did not attend the
meeting at the hotel on 7 December as a body, John Taylor sent messages as
their chairman concurring in the meeting's fundamental declaration of loyalty,
and the Association appointed a deputation to confer with Taylor and his
colleagues on joint measures for Birmingham's safety. There was therefore
some apparent ground for hoping that peace could now be patched up between
the parties, 'at least amongst all the reasonable part of them'.[76] The depredations of the Loyal True Blues must have cast serious doubt on such prospects,
and when the Dissenters as a body did reply formally to the resolutions of the
Association they made it quite clear that their position remained distinct. Led
once more by William Russell, they confirmed their loyalty to the Hanoverian
succession and to the constitution as defined by the principles of 1688, but
criticised the abuses which had crept into it during the past century and called
for parliamentary reform as the only remedy for the discontent in the country.
They declared themselves the enemies of sedition, but, in the face of the
government's prosecution of printers and booksellers, remained friends to the
liberty of the press. They would therefore concur in all constitutional measures
to encourage obedience to the law, but only 'when such assistance is rendered
necessary by overt acts'.[77]

At the end of 1792 the forces of reform and reaction were thus evenly
balanced in Birmingham, and this balance was sustained during the new year as
loyalists and Jacobins continued to keep pace with one another in their demonstrations. On 12 February 1793 an effigy of Tom Paine, labelled as 'Erskine's
client' and attended by two mock-Methodist chimney sweepers and a hangman
who carried a picture of a fox with a halter round its neck, was hanged, torn in
pieces and burnt. At the same time John Brooke, who since 1791 had replaced
Joseph Carles as the ringleader of the reactionaries, used the prevailing mood
to clinch his own election to the vacant coronership of Hemlingford Hundred by
impugning the loyalty of his opponent, William Whateley. The Loyal True
Blues, many of whom were no doubt among the claque which prevented
Whateley's supporters from voting at Warwick, were meeting again after their
temporary suspension of the previous December, and were now performing a
more controllable and more effective function in the fight against democracy by
compiling lists of suspected Jacobins for the benefit of the Association at the
hotel. During March they put pressure on the innkeepers, 120 of whom were
induced to close their doors to the constitutional societies, and towards the end
of the month they finally caught up with the leaders of the Birmingham Society
for Constitutional Information. Harrison, Kilmister and five others were
surprised on 20 March after a meeting at the Hare and Hounds in Hill Street by
a gang led by Mr Wooldridge, the town gaoler, Mr Barr, the constable, and Joe
Lyndon of the Minerva tavern, who had been the main instigator of the innkeepers' declaration. Harrison and Kilmister were beaten up, searched, robbed

and kept in solitary confinement before being interrogated by Joseph Carles for four hours on the following day.[78]

As the Birmingham society wrote on 6 February in its letter seeking affiliation with the Society for Constitutional Information in London,

> the interested and bigotted supporters of the exploded systems of corruption are continually throwing obstacles in the way of all Reform, and threaten us with rigorous prosecution and exhibit all the engines of power and Tyranny before us.[79]

Nevertheless, the letter continued, large numbers 'daily flock to the standard of Liberty', and the society was working hard to justify the claim. The mock execution of Paine was countered by a 'Last Dying Speech and Confession', which turned the tables on his assailants and showed that the Jacobins had a propagandist of some skill among their number by using a recital of the victim's supposed crimes to reiterate the salient points of his message at a halfpenny the sheet.[80] In March preparations began for a wider campaign. Early in the month the workmen in every manufactory received a broadsheet attacking both septennial and triennial Parliaments, exposing the iniquities of taxation and the corn Bill and calling for their support in a petition for reform.[81] This was followed on 12 March by a *Letter to the English Nation* pointing out that the war had already put ten thousand out of work in Birmingham, and warning that if France was unable to withstand her enemies unaided she would seek from the Americans a return for her support in their own revolution, in which case England would face once more the disaster she had suffered only ten years previously.[82] Five weeks later the Rev. John Edwards, preaching at the Union Chapel in Livery Street, the temporary home of the Old and New Meetings, likewise took the lesson of the American war and applied it to the General Fast on 19 April. In a sermon which demonstrated the ambivalence of such public rituals he developed the usual theme of collective sin, not into the conventional attack on atheism and sedition, but into an indictment of the nation's arrogance in entering upon a second unjust war, manifestly contrary to the designs which a benevolent creator was bringing to maturity in the world. Like its predecessor eighteen years before, this war too had been begun in iniquity, would be carried on with barbarian ferocity and would end in humiliation, disgrace and defeat. For such a war, said Edwards, responsibility lay not with the government but with a people who gave it their consent in ignorance of their own constitution, whose true principles, if only they were known, should make such injustice unthinkable.[83]

The visible effects of Jacobin agitation in Birmingham reached their peak during the summer of 1793. The petition for parliamentary reform which had occupied the constitutional society during the spring was supported by 2,720 signatures by the time Samuel Whitbread presented it on 2 May.[84] The plans for *Swinney's Birmingham and Stafford Chronicle* and for a possible third newspaper, which alarmed John Brooke, testify to the extent of the reformers' activities at this time, as does also the fact that the surviving copy of the *Letter to the English Nation* of the previous March is one of a batch subsequently reprinted for the Constitutional Society at Leeds.[85] On 10 June Maurice Margarot and Thomas Hardy acknowledged what seems to have been the first regular contact between the London Corresponding Society and the Birmingham Society for Constitutional Information when they welcomed 'the spirit of Freedom springing up in Birmingham'. They were confident that 'the zeal of your society and the increase of your numbers will soon do away the stigma thrown on your town by the unjustifiable behaviour of a Church and King Mob', and John Kilmister's reply was equally optimistic. 'The King of Birmingham (i.e. the Mob)' had been 'much indisposed' since the outbreak of war, and Kilmister raised high hopes that 'this affliction of his person may . . . probably create a revolution in his sentiments and enable him to discover the tricks that has been too successfully practiced upon him'.[86]

The expected 'revolution' was, however, still two years away;[87] and if the unemployment caused by the war did curtail the activities of the loyalists the closing months of the year were to show that the Jacobins would be equally affected. Already there were signs that progress had not been as uniformly encouraging as Kilmister claimed. The Birmingham reformers and the London Corresponding Society had tried to make contact with each other in March, when Harrison sent up a copy of the address to the manufacturers of the town; but Hardy's reply produced 'no answer, nor any correspondence' until 6 June,[88] when letters began to be exchanged on a comparatively settled basis.[89] Considering the discomfiture which Harrison and Kilmister had suffered at the hands of the Loyal True Blues on 20 March, this delay was only to be expected; but in April Harrison had given the Society for Constitutional Information an impression of Birmingham opinion rather different from that conveyed by his colleague to the London Corresponding Society two months later. 'We are,' he wrote,

> just now going on with our petition for a reform in our House of Commons— which I am sure would go on very rapidly if the people of this Town would let go their fears that have been too successfully excited by the late riots for Church and King.[90]

Harrison was nearer the mark than Kilmister. The mob was back on the streets on 2 August to celebrate the Allied victory at Valenciennes, and Birmingham was again threatened by serious disturbance on 21 and 22 October, when resistance to the collection of the special rate levied to compensate the victims of 1791 had to be broken up by troops from the new barracks at Ashsted.[91]

The expectations raised in the summer were not fulfilled. Though he wrapped the point up in quantities of invective against Burke's contempt for the Swinish Multitude and Pitt's 'War of Humanity', the chief burden of Kilmister's letter to the Society for Constitutional Information on 6 November was that Birmingham could not afford to send a delegate of its own to the Edinburgh convention. Kilmister tried hard to put a brave face on it. He still believed that the Birmingham society had done much good: it had tended to 'abate the pride, assuage the malice and confound many of the Enemies to Reform, particularly among the Dons of *Church and King*', and it had made 'many proselytes in the Cause of Liberty'. Nevertheless such consolations must have seemed hollow in the face of the mob's continued activity, and they squared ill with Kilmister's own complaint that the disruption of trade since the outbreak of war had

> driven a great number of our best members and Mechanics across the Atlantic. And those that remain are but little better situated than the wretched inhabitants of Flanders.[92]

The same impression is left by the slightly different account which Kilmister sent to Hardy in January 1794. This contained the same mixture of indignant rhetoric and apology, and the fact that it was written in reply to a letter sent over seven weeks earlier suggests that Birmingham's contact with the London Corresponding Society had remained sporadic. Birmingham had, it seems, been on the point of sending its own delegate to Edinburgh after all, when news arrived of the convention's forcible dissolution. Though circumstances had prevented an earlier answer to the London Corresponding Society's last letter, Kilmister and his colleagues intended to publish a string of resolutions on the convention later in the week. What effect they would have was hard to say, however, for Birmingham's trade was in a wretched state, and its people were reduced to beggary.[93]

The situation thus remained one of stalemate. Each side in Birmingham was able to deny mastery to the other; neither was strong enough to consolidate its own supremacy, and both were equally affected by the depressed state of the town's trade. Despite the continued attentions of loyalists and King's Messengers, who in May 1794 broke up a political club at James Parr's Cottage of Content in Ladywood,[94] the Birmingham Jacobins survived to enjoy a final revival of support between 1795 and 1797;[95] but the reformers could not claim to have established the kind of stronghold in the town which they had originally hoped to create. The limitations on its success were reflected in the nature of Jacobin agitation in the Birmingham area. Though the cause made rapid strides during the closing months of 1792, the fact remains that it was a Sheffield man who put the Birmingham Society for Constitutional Information on its feet. Similarly, the comparative quietness at this stage of the hardware towns of southern Staffordshire, where incipient unrest seems to have been temporarily forestalled,[96] stood in marked contrast to the ominous situation which had already developed in the Potteries. The same impression is also left by the language used by the Birmingham Jacobins. Apart from the conversations overheard at the Bell in Colmore Row during November 1792, which probably gained something in the telling, and apart from the flourishes which adorned the letters of the Birmingham leaders, especially those of John Kilmister, this remained a good deal tamer than that used elsewhere. It was Stockport, not Birmingham, which urged the immediate necessity of a national convention as the essential preliminary to any real reform, and was disappointed that the addresses of the London Corresponding Society hardly rose 'to that height which we expect from men sensible of their full claim to absolute and uncontrollable liberty, i.e. unaccountable to any power which they have not immediately constituted and appointed'. It was Norwich, not Birmingham, which asked whether the societies intended to abide by the moderate programme advocated by the Duke of Richmond and the Friends of the People, or whether it was 'their private design to rip up Monarchy by the roots and plant Democracy in its stead', as the Manchester society seemed to have intimated 'by addressing Mr. Paine as though they were intent on Republican principles only'.[97]

As the carefully chosen phrases of its original address show, the Birmingham society preferred to postpone such hard questions.[98] If there were those in the town whose thoughts did run to revolution they were offset by others, like 'Will Deepsee', 'Tom Would-be-right', 'Ned All-love' and 'Harry Clearsight' whose discussions spoke favourably of the Whig Friends of the People and explained the purpose of the Constitutional Society in terms of moderate reform and the *carrière ouverte aux talents*.[99] The strongest impression left by the Birmingham Society for Constitutional Information, in both its public and its private pronouncements, is in fact of a self-conscious penchant for high-sounding but rather unspecific indignation at the enormities of Old Corruption, as personified by the loyalist mob. Far from being consigned to its proper place in the past, the memory of the Priestley riots remained a present obsession which was regarded as providing in itself sufficient justification for the peculiarities of Birmingham Jacobinism. Sometimes this obsession showed itself simply as vindictive pleasure at the embarrassment of the local authorities, epecially when the cause of liberty was gaining ground;[100] its more usual and more characteristic form, however, was that of pretension to the martyr's crown. Thus, after the brawl at the Hare and Hounds in March 1793, Harrison told the Society for Constitutional Information that he had had 'the happiness to stretch my limbs on a bed of straw for the cause of liberty and truth', and Kilmister, who sent up his own detailed account of the incident as 'a few particulars which we doubt not you will peruse with much pleasure', was anxious to see it published in the *English Chronicle*.[101] The detention of its two leaders was, of course, the incident most likely to produce this kind of response, but the same tendency appeared in nearly all the Birmingham society's correspondence. It was almost as if the Jacobins in Birmingham were content to base their position not on the *Rights of Man*, nor even on the cause of reform in a more general sense, either of which would have entailed some degree of consistent commitment, but simply on the fact that their town was 'the very seat of persecution ... where Mob is King',[102] and that to be a member of the Birmingham Society for Constitutional Information was *ipso facto* to be a hero. It was this sense of complacency, coupled with a temporary slackening in the activities of the loyalists, which led Kilmister to overestimate the prospects of the society during the summer of 1793. Beneath it, however, the statements of the reformers remained hesitant. Whatever was imputed to them by their opponents, they contained no clear acceptance of the principle of universal suffrage before June 1793,[103] and even after that they never proclaimed it with the clarity and force achieved, for example, by *The Rights of Swine, an Address to the Poor*, which was published by the Stockport Friends of Universal Peace and the Rights of Man on 5 January 1794:

> Hearken! O ye poor of the land.—Do you *pet* and whine at oppression?—yes— Then as ye do, so did your fathers before you, and if you do no more your children may whine after you. Awake! Arise! arm yourself with truth and Reason. Lay seige to corruption and your unity and indivisibility shall teach your oppressors ... terrible things! Purge the representatives of the country ... Claim as your inalienable *Right* universal suffrage and Annual Parliaments, ... and whenever you have the gratification to chuse a representative, let him be from among the *lower order* of mankind. ... He will know how to sympathize with you and represent you in character. ... Then and not till then shall you experience universal peace and incessant plenty.[104]

Hopes that the artisans of Birmingham and the West Midlands would follow the example of their northern *confrères* in accepting the *Rights of Man* and rejecting wholesale the yoke of the past were thus not fulfilled. Opinion in the region remained balanced, its temper 'reformist' rather than 'revolutionary'. It did so not simply because the movement for reform lost its original leadership in the Priestley riots, nor even because when new leaders had been found the movement continued to be preoccupied with what had happened to it in 1791. This was itself more a symptom than a cause of the limited effectiveness of the Jacobin message in the Birmingham area. The real reason lay elsewhere: in this part of England the centre continued to hold for longer than it did in other places, despite the severe and complex strains to which it was subjected. The explanation for this lies in the shared achievements of the previous thirty years, which gave the West Midlands a usable past with which to confront the revolutionary crisis. It was thus possible to 'stabilise' local reactions in relation to the English democratic movement as a whole in the same kind of way that the latter was 'stabilised' in relation to French *sans-culotterie* by its ability to refer to still existing political traditions derived from the seventeenth century. The way in which this was done must be sought by considering the ways in which the evolving relationship between different patterns of life was perceived and discussed in the West Midlands, and the terms in which it was explained to the common people of the region.

NOTES

1 *Aris*, 10 November 1788.

2 *Aris*, 24 December 1787, 7, 21, 28 January, 4, 11, 18 February 1788, 4, 18 May 1789. 100 guineas had been sent to the London Abolition Society from a private meeting in Birmingham in November 1787, and extracts from Thomas Day's *Fragment of an Original Letter on the Slavery of the Negroes* (1776) were printed by the *Birmingham Gazette* in December. The following month a Birmingham Committee of Correspondence was formed, whose members included Charles Curtis, Spencer Madan and John Ryland of the established Church, Dr Priestley, William Russell, Charles Lloyd and Samuel Garbett. Following the lead given by Manchester, this called a public meeting to consider a petition to Parliament at the end of January. This was supported by sermons in all the town's churches and meeting houses the preceding Sunday; but though Priestley told the Rev. Newcombe Cappe of York that 'we are zealous and unanimous here' (letter to Cappe, 23 January 1788, *Life and Correspondence*, ed. J. T. Rutt, 2 vols, 1831, II, 7) the text of the Birmingham petition was somewhat cautious. It condemned the slave trade in principle, but 'would not presume to suggest any express mode of Parliamentary interference', and contented itself with asking that 'some relief may be found' and hoping for ultimate abolition. In reaction against 'the errors of some among us who are madly for abolishing that Trade which wiser Foreign Powers . . . would gladly get into their own hands', moves were made in May 1789 to petition again, this time merely for humane regulation of the trade. These, however, were repudiated by the original committee, which reaffirmed its position of the previous year.

3 Ill feeling could not be completely disguised, even at the centenary banquet itself. This was in fact largely the work of William Russell, and according to Priestley the Anglican clergy boycotted the occasion 'because we refused to drink *The Church and Constitution*'. (Priestley to Theophilus Lindsey, November 1788, *Life and Correspondence*, II, 14).

4 Parish, *Birmingham Library*, p. 16. In the library's minutes the title 'reverend' was blotted out from before the names of Priestley and of Radcliffe Scholefield of the Old Meeting.

5 Barlow, *Citizenship and Conscience*, p. 266.

6 Cited by F. W. Gibbs, *Joseph Priestley, Adventurer in Science and Champion of Truth* (London, 1965), p. 174. The exact source is not given.

7 *Aris*, 6 March, 2 October 1786.

8 See J. E. Hale, *The Centenary of the Cannon Street Sunday Schools* (1895), B.R.L. 130200, and H. New, *The Centenary of the Church of the Messiah* (*New Meeting Sunday Schools* (1888), B.R.L. 99004.

9 *Aris*, 30 July, 6, 13 August 1787.

10 For Birmingham's involvement in the movement for the repeal of the Test and Corporation Acts and its relationship to the Priestley riots see *V.C.H. Warwicks.*, VII, 279–284. I do not, however, entirely agree that the solidarity of the 'upper class "political nation"' was undisturbed by sectarian differences before 1787.

11 At the previous attempt, in 1787, the majority had been seventy-eight. See Lincoln, *Some Political and Social Ideas of English Dissent*, p. 266, n. 4.

12 For the co-ordination of the different shades of opinion within the London leadership itself and the care that was taken to keep the Dissenters' platform as broad as possible see Barlow, *Citizenship and Conscience*, pp. 253–6.

13 *Aris*, 18 October 1789.

14 *Aris*, 18 January 1790.

15 This had already caused some concern among the London Dissenters. As early as October 1789 Samuel Heywood had complained to William Russell of 'A most unaccountable ignorance and supineness' on the part of most Dissenters. Heywood welcomed the initiatives of the Midland Unitarians, particularly their plans to publish and distribute propaganda from Birmingham, which would help considerably to lighten the financial burden on the London committee. Nevertheless he urged Russell to concentrate on the Test laws only and not to be drawn into challenging all penal legislation on principle, which he feared would cost the movement the support of the Trinitarians. Heywood felt that the Midland District Association was too large to be a really effective political instrument, and that the personal attendance of provincial delegates in London was too ambitious a proposal at the present stage of the business. See Home Office Papers, H.O. 42/19, bundle of 'Select Birmingham papers', Heywood to Russell, 27 October, 25 November 1789.

16 *Aris*, 18 January 1790.

17 *Aris*, 24 May 1790.

18 George Walker, *The Dissenter's Plea* (Birmingham, 1790), B.R.L. 12437, especially pp. 1–10.

19 H.O. 42/19, 'Select Birmingham papers', Stone to Priestley, 11 March 1790.

20 George Croft, *The Test Laws Defended* (Birmingham, 1790), B.R.L. 6729; Spencer Madan, *The Principal Claims of the Dissenters Considered* (Birmingham, 1790), B.R.L. 14265.

21 *Aris*, 25 January, 1, 8 February 1790. Horsley had been the future earl's private tutor at Christ Church in 1768. See *D.N.B.*

22 Priestley to Theophilus Lindsey, 26 February 1790, *Life and Correspondence*, II, 58.

23 Priestley to Lindsey, 12 March 1790, *Life and Correspondence*, II, 58.

24 See above, pp. 20–21.

25 See below, pp. 261–2.

26 Sutton Coldfield.

27 John Nott, Button Burnisher, *Very Familiar Letters Addressed to Dr. Priestley in Answer to his Familiar Letters to the Inhabitants of Birmingham* (Birmingham, 1790), B.R.L. 66723, *passim*.

28 See R. B. Rose, 'The Priestley riots of 1791', *Past and Present*, 18 (November 1960), 68–88.

29 See above, pp. 142–3.

30 See below, p. 268.

31 *V.C.H. Warwicks.*, VII, 418, 475.

32 The most comprehensive account of these is James Walvin, 'English democratic societies and popular radicalism, 1791–1800' (University of York, unpublished D.Phil. thesis, 1969). This, however, is largely devoted to metropolitan developments, and though this concentration is offset by a survey of the provincial societies and their individual characteristics the work's particular case study of radicalism outside London is centred on Manchester, not Birmingham.

33 Treasury Solicitor's Papers, TS 11/1133, Minute book of the S.C.I., 2 May 1780–7 March 1783, entry for 24 January 1783.

34 TS 11/1133, entry for 25 October 1782; TS 11/961, Minute book of the S.C.I., 14

March 1783–14 March 1792, entry for 14 March 1783. A Rev. Mr Martin of Birmingham was listed in the society's minutes for 29 June 1792 (TS 11/962) and in the Treasury solicitors' own list of the society's country correspondents on 7 December the same year (TS 11/966/35110B).

35 TS 11/962, entries from 18 May to 29 June 1792. For Richard Phillips of the *Leicester Herald* see A. Temple Patterson, *Radical Leicester* (Leicester, 1954), pp. 67–73. Within the gross allocation for the Midlands the distribution was as follows: Rowe (Shrewsbury) 100, Fox (Derby) 200, *Leicester Herald* 100, Edwards (Birmingham) 150, Francis (Birmingham) 100, Martin (Birmingham) 100, Corrie (Bromsgrove) 100.

36 Anon. to John Reeves, 13 December 1792. Papers of the Association for the Preservation of Liberty and Property, British Museum, Add. MSS. 16922, f. 55.

37 The Shrewsbury Unitarians and their contacts are examined in G. M. Ditchfield, 'Some aspects of Unitarianism and radicalism, 1760–1810' (Cambridge, unpublished Ph.D. thesis, 1968).

38 In H.O. 42/22.

39 Schofield, *Lunar Society*, pp. 323–5.

40 See Eric Robinson, 'The Derby Philosophical Society', *Annals of Science*, IX (1953), 368–76. The Derby society had provoked division within its own membership by its address of sympathy with Dr Priestley in September 1791. For another example of radical sympathy among the younger associates of the Lunar circle see Eric Robinson, 'An English Jacobin: James Watt junior', *Cambridge Historical Journal*, XI (1953–55), 349–355.

41 H.O. 42/22, Nepean to Isaac Hawkins-Browne, 1 November 1792; see also 'Abstract of Papers relative to Seditious Persons' in H.O. 42/21.

42 Papers of the A.P.L.P., Add. MSS. 16927, f. 23, Richard Swanwick to John Reeves.

43 Birmingham—Add. MSS. 16919, f. 167; Belcher—TS 11/578/1893, bundle 1 (brief for the Crown), and B.R.L. 329314 (brief for the defendant); Tewkesbury—TS 11/964/3510, *First and Second Reports of the Committee of Secrecy of the House of Commons* (May, June 1794), appendix E, pp. 79–80, John Lloyd, of the Tewkesbury Society for Political and Moral Information, to Hardy, 6 July 1793.

44 See J. C. Wedgwood, *Staffordshire Parliamentary History*, vol. III, in *Trans. William Salt Arch. Soc.* (1933), pp. 7, 8.

45 H.O. 42/22, John Massey to Francis Freeling, 22 November 1792; TS 11/954/3498, Thomas Fenton to Chamberlayn and White, the Treasury solicitors, 17 December 1792.

46 See above, p. 62.

47 TS 11/962, S.C.I. minutes for 23 March 1792; list of affiliates from Sheffield.

48 TS 11/952/3496(2), Prosser to Adams, 26 November 1792; H.O. 43/4, Dundas to Edward Inge, town clerk of Coventry, 14 December 1792. The embarrassment felt by the corporation and its adherents as the polarity between loyalty and supposed subversion hardened can be seen in the example of Mr Piercy, the Coventry bookseller and former collaborator with Myles Swinney. Piercy was so alarmed lest his past record make him a target of prosecution that he fell over himself to make his excuses to the Attorney General. Yes, his daughter had sold one copy of Paine to a neighbour's servant; but this had been 'merely in the course of trade'; it was the only copy Piercy had in stock and he had no idea either of what it contained or that its sale was an offence. As a specimen of his own opinions and of those of the corporation Piercy enclosed a copy of his *Licentious Principles Exposed*, written the previous June. This admitted that the corporation had 'ardently wished' the repeal of the Test and Corporation Acts, but its members had done so as individuals on religious grounds only. The corporation had never acted as a body in the matter, and it had certainly never espoused levelling principles. (TS 11/954/3498, Piercy to Sir Archibald MacDonald, 19 December 1792.)

49 TS 11/964/3510, *First and Second Reports of Committee of Secrecy*, appendix E, pp. 87, 89, Harrison to the L.C.S., 20 August; Prosser to Harrison, 23 October 1793. Besides material exchanged with the L.C.S., Prosser also mentioned letters and a 'parcel of their publications' sent by a Mr Stuart. This was probably D. Stuart, who, as 'a reliable man' in the Birmingham society, had been entrusted with a letter from John Kilmister to the parent society the previous summer. See TS 11/953/3497, Kilmister to Adams, 18 June 1793.

50 H.O. 42/26, Letters from Robert Spillman, JP, 25, 26 August 1793; H.O. 43/4, Nepean to Spillman, 26 August 1793. According to Spillman the weavers had been well

organised for some time. They stopped work on the slightest provocation, forced their wages up at will and had an efficient strike fund. Their present dispute, which had arisen when one of the masters took an unlawful apprentice, reached its climax in a procession of garlanded marchers, complete with fife band and an ass, on which the blackleg apprentice's work was carried to the door of his offending master. Though several of the marchers were seized, they were rescued by their comrades. Democratic verses began to appear, and the crowd broke up only in order to recruit larger numbers 'from Coventry and other places of their residence'. The following day it met again, this time some 1,500 strong, and though it was dispersed the local authorities dared not proceed any further until a troop of Blues also arrived from Coventry.

51 R. B. Rose, 'The Priestley riots', pp. 75–80.

52 Sheffield—H.O. 42/19, James Wilkinson to Dundas, 23 July 1791; Manchester—see below; Leicester—H.O. 42/19, copy of John Eames to the Secretary at War, 23 July 1791; Wolverhampton—H.O. 43/3, Dundas to Colonel De Lancey, 29 July 1791; Bristol—H.O. 42/19, John Harris, mayor of Bristol, to Dundas, 21 July 1791.

53 *Cf.* H.O. 42/19, bundle marked 'Quarters of Troops', containing: (1) permanent quarters of forces in England and Scotland as of 1 July 1791; (2) lists giving disposition of troops relative to London and Bristol, with distances, routine, forced and emergency marching times. The detail of these lists, which are fair copies carefully produced, suggests that they were routine documents prepared at regular intervals in case of need—in other words, that the government already had contingency plans to meet trouble in London or Bristol; (3) a similar list relative to Birmingham, obviously drawn up in haste, and including places as far away as Winchester, Salisbury, York, Canterbury, Brighton, Norwich and Chichester; (4) log of orders sent between 16 and 23 July 1791 with regard to Birmingham; (5) memorandum concerning correspondence with commanding officers in different places with regard to possible disturbances in Bristol and in the north.

54 H.O. 42/19, Nepean to James Wilkinson, 25 July, Wilkinson to Dundas, 29 July 1791.

55 H.O. 42/19, Mr Swinnell to Robert Preston, 17 July 1791.

56 H.O. 42/19, Thomas Bayley and Henry Norris to ? Dundas and draft of reply, 19, 21 July, Bayley to Dundas, 27 July 1791.

57 *Aris*, 4 May 1792; H.O. 43/4, Dundas to Carles and Spencer, 23 May 1792; H.O. 42/20, Carles and Spencer to Dundas, 25 May 1792.

58 TS 11/952/3496(2), Ashton to Adams, 26 May 1792.

59 *V.C.H. Warwicks.*, vii, 282.

60 H.O. 42/20, Colonel De Lancey to Dundas, 13 June 1792.

61 For all this see *Parliamentary History*, xxx, 189; *The Correspondence of Edmund Burke*, vii (ed. P. J. Marshall and John A. Woods), 217, 328–35; *Aris*, 22, 29 October 1792, and the mass of papers on arms orders and movements from Birmingham between September and December 1792 in H.O. 42/21, 22 and 23. Maxwell's orders seem to have been concentrated on two makers, James Woolley and Thomas Gill. While the former soon became suspicious and gave up the work, Gill carried on, despite exposure in the newspapers, for nearly two months, claiming that since he had been persuaded to send a sample to the government, but had subsequently received no explicit command to stop production, he was justified in continuing. According to Woolley 3,000 complete daggers and another 700 blades had been delivered before Gill did rather ostentatiously call a halt. Besides his earnings on the completed part of the order, Gill also collected most of the credit for renouncing it. Understandably, Woolley was more than a little piqued by this, and may well have exaggerated his estimates. The same was probably true of his claim that twenty-four daggers of higher quality, including two with retractable blades, were still on order for David Blair of the Birmingham S.C.I.

62 H.O. 42/22, Nepean to Brooke, 6 November 1792.

63 Probably Thomas Hill, one of the two Hills who were among the twelve Birmingham men proposed for affiliation with the S.C.I. the following February. The other was George Hill, senior of Lower Temple Street, a huxter and buckle finisher, who became treasurer of the Birmingham society. See TS 11/962, S.C.I. minutes, 15 February 1793; H.O. 42/23, P. Hazlewood to John Brooke, 11 December 1792; *V.C.H. Warwicks.*, vii, 281.

64 H.O. 42/22, information on Jacobin activities in Birmingham, October and November 1792. This is the basis of the Birmingham entries in the 'Abstract of Papers Relative to Seditious Persons' in H.O. 42/21.

65 H.O. 42/23, J. Hurd to Nepean, 3 December 1792.
66 *Address, Declaration, Rules and Orders of the Birmingham Society for Constitutional Information, instituted 20th November 1792*, B.R.L. 64011.
67 H.O. 42/23, Hurd to Nepean, 3 December 1792. For the impact of the second part of the *Rights of Man* see G. A. Williams, *Artisans and Sans-culottes*, pp. 15, 16, and E. P. Thompson, *The Making of the English Working Class* (London, 1963), pp. 90–8.
68 H.O. 42/23, copy of Peter McGreory to Alexander MacQueen, n.d., December 1792.
69 *Aris*, 12 November 1792.
70 *Aris*, 3, 10 November 1792.
71 *A.O.P.*, Boulton to the Marquess of Stafford, 11 December 1792.
72 H.O. 42/23, Hurd to Thomas Williams, 4, 5 December, enclosed in Williams to George Rose, 6 December 1792.
73 See the replies to the Treasury solicitor's circular letter to provincial magistrates and attorneys on the prosecution of seditious booksellers in TS 11/954/3498.
74 *Aris*, 10 December 1792.
75 H.O. 42/23, P. Hazlewood to John Brooke, 11 December 1792.
76 *Aris*, 10 December 1792; *A.O.P.*, Boulton to the Marquess of Stafford, 11 December 1792.
77 *Aris*, 24 December 1792.
78 *Aris*, 4, 11, 18 February, 11, 18 March 1793; TS 11/953/3497, Kilmister to Adams, 25 March 1793.
79 TS 11/962, S.C.I. minutes, 15 February 1793.
80 Copy in TS 11/952/3496(2).
81 Copy in TS 11/953/3497, and see above, p. 214.
82 *A Letter to the English Nation, Wherein the Dreadful Consequences of War are Considered and Exposed*, B.R.L. 95842.
83 J. Edwards, *A Discourse Delivered on Friday April 19th 1793 at the Union Meeting in Livery Street, . . . being the Day Appointed for a General Fast*, B.R.L. 69233. For other anti-war fast sermons to the congregation at Union Chapel which developed an ideal of patriotism very different from the usual compound of evangelical chauvinism see David Jones, *Reasons for Peace* (25 February 1795), B.R.L. 4315, and John Edwards, the *Inattention of Christians to Set Days of Public Fasting Justifiable* (13 March 1796), B.R.L. 12380. *Cf.* also the Rev. J. H. Williams, vicar of Wellesbourne, *Piety, Charity and Loyalty Recommended in a Sermon on the Late Fast* (1793), B.R.L. 12438, which attacked the 'leaven of malice' in the loyal associations and looked forward to the day when the voice of the people would be heard 'not from a thousand inquisitorial associations, but in one legal assembly from their *own real representatives*'.
84 Simon Maccoby, *English Radicalism, 1786–1832* (London, 1955), p. 68.
85 Probably another example of Harrison's influence: besides his Birmingham and Sheffield connections he had also presided for a time over the Jacobin club at Bradford. See H.O. 42/23, P. Hazlewood to John Brooke, 11 December 1792.
86 TS 11/954/3498, Margarot and Hardy to Kilmister, 10 June 1793; TS 11/965/3510A, Kilmister to Hardy, 18 June 1793.
87 See below, pp. 266–8, and R. B. Rose, 'The origins of working class radicalism in Birmingham', *Labour History* (Canberra, Australia), 4 (November 1965), 6–14.
88 TS 11/965/3510A, George Lynam's report to Nepean of L.C.S. committee meeting, 21 March 1793; TS 11/953/3497, abridgements of Lynam's reports in 'Index to bundle H, being general papers of the L.C.S. and S.C.I. for 1793', items 12, 16, 23. George Lynam, a clerk employed by James Yates & Co. of Birmingham, had been used by Nepean in the course of his investigation of the Birmingham arms trade (*cf.* H.O. 42/22, Nepean to Brooke, 26 October 1792) and had now been planted in the L.C.S.
89 But *cf.* Add. MSS 27812, Journal of the L.C.S., 2 April 1792–2 January 1794, whose entries for 2 and 30 May 1793 mention respectively propaganda sent to Birmingham and a circular letter from Birmingham on the rejection of Lord Grey's motion for parliamentary reform. *Cf.* also TS 11/965/3510A, 'Calendar of Papers of 1793', which has an entry at 13 May 1793 for a printed letter and resolutions from Birmingham, annotated as not yet copied. Though personal contact had not yet been properly established, Birmingham was clearly already an active participant in the general exchange of printed material.

90 TS 11/953/3497, Harrison to Adams, 17 April 1793.

91 *V.C.H. Warwicks.*, vii, 283; *Aris*, 28 October 1793.

92 TS 11/953/3497, Kilmister to Adams, 6 November 1793.

93 TS 11/959/3503(2), 'Account of bundle D, being Hardy's papers of 1794', Kilmister to Hardy, 12 January 1794.

94 *V.C.H. Warwicks.*, vii, 282.

95 See below, pp. 266–9.

96 H.O. 42/20, Sir Edward Lyttleton to Dundas, 18 June 1792, regarding his anxiety to prevent the presentation of 'an absurd tho' well meant address' from the manufacturers of Wolverhampton, the exceptionable part of which contained 'a strange charge of insolence on Peers and of tumult on Commons'; H.O. 42/22, William Chrees to Francis Freeling, 23 November 1792: Wolverhampton retains its boasted peace and loyalty; Add. mss 16920, f. 135: Wednesbury Constitutional Society's offer to help the A.P.L.P., 5 December 1792.

97 TS 11/965/3510A, P. W. Frost to Hardy, 27 September 1792, George Knapp and Isaac Saint to Hardy, 11 November 1792.

98 It was not, of course, alone in this. The men of Norwich found even the position of Sheffield ambiguous at this time, and both the L.C.S. and the S.C.I. were trying hard to restrain their more zealous associates. *Cf.* the answer sent by the former on 14 December 1792 when Norwich asked for guidance on the correct attitude to addresses of attachment to the constitution. This still spoke in terms of restoration and 'ancient purity' (TS 11/953/3497, 'Index to bundle B, being Hardy's papers for 1792', item 52). Four months later, when Norwich tried to probe the S.C.I.'s attitude to a national convention, the myth of the Ancient Constitution had been diluted to some extent, but still the society tried to ward off the issue with a promise to call a convention when the time was ripe, and with the sweeping but rather unspecific and flustered assertion that in the meantime the societies were 'not a handful of individuals unworthy of attention or consideration who desire the restoration of the ancient liberties of England, but on the contrary, a host of well meaning men, who in the different Towns and Counties ... are silently but seriously anxious for a Reformation in the Government'. (TS 11/959/3505, J. Frost to the Norwich societies, 12 April 1793.)

99 *Address to the Association for the Protection of Liberty and Property,* and *Observations on Constitutional Societies among the Middling and Lower Classes,* both by 'A Friend to Liberty and Property', B.R.L. 64351 and 589747.

100 *Cf.* H.O. 42/23, copy of Peter McGreory to Alexander MacQueen, n.d., December 1792. The five thousand converts to Paine and Priestley made in the last two months had made the Churchmen look very foolish, especially Joseph Carles, the instigator of the Priestley riots, who had so far succumbed to his weakness for liquor that he seemed about to come to an appropriately horrible end.

101 TS 11/953/3497, Harrison to Adams, Kilmister to Adams, 25 March 1793. Though the S.C.I. advised the two of them to seek redress in the courts, it regarded the incident with some detachment. The subscription which was eventually opened for Harrison in November raised only £5. (TS 11/962, S.C.I. minutes, 8 November 1793.) The L.C.S. was equally cool: it agreed that Harrison had been 'extreemly ill used' but 'did not come to any determination about him', and postponed action until he arrived in London (Add. mss 27812, L.C.S. journal and minutes, i, 8 August 1793).

102 Cited by G. A. Williams, *Artisans and Sansculottes,* p. 65, where the same point is suggested. *Cf.* E. P. Thompson, *The Making of the English Working Class,* p. 123, on self-dramatisation, 'the characteristic vice of the English Jacobins'.

103 *V.C.H. Warwicks.*, vii, 282.

104 Copy in TS 11/954/3498.

PART FOUR

'TWO PHASES OF ENGLISH LIFE'

X

'TWO PHASES OF ENGLISH LIFE'

Though the underlying causes of what was happening were not yet clearly understood, it was the provision riots of the mid-1760s which first brought opinion at large to recognise that relationships between the different parts of English society which had hitherto been accepted as constant were already in the process of fundamental and irrevocable alteration. Before turning to the particular question of the reactions of observers in the West Midlands to what seemed to be taking place it will therefore be well to consider briefly the causes and consequences of the widespread disturbances which, in the early autumn of 1766, marked the convergence both of long- and short-term tendencies and of serious misjudgement by the authorities of the actual situation that faced them.[1]

With the exception of the years 1740–43, social tension in the sense of acute and widespread dissatisfaction at the ordering of society itself had remained at a comparatively low level during the first half of the eighteenth century. Wage rates had remained stable, while provision prices had actually tended to fall slightly; the disruptive effects of population growth and movement, like those of industrial change, had not yet assumed major proportions, and while English society continued to be characterised by individual violence and brutality, these seldom took forms which seriously threatened the whole security of the established order. At the same time, however, changes were already taking place in the organisation of the economy whose social implications, masked for the present, were to become apparent only in the years after 1750. The good seasons and abundant yields which meant low provision prices and rising real wages to the labourer meant reduced profits, and therefore adversity, to the producer. By eliminating many of the smaller and less adaptable of the latter, by causing others to exchange their freeholds for secure tenancies from landlords who would shield them from the worst effects of difficult years, and by acting generally as a spur to the adoption of more efficient farming methods, this period of difficulty produced deep-seated alterations in the structure of landed society. At the same time an equally important development was taking place in the system of supply as the middleman, taking advantage of the fact that the laws which were supposed to control his activities were both difficult to enforce and only called into play when rising prices threatened to provoke direct protest, entrenched his position as an indispensable intermediary between producer and consumer.

After 1750 the social consequences of these developments became increasingly apparent. Though the fact was not yet realised, the country's population was now increasing decisively; and this, combined with the effects of deteriorating climatic conditions and animal epidemics, meant that provision prices rose once more to cancel the improvement in conditions and expectations previously enjoyed by the poor. At the same time, while the new commercial agriculture did not necessarily deprive the latter of employment outright, its more specialised requirements did limit the variety of support which had hitherto served the labourer as a hedge against adversity. The chief beneficiaries of changing conditions were, of course, the large farmers and the middlemen whose profits were enhanced by the expansion of the urban market, and of these the middlemen in particular became the object of almost universal suspicion. On one hand, both the poor themselves and manufacturing interests bent on lowering their costs, but not yet strong enough to confront the landed interest proper, were united in their attribution of rising prices to artificial scarcity deliberately induced for private gain by manipulation of the market. On the other hand, the landed interest added its own voice to the mounting volume of criticism. In part the attitude of the gentry was simply an expression of distaste for the aspirations of a new and therefore 'unnatural' element in the social order, but it also reflected more particular considerations. An attack on the middlemen gave the landowners a way of demonstrating unease which distracted attention from their own part in the course of agricultural change. At the same time it concealed a growing uncertainty about the merits of the bounty system on exported grain which might otherwise have marred the public solidarity of the landed interest. Most specifically, it provided a means, entirely in keeping with the moral premises of paternalism, by which to avert a possible repetition in the mid-'60s of the dangerous situation which had threatened to develop in some parts of the country during 1756 and 1757, when militia riots had coincided and coalesced with disturbances over the price of provisions in a way which seemed for a while to presage a general rising of both middling and lower orders against their rulers.

By creating conditions of full employment and by supporting the older domestic industries at capacity while it lasted, the Seven Years War maintained the expectations of the poor for the time being, and indeed added to them in the case of the significant section of the population whose military experience not only gave it inflated hopes for the future but also made it less likely to accept adversity with resignation. As a result, the rapid downturn in prospects after 1763 was the more drastic in its consequences. The economic regression which followed the return of peace caused widespread unemployment, which was made doubly severe by the effect of colonial non-importation agreements during the Stamp Act crisis of 1765–66. The consequences of these particular developments were further aggravated by the early repercussions of a more fundamental realignment of trade which kept overseas markets uncertain and exports depressed throughout the decade. Combined with a marked increase of provision prices after 1764, these conditions produced a rapid rise in social tension which reached its climax in the riots of 1766.

There were, however, more immediate and specific influences at work than economic tendencies and social disappointments; for the government, which acted sensibly when disturbances provoked by the movement of grain to West Country ports during January and February 1766 were prevented from spreading by the timely imposition of an embargo on exports, mishandled the situation badly in the autumn. As was usually the case with an emergency measure which impinged directly on the economic concerns of the landed interest, the embargo of 26 February 1766 was imposed reluctantly and with an eye not only on the possibility of further disturbances in the vicinity of the outports but also on the danger that these would be compounded by widespread rebellion in the inland manufacturing areas, which were suffering at the time from the economic repercussions of the Stamp Act crisis. In its primary objective of averting this danger the prohibition of exports was successful, but it did little to reduce prices during a summer which was unusually cold and wet. Nor could it prevent the speculative movement of grain by dealers looking for large profits from overseas sale once the ports were opened again. This, combined with continued scarcity, provoked a second outbreak of riots during the first fortnight of August. After this, however, prospects seemed to improve dramatically. The rain of the previous three months gave way to a late summer heat-wave which raised belated expectations of a bumper harvest, and prices began to fall as dealers who had hitherto withheld stocks in anticipation of high profits in the autumn released them on to the market. By this time, too, the ending of the colonial non-importation agreements following the repeal of the Stamp Act had removed the immediate threat of trouble from the manufacturing areas. The newly formed and fissiparous Chatham Ministry was therefore tempted to gamble on the continued improvement of the situation. Perhaps because Ministers were genuinely misled by optimistic estimates of the coming harvest, perhaps because they were reluctant to jeopardise England's position in the European grain market any longer, but most probably because they were anxious to increase their chances of political survival by conciliating the landed interest and broadening their independent support at Westminster, the export embargo was lifted on 26 August.

The consequences were disastrous. Most of western Europe had been equally affected by the poor growing season earlier in the year, and once the English trade was freed, grain which had been amassed at the ports in hopes of just such an event flooded out of the country to command famine prices in Continental markets. Meanwhile the true state of affairs at home was revealed. The reports which had so lately raised hopes of abundance had been based on the size of the standing crop, swollen by the excessive moisture of past months, not on its weight and density. Observers who warned that this was the case had so far been ignored; but by 26 September, when the ports were closed again, it was clear that the pessimists had been right. The yield of the harvest fell far below expectations, and though conditions in northern counties were less severe, the southern half of the country was faced with the prospect of real dearth. This, however, was not the worst. Not only had the Ministry allowed the country's reserve stocks of grain to be seriously depleted by opening the ports, it had also proclaimed the old Edwardian statutes against forestalling, regrating and engrossing on 10 September in the hope that this reminder of traditional social duties would be sufficient to meet what at the time was expected to be mild protest at most. The effect of this, combined with the optimism about the harvest which was still prevalent, was tantamount to an official declaration that any scarcity which might ensue would be the deliberate result of pure selfishness on the part of those who controlled and supplied the market. It gave the poor virtual *carte blanche* to regulate markets for themselves, and in the riots which followed it slowed the response of the local authorities, whose usual sensitivity to social disturbance was on this occasion confused by the temptation to allow the energies of protest to spend themselves on the detested middlemen rather than in more destructive paths. As a result the accepted framework of the commonwealth was strained almost to breaking point. Bewildered country magistrates found themselves facing a genuine and serious crisis of scarcity, in which their only recourse was to paternalist legislation designed to do no more than control mild protest by the supervision of local markets on the assumption that adequate supplies were in fact available. When this failed they had no alternative in most cases but to hope that the violence would confine itself to the victims apparently half sanctioned already by the proclamation of 10 September. For its own part, the central government was equally devoid of recourse as the situation threatened to get out of hand in large areas of the country. For good reasons it was reluctant to use the militia against the rioters, either by itself or in combination with the army, and the available resources of the latter, which were almost completely unprepared when the emergency began, had been severely stretched before it ended.

By the end of October order had been restored, and though individual incidents were reported after that, there was no widespread recurrence of trouble. Even though prices remained high and discontent vocal for the next two years, the existence of genuine scarcity beyond the immediate responsibility or remedy of any particular agency was now recognised. To some extent distress was alleviated by massive imports of grain during 1767 and 1768, and social tension in the country at large was dissipated by a combination of export by emigration to the Thirteen Colonies, transfer by immigration to London and placation by token supervision of the middlemen. But though a semblance of normality was thus restored with conventional social assumptions still apparently intact, the events of 1766 had far-reaching effects. Besides pointing to the futility of blaming one particular group for the kind of situation which had developed in the country, to the ineffectiveness of the old legislation as a remedy for it, and therefore to the need for a more fundamental appraisal of the changes which were taking place in English society, the crisis must also have caused at least some people to wonder whether too much supervision of economic processes, no matter how well intentioned, was not worse than none at all. The first consequence of all this can be seen in 1772, when the old laws which had been proclaimed in 1766 were removed from the statute book.

By the 1760s the explicitly normative view of social relationships, derived ultimately from medieval ideas of theocentric order, and transmitted to eighteenth century England via the precept and practice of the Tudor commonwealth, was thus considerably at variance with the real functioning of the economy, and the belief that the latter could, or even should, be controlled by such principles was already being abandoned in practice when Adam Smith's *Wealth of Nations* was published in 1776.[2] The general movement of contemporary opinion did not, however, change direction so tidily, and it would therefore be unrealistic to look for a particular moment at which the traditional, paternalist view of society was generally discarded in favour of an alternative based on the propositions of the new political economy. The latter did not advocate the implementation of any definitive 'social model' of its own devising. Its purpose was not to suggest how a particular society 'ought' to be arranged but to provide a general explanation of the way in which economic relationships functioned in any social circumstances, in the belief that it was through the free play of those relationships in accord with the natural designs of a benevolent

Creator, and not by obedience to 'intrusive moral imperatives', that society would ultimately and indirectly achieve its higher purposes. Of the significance of the 'new moral order' implied by this scheme of thought there can be no doubt. Nevertheless the traditional view still provided the conceptual framework within which the mutual obligations of society were conventionally expressed. The old code was still being invoked by local magistrates as a social palliative long after its official repeal; and since the very nature of the premises on which the new political economy rested meant that its early advocates were not primarily concerned to give explicit guidance to the moral aspects of social relationships as these were still understood by the greater part of the population, the task of legitimising changes in those relationships continued to be discharged as best it could be by taking advantage of the very considerable adaptability of the existing order. That the reaction to change of those immediately affected should have shown little theoretical grasp of what was happening was therefore only to be expected. Produced as they were in a context of scarcity, distress and what looked like a declining rural population, for which urban growth seemed poor compensation, most of the early remedies which were proposed for the ills of the time were backward-looking. It was some time before accepted commonplaces began to be revised and more positive conclusions entertained. Even then most local commentators, groping towards an understanding of social change with limited information and less analytic skill, continued to conceive the problem in terms of a malaise in the traditional order of rural society. Not until the 1790s was any really deliberate effort made to come to terms with the circumstances of the new manufacturing towns, and this task itself was addressed not by the proposal of new ideas but once more by adapting old values to an urban role in the best ways that could be managed.

As might be expected, the usual response of West Midland opinion to scarcity and the disturbances which it brought in its train during the 1760s was to ring the changes on the malpractices either of the large farmers or of the middlemen or of both groups together. All the possible culprits were denounced, for example, in the letter from Broseley against cheese factors, flour millers and large farmers which the *Birmingham Gazette* printed on 29 October 1764, and 'A.B.' of Lichfield laid much the same charges two years later when he complained that

> It might formerly be supposed that a set of men educated in an honest rustic simplicity would not entertain a wish to injure, much less to starve the industrious poor, but from the reduction of many small farms to one great one, the numbers of the Farmers are lessened and their wealth increased, and therewith their manners are greatly altered.[3]

By thus inviting his readers to condemn the pride and ostentation of a group of renegades who had forgotten their duty to the common weal 'A.B.' increased the appeal of his argument and conformed to the widely held opinion that it was 'luxury' that lay at the root of the ills from which society was suffering. This characteristic disposition to seek an underlying moral cause rather than a purely physical or economic explanation for social unrest was, however, capable of wide variation, depending on which precise group was accused of luxurious living in any particular case. The argument could therefore be used as easily to support special pleading on behalf of the farmers and middlemen as it could be to condemn them. 'Benevolus', for example, who wrote to the *Coventry Mercury* in October 1764, sought to exonerate the middlemen by censuring both the self-indulgence of the common people and the wealth of the farmers,[4] and 'A Constant Reader', who defended enclosures in the *Birmingham Gazette* of 26 August 1771, had no doubt at all where the real explanation lay for the increase in poor rates. Admittedly some landlords were as grasping as Ahab, and certainly a number of other contributory factors were also involved; but bad harvests were beyond anyone's control, and discrepancies in weights and measures, like improper marketing, 'may be regulated by our legislators'. In the final analysis 'the most irremediable cause' arose 'from the Pride, Luxury, Extravagance and Want of Shame in the Lower Class, to some of whom formerly the thought of being on a Parish was next to Death itself'. The conventional reaction, which was more concerned to condemn the supposed moral delinquency of this or that section of society than to examine realistically its circumstances and place in the economy, thus did little to clarify the problems at issue, and it is the other aspects of these letters which deserve attention. 'A Constant Reader' provides a good example in his justification of enclosures. This was based not only on the obvious fact that they increased the productivity and value of land but also on the argument that, properly controlled, enclosure would encourage settlement rather than the reverse. Like his confidence that laws could be passed to regulate the scale of weights and measures and the system of distribution, this placed the writer among those who maintained that the way to cure the ills of society was not simply to try and arrest its development but to welcome the sources of agricultural improvement, and so to guide them that instead of furthering the process of corruption the wealth they produced would encourage the kind of hardy and self-sufficient population which would replenish the nation's military resources in wartime, and in peace bring to it a soundly based and virtuous prosperity.

This approach to the preservation of the nation's stock found a prominent advocate in Josiah Tucker, Dean of Gloucester, whose *Elements of Commerce and Theory of Taxes* (1755)[5] envisaged a reformed social order, composed in its principal parts of a population of self-sufficient freeholders, fully occupied in agriculture and domestic manufacture, governed by 'a respectable number of new independent Families possessing from one hundred to one thousand pounds a year'. The latter were to be 'raised up' by altering the laws of inheritance so as to bring about the 'dismembring' of 'most of the great *unwieldy* Estates throughout the kingdom'. The former was to be created partly by policies designed to promote population by discouraging celibacy and encouraging marriage and the immigration of skilled foreigners, but mainly by selective subsidisation[6] of the process of enclosure in combination with the systematic promotion of canals and turnpikes in order to encourage settlement. The direct influence of these ideas was limited, for the *Elements* were printed only for private circulation. Tucker's other writings were prolific, however; he was also a frequent contributor to both the London and the provincial press, and he was a prominent figure in his own part of the country. It was through these less systematic channels that his ideas became more widely known. During the 1760s they were explicitly recommended by at least one commentator in the Birmingham and Coventry papers,[7] and several other correspondents who deplored the apparent decline in the country's rural population at this time proposed to reverse the trend by encouraging enclosure as part of a constructive policy to increase the value of the land, which they reckoned in terms not simply of the cash profit which it could produce but also of the number of people who could be independently settled on a given area.

The most conspicuous example of the influence these ideas exerted in the West Midlands was their effect on the thinking of Samuel Garbett. Garbett set out his own views on the social and economic development of the country in a draft paper prepared for the Earl of Shelburne in May 1766 on 'The Value of Land, Labour, the Number of People, the Tendency of Manufactures and the Consequence of Foreign Trade'.[8] As a manufacturer himself, whose most immediate concern in the question was his labour costs, Garbett's perspective was rather different from that of the Dean of Gloucester, but at this stage at least his conclusions and suggestions were very similar to those of Tucker.[9] Like Tucker, he saw the situation as a series of policy problems specifically requiring the attention of the State; he shared the contemporary belief that the country's population had fallen in recent years, and he based his argument on good late-mercantilist principles. Since 'the number of people in any State constitutes the value of land, or Real Wealth', 'the criterion by which all commerce should be tried by the legislator' was its ability to promote population and employ sailors, and by this criterion Garbett found the recent economic per- formance of Britain wanting, despite its impressive appearance. 'Our land and the immediate products of it are by commerce, *not by populousness*, raised in their value of late years.' As population had not increased in proportion to the expansion of commerce, wages had risen in response to the increased demand for workers in manufactures. The consequences of this would be felt not only in the loss of men but also in 'raising the price of labour and consequently increasing idleness'. Industry and agriculture would both suffer; for the labour needs of the former were being satisfied at the expense of the class of cottagers and yeomen farmers living on incomes of between £20 and £200 a year, and in the process a social asset was being turned into a liability. To prevent this degeneration, Garbett proposed the division of the Crown forests into small- holdings, offered his services if the scheme was adopted and suggested that the Forest of Dean would provide a suitable site for a preliminary trial of the project. A year later Garbett himself volunteered to support the cost of an experimental enclosure of this kind in Staffordshire,[10] and the idea does seem to have evoked some similar response from other private individuals, such as the 'opulent farmer' turned landowner in Gloucestershire, whose plans for settling his labourers in new cottages on half-acre plots inspired in the *Birmingham Gazette* of 20 July 1772 the hopeful belief that

> political, like natural evils, if left alone will in many cases provide a remedy for themselves; a truth which begins to be verified in the case of engrossing farms and destroying the houses thereon, . . . it having been found by experiment that land cannot be cultivated without hands, and that the possible or contingent burden of Poor-tax is not comparable to the real and substantial evil of depopu- lation.

A year and a half after he had first written to Shelburne on the subject, however, Garbett was still lamenting the 'present invincible prejudices . . . against improving lands at home' and the absence of any 'great line to remove the storm that hath for years been forming by the wealthy speculating deeply on provisions dexterously to make profits, and the Gentlemen indecently and weakly at least looking on, if not assisting the game'.[11] Such anxiety from one of the best informed people in the country, and one who made it his abiding concern to secure the recognition of economic affairs as a great object of policy, testifies eloquently to the seriousness of those who were seeking solutions to the problems of social change through conservationist regulation of the processes apparently involved. It will therefore not be sufficient to pass over such solutions as mere misconceived anachronisms whose essential irrelevance was soon to be revealed by the course of history. In their proper place the shortcomings of the conservationist view must be recognised, but to do this and nothing else would be to make unfair use of the advantages of hindsight and to ignore the need to relate opinion to the particular circumstances which produced it. From the latter point of view, the proposal of an essentially rural solution to what was still regarded as an essentially rural problem was not merely to be expected; it also made sense. Since the direction in which the country's population level was in fact beginning to move was not yet generally recognised, and since the full significance of innovation in technology and industrial organisation was likewise not yet commonly appreciated, the growth of the new manufacturing towns was at this stage no more accepted by most people as irreversible than its true causes were understood by them. What was clear was simply that the towns were growing; that the recent past had witnessed a major decline in the numbers of small farmers,[12] particularly on the heavy clays of the Midlands, and that these two developments in combination seemed to threaten the integrity of society. To say the least, the relationship of enclosure to this threat was open to more than one interpretation. The decline in the position of the small farmer could well have other causes, such as high costs and limited opportunities, especially when it preceded the main period of parliamentary enclosure. Far from compounding such difficulties, indeed, enclosure might well provide the best means of coping with them, particularly while its cost remained low enough to place it within the reach of small as well as great landowners. In Warwickshire itself, in fact, the parishes most affected during the early years of parliamentary enclosure were those in which small owners were strong, and far from being oppressed by the process it was frequently they who initiated it.[13] These considerations all suggest that whatever may have been the case twenty years later, when increased costs did begin to bear with disproportionate weight on the smaller owners in the county, the proposal to treat the ills of rural society by harnessing the process of enclosure to desirable ends was not, in the circumstances of the 1760s and 1770s, as obviously backward-looking as it may seem.

Nevertheless the practical effectiveness of such an approach was limited. Despite the distinction which they made between personal gain and profit to the commonwealth, the advocates of regulation still couched their own proposals too deeply in the language of private property and initiative ever to put their assumptions to any serious test. Though they condemned the process of enclosure when it was applied for private gain to land whose increased yield could command sufficient profit in urban markets to repay the expense involved, they nevertheless took it for granted that because existing enclosures had in fact proved profitable the process would continue to produce the same result even when it had been subordinated to the requirements of a comprehensive scheme of rural resettlement. The question thus begged was never faced, and in Warwickshire at least the reality for small owners, reflected in the increasing numbers of lesser estates which were sold up before, during or immediately after enclosure from the 1780s onwards, was that profits proved to be a good deal less certain than a formidable rise in the cost of the process.[14]

Besides, as an answer to the main problem, there was a more basic reason why the conservationist approach was of only limited value. However well conceived and indeed feasible it may have seemed in its own terms, its assumptions and intentions contained neither positive recognition of the manufacturing towns nor any constructive purpose for them. Though it argued from the incontrovertible fact that improved farming meant that the land could support greater numbers, the proposal to regulate enclosures so as to promote settlement was intended to encourage a population employed in husbandry or domestic manufacture, evenly distributed between small, self-sufficient communities on holdings of controlled size, not one which lived in large towns and worked collectively in occupations which had little or no direct contact with the land. The real relationship between urban immigration, enclosure and rural distress was not perceived—namely that far from devouring a population which was declining in numbers and being driven wholesale from the land, the towns, where they were accessible, offered the best recourse for the surplus of a population which was now growing more rapidly than could be absorbed entirely by an expansion in rural employment.[15] Individual projects, such as that of the Gloucestershire landlord which won the *Birmingham Gazette*'s approval in July 1772, may have brought some local relief. But the argument that 'land cannot be cultivated without hands, and that the possible or contingent burden of Poor-tax is not comparable with the real and substantial evils of depopulation', looked towards the expedient adopted by the Speenhamland Justices in 1795. Whether the latter is better regarded as a rational attempt to deal with the problem of maintaining the body of surplus rural labour which was as yet unemployable in industry, or merely as 'an instinctive escape of country gentlemen into the world they knew best',[16] the approach it reflected did little to help the traditional order comprehend the growth of the manufacturing towns.

On the face of it, much the same was true of the suggestion made in December 1773 by 'Humanus', a 'friend to the poor cottager, the country and town labourer, the manufacturer & c.' Once again the value of enclosure was stressed as a means of increasing production and employment, and Humanus asked for the inclusion of smallholdings in the plans of future awards. If this were done, or if some of the affected land were set aside for allotments or parish gardens,

> The poor tradesman, weary with confinement, would be much refreshed by such airy profitable exercise, and if the plot is not too scanty, it helps greatly to keep a pig or a cow, which if he can raise, and is blessed with health and success, it so excites his diligence that he seems above want, and is likely to be kept from it.[17]

The intent of this suggestion, however, differed noticeably from that of those so far made by other contributors, and it did so in ways which imply some recognition of changing circumstances. Humanus made his proposals as a means of compensation for losses incurred in an accepted process, not as a plan to rectify or reverse the process itself. He was specifically concerned with the 'poor tradesman, weary with confinement', not with an idealised population of self-sufficient owner-occupiers. And if he was anxious to see the town labourer get some fresh air and retain his connection with the soil the intention was not to turn him back into a yeoman but to enable him to keep some tincture of old virtues in his new surroundings, by giving him both the chance to raise himself above want by his own efforts and the incentive of his own success and self-respect to remain so. Whether or not 'three acres and a cow' was the best or most practicable way of providing this incentive is another question; but it was through such practical concern for the condition and morale of the labouring poor, rather than through comprehensive schemes to supervise the entire development of society, that the more perceptive writers were led to some awareness of what was really happening, and therefore to a review of previously accepted commonplaces. No clear-cut distinction appeared between 'old' and 'new' attitudes, and the latter were often either hinted at unconsciously or, if deliberately assumed, were not fully explored, but it was this process which prepared the way for the reappraisal of more fundamental ideas. The course taken by this preliminary revision can be seen particularly clearly in the gradual change which took place in accepted attitudes to the price of labour.[18]

According to conventional wisdom the labouring poor, being almost by definition work-shy, would perform their allotted tasks only under threat of severe privation. Though it might deplore the anti-social activities of forestallers, regraters and the engrossers of farms, a large part of conservative opinion therefore still reserved its severest strictures for the 'Pride, Luxury, Extravagance and Want of Shame in the Lower Class', and condemned any move to relieve distress by bringing wages into line with current prices as 'raising the price of labour and consequently increasing idleness'. As the latter expression from Samuel Garbett shows, this basic attitude was not confined to the merely reactionary, and since the attribution of idleness and improvidence to the poor lent itself as easily to a superficial justification of the harsher aspects of the new political economy as it did to the suppositions of the old, it still had a long future ahead of it. It was, however, hardly consistent to go on regarding the poor as almost a separate species, congenitally improvident, while proposing to explain the economic evolution of society in terms of provident instincts and a spirit of emulation natural to all men without distinction. Other writers there-fore rejected the usual subsistence view of wages, even though their anxiety to avoid either raising the cost of manufactures or disturbing the social order still caused them to shy away from the idea of actually giving the labourer more for his hire. Instead they recommended a reduction of provision prices, which they considered to be artificially inflated by the monopolistic tendencies of large-scale production, as the best way of improving real wages, restoring the morale of the labourer and reducing the cost of the country's manufactures.[19]

As it stood, this school of thought was more clearly conservative than any, for what it was in fact proposing was an artificially contrived return to the conditions which had prevailed for most of the first half of the century. Though the advocates of this approach thus joined the general call for regulation, they nevertheless did so from a point of view not only more positively disposed to the labourer, to whom incentives to 'hope, emulation and industry' meant as much as to any man, but also more clearly aware of the interconnectedness of industry and agriculture, and of the importance of free circulation as a stimulus to both. The conclusions drawn from these elements had so far been uniformly orthodox, but at least one contribution to the local debate contained signs that they were capable of yielding very different results if any change took place in the basic assumptions within which they were discussed. Like most of his contemporaries, 'A.M.', writing in *Jopson's Coventry Mercury* of 24 October 1768, warned that if prices were not controlled the circulation of money would be slowed, consumption reduced and a great encouragement of employment and expansion removed. He was, however, going on ground rather different from other correspondents. Instead of deploring the destructive effects of commercial agriculture on a declining population he attributed the crisis in provision prices to the failure of land under cultivation to keep pace with population growth. More important still was the moral basis of his argument, or rather its absence in any explicitly normative sense. Though he followed the general example by calling for regulation, and referred to the State's 'duty' in this respect, the word did not really carry the traditional moral injunction, not even as a device to awaken the consciences of his readers; for the duty which 'A.M.' invoked was simply that of ensuring

> that the several conditions of men have the full enjoyment and fruition of all that the Great Author of their Being has entitled them to, from the immutable laws he has established for their subsistence, preservation, and increase.

The State's fundamental obligation, in fact, was not to govern society according to any distinct or prior moral imperative but simply to guarantee the material freedom of its members, since it was for their pursuit of happiness that society had first been instituted by a benevolent Creator, and since it could be assumed that any 'higher' purpose would best be achieved by fulfilling that original intention.

Such an argument challenged the entire moral framework within which the development of society had so far been discussed. Its optimistic implications ran clean counter to the outlook of those who saw the problem in terms of the luxury and indolence of the age and called on the authorities for protection against the corrupting effects of material wealth and private gain. In retrospect, the proposition that whatever moral task had been reserved for men by the 'Great Author of their Being' would be automatically served by their 'full enjoyment and fruition' of the earth and all that was in it may seem as naive as the traditionalists' belief that the means of improvement and the sources of wealth could be harnessed to the preservation of an obsolescent model of society. At the time, however, this hardly mattered. Quite apart from the positive sanction which it gave to the values of economic growth and the consumer society, the proposition made a powerful aesthetic appeal to one of the strongest tendencies of contemporary thought, the assumption of a perfect unison in creation between God, man and Nature, and its symmetry resolved at one stroke the dilemmas which perplexed more traditional commentators. Though 'A.M.' in 1768 failed to grasp the full import of his own argument, it was but a short step from the proposition that the State's economic regulations should approximate to immutable laws to the conclusion that those laws would operate best if left to themselves. It is therefore not surprising that the reception of the new political economy should have been so swift. The highway of its triumph had been made straight, and the publication of Adam Smith's *Wealth of Nations* in March 1776 represented a final synthesis and reformulation of previous trains of thought as much as it did a new starting point. The old laws against forestalling and regrating had already been repealed for four years; recent writers on the price of provisions were already using analogies drawn from physical phenomena to justify the unrestricted operation of the market,[20] and barely five months after Smith's work appeared its message was being paraphrased and made available to readers of *Jopson's Coventry Mercury* in 'Thoughts on Commerce and the Riches of a State'. Unlike most contributions to the local discussion of economic problems, this deliberately avoided any involvement in the pros and cons of particular policy, and concentrated on establishing a set of general principles. Starting from the relationship between supply and demand ('Commerce flows from want and from abundance'), it emphasised the interdependence of commerce and agriculture and the importance of increased consumer demand in relation to economic growth, reaching the crux of its argument with the statement that

> In considering the riches of a State, we must pay attention to the annual reproduction, and to the annual consumption. In every State, man consumes by enjoyment, and what he has consumed is reproduced by vegetation and manufactures.[21]

It was this relationship between production and consumption which was the basic criterion of prosperity or decay; and since it had a built-in tendency to equilibrium if left to operate without restraint for a sufficient period of time, the essay concluded that the benign laws of economics would eventually bring to society a degree of prosperity and distributive justice as near perfect as was appropriate to the real deserts of its individual members:

> Thus would nature, if allowed the freedom of her own operations, treat all men with the impartiality of an affectionate mother, by remedying defects and abuses whenever they occur, by distributing good and evil among her children in proportion to their activity and their prudence, and by permitting no more inequality between them than what is sufficient for keeping industry and want in action. But it frequently happens that the desire, however respectable in itself, of attaining the summit of possible perfection and happiness, is attended with fatal consequences. This it is which has so often misled legislators and created physical obstacles to that natural equilibrium towards which there is a perpetual tendency, both in the moral and physical world.[22]

Once such general principles had been stated, those more practically concerned with the particular tasks of social policy were soon able to adapt what was fact becoming the new orthodoxy to their own purposes, even though these themselves were still envisioned in traditional terms. Once again, the results can be seen most clearly in the continuing discussion of the price of labour, contributors to which now found themselves able to recommend the previously unthinkable step of raising money wages without seeming to threaten the stability of society by so doing. 'Reasons for the late Increase of the Poor Rates, or a Comparative View of the Price of Labour and Provisions' in *Jopson's Coventry Mercury* of 17 February 1777, for example, began on familiar enough lines with the fundamental importance of the agricultural labourer, from whose strength and industry alone the land derived its real value, and continued by contrasting the condition of the Elizabethan worker, secure in the provision of four acres to every cottage, with the unhappy lot of his eighteenth century descendant. As the article developed, however, its emphasis changed. Far from being by nature idle, English labourers would work as hard as any man if properly encouraged, and 'the bad policy of considering them as an encumbrance has had the worst effect imaginable'. Though he hastened to assure his readers that he was 'one of the last men who would wish to unhinge order, or loosen the bands of society', the writer therefore proposed that wages should be raised to a degree commensurate with recent increases in the rental value of land by relating daily rates of pay directly to the current price of wheat. Admittedly this would involve some increase in wage bills, but this would be more than offset by the improved morale of the labourer and the saving in the poor rates which that would make possible.

By some at least, the same argument was extended to include the town labourer as well. Thus 'Reasons for the late Increase of the Poor Rates' provoked an immediate rejoinder which acknowledged the previous writer's 'charity to the industrious poor labourer' but thought him 'extremely negligent in overlooking the ingenious mechanic':

> Whoever takes a view of our farmers' labourers in general will find they live as neat and comfortable as any working poor in Europe, whilst those who will but examine the habitations of our poor manufacturers in any of our great towns, will find them to be the most miserable set of working people on earth. . . . Therefore, if any body of men are absurd in their conduct towards working hands, it must be the masters of our manufactories who are guilty and not the farmers; for the farmers' labourers do not fall upon the parishes in an equal proportion to the manufacturers. No people, it is true, work harder than our English labourers, who therefore ought to be well payed, and as no people on earth are more ingenious and clever than our manufacturers, consequently they ought not to be overlooked, but are entitled to have their wages raised as well as the labourers.[23]

These signs of a different outlook were, however, still counterbalanced by the uneasiness which many continued to feel about the course the country's economic development seemed to be taking. The opinion that prosperity derived from the productive superiority of a few advanced manufactures was too narrowly based to last, and that speculative wealth gained 'by commerce, not by populousness' was an unsafe bottom in which to venture the nation's future, still found many advocates, especially during the discussion of William Pitt's commercial policies in the 1780s.[24] Similarly, the growth of the manufacturing towns was still widely regarded as a pernicious distortion of the natural course of social development, and the conditions which this growth was creating continued to be discussed not as posing distinct problems of their own but as special cases of the general rural situation, which was still taken as that for which remedies were fundamentally needed.

The same general disposition extended far beyond the immediate bounds of political economy. It inspired Priscilla Pointon of Lichfield, who moralised in 1770 about the blessings of country mediocrity, to advise her readers that 'In humble cots contentment's found';[25] it was equally implicit in such popular celebrations of idealised rusticity as 'Content' by John Crane of Bromsgrove, toyman, bookseller and loyalist versifier, who bade 'cash' to 'keep away till thou canst yield content',[26] and it moved Sir Roger Newdigate to set down his thoughts on *bon ton*:

A pestilent nuisance, ... in my opinion much more to be dreaded than those things which have set my countrymen in such frights from time to time, as earthquakes, murrains, invasions, flat bottom boats, the Cyder Act, Cock Lane Ghost, Mr. Wilkes;—and this being too is of French extraction, as I judge by its name. ... I would find no fault with it if it was permitted only to dress ye heads of the Males and Females, shape a ruffle, roll a stocking, or add a dish to ye second course or dessert, ... but when Bon Ton laughs at ye Scriptures, sets its votary to cards on Sundays, and whispers to ye vapourish dame, ... then it is to be feared indeed; and yet so artful is it that it introduces itself everywhere. I wish it is not sometimes to be discovered peeping into ye House of Lords and Commons, and the Courts of Justice, and I'm sure it has intruded its odious hypocritical form into ye Royal Presence. Hitherto I bless my stars that it has not travelled more than fifty miles from London (at least to make no stay), or we shd. not now be enjoying our plumb broth, Xmas pyes, our honest neighbours and tenants and the poor. . . .[27]

The occasion of Miss Pointon's coy admonition, which was addressed 'to a young Tradesman, who complained that he had secretly languished for a Lady of Distinction in the neighbourhood without the least hope of a favourable return', was, however, more expressive of reality than the pastoral conceit which it tried to sustain. Conventionally acceptable or not, such ambition and its social and economic by-products were integral to the progress of a community whose dominant characteristic was anything but arcadian placidity. Similarly, Sir Roger Newdigate's condemnation of *bon ton* did him credit as the very model of a Fine Old English Gentleman; but though he stood by the venerable code of his kind, such values in their existing forms were ceasing to bear much relation to a changing world, which, if it did not discard the niceties altogether by avowing an open preference for 'cash' over 'contentment', at least showed signs of measuring the latter in terms of the former, and bade the poor look after themselves. If the dangers implicit in the growth of the towns were to be avoided it would not be enough to reiterate time-honoured precepts in the resuscitated language of the past. The known example would have to be adapted in order to preserve traditional virtues intact in changed circumstances.

In the attempting of this task the Birmingham area started with several advantages. The strong elements of conservatism and practical individualism, which, despite the breadth and sophistication of its newly acquired articulacy, continued to modify the potential radicalism of the area's artisan population, the nature of the area's trades themselves, and the proven effectiveness of the close relationship which existed between Birmingham and its surroundings, all made it possible to retain the traditional metaphors of social hierarchy without losing touch too blatantly with reality. These metaphors were further supported by the rehabilitation of 'luxury', hitherto deplored as the very root of disorder, as a provider of employment and a guarantor of the interdependence of the different ranks of society. There were, of course, obstacles as well. By 1795, when signs of real class cleavage and of a breakdown in the understanding which had hitherto existed between town and county were clearly visible in Birmingham, the explanations of the social role of luxury offered to the people in previous years were replaced by an extolling of 'frugality' which must have sounded very hollow, despite its acompanying dose of evangelical piety. But nevertheless an accommodation of sorts was achieved. As a systematic revision of the old order it left a lot to be desired; as a practical mixture which could be underpinned by appealing to the region's collective sense of pride in its own past experience it answered its purpose well enough, and it only threatened to break down when it was subjected to severe strain on too many fronts at once.

The mixture of traditional and progressive characteristics which were combined in the tavern clubs and cliques formed in Birmingham from the 1760s onwards, and clearly displayed in the discussions of the Free Debating Society and its various offshoots, was equally apparent at the same stage in the response of the small manufacturers to far-reaching changes in the scale and structure of Birmingham's trades. As the larger firms began not only to sell but also to produce their own goods, instead of merely marketing the wares of independent workshops,[28] the lesser masters felt themselves threatened in much the same way as did the small landowner confronted by enclosure and the engrossing tenant farmer. Attention was drawn to this situation by a long 'Address to Manufacturers in General' in the *Birmingham Gazette* of 26 September 1763. This was 'intended to promote that spirit of unanimity and concern for their general interest, without which no trade or society can happily exist', and it pointed out the danger of allowing trade to fall into the hands of a few monopolist firms which combined the previously separate functions of merchant and manufacturer. The natural order of things was that trade should be 'carried on by a variety of hands who have *each* a prospect of becoming independent in proportion to their conduct and abilities'. The composite firm, however, would be able to undersell the merchants pure and simple who traded fairly with the independent masters; the fair traders would have to pass profit reductions on to their suppliers in order to stay in business, and they would ultimately be forced to follow the example of the composites. 'What then will become of the *poor manufacturers*? Will they be merchants too? Yes—Merchants' clerks, runners, journeymen, and slaves.' Certainly there was no way of preventing the merchant turning manufacturer:

> but it is equally certain that to serve such merchants . . . is not in the interest of the meanest manufacturer; and if he would keep the power in his own hands to support his family comfortably, and maintain the character of an honest man, he will not do it. . . . Can it be honest in any man to empower one customer to sell his goods cheaper than another? Does he not by that means put it out of the power of everybody else to deal with him? The case is exactly *the same as if we sold our goods cheaper to one than another* so long as we serve any merchant or dealer who is himself a manufacturer; for in doing so, we empower him to injure every other fair dealer who has not the same advantage.

To forestall this threat the small men would have to put aside their present 'pitiful jealousy of each other' and learn to unite their interests. 'Many advantages would accrue to them by becoming an amicable society and frequently meeting and conversing together', and as a first step towards this end the manufacturers of Birmingham, Wolverhampton, Walsall, Bilston and the other Black Country towns were called to a meeting on 13 October 'in order that a free correspondence and good understanding may be maintained through every branch of the hardware and toy trades'.[29]

The fears of the manufacturers that monopolistic combines would deprive them of status and livelihood proved to be largely unfounded. The expansion and diversity of Birmingham's trades were sufficient to accommodate both the great firms and the small masters who sold their goods through factors and merchants, and since the artisans of the town could therefore still find a place for themselves in the existing social order they were able to sustain their belief in its underlying principles. This belief was the more realistic because the nature of Birmingham's trades made their prosperity peculiarly dependent on those principles. It was a commonplace of the loyalist resolutions which followed the royal proclamation in November 1792 that there would be different ranks and degrees of men in every system of government, but that 'in such as are well regulated' these would tend, not 'to the encouragement of Pride and Oppression', but to the promotion of industry and provision for the wants[30]

> of the Artificer, the Labourer, and the Indigent: and therefore the adoption of any visionary scheme of Equalization would deprive by its effects the lower orders of those means of subsistence they now enjoy.

In Birmingham this argument was stated with no compunction at all:

> If we had no Nobility, Gentry, or Rich People, who would consume the Manufactures of Birmingham? Our Manufactures are principally Luxuries or Superfluities: and if we mind our own interest, we should be among the last to injure or chace away the Consumers of them.[31]

This prompts a speculation on the particular reasons for the presence of the mob in 1791 and for the ease with which it was turned against the Dissenters. The most exhaustive and authoritative account[32] of the Priestley riots finds their underlying cause in the temporary conjunction during the transitional period of Birmingham's development between traditional prejudices and the new social tensions set up by industrial growth. As a general explanation of the context of the disturbances this conclusion is convincing. It disposes effectively of the unverifiable view that the riots were part of a premeditated plan devised by the government to clip the Dissenters' wings, and by confining the role of interested participation by the authorities to local provocation and exploitation of the outbreak it seeks to achieve a proper balance between religious and political motives on one hand and social and economic factors on the other. Quite apart from the considerable case that can be made for government complicity after the event,[33] however, this account is open to the objection that though it mentions them in the course of its examination of the social and economic factors involved in the riots, it nevertheless treats the religious and political prejudices of the mob simply as phenomena whose existence as part of the very nature of Birmingham can be regarded as axiomatic. The conjunction of the riots' different elements in the venting of latent class hatred against the Dissenters thus tends to appear as the logical result of a process which requires no further elucidation. As a result 'the Mob' in 1791 gets taken for granted,[34] and the need to ask how the overlap between traditional prejudices and new social and economic tensions may have actually occurred in the consciousness of the rioters themselves escapes unnoticed. It is in this respect that the nature of Birmingham's trades and their state in 1791 become important contingent factors in a full explanation of the riots, just as it was in the aftermath of the latter, when those involved had to be brought under control before they pursued the logic of their action beyond its desirable limits, that the same characteristics were most systematically exploited by the propagandists of subordination.

Because of its dependence on superfluities Birmingham had a special interest not only in the established order but also in established fashions. This was particularly so in the case of the buckle and the button, two of the town's staple products. By the end of the eighteenth century buckled shoes and polished metal buttons had been necessary accessories of respectable dress for so long that what had begun as a fashion had become an institution, part of the accepted way of life. As such, these essential ornaments could support an infinite range of ephemeral variation without forfeiting their basic position, and Birmingham had long grown used to taking the effects of such passing fancies in its stride. From about 1786 onwards, however, polished buckles and buttons began to give place altogether to laced shoes or slippers and covered buttons. This total change in dress, which came to be associated in the common mind with new-fangled ideas and events on the other side of the Channel, had dire effects in Birmingham and its neighbourhood. By December 1791, when delegates from Birmingham, Walsall and Wolverhampton petitioned the Prince of Wales, as an arbiter of fashion, to renounce the shoestring, twenty thousand men were said to be out of work in the buckle trade, whose entire future was in jeopardy.[35] Conditions among the button makers were admittedly not quite so bad: the indispensable button could hardly have been overtaken by the kind of calamity which befell the buckle, and between them the American market, changes in women's dress and the coming vogue for gilt buttons ensured the trade's recovery.[36] But nevertheless it was hard hit for a time, and even though what was threatened in this case was not the actual making but only the finishing of the goods, the public was warned at least twice during the winter of 1790–91 that

> Many thousands of industrious men and women are become almost destitute of employment by the general use now made of buttons unlawfully covered, and which from our example is also become the prevailing fashion abroad.[37]

William Hutton dated the era of the buckle, like that of the constitution, from 1688.[38] Both were now threatened, and anxiety for the established order and the established fashion easily became synonymous, especially when the livelihood of thousands was at stake. The relationship between social and political upheaval, changing ideas and fashion is difficult to demonstrate factually; but in these latter days of hair, beads and unisex it is perhaps easier to appreciate than in more settled times, and contemporaries certainly made the connection in the 1790s,[39] when the wearing of laced shoes and covered buttons was regarded as a badge not only of dubious personal tendencies but of political subversion as well. The *Birmingham Gazette* of 10 May 1790 contrasted 'the Manly buckle' with 'that most ridiculous of all ridiculous fashions, the *effeminate* shoestring' as worn by 'a very few incorrigible petits maitres, against whom the shafts of ridicule[40] are pointed in vain'. When Fashion eschewed 'foreign or unprofitable ornaments' in favour of British manufacturers, the buckle makers told the Prince of Wales in December 1791, she assumed the nobler form of patriotism. Taste which both decorated the persons of the rich and fed the hungry poor deserved the name of humanity: no doubt His Royal Highness would prefer 'the blessings of the starving manufacturer to the encomiums of the drawing room'. By implication the replacement of buckles and buttons by foreign frippery was part of a conspiracy to starve the loyal British artisan. The figure of twenty thousand jobless in the Birmingham area which the buckle makers claimed in their petition was undoubtedly exaggerated, and the number who were out of work the previous July was not mentioned; but serious unemployment, apparently caused in this way among workmen whose immediate and superficial resentments could so easily lead them to turn on the intellectuals of Birmingham as the imagined authors of their plight, may well explain the availability of the mob in 1791. The choice of 'Job Nott, Buckle-maker', and 'John Nott, Button Burnisher' as pseudonyms by local anti-Jacobin pamphleteers was probably not fortuitous, and the moral was succinctly put by the last couplet of 'Lines on the Bucklemakers' Petition' by 'Tutania' in January 1792:

> Success to the ARTS, and again and again,
> GOOD ORDERS to those who good order maintain.[41]

By that time the mob had served its turn and had to be set aside as quietly as possible.

The Old Meeting and the houses of the Dissenters were not the only victims of the riots. 'That deference for the law which prevailed in this place'[42] also perished, and before many months had passed the two-edged weapon of July 1791 was turning in the hands of those who had first wielded it. In the spring of 1793 Samuel Garbett feared that the mob might be raised as easily 'by a cry against Parliament and Country Gentlemen' as by Church and King. During the previous winter he had heard 'Children cry "God save the King and Huzza, Tom Paine for ever", and others cry "No Presbyterians and Tom Paine for ever"'.[43] Similar garbled slogans were bandied about in other places too. 'A Card', circulated at the Newcastle under Lyme by-election in September 1792, ran the whole gamut from traditional local feuds to the French revolution and the *Rights of Man*:

> No Peer's Interference.
> No perjured Peer.
> No Eg-rt-n.
> No Runaway.
> No Henry T--k--n.
> No Pickpocket.
> No Pictures heels upwards.
> No Rascal that will dare to defend himself,
> or attempt it, against Butcher Salt.
> No Bastille.
> No Constraint.
> The Poor equal to the Rich when called upon oath.[44]

The antidote in this particular case was characteristic. It was the egregious Job Nott who was telling the working people of the West Midlands how to behave themselves, and at the beginning of 1793 John Massey, election agent for the Marquess of Stafford, distributed a thousand copies of Job's *Humble Advice* in Newcastle, along with other equally improving literature.[45] Job encouraged his readers to think of themselves and their occupations in terms of an expansion of the traditional order, which was adapted to urban circumstances, and in which the self-respect of the independent artificer was reassured. There was 'a great chain from the King to the Poor Man'; equality was a reward in the next world for dutiful deference here and now, and there 'must be Workmen,

Masters, Factors, and Merchants to distribute all sorts of goods to shopkeepers
at home and abroad, who can distribute them to the Consumers, and so all
sorts of people find employment and profit'.[46] Within this expanded hierarchy
there was room for a more permissive attitude to luxury, emulation and individual advancement. For from being harbingers of political corruption and
social disintegration, as some had feared, these now appeared as guarantees of
stability, bonds sufficiently compelling yet sufficiently flexible to retain their
hold even as society itself changed beneath them. The apologia for luxury was
stressed, and Job explained the economic function of the upper classes with
luminous candour:

> What use would it be for us poor artificers to make Buckles, Buttons, and a
> thousand fine things, if there was not Nobility and Gentry to wear them when we
> had done?

Thus the visionary distinction between the 'useful' and 'ornamental' branches
of society, so sharply drawn by Volney's *Ruines*, was denied, and 'Wealthy
Inhabitants' were advised to support the constitution which had watched over
their own climb to eminence so that 'other poor industrious men may be
protected by it while they rise in the world as you have done'.[47]

This, however, was not the whole of Job's message. The new townspeople of
the West Midlands had also to be weaned away from many of the practical
freedoms which they had enjoyed or aspired to as countrymen. They had to be
encouraged to submit willingly to tighter discipline as minor participants in the
development of one of the fastest-growing regions in the kingdom, but they had
also to be left with their self-respect unimpaired if traditional virtues were to
survive the transition. To achieve this, Job Nott used his own example to erase
from his readers' minds their awkward memories of country life and to replace
them with something more suitable. He recalled the precepts of his venerable
master and his own exemplary apprenticeship, and, having completed his time,
recollected the holiday spree in the countryside which followed. In this he put
himself through a veritable chapter of accidents during which he shed his own
rustic aspirations in a variety of ridiculous scrapes, and emerged, bloody but
unbowed, having learnt the good sense of not meddling in things he did not
understand.

As an apprentice Job had been 'the pick of the bunch', clean, tidy at his
work, and, above all, punctual; for, as his master used to say, 'A tradesman
without punctuality was like a rusty weathercock that would not turn upon
its centre. There was no dependence on 't.' Master was an Anglican, but,
possibly as a gesture of conciliation, his wife was cast as a Dissenter. Although
presumably of the 'sleepy quiet'[48] kind, and 'a good sort of woman', she was
depicted as slightly scatterbrained, inclined to pettishness and hasty conclusions.
One of her tantrums, diagnosed by Master to have been brought on by disreput-
able literature from 'The Poison Shop', [49] was used as the occasion for a series
of simple homilies on popular grievances, the game laws among them:

> What advantages would it be to us Birmingham people to have a right to go
> a shooting? None, but evidently a disadvantage. If I want a hare for a Christening
> Dinner, I can get one for four shillings, and I fancy I should lose more time by
> neglecting my business to go and shoot one, beside the expense of powder and shot,
> and the danger of my gun going off at half cock, or in shooting across the road

and blowing the brains of some worthy man out. . . . Upon the whole, depend
upon it, the Game Laws serve to make men industrious, and to keep them at
their work.

Once his time was up, Job allowed himself a fortnight's holiday trip to Wolverhampton and Walsall to see a bit of the world, and to taste the delights of
country life for himself. He started out in style, dressed in a new suit of clothes
and driving a chaise which he hired from a livery stable. The affair of 'The
One Horse Chaise' ended in a crash which put paid to Job's carriage and
involved him in a quarrel with its owner. Nothing daunted, Job kept the horse,
set off once more and was soon involved in 'The Hunting Business'. As he rode
towards Sutton Coldfield a hunt crossed the road, and Job joined in. None too
sure of his seat, and bawling incomprehensible hunting whoops, he was thrown
at the first fence, landed in a mud puddle and lost his horse completely. This
time, however, Job had an answer to the jeers of the huntin' gentlemen:

> But I can't say I am mightily pleased with these Hunting Country Gentlemen
> for running the rig on us Birmingham folks, tho' we mayn't all be quite so polite
> as they are. I was as well or better dressed than any one of 'em, and for aught
> I saw, till I was thrown, rode as fast, tho' to be sure I did not sometime sit quite
> so tight on the saddle. . . . Besides the COUNTRY GENTLEMEN should consider that
> if it wasn't for me, and such as me, perhaps they might not have so much money
> to hunt with. . . . Don't they sell their farms for double price in consequence of
> the quantity of provisions devoured in this place, so that I think there isn't much
> to laugh at. Methinks if Mr. Pitt was to neglect the trade, and trade should be
> dead, and population didn't go on in the manner it does here, these laughing
> Gents might laugh at tother side the mouth, and mayhap some of their children
> or grand-children be glad to be Bucklemakers, and then they might happen to be
> in the same condition as Job Nott. Gentlefolk should consider these things a little.

Job decided that it was safer to walk, but he was not yet done with country
pursuits. After various other adventures, he was tempted to try his hand with a
borrowed gun. 'The Shooting Business' finally cured him, for he had the mis-
fortune to knock off an old lawyer's wig, had his gun smashed, and was lucky
to get away with only a horsewhipping.

Job now knew where he belonged, and 'finding that nothing agreed with me
half so well as work, I went back to the shop again, and set to hard and fast'. In
due course he became a master himself, and set out his own simple commercial
principles: to pay as good wages as he could afford; to get buckles up as good
and cheap as possible, for 'A nimble ninepence is better than a slow shilling,
both for master and man'; to pay his men on Saturday afternoons at five o'clock
so as to minimise their chances of drinking their wages away before the week-
end, but to give them a small instalment on the previous Thursday morning so
that wives would have time to go to market; never to run his business on credit;
to avoid all traffic in bills, which was a sure way to ruin and suicide, and, finally,
to make a clean breast of any trouble that should arise, so that other people's
property would not be jeopardised by his own difficulties.[50]

Job's task was made easier by the fact that he could appeal to the pride of his
fellow townsmen in their considerable achievements during the past thirty or
forty years. He noticed that the streets of Paris were unpaved, which led him to
dwell fervently on the blessings of England in general, and of Birmingham,

whose streets had been paved since 1769, in particular. The Blue Coat School, the Hospital, the Free School, the Sunday schools, the Dispensary, all were praised, and especially the latter, whose opening in 1792 gave 'the opulent... an opportunity to feel the real luxury of doing good'. But Birmingham was not only a place to be grateful for; its people could be proud of its political significance as well. Its petitions and remonstrances were 'instantly attended to by the King and his Ministers', and

> I have heard that Sir Robert Lawley should say that whenever he waited on Mr. Pitt on Birmingham business, he never was suffered to wait a moment. It was only to announce the *Warwickshire* Member, and the doors flew open directly.[51]

The spirit and unanimity of Birmingham people in county politics was praised, and though this same spirit may have led them into pardonable excesses in 1791 they could hardly be blamed for what was obviously the work of a few hardened criminals. Such violence was quite out of keeping with the town's true character:

> I believe there never was a place of its size as remarkable for a quiet and peacable character. A many years ago, when we chose to shew the Country Gentlemen the odds on't, and brought in Sir Charles Holte because we would bring him in, there was twenty thousand people assembled, and yet not a shin broke or a toe trod upon as you may say.[52]

Thus was the most significant achievement of all, the first effective demonstration by Birmingham people of their own articulacy and assertiveness, appropriated to the cause of law and order.

Job did not have the field to himself, however, and much of what he had to say to his 'brother artificers' would have been more appropriately addressed to Harriet Beecher Stowe's Uncle Tom than to the heirs of Freeborn John. The latter can hardly have taken kindly to such fancies as Job's notion that fine ladies' feet should be kissed because they were adorned by Birmingham buckles,[53] and the Bucklemaker's advice had to make its way against the chiliastic denunciation of his 'Elder Brother', John Nott, Button Maker. Urged on by the ghost of his father, who had 'died on the 20th day of July in the year of the great riots in Birmingham, of a broken heart, aged 91', and who now returned from the grave to proclaim the coming downfall of Antichrist, John appealed to a Bunyanesque jury consisting of

> Manlove and Goodwill; Manpatience and Manpeace; Man-Human and Man-Moderate; John Manly and Job Firm; David No-coward; Peter Notbefrighted; Daniel the Prophet, and some other worthies,

who condemned his brother's production as 'a false, wicked, seditious and treasonable writing against the rights of man and truth'.[54] By 1795 Job Nott's arguments were wearing thin. Not even the good offices with the Prince of Wales of Matthew Boulton and his agents could procure the rehabilitation of the buckle,[55] and claims that Birmingham was 'flourishing beyond all measure' no longer rang true. At the same time, the links between town and county to which Job so gratefully drew attention were ceasing to guarantee that Birmingham business would automatically be the first concern of the Warwickshire Members, and a sense of betrayal began to appear in the town's remonstrances:

"What", says the Secretary-at-War, "a cry of distress and poverty had been raised . . . he believed it not". It is possible that either of the Members for this County of Warwick could have been present, and yet make no reply?

The writer of this 'Appeal to Manufacturers' also noticed another change wrought on Birmingham by 'the policy of the times', less obvious perhaps than the simple decline of trade but ultimately more pernicious, and one for which responsibility could be more immediately assigned. This was the increasing physical segregation of what were now called 'working manufacturers', dependent on one specialised source of support alone, and their confinement to certain parts of the town. It was, for example, distressing to find in the minutes of the Handsworth Parish Vestry for December 1794 a resolution which proposed to 'prevent the evil consequences likely to arise from the great number of Club, and other small houses, intended to be built in this Parish' by removing 'all likely to become chargeable that shall come to reside in the Parish . . . without a certificate', and doubly disappointing to discover that this had the support of none other than Matthew Boulton himself:

> Had these resolutions been the result of the deliberations of *Country Gentlemen,* I should have felt no surprise; but when I see affixed to them the name of one of the most *justly* celebrated manufacturers in his M---y's dominions, I must say, there is too much truth in the assertion which states that "It is often more difficult for a poor man to pass the artificial boundary of a parish than an arm of the sea, or a ridge of high mountains".[56]

Birmingham people, it seemed, could no longer even trust their own leaders to keep faith with the town.

Against such a background, the advice offered in 1794 by James Morfitt stands out as peculiarly provocative. In a blatant *volte-face* from the propaganda of previous years this local barrister, who may have had a hand in the earlier Nott pamphlets, urged his fellow townsmen to shun the snare of luxury and embrace instead 'the Glories of FRUGALITY'.[57] During the famine months of the following summer most of Morfitt's 'sons of Commerce' had little choice in the matter, but his alternative was not accepted without a fight. In June handbills were circulated calling the people to arms, and a crowd a thousand strong ransacked Birmingham's bakeries and stormed James Pickard's mill on Snow Hill in protest against the price of flour and a reduction in the size of loaves. The outbreak, which threatened to spread to Dudley, Stourbridge and Bromsgrove, was brought under control by regular troops from Ashted barracks, reinforced by the Aston detachment of the newly formed Warwickshire Yeomanry; but two of the rioters were shot,[58] and the most that could be done to avert future trouble was to organise a sale of cheap flour, to set up various emergency measures of charitable relief and to try to convince the lower orders 'that their superiors shared in the scarcity of the times and had retrenched their superfluities'.[59] The arrangements which were made at the end of July to convoy grain to the town under armed escort from as far away as Abingdon, Woodstock, Banbury, Towcester and Burford came none too soon. The situation remained 'tolerably quiet', but by this time Birmingham was down to its last fortnight's supplies, and Matthew Boulton, who was concerned only to 'supply them with food and preserve peace', found 'an evident insolence and ingratitude visible amongst the very lowest class of people, who attribute our charity to fear'.[60]

In these conditions the Jacobins regained some of the ground they had lost since 1793. According to John Kilmister,

> In the late disturbances in Birmingham, the chief argument of the Rioters to the magistrates was "You did not shoot us when we were rioting for Church and King & pulling down the presbyterians meetings and dwelling houses, but gave us plenty of good ale & spirits to urge us on. Now we are rioting for a big loaf we must be shot at & cut up like Bacon Pigs".[61]

In November a petition against the impending passage of the Two Acts carrying 3,400 signatures was forwarded to the London Corresponding Society for prospective presentation to Parliament.[62] The following March John Gale Jones and John Binns arrived in Birmingham as guests of Edward Corn, warden of the New Meeting,[63] and as delegates to advise 'The Birmingham United Corresponding Society' on the proper tactics for survival under the new treason and sedition laws. Both the meetings held by the delegates proved difficult to keep below the maximum of fifty now allowed by the law. At the Swan in Swallow Street, John Binns was able to disband his audience before the magistrates arrived, but he reported with undisguised pleasure that it had overflowed onto the stairs of the house. At the Bell in Suffolk Street, John Gale Jones was less lucky in dodging the Justices. His meeting, which according to the *Birmingham Gazette* numbered about seventy, was interrupted by a magistrate who engaged Jones in a bout of logic chopping over the nature of reform. After this, the royal proclamation against treason and sedition was read, 'the assembly with some reluctance taking off their hats' and greeting it with low hisses, contempt and laughter. Jones thought it wise to yield to the authority of the law and left the meeting, 'which seemed strongly inclined to stay',[64] but on the pretext of this incident both he and Binns were arrested and committed for trial at Warwick assizes. Their trials were, however, postponed, and since they were allowed bail they were able to use the interval to sustain the Birmingham society.[65]

This was now attracting attention in other parts of the Black Country which had hitherto been silent. At the end of July the London Corresponding Society was in touch with three small clubs at Wolverhampton, Coseley and Sedgley, which were anxious to do whatever they could for the delegates,[66] and at the same time further news arrived from Birmingham itself. Binns was acting as treasurer of the society, whose new secretary, 'Citizen Bullock', was proving to be both an inspiring speaker and an energetic fund raiser.[67] In due course £39 5*s* was sent up to the parent society in London, which was 'happy to hear from Citn. Binns that your society increases so rapidly'.[68] After this there is little substantial evidence on the Birmingham Jacobins, but they were still meeting the following summer, when they played their part in county agitation against the Ministry during August by collecting 4,500 signatures on a supporting petition from Birmingham.[69] At the same time the assize jury at Warwick vindicated the position of the London Corresponding Society by acquitting John Binns of the charges brought against him in March 1796. Warwickshire juries had not been known for their impartiality in the past, and such a verdict in the first major test of the Two Acts seemed well worthy of celebration. It earned the jury an address of thanks from the London Corresponding Society, and Binns hastened to put his account of the trial in the hands of James Belcher, Birmingham's Unitarian printer, for publication and distribution to booksellers and newspapermen in most other parts of the country.[70]

Too much should not be made of all this, however. When they left London in March 1796 Binns and Jones had been instructed to warn the affiliated societies against becoming absorbed in the agitation of other groups, and especially against allowing the Whig Club's plans to associate for the repeal of the Two Acts alone to divert them from their own objectives.[71] Conversely, the complaint about the price of the London Corresponding Society's *Moral and Political Magazine*, which marred Jones's otherwise encouraging report from Birmingham at the beginning of August 1796,[72] suggests that while the Birmingham society had maintained its own position, it was finding it difficult after all to widen its regular circle of interest in the town. Despite their involvement, the petitions of November 1795 and August 1797 are therefore better regarded as general expressions of concern at the state of the country and the policies of the Ministry than as indicators of committed support for the Birmingham Jacobins. The same concern may help to explain the Warwickshire jury's departure from the traditions of its predecessors in 1797, and in any case, the victory represented by Binns's acquittal was in practical terms a pyrrhic one, for it exhausted the remaining resources of his supporters. Before his trial Binns was writing anxiously to warn the executive committee of the London Corresponding Society that he had 'not a guinea to bring a witness, to fee counsel or to give Mr Jones', and though the committee set aside seventy guineas for the defence of its delegates this was far from sufficient. After his acquittal Binns was still asking for money to discharge the various debts which he had unavoidably contracted and to pay for the publication of his trial.[73] He claimed in September 1797 that the Birmingham society was 'daily increasing in numbers'; but though the parent society in London was still receiving letters which indicated the vigorous, if leaderless, survival of political clubs in other parts of the country, the last known meeting of Birmingham's Jacobins was a supper party, attended by fifteen of them, at Parr's Cottage of Content after the petition meeting at Warwick in August 1797; and this, symbolically, was disturbed by a gang of drunken loyalists from the White Horse in Friday Street.[74]

NOTES

1 The following account of the provision riots of the mid-1760s is based on W. J. Shelton, *English Hunger and Industrial Disorders*.

2 For the points raised in this paragraph see the discussion between E. P. Thompson, 'The moral economy of the English crowd in the eighteenth century', and A. W. Coats, 'Plebs, paternalists and political economists', in *Past and Present*, 50 (February 1971), 76–136, and 54 (February 1972), 130–3 respectively.

3 *Aris*, 8 September 1766.

4 *Jopson*, 22 October 1764.

5 Reprinted in R. L. Schuyler, ed., *Josiah Tucker: a Selection from his Economic and Political Writings* (2nd edn, New York, 1966), pp. 55–219.

6 Enclosures which had the consent of two-thirds of those affected were to be adopted

'as a truly *National Concern*', and to have their costs defrayed out of public revenue, provided always that the proprietors gave reasonable security against injustice and oppression.

7 By 'A.B.' in *Jopson*, 1 February 1768.

8 *Garbett–Lansdowne Letters*, 1, Garbett to Shelburne, 23 May 1766.

9 For the development of Garbett's ideas see P. S. Bebbington, 'Samuel Garbett, 1717–1803, a Birmingham pioneer' (University of Birmingham, M.Comm. thesis, 1938).

10 *Garbett–Lansdowne Letters*, 1, Garbett to Shelburne, 17 August 1767.

11 *Garbett–Lansdowne Letters*, 1, Garbett to Shelburne, 24 November 1767.

12 For a succinct guide to the extensive body of detailed and highly localised research which has been devoted to this question see G. E. Mingay, *Enclosure and the Small Farmer in the Age of the Industrial Revolution* (London, 1968).

13 See J. M. Martin, 'The parliamentary enclosure movement and rural society in Warwickshire', *Agric. Hist. Rev.*, xv (1967), 19–39.

14 See J. M. Martin, 'The cost of parliamentary enclosure in Warwickshire', *U.B.H.J.*, ix (1963–4), 144–62.

15 See J. D. Chambers, 'Enclosure and labour supply in the industrial revolution', *Econ. Hist. Rev.*, 2nd series, v (1953), 319–43.

16 See M. Blaug, 'The myth of the old poor law and the making of the new', *Journ. Econ. Hist.*, xxiii (1963), 151–84, and comment by E. J. Hobsbawm and G. Rudé, *Captain Swing* (London, 1968), p. 50.

17 *Aris*, 20 December 1773. The development of such schemes is considered by D. C. Barnett, 'Allotments and the problem of rural poverty, 1780–1840', in E. L. Jones and G. E. Mingay, eds., *Land, Labour and Population in the Industrial Revolution* (London, 1967), pp. 162–86.

18 On the wider context within which local discussion of this question took place see E. W. Gilboy, *Wages in Eighteenth Century England* (Cambridge, Mass., 1934), and three articles by A. W. Coats: 'Changing attitudes to labour in the mid-eighteenth century', *Econ. Hist. Rev.*, 2nd series, xi (1958–9), 35–51; 'Economic thought and poor law policy in the eighteenth century', *Econ. Hist. Rev.*, 2nd series, xiii (1960–61), 39–51, and 'The classical economists and the labourer', in *Land, Labour and Population in the Industrial Revolution*, pp. 100–30.

19 See, for example, articles in *Aris*, 27 April 1767 and *Jopson*, 30 May 1772.

20 *Cf.* Examples cited by E. P. Thompson, 'The moral economy of the English crowd', p. 81.

21 *Cf. Wealth of Nations* (ed. E. Cannan, London, 1904), p. 464: 'There is another balance indeed, ... very different from the balance of trade, and which, according as it happens to be either favourable or unfavourable, necessarily occasions the prosperity or decay of every nation. This is the balance of the annual produce and consumption.' The text presented by Cannan is that of the fifth edition of Smith's work, published in 1789. The passage above had, however, remained unaffected by changes subsequent to the first edition in 1776.

22 *Jopson*, 19 August 1776.

23 *Jopson*, 24 February 1777.

24 Even the *Wealth of Nations* itself remained 'conspicuously little influenced by contemporary events' in technology and industrial organisation. It showed little curiosity about the precise sources of entrepreneurial activity, as distinct from 'the common urge of self-interest and the wholesome practice of competition', and its argument did not fully acknowledge the significance of innovation as a permanent economic asset. When the success of the new manufactures was mentioned, in Smith's discussion of wages and profit in different employments of labour and stock (Book 1, ch. 10, pt 1), it was accorded only a rather qualified recognition, and was still treated implicitly as an aberration from the natural course of development. *Cf.* in particular Smith's comparison of the novelty trades of Birmingham, where demand arose entirely 'from fashion and fancy' and profit therefore depended on continuous and inherently expensive innovation, with those of Sheffield, where demand arose 'chiefly from use or necessity' and profits, though perhaps not so individually conspicuous, were more valuable in the aggregate (Cannan edn, pp. 114–15). In general, *cf.* also R. Koebner, 'Adam Smith and the industrial revolution', *Econ. Hist. Rev.*, 2nd series, xi (1958–59), 381–91.

25 Priscilla Pointon, *Poems on Several Occasions* (1770), B.R.L. 5856, p. 23.

26 *The Crumbs, by a Bird at Bromsgrove* [John Crane] (1793), B.R.L. 317009:

> Said Joe, snug seated, by a rousing fire,
> To his own self, what more can I desire?
> Cash keep away till thou canst yield content,
> 'Tis just enough what providence has sent.
> My little farm supplies my house with food,
> Content shakes spices o'er it and makes it good.

For Crane see 'Worcestershire worthies, *c.* 1750–1836' in the *Bromsgrove Messenger*, 11 March 1911, B.R.L. 317017.

27 *Newdigate*, CR 136/2592. The manuscript is undated and incomplete.

28 For this development see Eric Robinson, 'Boulton and Fothergill, 1762–82, and the Birmingham export of hardware', *U.B.H.J.*, vii, No. 1 (1959), 60–79.

29 *Aris*, 10 October 1763.

30 *Jopson*, 22 December 1793, resolutions from Rugby.

31 *Address to the Inhabitants of Birmingham* from 'A Friend to Birmingham and the Constitution', 29 April 1793, B.R.L. 325311.

32 That of R. B. Rose in *Past and Present*, No. 18 (November 1960).

33 For the Crown's reluctance to expose the local magistrates in the courts by proceeding against the rioters as vigorously as it might have done, see contents of H.O. 42/19 and TS 11/932/3304.

34 This is particularly apparent in Professor Rose's account of Birmingham politics in *V.C.H. Warwicks.*, vii, 279 ff., which presents the Priestley riots as conforming to type within a long and notorious history of sporadic violence. When one half of the established pattern of Birmingham politics, 'a "political nation" of merchants and manufacturers with a strong leaven of dissent', began to break up in the later 1780s, what more apparently predictable than to find the other half, 'an unruly populace with strong "Church and King"', and even, in the early years, Jacobite proclivities', turning on the Dissenters? This, however, glosses over part of reality. It abstracts the mob from particular circumstances and regards it as a phenomenon whose continuous presence, being implicit in the very nature of Birmingham, needs no further explanation. Against the unruly side of Birmingham's past must be weighed the pride which people took in the town's reputation for comparative orderliness, combined with freedom from superfluous authority. As more than one local commentator pointed out, this had been well borne out in the most conspicuous event in Birmingham's recent past: its part in the Warwickshire election of 1774, which was eminently an example of what could be achieved by orderly behaviour within the law. This is not to deny that the town's unanimity on that occasion was soon to be impaired by reactions to the American war, or that the hostility to Dissent which erupted in 1791 can in some respects be traced back to the same period. Nevertheless there had been no open signs of tension before 1785; and however much it may have conformed to type, the mob which hounded the Dissenters in 1791 was induced to behave the way it did for particular reasons of recent origin. If indeed there was any place in the West Midlands where the 'pattern of politics' alone might have been advanced automatically as a sufficient explanation for trouble between Church and Dissent it was Coventry, not Birmingham.

35 *Aris*, 26 December 1791.

36 *V.C.H. Warwicks.*, vii, 102.

37 *Aris*, 15 November 1790. A similar warning was issued on 21 March 1791, and in both cases attention was drawn to the several statutes, dating from the turn of the previous century, which enshrined the wearing of polished buttons in the law of the land.

38 Hutton, *History of Birmingham* (2nd edn), pp. 77–8.

39 In November 1792 it was corroborated by the Jacobins themselves, in the opening address of the Birmingham Society for Constitutional Information: ' . . . For it is a well known matter of fact that some free nations abroad, and free people at home, have refused some articles of Birmingham Manufacture on that very account, and have substituted Vigo Buttons, which may be made anywhere, and Shoestrings, to answer the same purpose, besides endeavouring to carry the trade from the town into other countries where the mind of man can enjoy true and real liberty.'

40 *Cf.* 'Shoestrings', by John Crane of Bromsgrove, *The Crumbs*, p. 18:

> 'Oh!' cry'd the Insteps, 'who could bear
> The weight that these two Buckles are?'

The angry Buckles roar'd it out,
'Why you before you had the gout!
For robbing poor men of employ
Your lot is in your strings to die.
We shall be worn, and still will sell
To all who wish poor artists well.'

41 *Swinney*, 5 January 1792. Tutania was one of the soft metal alloys used in the trade.

42 *Garbett–Lansdowne Letters*, III, Garbett to Lansdowne, 23 July 1791.

43 *Garbett–Lansdowne Letters*, III, Garbett to Lansdowne, 30 April 1793, 8 December 1792.

44 Stafford, William Salt Library, Fletcher-Boughey MSS, D 1788/P2B1/3.

45 Stafford, County Record Office, Leveson-Gower MSS, D 593 S/16/10/5, account of John Massey for election expenses at Newcastle under Lyme, 1790–93, invoice of James Smith, stationer, of Newcastle, for printing and distribution of songs and pamphlets, December 1792–January 1793.

46 *More Advice from Job Nott* (4th edn, 1795), B.R.L. 63933, p. 6.

47 *Job Nott's Humble Advice, with a Suitable Postscript* (5th edn, 1793), B.R.L. 63934, pp. 2–3. Exactly how effective this line of argument was is impossible to measure. It would be an exaggeration to suggest that Birmingham people felt themselves to be in the same degree of clientage to aristocratic society as that which existed among the luxury tradesmen of pre-radical Westminster (see N. Rogers, 'Aristocratic clientage, trade and independency: popular politics in pre-radical Westminster', *Past and Present*, 61 (November 1973), 70–106); but though the comparison is a long one, it is perhaps worth setting the ambiguous reactions of Birmingham alongside those of the Electorate of Mainz, in Germany. Here a somewhat similar dependence on conspicuous consumption and established social relationships was demonstrably linked, contrary to the suppositions both of contemporaries and of historians in search of a single democratic revolution, to a marked lack of popular enthusiasm for French freedom. For example, compare the frequently expressed attitude towards the toy trade which was taken up by Birmingham's anti-Jacobin propagandists with the complaint of Georg Forster, a prominent Mainzer radical, at 'a swarm of craftsmen, shopkeepers, artists, servants and dependants, who all see in the person of their master their ideal of what a man should be, and the model which they should all seek to copy. If idleness and pleasure stand at the head of the people as their standards, is it not inevitable that the morals of the working class must deteriorate in the long run?' (Quoted, T. C. W. Blanning, *Reform and Revolution in Mainz, 1743–1803*, Cambridge, 1974, p. 293.)

48 See above, p. 148.

49 Probably the premises of William and James Belcher, the Unitarian booksellers.

50 *The Life and Adventures of Job Nott, Bucklemaker, of Birmingham* (1793), B.R.L. 63937, *passim*. Though its purpose is no longer so urgent or explicit, and though the medium has changed, Job Nott's task is still being performed most conspicuously and influentially by the British Broadcasting Corporation's long-running serial 'The Archers: an everyday story of country folk'. Today the situation is addressed from the other end on, and the country is explained to the town rather than vice versa; but the programme still supplies the same underlying need to provide in popular terms an acceptable accommodation between different patterns of life. Appropriately 'The Archers' is produced in the B.B.C.'s Birmingham studios.

51 *Humble Advice*, p. 5.

52 *Life and Adventures*, p. 17.

53 *Life and Adventures*, pp. 2–3: 'I used to look at my vice, tools, and bench, with as much pleasure as mayhap Mr. Richards does at his Grand Toy Shop, where I once saw him reaching out of the window a pair of plate buckles, and put into a fine Lady's hands, who little thought that the poor dirty lad as was peeping in did most at making of 'em. I declare it had such an effect on me that I could have gladly have kissed her foot. And I directly thought to myself, this is the blessing of having rich people in the nation. They wear the fine things as us poor folks get our bread by making.'

54 *An Appeal to the Inhabitants of Birmingham, designed as an Answer to Job Nott Bucklemaker, by his Elder Brother, John Nott, Button Maker, and First Cousin to John Nott Button Burnisher* (Birmingham, 1792), B.R.L. 12381, pp. 4. 16–17. The appropriation of the Nott pseudonym by the Jacobins was as much in accord with reality as its use by

their loyalist opponents. The *Birmingham Gazette* of 20 February 1792 reported a wage dispute between the button makers and their masters which had provoked potentially riotous demonstrations. In fact the whole elaborate fiction, and especially the Jacobins' introduction of a disintegration of the original Nott family in 1791, points back to the specific context within which propaganda on both sides was conceived.

55 *A.O.P.*, John Newcomb of Pall Mall to Boulton, 24 December 1793: the Prince of Wales will try to persuade the Queen, princesses and other ladies to wear buckles for Christmas. The Prince has ordered buckles himself; so has Mrs Fitzherbert. Also William Smith to Boulton, 18 January 1794, re. publicity for Spitalfields silks, metal buttons and shoe buckles in press reports of celebrations of Queen Charlotte's birthday.

56 *An Appeal to Manufacturers on the Present State of Trade* (1795), B.R.L. 67417, pp. 5, 8–10. Boulton was in fact threatened with reprisals later in the year: *cf. A.O.P.*, Garbett to Boulton, 5 November 1795, warning him of rumours that a club in Deritend, 11,000 strong, was planning to level some parks, including Boulton's, because he had turned a poor family with smallpox out of doors.

57 *Cf.* 'Lines on Commerce' in *Poetical Sketches by James Morfitt, Esq., Barrister, with Additional Pieces, chiefly by Joseph Weston* (1794), B.R.L. 2469, p. 27:

> *Offspring of trade*, Oh Birmingham beware
> Of Luxury the syren! Shun her snare.
> Let other towns in empty splendour shine,
> The Glories of FRUGALITY be thine.
> This friend to trade, ye sons of commerce know,
> Guards it when high and raises it when low.

58 *V.C.H. Warwicks.*, VII, 284; E. P. Thompson, 'The moral economy of the English crowd', p. 107.

59 *A.O.P.*, Heneage Legge to Boulton, 16 July 1795.

60 *Garbett–Lansdowne Letters*, IV, copies of letters from Garbett to Heneage Legge, 22 July–1 August 1795; *A.O.P.*, Boulton to Legge, 27 July 1795.

61 Add. MSS 27813, ff. 73–5, Kilmister (named as writer on verso of f. 148) to L.C.S., 10 July 1795.

62 Add. MSS 27815, f. 19, Minutes of L.C.S. executive committee, 23 November 1795.

63 For Corn see *Miscellaneous Papers of Edward Corn of Birmingham* (1777–1832), B.R.L. 387323, and *Poems by Edward Corn . . . with notes on the Old and New Meetings . . . etc.* (1754–1826), B.R.L. 444238. Corn's connections with Binns and Jones are apparent from the lists and accounts in 'Seditious Papers found in Binn's Box' TS 11/959/3505, and from his letter to John Ashley of the L.C.S., 24 April 1796, Add. MSS 27815, ff. 47–8.

64 *Trial of John Binns* (Birmingham, 1797), B.R.L. 57689; TS 11/959/3505, 'Seditious Papers found Binns's Box': reports to L.C.S. from Binns and Jones, 14 March and 'Plain Statement' from L.C.S. of 'motives and conduct in sending deputies to visit the society in Birmingham', 21 March 1796; Langford, *Birm. Life*, II, 172.

65 Had the government acted promptly it would probably have had no difficulty in securing convictions; but possibly because it had misgivings about leaving two such important trials in local hands, possibly as a deliberate move to burden the L.C.S. with added expense, the Crown removed both cases to the central courts in July 1796 (Add. MSS 27815, ff. 105, 110). The delay gave the delegates time to prepare their defence. In the event they were tried separately; Jones was convicted on 9 April 1797, though no sentence was passed on him; Binns, who was tried at Warwick after all on 15 August 1797, was defended by Samuel Romilly and acquitted. *Cf.* Mary Thale, ed., *The Autobiography of Francis Place* (Cambridge, 1972), p. 150.

66 Add. MSS 27815, ff. 108–10, John Bates junior of Wolverhampton to L.C.S., 31 July 1796, on behalf of the three clubs, and draft reply to Coseley and Sedgley. Support also came from many other parts of the country, including Manchester, Norwich, Melbourne (Derbyshire), Exeter, Portsmouth and Coventry. In addition, Hereford sent help independently to another Birmingham victim, a jobbing smith called Bathurst, who was arrested with Binns and Jones but for whom the L.C.S. could not afford bail. Add. MSS 27815, *passim*; Langford, *Birm. Life*, II, 172.

67 Add. MSS 27815, f. 111, Gale-Jones to John Ashley, 2 August 1796. At this point Jones left Birmingham. Binns stayed on until September 1797.

68 Add. MSS 27815, f. 137, undated draft acknowledging the money, presumably to

Bullock and probably shortly after 12 August 1796, when the L.C.S. executive committee
minuted a report from Binns on his activities in Birmingham (f. 118).

69 *V.C.H. Warwicks.*, VII, 284.

70 Add. MSS 27815, ff. 173–4; lists and accounts, September 1797, in Binns's papers,
TS 11/959/3505.

71 Instruction No. 8 in L.C.S., 'Plain Statement of Motives and Conduct', 21 March
1796, in Binns's papers.

72 Add. MSS 27815, f. 111: 'Respecting the magazine, I may have been misinformed,
but it was from citizens Clarke and Kilmister that I heard the complaint—not indeed
from those who are *members* but from those who are *not* members of the society, who,
having seen the printed handbills wherein the magazine is declared to be 4½d desire to
have it at the same rate or refuse to purchase'. The price to the public was 6d.

73 Add. MSS 27815, ff. 148–50, 155, 170–1: Binns to L.C.S., n.d.: report of executive
committee, 3 March 1797; Binns to L.C.S., 19 August 1797.

74 *V.C.H. Warwicks.*, VII, 284; Langford, *Birm. Life*, II, 173–4.

CONCLUSION

It is time to take stock. The part played by Birmingham and the West Midlands in the history of late eighteenth century England was distinguished not by any one overriding characteristic but by a closely meshed combination of lesser traits. For this reason the region cannot advance any obvious single claim to significance in the affairs of the nation. The course of its social and economic development, though of prime importance both for its own life and ultimately for that of the country at large, was not set apart by any drastic discontinuity from the past, nor was the process of change marked yet by the polarities whose emergence in the north and north-west was already attracting the concerned attention of contemporaries. The same is true of the political reactions of the West Midlands. Here too there was no one dominant characteristic, comparable, for example, to the effects of urban penetration on the affairs of Middlesex, or to the interplay between the freeholders of Yorkshire and the ascendancy of the Marquess of Rockingham in that county, by which the region can be closely and visibly associated with the course of major events. The controversies of George III's early years left the Birmingham area largely untouched, though the remonstrance against the cider tax in 1762–63 did affect its south-western parts. During the Stamp Act crisis, which might have been expected to produce a more definite response in view of the heavy dependence of the West Midland iron industry on the American market, the region's reactions were directed through the urgent but discreet use of personal contact and influence rather than through open demonstration and formal testimony, and the publicity which they did receive was carefully screened lest it should jeopardise the success of other projects. The repercussions of 'Wilkes and liberty', though of major importance in the West Midlands' own political history, were filtered indirectly through a complex set of local circumstances, and made little overall difference to the actual course of a movement which at every stage continued to be centred in London and Middlesex. Similarly, the Warwickshire contest of 1774, for all its local and regional significance, did no more to affect the cast of national politics at the time than did any of the other piecemeal exceptions to the prevalent pattern. Even within the Birmingham area itself several more years passed before the confusions surrounding the election and the divisions over America which followed it had settled sufficiently to allow the result of the contest to be put to deliberate use. After 1780 the same absence of simple relationships to the questions of the day continued. During the years of the Yorkshire Association, the chief prototype of large-scale extra-parliamentary organisation in British politics, and the first to derive its main impetus from outside the capital, neither Birmingham nor any of its surrounding counties made any move to participate in the objectives of Christopher Wyvill and his colleagues, though the prospect of doing so was raised on more than one occasion. Even in response to the commercial policies of the younger Pitt, when the region came closest to concerted support for a wider movement, and when the part played by the industrial leaders of the West Midlands in the establishment of the General Chamber of Manufacturers did involve them in important questions of theoretical and practical politics, their reactions, though conducted on a larger and more elaborate scale, were still essentially those of 1766. Finally, the role of the Birmingham area in the revolutionary crisis of the 1790s was as ambiguous as its part in any preceding episode, despite the early prominence of its dissenting congregations, the significance, both symbolic and material, of the Priestley riots, the reconstruction of the local reform movement in their aftermath and the high hopes which this success raised among reformers elsewhere. Throughout the story from 1760 onwards there is no unmistakable series of landmarks of national proportion by which the history of Birmingham and the West Midlands can be associated with that of the country at large. Instead there is a steady accumulation of smaller reactions, whose relationship to each other and to the course of general events must be traced as much through the internal minutiae of local affairs as through their immediate repercussions on a more extensive scale.

Nevertheless the West Midlands deserve attention. The adage that, between them, Yorkshire and Middlesex made up half England may have been true at the time; but, if only unintentionally, Edmund Burke's warning that the opinion of the two most prominent of the country's new manufacturing areas should not be taken for that of the whole nation was more prophetic. The importance in the history of nineteenth century England of the differing patterns of social and political response manifested in the Birmingham area and in industrial Lancashire is well known.[1] The broad truth of the proposition that 'whoever says Industrial Revolution says cotton'[2] has meant, however, that in the general historiography of social change it is the second of those regions which has been accorded the greater prominence, just as the contemporary significance of Yorkshire and Middlesex has been reflected in the priorities of those who have studied the wider extension of politics during the later eighteenth century. On neither count have the origins and nature of the 'Birmingham' pattern of provincial response during the next hundred years qualified for similar examination. Yet though the course of social change in the West Midlands may not have been marked by any one predominant feature, and though the region cannot be positively associated with any of the major phases of contemporary politics, it nevertheless acquired, through the interaction of its own affairs with the larger issues of the day, its own distinctive sense of experience and identity. The formation of this, at a level intermediate between that of the local community and of the nation at large, would claim consideration, even if the seminal place of Birmingham and its surrounding counties in the subsequent course of English history were left out of account.

The study began by considering two conspicuous examples of the problem of accommodation which was created as Birmingham's internal affairs impinged on those of its surrounding communities. These were important because they provided the local component without which the town's reactions to larger events can be only partially understood. In the case of the General Hospital, one of Birmingham's earliest and most important independent initiatives, they were satisfactorily solved. Despite appearances to the contrary, the problems raised by the town's local government were more awkward. During the later 1780s these involved Birmingham in a difference with the Warwickshire authorities over the question of criminal administration which helped to frustrate efforts to provide the town with its own magistracy and an effective system of internal police. At the same time they provoked a furious quarrel over the rating of tenement property, whose religious and ideological overtones played an important part in the prelude to the Priestley riots. After the riots the local reinforcement of the county Bench appeared to provide an answer to the problem of control in Birmingham which was in keeping with past practice, but it left much to be desired as a full solution. This fact was reflected in popular reactions at the time, and it constituted a serious limitation on the extent to which Birmingham could continue to rely on its previous tradition of close integration with its surroundings. In this instance at least, difficulties were postponed, not resolved.

The most general object of continuous attention in the West Midlands as a whole was not, however, the particular problems which attended the growth of Birmingham but the major developments in physical communication that were taking place within the region. The promotion and building of the canals and, in a lesser and rather different way, of the turnpike roads, not only made the component parts of the West Midlands aware of their interdependence and brought them together in enterprises of major significance. They also made the region as a whole more conscious of its relationships with other parts of the country; by multiplying its direct connections with a wider world they increased the speed and sensitivity of its reactions to developments elsewhere, and by the same token they decreased its deference to London as the usual source of authentic information and example in public affairs. The result of this was to accentuate the West Midlands' conscious contribution to the tension which was beginning to develop between the assumed hegemony of the capital and the ambitions of what can henceforward be properly called the provinces. This showed itself in many forms, but it was most clearly articulated in the manufacturers' reactions to the commercial policies of the younger Pitt, which culminated in the formation of the General Chamber of Manufacturers in 1785. The first part of the study therefore ended by examining the distinctive part the West Midlands played in the paradoxical history of the chamber, and by emphasising in particular the importance for the widening of accepted political practice of the problems of representational theory, constitutional legality and tactical timing which the leading manufacturers encountered, not just in their efforts to establish their credentials at Westminster, but also in the mobilisation and maintenance of supporting opinion in their own localities.

After this opening survey of the local and regional issues through which Birmingham and the West Midlands were discovering where their common interests lay, both with regard to their own affairs and to those of other parts of the country, the study reached its main focus of attention in part two, which was devoted to the development of mental communications. Examination of the three main newspapers which served the region showed that each of them had already established for itself a distinct character and role in the positive formation of public attitudes, even though the leading techniques of 'opinion' journalism in the modern sense were as yet virtually unexplored. Following this, attention was turned to the wide range of opportunities for social meeting through which information could be exchanged and ideas could affect each other. Some of these, like the triennial festivals of oratorio which supported the General Hospital, turned it into an important and fashionable charity and came to symbolise in a unique way Birmingham's aspirations to future greatness, were recognised institutions whose continuous histories are easily accessible. Others, like the Birmingham Bean Club, which provided a long-established connection between the leaders of the town and the landowners of its surrounding counties, were less visible, but nevertheless played a crucial part in consolidating the new centre's place in the established structure of society and politics. Still others, among them most of the lesser groups which were formed within the Birmingham area's artisan population, were individually more ephemeral but nevertheless represented a continuous and increasingly important element in the life of the region. The progressive broadening of articulate popular consciousness which became apparent in Birmingham and the Black Country from the 1760s onwards was indeed the most significant aspect of the whole enquiry into 'the means of communication and the creation of opinion'. Those who promoted the oratorio festivals or, like Matthew Boulton, sponsored Birmingham's New Street theatre, did so because they hoped thereby to enhance the reputation of the town, to reinforce its social and political connections and, especially in the case of the stage, to satisfy the demand for entertainment in ways which would enable it to be used as a positive instrument of social and industrial policy. Alongside these formal promotions, however, there developed a vigorous if less seemly popular culture which played at least as much part in shaping the attitudes of ordinary people as did the supervised offerings of their betters.

The significance of this first became clear during the crowded years between 1768 and 1774, when groups like the Free Debating Society at the Red Lion in Digbeth, or 'poet' John Freeth's circle at the Leicester Arms took up with enthusiasm the cause of 'independent' opposition which had developed in several of the West Midlands' parliamentary constituencies, particularly in the city and county of Worcester. By so doing they not only contributed an important ingredient to the context of the Warwickshire contest of 1774 but also demonstrated the effectiveness with which Birmingham was now acting as a relay in the transference of popular reactions between different parts of the region. The enhanced awareness that showed itself in these interactions was not, however, confined to local politics. In their questions and resolutions, which combined a basic traditionalism with a self-assertive curiosity which was quite new, Birmingham's debating societies showed an almost universal range of interest. Since this could not have been sustained without extensive access to printed material of all kinds and without a contagious enthusiasm for reading and enquiry, the second part of the study ended by examining these two aspects of the situation. The investigation of the first embraced not only the development of libraries of all kinds in the Birmingham area, but also the nature and growth of printing and publishing in the town and the appearance for the first time in the later 1760s of local periodicals pursuing definite political and educational objectives. By itself, however, a demonstration of the accessibility of books, pamphlets and periodicals would have delineated only part of the growth of a wider reading public in the area. More important were the channels through which the interest in enquiry itself was communicated, not only to Birmingham's 'middle class' readership but also to an increasing section of the town's artisan population. Examination of these involved a consideration of the travelling lecturers and other showmen, both serious and comic, scientific and thaumaturgic, who visited the town and its surroundings, and of the numerous opportunities for practical education which were available throughout the West Midlands. Above all, it drew attention once again to the role of the overlapping groups which formed among the individuals who had a hand in all these activities. Together these groups constituted a recognisable element within the community, whose attitudes and influence can be traced not only through the membership of local Masonic lodges and other fraternities but also through the activities of more specific cliques, like the Birmingham Book Club, which provide a continuous link between the first beginnings of popular consciousness in the town in the mid-eighteenth century, the democratic agitation of the 1790s and the re-emergence of a distinctive Birmingham radicalism in the years before the passing of the Great Reform Act. The example of the Book Club raised questions about the place of such groups in the finely graded scale of status which governed social relationships among those employed in Birmingham's many trades, and therefore about the extent to which the characteristics of the better known societies were reproduced among the lesser clubs which were formed among the town's working people. Finally, the examination considered the whole nature of the popular articulacy which had developed in the Birmingham area during the second half of the century. By the 1790s the existence of this was a recognised fact; but though its importance as a new and major factor in the life of the region was attested both by its own authentic productions and by the artificial responses which it provoked, its social and political manifestations remained ambiguous. They were part radical, certainly, and they did contain some features which were suggestive of 'working class' solidarity. But they were also still part traditional, and, more conspicuously than either, they were individualist rather than collective, and therefore in the final analysis more compatible with the adaptation than with the rejection of the existing social order.

The oustanding event in the political experience of the Birmingham area during the thirty years which preceded the impact of the French revolution was the unexpected return of Sir Charles Holte in the contested Warwickshire election of 1774. This result, which demonstrated for the first time the influence that could be exerted in county politics by the voting power of its north-western parts, has usually been regarded as the first political achievement of a newly formed Birmingham manufacturing interest. In fact it upset the manufacturers' calculations, such as they were, for it was brought about in circumstances of considerable confusion by a movement of opposition which, though it found fully effective expression only in Warwickshire, had developed in many parts of the West Midlands during the years before the election. This movement, which was in effect a belated manifestation of the 'country' view of politics, expressed itself not in terms of commercial interest but in the traditional language of 'independence' and freeholders' rights, and it was reinforced by the indirect repercussions of the Wilkite movement. Since 1769 these had affected several local parliamentary constituencies; they had impinged markedly on the political consciousness of Birmingham people, and they were closely associated with the early agencies of popular articulacy in the area. The Warwickshire contest of 1774 thus took place against a background of considerable popular interest, which could claim with some truth to have been justified by the result. This situation was clearly capable of radical development. During the American war pamphlets and tracts favourable to the colonial cause were available in bulk and at low price from at least one of Birmingham's printers and booksellers. In 1775 bitter recriminations over the town's petitions for and against the measures of the North Ministry were specifically linked with the sides taken in the county a year earlier. In 1776 the *Birmingham and Stafford Chronicle* used discussion of Richard Price's *Observations on Civil Liberty* as a platform for a lengthy digression of its own on the nature of representation and the rights of petitioners. Though Birmingham responded well enough two years later to the call for subscriptions to augment the forces of the Crown, the proposals which were made for the town's contribution to the national effort met with considerable opposition before they were adopted.

The result of the 1774 election could also be turned to more conservative ends, however. Its radical component was still tentative: in its own sources it had looked to the past, and though some may have been eager to press forward on to new ground there were many more for whom the victory over 'Lordly power' was a vindication of existing liberties, not an argument for further change. This point of view was taken up by Birmingham's leaders; for though they were not its original creators, it was the merchants and manufacturers of the town who were the eventual beneficiaries of the position won in 1774. To begin with, they were handicapped by mutual divisions over the American question, but by the mid-1780s they had used the influence demonstrated by Holte's success to gain for their interests a very satisfactory integration into the existing structure of politics. In the process of achieving this the real element of popular participation, which had been present in 1774, and which might have proved troublesome if subsequent elections had been allowed to reach the hustings, was replaced by a surrogate. The return of Sir Charles Holte as Member for Warwickshire was held up to posterity as an example of what Birmingham people could do, if they chose to exert themselves, by lawful use of their existing liberties. The victory was sufficient in itself; the stewardship of its fruits was demonstrably in good hands, and since it was defensible if need be by the same means by which it had first been won there was no justification for more radical action. The tradition of 1774 was thus kept alive, but in a modified and acceptable form. Like the development of popular articulacy, with which it was in any case closely associated during its first formative phase, the political experience of the Birmingham area thus lent itself as easily to the justification, or at most the adaptation, of the existing order, as it did to the demand for drastic change.

During the last ten years of the century Birmingham and the West Midlands occupied an important place in the strategic plans of the English democratic movement. But though the emissaries who came south from Sheffield and Manchester in 1792 had considerable success in repairing the damage inflicted on Birmingham's own reformers by the Priestley riots, they were unable at any stage to win the commanding position which they had hoped to achieve in the area. The forces of reform and reaction remained evenly balanced in Birmingham, so that each was able to deny mastery to the other. Even more telling than this was the fact that, for all their rhetoric, the town's Jacobins themselves remained obsessed with the memory of 1791. The temptation to self-dramatisation which this placed before them distracted them from grasping the full import of the democratic message as a basis for future belief and action rather than a recompense for past wrongs, and their stance was in reality never as uncompromising as that of their colleagues elsewhere. Behind its immediate manifestations, however, there were deeper reasons for the ambiguity of the Birmingham area's response to the events of the 1790s. In the final part of the study, these were sought in the whole way in which the basic transition from rural to urban and industrial society was perceived and explained in the West Midlands. Though they made sense in their own terms, the initial remedies proposed in the 1760s for the ills of society were of limited utility because they did not yet fully comprehend the nature of the changes that were taking place within it, and in particular because they contained no positive recognition of the growing towns. Despite this deficiency, however, they established the basic categories in which the problems of the latter continued to be discussed. It did become possible for practical commentators to suggest more constructive approaches as basic concepts of the nature and purpose of society in general were re-examined in the light of the new political economy; but since the premises of the latter meant that it did not propose any explicit social model of its own, the task of explaining and legitimising the changes in social relationships entailed in the growth of the manufacturing towns had still to be carried out as well as possible by the adaptation of traditional patterns and values to urban and industrial circumstances. In Birmingham and the West Midlands it proved possible to do this sufficiently effectively to avert or at least to mitigate the most divisive aspects of the revolutionary crisis.

To say this is not to claim that the adaptation was in any systematic sense complete, or that the 'usable past' on which its practical acceptability rested had any objective validity. However convincing it may have seemed during the prosperity and apparent harmony of the 1780s, the conservative version of the region's recent history was beginning to look decidedly threadbare by the time ten more years had passed. In 1797, indeed, it seemed that Birmingham, its impulse to reform muzzled by loyalist bigotry, remained poised between the bitterness of the unemployed chapemaker, who could only 'suffer and be dumb, and hope for happiness in worlds to come', and the cant of a transformed Job Nott, who, having set aside his earlier temporal complacency, was now exhorting his readers to

> Be comforted, nor think these plagues are sent
> For your destruction, but for chastisement.
> Heav'n oft in mercy punisheth, that sin
> May feel its own demerits from within,
> And urge not utter ruin. Turn to God,
> And draw a blessing from his Iron Rod.[3]

Yet a third alternative did exist, at once rooted in the past and more indicative of the future development of Birmingham radicalism than the final phase in the history of the local Jacobins. This was most clearly expressed in the traditions of the Birmingham Book Club and in the declaration of James Lucock's

Birmingham Brotherly Society of 1796, whose undertaking to teach as 'subjects
for improvement... whatever may be generally useful to a manufacturer, or
as furnishing principles for active benevolence and integrity' bespeaks the step
from the tocsin of revolution to the gospel of self-help which many of the town's
reformers had already taken:

> Such being the leading motives of our association, we pledge ourselves to each
> other to endeavour to carry them into effect. We will endeavour to make our-
> selves as useful as we can and will be careful that our example for steadiness
> and general propriety be such as will be proper for imitation to the best of our
> judgement. We engage to behave with civility and respect to each other, to con-
> sider each other as desirable companions and as brothers, to go hand in hand in
> our improvements and amusements, and to study each other's welfare and happi-
> ness. We will avoid all levity or trifling unmanly behaviour, all finery and foppish-
> ness in our dress, all bad company and gaming. We will consider industry in our
> callings as an indispensable duty and obedience to parents or masters as not less
> necessary and binding. We will love and cultivate honesty and truth, and in every
> respect strive to gain the confidence of our friends and the esteem of all who
> know us.[4]

Birmingham and its surrounding area achieved the adaptation of traditional
values to urban and industrial life, if not with theoretical perfection, then at
least with appreciable practical success. 'The social and political state of that
town,' Richard Cobden was later to write, 'is far more healthy than that of
Manchester. There is a freer intercourse between all classes than in the Lancashire town, where a great and impassable gulf separates the workman and the
employer.'[5] Job Nott, it seems, had been substantially vindicated, and the fact
is important. 'Birmingham... should have been a natural for Artisan jacobinism, with its myriad small workshops and "every man... stinking of train-oil
and emery"';[6] yet 'it was, comparatively, silent'. As has been seen, this cannot
be explained by the supposed 'decapitation' of the local movement by the
Priestley riots. If Birmingham people showed less conspicuous interest in the
'Artisan' cause during the 1790s than historians might expect from the nature
of the town, it was because the local 'pre-industrial' sense of community, which
worked in favour of Jacobinism in other places, conspicuously in Sheffield and
Norwich, worked against the cause in the West Midlands. This sense of regional
community was deliberately fostered by Birmingham's anti-Jacobin pamphleteers in order to avert, or at least to conceal for a time, 'the *polarization* of
English political society, which left artisans isolated'. At first sight, it might
seem surprising that it was possible to do this: that what was involved was
entirely a matter of illusion, whose maintenance for any length of time was
surely incompatible with the level of education and political sophistication
which the town's artisans had attained by the end of the century. To have
attained some degree of education and political awareness, however, no more
entailed the necessary espousal of an unalloyed Painite radicalism by a late
eighteenth century tradesman than it requires an analogous reaction by his
counterpart today; and while it may be legitimate to assume in other places
that the politically conscious artisan of the 1790s was *ipso facto* immune from
the blandishments of tradition and subordination, this was not the case in the
Birmingham area. Here, both as regards the agencies through which it was
formed and as regards the immediate political experience which it assimilated,

the development of popular articulacy during the second half of the eighteenth century took place in a context which tempered its radical potential with a highly adaptable admixture of practical conservatism. Birmingham's anti-Jacobin pamphleteers themselves bore witness to this fact by fitting their message very carefully to the particular susceptibilities which their intended readership had acquired during the previous thirty years. Mawkish, stuffed with humbug, scurrilous, in places downright obscene the arguments of Job Nott and his fellows may have been. They were also well directed, and they contained enough grains of truth to be plausible. It is in the achievements of Birmingham and the West Midlands during the last four decades of the eighteenth century, in the grafting of new developments on to older patterns of life, and perhaps above all in the events which surrounded the Warwickshire election of 1774, that the roots are to be found of that tradition of popular but orderly participation, embracing all levels of the community, which remained the characteristic response of one of the great provincial cities which exerted such a profound influence on the development of British society and politics in the nineteenth century.

NOTES

1 See, for example, Asa Briggs, *The Age of Improvement* (London, 1959), pp. 208–9.
2 E. J. Hobsbawm, *Industry and Empire: an Economic History of Britain since 1750* (London, 1968), p. 40.
3 *More Advice from Job Nott* (1795), B.R.L. 63933, p. 8; *Thoughts on the Taxing of Slippers Continued: An Address to the Bucklemakers at Large* (1795), B.R.L. 63696, p. 4.
4 Rules and declaration of the Birmingham Brotherly Society, in minute books of the Birmingham Unitarian Brotherly Benefit Society, I, 3–5, 7–8.
5 John Morley, *Life of Cobden* (1910), p. 663, cited by *V.C.H. Warwicks.*, VII, 223.
6 This and subsequent quotations are from G. A. Williams, *Artisans and Sans-culottes*, pp. 63–4.

APPENDICES

I THE CIRCULATING AREAS OF THE WEST MIDLANDS' NEWSPAPERS

This brief account is based on the agencies listed by the papers themselves, supplemented by M. J. Wise, 'Birmingham and its trade relations in the early eighteenth century', *U.B.H.J.*, II (1949–50), No. 1, 53–79; Hill, *Bookmakers*; G. A. Cranfield, *Development of the Provincial Newspaper*, and the same author's *Handlist of English Provincial Newspapers and Periodicals, 1700–60*.

By 1743, two years after its first appearance, *Aris* was listing agencies in Shrewsbury, Bridgnorth, Worcester, Leominster, Warwick and Wolverhampton. Despite its agency in Worcester itself, the paper's circulation was limited in south Worcestershire, partly by the physical barrier of the Clent hills and partly because here it overlapped with the territory of the much older *Worcester Journal*. Nevertheless the situation of these early outlets, which reflect the importance of the river Severn in the structure of communications in the West Midlands at the time, delineated the basis of the *Birmingham Gazette*'s future sphere of influence. By 1760 the first of an eventual five agencies had been established in London; the paper's development towards the Severn had been consolidated, as had its circulation in the Black Country; an important extension had been made into northern Staffordshire, and a further addition, based on Stratford on Avon, had been made in the northern Cotswolds and the Vale of Evesham, which had previously been served intermittently by a paper published in Stratford itself. During the next thirty years the same progress continued. More agencies were added in London, and Aris's outlets in his own hinterland of Warwickshire, Staffordshire and north Worcestershire were substantially increased. After the mid-1770s, however, the most significant development was the establishment of agencies in other important provincial centres. Leicester, Burton on Trent, Derby, Sheffield and Chester had all been added to the list by 1788, and by 1790, when it was being sent post-free to any part of the kingdom, the principal Birmingham paper could genuinely claim to be of more than regional significance.

While the *Birmingham Gazette* looked westward towards the Severn, its contemporary, the *Coventry Mercury*, set its sights initially in the opposite direction, and had greater difficulty in establishing an extended circulation. For a short time it appeared as *Jopson's Coventry and Northampton Mercury, or Weekly Country Journal*, but this extension was not sustained, probably because it entailed a sally into the territory of *Dicey's Northampton Mercury*, one of the outstanding successes of provincial journalism during the first half of the century, and one whose Whiggish politics were very different from Jopson's own. For a while after 1743 Warwick was substituted for Northampton on Jopson's masthead, but by 1758 this too had been dropped, and during the 1760s the paper seems to have remained local in its circulation. By 1776, however, the *Coventry Mercury* was claiming a range which overlapped to some extent with that of the *Birmingham Gazette*, but which was once more principally directed eastwards through Leicestershire and Rutland to the southern parts of Lincolnshire, and south-eastwards into north Oxfordshire and Northamptonshire. This was confirmed by the specific agents the paper listed during the 1780s, and from 1787 onwards its more westerly circulation may also have received some assistance from the proprietorship of N. Rollason, a member of the family which was now running the successful *Birmingham Gazette*.

The absence of surviving copies, and the fact that it did not list its agents in detail with any regularity until the 1790s, makes conclusions about the range of *Swinney* more difficult to reach. Swinney's own claims were remarkable, however. On 25 July 1776, for example, he not only listed nine counties in his regular delivery network but also mentioned 'parts of Wales', stated that his paper was filed by coffee houses in practically every centre of any size from Edinburgh southwards and claimed a regular news and advertisement service in Ireland as well. This, however, was probably for the most part public relations designed to soften the fact that he had just raised the price of his paper, and a more realistic impression is probably given by the outlets which he had used to distribute a cheap abridgment of Richard Price's *Observations on Civil Liberty* two months earlier. These covered much the same area as the agencies of the *Birmingham Gazette*. Nevertheless Swinney was an influential and adventurous journalist. To a greater degree than his immediate competitor he collaborated with partners in other parts of the region, most permanently with S. Boden of Stafford and most significantly with J. W. Piercy of Coventry between 1778 and 1781. In the 1790s, when his paper was brought to the attention of the Home Office as a potential acquisition for propaganda purposes, the sixty agencies which he was then listing suggest an impressive circulation range, from as far north as Manchester to as far south as Monmouth and Swansea.

II BIRMINGHAM AND THE WORCESTERSHIRE PETITION IN REDRESS OF GRIEVANCES, 1769

Sources

Worcestershire petition in redress of grievances: Public Record Office, Home Office Papers, H.O. 55/2/4.

Birmingham section of *Sketchley's Birmingham, Walsall and Wolverhampton Directory* (Birmingham, 1767).

Notebook, titled 'Book Society at Freeth's, Bell Street, Birmingham', containing membership lists for the Birmingham Book Club, in Birmingham Book Club records, District Bank, Bennett's Hill, Birmingham 1. The earliest list, that for 1775, was used.

Names in notices regarding the Birmingham conciliatory petition of 1775 in *Aris*, 23 January, 20 February 1775.

Matthew Boulton's list of 'names to petition of the inhabitants of the town and neighbourhood of Birmingham to North America', 1775, in *A.O.P.*, America box.

Old Meeting House, Register of Resolutions of the General Assembly of Subscribers, 1771–91, B.R.L. 641586, signatures to letter of invitation to the Rev. Mr Walker, 25 December 1771.

The names on the petition were listed and numbered in sequence. At the same time the positioning of the names on the petition's different skins was also recorded. The list was then rearranged alphabetically to facilitate comparison with the other sources listed above. Identifications were classified as probable or possible according to the degree of certainty involved. For example, identifications could obviously be treated with more confidence in the case of names like Kimberly Moore or James Dolphin than they could in the case of Jones, Smith or Brown. However, as a pattern of distribution became clearer the more common names could be treated with more certainty when they appeared in close juxtaposition to groups of more probable identifications. Thus, when a close concentration of probables on the same skin suggested that that particular duplicate of the petition had circulated specifically in Birmingham, other names in the same position on the roll could be regarded more positively. The petition had five skins in total, the heading plus four duplicates, and the basic comparison with *Sketchley's Birmingham Directory* produced 153 identifications, 102 of them possible and fifty-one probable. These were distributed as follows:

Skin 1. Not many at all, apart from a small and fairly close group of three (Samuel Skey, John Rickards and John Skey) at 24, 38 and 41, and a probable (Thomas Gem) at 313.

Skin 2. An even distribution of possibles, which must be treated with caution, between 330 and 562, and one probable, John Oseland, at 382. Then a small but close bunch of possibles, including one probable, Thomas Hanson, between 670 and 675.

Skin 3. An even distribution of possibles between 690 and 822, followed on the second half of the skin, between *c.* 820 and 920, by a strong concentration of probables, often in direct sequence.

Skin 4. A wide scattering of possibles and some probables throughout, with one fairly substantial group between 982 and 997.

Skin 5. Again a scattering of possibles and one probable, Thomas Rock, at 1194; then, at the end, four probables between 1399 and 1426.

This suggests that skin 3 circulated for some time in Birmingham and its immediate neighbourhood, and that skin 4 probably also did so for a while. The probables whose names appeared outside the main groupings were most of them men who might be expected to do a fair amount of travelling in the course of their work. Of those mentioned above, for example, John Rickards and Thomas Gem were attornies, John Oseland was a merchant, Thomas Hanson was a button maker and Thomas Rock an ironmonger. In addition to these, Philip Pardoe at 1399 was listed by Sketchley as the Worcester carrier, Thomas Highway at 1406 was another attorney and Francis Highway at 1426 was a tanner. Of the trades listed by Sketchley, the following were represented: seventeen button makers, sixteen miscellaneous, fourteen innkeepers and publicans, eight shoemakers, seven buckle makers, six attorneys, six merchants, five tailors, five bakers, five ironmongers, four black, white and jobbing smiths, four cutters, four platers, three gun and pistol makers, three peruke makers, two each of apothecaries and surgeons, butchers, brass and iron candlestick makers, clock makers and founders, comb makers, grocers, jack makers, linen and woollen drapers, maltsters, thread makers, watch chain makers, one each of brass founders, brushmakers, buckle cutters, carpenters, chape makers, cock founders, curriers, factors and chapmen, file cutters, fork forgers and filers, hinge makers, japanners, jewellers, lapidaries, locksmiths, 'professors of the polite arts', sadlers, staymakers, steel snuffer makers, steel spur makers, sword blade makers, toymakers, upholsterers, wire drawers.

Of the houses kept by the innkeepers and publicans, thirteen were named: the Red Lion, Thomas Street; the Coach and Horses, Chapel Street; the Blue Ball, Snow Hill; the Hog in Armour, Lichfield Street; the Cutler's Arms, John Street; the Tyger, Snow Hill; the Lamp, Brickhill Lane; the Coach and Horses, Edgbaston Street; the Pitt's Head, Snow Hill; the Mogul's Head, Dale End; the Key, Edgbaston Street; the Lamp, New Hinckleys; the Dog, Spiceal Street.

The other comparisons produced the following results:

Birmingham Book Club membership. A possible total of eight out of twenty-four members as of 1775: William Price, A. Walker, W. Wright, J. Benton, J. Bedford, J. Bedford, S. Bedford, J. Wright.

Organisers of the Conciliatory Petition, 1775. Four out of eighteen: W. Russell, Joseph Wilkinson, Joseph Smith and John Richards.

Boulton's 'names to petition', 1775. Possibly thirteen out of eighty-seven: Luke Bell, Samuel Ford, Thomas Gem, John Goodall, Thomas Rock, John Meredith, Edward Palmer, Thomas Price, Thomas Smith, John Taylor, William Taylor, John Tovey, William Smith.

Subscribers to the Old Meeting, 1771. Possibly fourteen out of 107, not counting women: Thomas Lee, John Webb, Benjamin Wright, J. Brown, Edward Fereday, John Allen, William Baylis, John Lane, Richard Smith, Thomas Powell, Thomas Russell, John Rickards, — Walford, W. Hunt.

The results of these subsidiary comparisons make it clear that while there is good evidence for Birmingham's general involvement in political discussion and activity during the late 1760s and early 1770s, and while the high proportion of involvement on the part of the Birmingham Book Club stands out, there is no real basis yet for attributing consistent and continuous patterns of political behaviour to particular groups. On the basis of the Worcestershire petition of 1769, for example, the political involvement of the Old Meeting subscribers as a body was slight; and the fact that names which can be linked to the Worcestershire petition in 1769 can also be associated with both sides of the American question in 1775 bears out the considerable degree of confusion and uncertainty which was demonstrated by the circumstances of the Warwickshire election in 1774.

III BIRMINGHAM AND THE WARWICKSHIRE ELECTION OF 1774

The Poll of the Freeholders of Warwickshire, 1774 (Coventry, 1775) in Coventry City Libraries, Coventry and North Warwickshire Collection.

W. K. R. Bedford, *Notes from the Minute Book of the Birmingham Bean Club, 1754–1836,* B.R.L. 131399.

Birmingham Book Club, list of members, 1775.

Old Meeting Register, invitation to the Rev. Mr Walker, 25 December 1771.

Matthew Boulton's list of 'names to petition', 1775.

Visitation Return, Diocese of Coventry and Lichfield, 1772, Lichfield Joint Record Office, B/V/5.

Mary Ransome, ed., *The State of the Bishopric of Worcester, 1782–1808* (Worcestershire Historical Society Publications, new series, 6, 1968).

Voting of Bean Club membership
1 *Club attendance and elections*
to end of 1774

Total attendance and elections, sixty-three; total attributable vote in 1774, eighteen, possibly twenty-four. Of these, for Holte and Skipwith, nine, possibly thirteen; for Skipwith and Mordaunt, nine; for Holte only, possibly two; for Mordaunt only, nil. Place of freehold is given in brackets where it differs from that of residence.

Holte and Skipwith:

> Samuel Aris, Birmingham
> Egerton Bagot, Aston
> ?John Ball, Birmingham
> Henry Carver, Birmingham
> ?William Freer, Atherstone
> John Ingram, Little Woolford
> John Ludford, Ansley
> Rowland Okeover, Manceter (Weddington)
> ?Charles Stuart, Birmingham
> Miller Sadler, Over Whitacre
> Joseph Scott, Sheldon (Sutton Coldfield)
> ?William Wright, Birmingham
> Christopher Wren, Wroxall

Skipwith and Mordaunt:

> Thomas Faulconbridge, Birmingham
> John Fothergill, Moreton Bagot (Handsworth)
> Hon. Charles Finch, Polesworth
> George Holloway, Henley in Arden (Birmingham)
> John Meredith, Birmingham
> Thomas Orton, Barnacle (Bulkington)
> Edward Palmer, Solihull (Birmingham)
> William Tovey, Kenilworth
> Matthew Wise, Leamington Priors

Holte:

> ?Thomas Cooper, Birmingham
> ?James Cooke, Birmingham

Voting of Bean Club membership
II   *Club attendance and elections*
1775–82

Total attendance and elections, seventy-one; total attributable vote in 1774, eighteen, possibly twenty-three. Of these, for Holte and Skipwith, fourteen, possibly eighteen; for Skipwith and Mordaunt, four; for Holte only, possibly one; for Mordaunt only, nil. Brackets preceding name give first year of appearance in minutes.

Holte and Skipwith:

> (1775) Richard Astley, Kingsbury
> (1778) Charles Bowyer Adderley, Lea Marston
> ?(1778) John/Stephen/Charles Bedford, Birmingham (Aston)
> ?   John Ball, Birmingham
> (1775) William John Banner, Birmingham (Tanworth)
> (1775) William Dilke, Maxstoke
> ?(1780) William Dickenson, Birmingham (Tamworth)
> ?(1780) John Evans, Birmingham
> (1775) Richard Geast, Shustock
> (1777) Joseph Green, Birmingham
> (1779) John Holyoake, M.D., Warwick

(1779) John Ludford, Ansley
(1775) James Male, Birmingham
(1775) Thomas Rock, Birmingham
(1775) John Smith, M.D., Winchester (Corley)
(1777) Rev. Dr Benjamin Spencer, Aston
(1781) Sir Robert Lawley, Sutton Coldfield
(1782) Francis Parrott, Birmingham (Bedworth)

Skipwith and Mordaunt:

(1775) Joseph Carles, Handsworth (Birmingham)
Thomas Orton, Bulkington (Barnacle)
Edward Palmer, Birmingham (Solihull)
(1779) Rev. George Smith, Handsworth (Whitchurch)

Holte:

?(1780) Thomas Smallwood, Birmingham

The difference between the more or less even division of votes in the attendance up to the end of 1774 and the heavy preponderance for Holte and Skipwith among those who were active in the club during the following period is most marked, as is also the fact that nearly all the Holte and Skipwith votes in the second list seem to have been new to the club. At least, they did not appear in the minutes before 1775, and the overlap between the two lists is surprisingly small. The influx of Holte and Skipwith votes in 1775 was particularly large.

The Birmingham Book Club

A possible total of ten votes can be attributed out of a membership of twenty-four, all of them for Holte and Skipwith: W. Wright, Joseph Guest, John Benton, John Bedford, James Bedford, Stephen Bedford, Jonathan Francis, John Lane, William Piddock, James Wright. All lived and held their freeholds in either Birmingham or Aston except Jonathan Francis, who held his at his home in Hartshill.

Subscribers to the Old Meeting

A possible twenty-seven votes out of a total of 107 named subscribers, twenty-one for Holte and Skipwith, four for Holte alone, one for Skipwith and Mordaunt and one for Mordaunt alone:

For Holte and Skipwith:

Benjamin Richards, Samuel Harvey, Joseph Webster, Joseph May, William Corden, James Jackson, Thomas Parkes, John Allen, Daniel Gill, Ambrose Foxall, William Baylis, John Lane, Thomas Parkes, Samuel Harvey junior, John Walford, John Simcox, Benjamin Giles, George Humphreys, Henry Venour, Michael Lakin, William Parkes.

For Holte only:

Robert French, John Gill, Thomas Russell, Thomas Cotterell.

For Skipwith and Mordaunt:

John Rickards.

For Mordaunt only:

William Bache.

All lived and held their freeholds in Birmingham or Aston, except William Baylis, who held his freehold in Aston but lived in Handsworth; Thomas Russell, a freeholder in Birmingham but resident in Wednesbury; George Humphreys, who held his freehold in Tanworth, though he lived in Birmingham; Thomas Cotterell, who lived and held freehold in Solihull, and William Parkes, who held freehold in Birmingham but lived at Sutton Coldfield.

Boulton's 'names to petition', 1775

Twenty-three attributable votes out of a total of eighty-seven on the list, twelve for Holte and Skipwith, three for Holte only, seven for Skipwith and Mordaunt and one for Mordaunt only:

For Holte and Skipwith:

George Calley, freehold and lived in Birmingham
William Capper, freehold at Kingsbury, lived in Birmingham
William Dickenson, freehold at Tamworth, lived in Birmingham
Joseph Green, freehold and lived in Birmingham
James Male, freehold and lived in Birmingham
Thomas Rock, freehold and lived in Birmingham
William Noble, freehold and lived in Birmingham
John Simcox, freehold and lived in Aston
Thomas Smith, freehold and lived in Birmingham
William Smith, freehold and lived in Birmingham
John Taylor, freehold at Edgbaston, lived in Birmingham
William Vale, freehold at Stratford on Avon, lived in Birmingham

For Holte only:

Isaac Anderton, freehold and lived in Birmingham
James Cooke, freehold and lived in Birmingham
Edward Hunt, freehold and lived in Birmingham

For Skipwith and Mordaunt:

Joseph Carles, freehold at Birmingham, lived in Handsworth
Thomas Faulconbridge, freehold and lived in Birmingham
John Fothergill, freehold at Moreton Bagot, lived in Handsworth
William Holden, freehold and lived in Birmingham
John Meredith, freehold and lived in Birmingham
Thomas Orton, freehold at Barnacle, lived in Bulkington
Edward Palmer, freehold at Solihull, lived in Birmingham

For Mordaunt only:

Luke Bell, freehold and lived in Birmingham

The course of the poll at Warwick,
20–31 October 1774

(*a*) Each day's poll and (*b*) cumulative totals. There was no polling on 23 and 30 October.

	Holte		Skipwith		Mordaunt	
	(*a*)	(*b*)	(*a*)	(*b*)	(*a*)	(*b*)
20 October	164	164	370	370	270	270
21 October	339	503	815	1,185	580	787
22 October	427	930	764	1,949	466	1,253
24 October	257	1,187	387	2,336	242	1,495
25 October	200	1,387	206	2,542	72	1,567
26 October	168	1,555	145	2,687	46	1,613
27 October	107	1,662	108	2,795	62	1,675
28 October	84	1,746	79	2,874	58	1,733
29 October	72	1,818	57	2,931	28	1,761
31 October	27	1,845	23	2,954	26	1,787

As the sitting candidate, and supported by both sides, Skipwith polled well throughout. Mordaunt polled strongly on the first four days, but his bolt was then shot. His daily total fell from 242 on 24 October to seventy-two on the 25th, and dwindled still further on the remaining five days. On a daily basis, Holte never polled so strongly as the other two candidates, but his support was more sustained and evenly spread, particularly towards the end. The crucial period was 24–28 October, when Holte gradually over-hauled Mordaunt.

Votes for each candidate in each hundred

	Holte	Skipwith	Mordaunt
Barlichway	189	410	333
Hemlingford	1,175	1,099	315
Kington	229	601	487
Knightlow	252	844	653

Voting of the main places in the Birmingham area

	Holte	Skipwith	Mordaunt
Henley in Arden (Barlichway hundred)	25	48	30
Warwick (Kington hundred)	43	151	122
Kenilworth (Knightlow hundred)	13	66	56
Aston (Hemlingford hundred)	134	99	8
Atherstone (Hemlingford hundred)	27	25	10
Birmingham (Hemlingford hundred)	366	267	39
Coleshill (Hemlingford hundred)	17	32	18
Nuneaton (Hemlingford hundred)	63	85	31
Solihull (Hemlingford hundred)	60	60	16
Sutton Coldfield (Hemlingford hundred)	107	80	3
Tamworth (Hemlingford hundred)	106	90	4

In the Coventry and Lichfield Visitation return of 1772 Kenilworth was described as containing one decayed meeting of Presbyterians; the parish of Manceter, which included Atherstone, Hartshill, Oldbury and Ridge Lane, reported a strong scattering of Presbyterians and Quakers, mainly at Atherstone, where there were both Presbyterian and Quaker meetings, and at Hartshill, where there was a second Quaker meeting; Nuneaton reported one family of Quakers and some of Presbyterians, who attended meetings at Chilvers Coton and Bedworth; Sutton Coldfield, a large parish which included several dispersed farms and hamlets, reported one family of Quakers and a poorly attended meeting at Wigginshill, and also an Independent meeting in Sutton Coldfield itself which was shared with a growing Methodist congregation; Tamworth, another large parish, reported two families of Quakers and a small meeting, and thirty families of Presbyterians and a meeting.

Places of some size outside Hemlingford
returning a majority for Holte
and Skipwith

Barlichway Hundred:

	Holte	Skipwith	Mordaunt
Beaudesert	8	10	5
Bidford (patron of living, Sir Francis Skipwith)	19	27	8
Lapworth	19	17	6
Packwood	5	4	0
Rowington	8	10	7
Wooton Wawen	9	10	5
Ullenhall	10	5	1

Also sizable minorities for Holte at:

	Holte	Skipwith	Mordaunt
Henley in Arden	25	48	30
Stratford on Avon	35	83	64
Studley	11	25	17

Kington Hundred:

	Holte	Skipwith	Mordaunt
Ascott	5	7	2
Bourton on the Heath	5	4	0
Cherrington	13	19	8
Shuckburgh Lower	5	6	1
Stourton	17	18	5
Stretton on Fosse	11	14	7
Tanworth (patron of living, Lord Archer; several of the freeholders resident in Birmingham area)	54	54	8
Whichford	14	15	0
Willington	5	5	0
Woolford Little	5	6	1

Also a sizable minority for Holte at:

	Holte	Skipwith	Mordaunt
Warwick	43	151	122

Knightlow Hundred:

Clifton	6	6	1
Flecknow	16	12	2
Grandborough	9	11	5
Napton on the Hill (described, 1772, as a large open-field parish, four families of 'Anabaptists' and a meeting)	52	69	31
Willoughby	8	10	4
Arley	9	8	2
Long Itchington	5	8	4
Sawbridge	6	9	4

*Places inside Hemlingford Hundred returning
a majority for Skipwith and Mordaunt*

	Holte	Skipwith	Mordaunt
Berkswell (described, 1772, as a large parish—some Dissenters, but number not great and not increasing)	10	35	29
Bickenhill	6	15	13
Chilvers Coton (patron of living, Sir Roger Newdigate)	9	17	12
Coleshill	17	32	18
Hampton in Arden and Kinwalsey	5	11	8
Meriden (in 1772 reported one small family of Quakers only)	4	24	22
Polesworth	9	10	12
And at Nether Whitacre an exact balance	11	10	11

BIBLIOGRAPHY

MANUSCRIPT SOURCES

British Museum:

Papers of the Association for the Preservation of Liberty and Property against Levellers and Republicans: Additional Manuscripts 16919–16931.
Place manuscripts, papers of the London Corresponding Society: Additional Manuscripts 27811–17.

Public Record Office:

Chatham Papers: Secret Service Accounts, P.R.O. 30/8/229.
State Papers Domestic, George III: S. P. 37.
Home Office Papers, Domestic and General Correspondence, George III: H.O. 42.
Home Office Papers, Entry Books, 1782–1898: H.O. 43.
Home Office Papers, Addresses (Miscellaneous): H.O. 55.
Treasury Solicitor's Papers: T.S. 11:

   T.S. 11/578/1893, *Rex* v. *Belcher.*
   T.S. 11/932/3304, Papers on the Priestley riots.
   T.S. 11/951/3495–966/3510B, Papers of the London Corresponding Society and the Society for Constitutional Information.
   T.S. 11/961, 962, 1133, Minute books of the Society for Constitutional Information.

Barlaston: Wedgwood MSS.
Birmingham, Central Reference Library:

Letters, etc, chiefly from Samuel Garbett to the Earl of Shelburne, later Marquess of Lansdowne, 1766–1802: photostat copies of original MSS in William L. Clements Library, Ann Arbor, Mich.
Hutton-Beale MSS.
Lucock, James, 'Narrative of the Proceedings Relative to the Erection of the Old Meeting Sunday Schools, Birmingham, and of Various Occurrences therewith connected.'
Minute books of the Birmingham Unitarian Brotherly Benefit Society, vol. I.
Old Meeting House, Register of resolutions of the General Assembly of Subscribers, 1771–91.
Rules of the Insurance Society belonging to Soho Manufactory, Boulton & Watt MSS, Misc. W/1.
Brief for the Defendant: *Rex* v. *William Belcher of Birmingham, bookseller,* for publishing seditious works, Warwick summer assizes, 1792.
Miscellaneous papers of Edward Corn, Warden of the New Meeting, with notes on the New Meeting (1777–1832).
The commonplace books of Sarah Moody Breedon, 1793–*c.* 1850.
Volume in the handwriting of James Bissett containing many original songs, etc, 1796–*c.* 1805.

Birmingham, the Assay Office: Boulton & Watt MSS.
Birmingham, District Bank, Bennett's Hill: Records of the Birmingham Book Club.
Lichfield, Joint Record Office: Visitation returns, Diocese of Coventry and Lichfield,
   1772.
Manchester, John Rylands University Library: Copies of Wedgwood MSS, English MSS,
   1101–10.
Northampton, Northants Record Office: Fitzwilliam (Milton) Burke MSS.
Stafford, Staffordshire Record Office:

   Dartmouth MSS.
   Dyott MSS.
   Leveson-Gower MSS.

Stafford, William Salt Library:

   Fletcher-Boughey MSS.
   The Diary of Samuel Pipe-Wolferstan of Statfold, Staffordshire (made available in
      typescript).

Warwick, Warwickshire Record Office: Newdigate MSS.

MANUSCRIPT SOURCES: PRINTED COLLECTIONS

Public Record Office, *Calendar of Home Office Papers, George III.*
Royal Commission on Historical Manuscripts:

   Fourteenth Report, appendix x (1895): *H.M.C. Dartmouth* II.
   Fifteenth Report, appendix I (1896): *H.M.C. Dartmouth* III.
   68 (1911): *H.M.C. Denbigh* v.
   Joint Publication No. 8 (with the Dugdale Society, 1965): Levi Fox, ed., *The
      Correspondence of the Rev. Joseph Greene, Parson, Schoolmaster and Antiquary,
      1712–90.*

The Correspondence of Edmund Burke:
   Vol. II, ed. L. S. Sutherland (Cambridge and Chicago, 1960).
   Vol. III, ed. G. H. Guttridge (1961).
   Vol. VII, ed. P. J. Marshall and J. A. Woods (1968).

Curnock, N., ed., *The Journal of John Wesley* (8 vols, London, 1915; repr. 1960).
Farrer, K. E., ed., *The Letters of Josiah Wedgwood* (2 vols, privately printed, 1903).
—*The Correspondence of Josiah Wedgwood, 1781–94* (privately printed, 1906).
Finer, A., and Savage, G., eds., *The Selected Letters of Josiah Wedgwood* (London,
   1965).
Rutt, J. T., ed., *The Theological and Miscellaneous Works of Joseph Priestley*, vol. I
   (London, in two parts, 1831–32).
Telford, J., ed., *The Letters of the Revd. John Wesley* (8 vols., London, 1931; repr.
   1960).
Wyvill, C., *Political Papers, Chiefly Respecting the Attempt of the County of York and
   Other Considerable Districts to Effect a Reformation of the Parliament of Great
   Britain* (6 vols, York, 1794–1808).

CONTEMPORARY PRINTED WORKS

Official and semi-official publications:

   Journals of the House of Commons, vol. XXX.
   Cobbett, W., Wright, J., *The Parliamentary History of England from the Earliest
      Period to 1803* (London, 1806–20).

First and Second Reports of the Committee of Secrecy of the House of Commons (London, 1794).

Newspapers:

Aris's Birmingham Gazette.
Swinney's Birmingham and Stafford Chronicle.
Jopson's Coventry Mercury.
Piercy's Coventry Gazette.
Berrow's Worcester Journal (used selectively only, during 1768–69 and 1773–75).

Printed works in Central Reference Library, Birmingham:

1 Local periodicals

The Birmingham Register, or Entertaining Museum, vols. I (1765), II (1766, Nos. 1–15).
The Repository, or Weekly General Entertainer (1770, reissued 1772 as *The Winter's Evening's Entertainer*).
The British Museum, or Universal Register of Literature, Politics and Poetry, Containing Instruction and Entertainment for the Fair Sex, the Gentleman and the Mechanic (1771).

2 Topical verse

Corn, Edward, *Poems, by Edward Corn of Birmingham, with Notes on the Old and New Meetings and Newspaper Cuttings of Poems and Drama, 1754–1826.*
Crane, John, *The Crumbs, by a Bird at Bromsgrove* (1793).
Davis, George, *Saint Monday, or Scenes from Low Life* (1790).
Freeth, John, *The Political Songster, 1766.*
—*Inland Navigation: an Ode Inscribed to the Inhabitants of Birmingham and the Proprietors of the Canal* (1769).
—*The Political Songster, 1771, Addressed to the Sons of Freedom and Lovers of Humour.*
—*The Warwickshire Medley, or Convivial Songster* (1780).
—*Modern Songs on Various Subjects* (1782).
—*A Touch on the Times, or the Modern Songster* (1783).
—*The Political Songster, or a Touch on the Times on Various Subjects, Adapted to Common Tunes* (1784).
—*The Political Songster, 1786*; also the same for 1790 (three separate editions, all with internal differences).
—*New Songs on the Present Times* (1793).
—*The Annual Political Songster, 1794.*
—'Freeth's invitation cards, 1770–1801': photostat copies of rhyming invitations sent by Freeth as host of the Birmingham Book Club.
Morfitt, James, *Poetical Sketches by James Morfitt, Esq., Barrister, with Additional Pieces, Chiefly by Joseph Weston* (1794).
Navigation, a Mock Heroic on the Present Contest (the Birmingham and Fazeley Canal Bill, 1783).
Pointon, Priscilla, *Poems on Several Occasions* (1770).

3 Vernacular tracts

Alexander Armstrong, Whip Maker; Abel Sharp, Spur Maker, *Very Familiar Letters to John Nott, Button Burnisher, in reply to his Very Familiar Letters to Dr. Priestley* (1790).
Cutter, Thomas, *A Flogging for Job Nott by Thomas Cutter (formerly a Drummer in the 7th Regiment* (1793).
Noboddy, Nicholas, *A Wurd or 2 of Good Counsil to Abowt Hafe a Duzzen*

Diffrunt Sorts o Fokes, by Nicholas Noboddy, Brass Candlestick Maker (*First Cousin to Job Nott the Buckel Maker, and Sum Kin of John Nott the Button Burnisher* (1792).

Nott, John, Button Burnisher, *Very Familiar Letters to Dr. Priestley in Answer to his Familiar Letters to the Inhabitants of Birmingham* (1790).

'*Not* Button Burnisher', John, *A Letter of Advice to the Revd. J. Edwards, with Remarks on his late Productions* (1792).

Nott, John, Button Maker, *An Appeal to the Inhabitants of Birmingham, Designed as an Answer to Job Nott, Bucklemaker, by his Elder Brother, John Nott, Button Maker, and First Cousin to John Nott, Button Burnisher* (1792).

Nott, Job, Bucklemaker, *The Life and Adventures of the Celebrated Job Nott, Bucklemaker, of Birmingham, First Cousin to the Celebrated Button Burnisher* (1793).

—*Job Nott's Humble Advice, with a Suitable Postscript* (5th edn, 1793).

—*More Advice from Job Nott* (4th edn, 1795).

4 Sermons

Croft, George, *The Test Laws Defended* (1790).

Edwards, J., *A Discourse Delivered on Friday April 19th 1793 at the Union Meeting in Livery Street, . . . Being the Day Appointed for a General Fast* (1793).

—*The Inattention of Christians to Set Days of Public Fasting Justifiable* (1796).

Jones, David, *Reasons For Peace, Stated in a Discourse Delivered in the Union Chapel, Birmingham, on Wednesday, February 25th 1795* (1795).

Madan, Spencer, *The Principal Claims of the Dissenters Considered* (1790).

Riland, John, *The Sinful State of the Nation; and the Expectation of God's Judgement upon it, with the Way to Save us from Ruin, Considered in Two Discourses Preached in St. Mary's Chapel, Birmingham, 1775* (1776).

Williams, J. H. *Piety, Charity and Loyalty Recommended in a Sermon on the Late Fast* (1793).

5 Miscellaneous

An Account of the Manner in which a Standing Commercial Committee was Established at Birmingham for the Purpose of Watching Over and Conducting the Public Interests of the Town and Neighbourhood (1784).

'A Friend to Liberty and Property', *An Address to the Association for the Protection of Liberty and Property against Republicans and Levellers, held at the Hotel in Birmingham* (1792).

Observations on Constitutional Societies among the Middling and Lower Classes, addressed to the Association for the Protection of Liberty and Property . . . in Birmingham (1792).

'A Friend to Birmingham and the Constitution', *Address to the Inhabitants of Birmingham 29th April 1793* (1793).

Address, Declaration and Rules of the Birmingham Society for Constitutional Information, Instituted 20th November 1792 (1792).

An Appeal to Manufacturers on the Present State of Trade (1795).

A Letter to the English Nation, Wherein the Dreadful Consequences of War are Considered and Exposed (1793).

Binns, J., *The Trial of John Binns* (1797).

Calcott, W., *Thoughts Moral and Divine* (1758).

Hutton, W., *A History of Birmingham* (1781; 2nd edn, 1783; 3rd edn, 1793).

—*Courts of Requests, their Nature, Utility and Powers Determined, with a Variety of Cases Determined in that of Birmingham* (1787).

—*A Dissertation on Juries with a Description of the Hundred Court* (1789, as an appendix to *Courts of Requests*).

Thoughts on the Taxing of Slippers Continued: an Address to the Bucklemakers at Large (1795).

Voltaire's Creed Proved Insufficient for Man's Salvation, in Five Letters to Anonymous, four of which have appeared in the Warwickshire Journal, by the Objector (1771).

Walker, G., *The Dissenter's Plea* (1790).

6 Library catalogues

Catalogue of Lucas's Circulating Library (1788).
Catalogue of St Philip's Parish Library (1795).
Catalogue of Lowe's Circulating Library (1796).

7 Trades directories of Birmingham and the hardware district

Sketchley's Birmingham, Wolverhampton and Walsall Directory (1767). Used intensively in connection with Worcestershire petition in redress of grievances, 1769.

Other directories consulted, primarily in connection with educational developments noticed in chapter VI, are listed here by printer and date: Swinney, 1775; Pearson and Rollason, 1777, 1780, 1781; Pye, 1785, 1787, 1788, 1791; Ward, 1790; *New Universal British*, 1791.

Other contemporary printed works:

Bentley, Thomas, *A Short View of the General Advantages of Inland Navigations, with a Plan of the Navigable Canal Intended for a Communication between the Ports of Liverpool and Hull* (Liverpool, 1766). Reprinted as an appendix to K. E. Farrer, ed., *The Correspondence of Josiah Wedgwood, 1781–94*, q.v.

Field, W., *A Second Letter to the Inhabitants of Warwick, in Reply to Remarks on the First Letter, and Upon a Letter to the Printer of the Birmingham Gazette from the Revd. Vicar and Curate of St. Nicholas* (1791). In Cambridge University Library, *Collected Tracts on the Test and Corporation Acts*, III, No. 13.

Jacob, G., *A New Law Dictionary* (7th edn, London, 1756).

Morfitt, J., *Supplementary Gleanings Collected in the Years 1782 and 1783 on the Warwickshire Station, Including the Communications of J. Morfitt, Esq.* (London, 1805). In Coventry City Libraries, Coventry and North Warwickshire Collection.

The Chronicles of the Times at Coventry During the Reign of Nebuchadnezzar the Third, King of Utopia (Coventry, 1776). Reprinted as an appendix to T. W. Whitley, *The Parliamentary Representation of the City of Coventry*, q.v.

The Poll of the Freeholders of Warwickshire, 1774 (Coventry, 1775). In Coventry City Libraries, Coventry and North Warwickshire Collection.

POST-CONTEMPORARY LOCAL SOURCES

A Brief Sketch of the History of the Birmingham Book Club (Birmingham, 1864).

An Eighteenth Century Shelf-List of the Parochial Library at King's Norton (TS, Birmingham Reference Library, 1960).

Bedford, W. K. R., 'Notes from the Minute Book of the Bean Club, 1754–1836', (MS notes, 1889, in Birmingham Reference Library).

Brassington, W. S., 'Correspondence and newspaper cuttings, etc, relating to Kings Norton Parish Library, with an annotated catalogue' (MS notes and cuttings, 1897, in Birmingham Reference Library).

The Catalogue of the Birmingham Collection (Birmingham, 1918).

Clark, Thomas, junior, *Biographical Tribute to the Memory of James Lucock, Father of Sunday School Instruction in Birmingham* (Birmingham, 1835).

Dudley, T. B., ed., *Memoir of James Bissett, Written by Himself* (Birmingham, 1904).
Early Records of St. Paul's Lodge, No. 43 (n.d., in Birmingham Reference Library).
Hale, J. E., *The Centenary of the Cannon Street Sunday Schools* (Birmingham, 1895).
Langford, J. A., 'John Freeth, the Birmingham ballad maker', *Mid-England*, I (1880–81). In Birmingham Reference Library.
New, H., *The Centenary of the Church of the Messiah (New Meeting) Sunday Schools* (Birmingham, 1888).
Remarks on the Character of the Late James Lucock (Birmingham, 1835).
Stone, J. B., 'Annals of the Bean Club' (MS, 1904, in Birmingham Reference Library).
Timmins, S., *The Centenary of the Birmingham Library, 1779–1879* (Birmingham, 1879).
'Worcestershire Worthies c. 1750–1836', *Bromsgrove Messenger*, 11 March 1911 (in Birmingham Reference Library).

SECONDARY SOURCES: BOOKS

Albert, W., *The Turnpike Road System in England, 1663–1840* (Cambridge, 1972).
Allen, W., *George Eliot* (London, 1965).
Armytage, W. H. G., *Four Hundred Years of English Education* (2nd edn, Cambridge, 1970).
Ashmun, M., *The Singing Swan: an Account of Anna Seward and her Acquaintance with Dr. Johnson, Boswell and Others of their Time* (New Haven, Conn., 1931).
Ashton, T. S., *Iron and Steel in the Industrial Revolution* (2nd edn, Manchester, 1951).
Aspinall, A., *Politics and the Press, c. 1780–1850* (London, 1949).
Bailyn, B., *The Ideological Origins of the American Revolution* (Cambridge, Mass., 1967).
—*The Origins of American Politics* (New York, 1968).
Barlow, R. B., *Citizenship and Conscience: a Study in the Theory and Practice of Religious Toleration in England during the Eighteenth Century* (Philadelphia, 1963).
Bennett, W., *John Baskerville, the Birmingham Printer: his Press, Relations and Friends* (2 vols, Birmingham, 1937).
Black, E. C., *The Association: British Extraparliamentary Political Organization, 1769–1793* (Cambridge, Mass., 1963).
Blanning, T. C. W., *Reform and Revolution in Mainz, 1743–1803* (Cambridge, 1974).
Brinton, C., *English Political Thought in the Nineteenth Century* (London, 1933; repr. New York, 1962).
Bowden, Witt, *Industrial Society in England towards the End of the Eighteenth Century* (2nd edn, London, 1965).
Butterfield, H., *George III, Lord North and the People, 1779–80* (London, 1949).
Cannon, J., *Parliamentary Reform, 1640–1832* (Cambridge, 1973).
Christie, I. R., *The End of North's Ministry, 1780–82* (London, 1958).
—*Wilkes, Wyvil and Reform: the Parliamentary Reform Movement in British Politics, 1760–85* (London, 1962).
—*Crisis of Empire: Great Britain and the American Colonies, 1754–83* (London, 1966).
—*Myth and Reality in late Eighteenth Century British Politics, and other Papers* (London, 1970).
Clark, D. M., *British Opinion and the American Revolution* (2nd edn, New York, 1966).
Court, W. H. B., *The Rise of the Midlands Industries, 1650–1838* (2nd edn, Oxford, 1953).
Cranfield, G. A., *The Development of the Provincial Newspaper, 1700–60* (Oxford, 1962).
—*Handlist of English Provincial Newspapers and Periodicals, 1700–60* (Cambridge Bibliographical Society Monographs, No. 2, 1952).

Darnton, R., *Mesmerism and the End of the Enlightenment in France* (Cambridge, Mass., 1969).

DeCastro, J. P., *The Gordon Riots* (Oxford, 1926).

Donoughue, B., *British Politics and the American Revolution; the Path to War, 1773–1775* (London, 1964).

Ehrman, J., *The Younger Pitt: the Years of Acclaim* (London, 1969).

Gaskell, P., *John Baskerville, a Bibliography* (Cambridge, 1959).

Gibbs, F. W., *Joseph Priestley, Adventurer in Science and Champion of Truth* (London, 1965).

Gilboy, E. W., *Wages in Eighteenth Century England* (Cambridge, Mass., 1934).

Gill, C., *A History of Birmingham*, vol. I. *Manor and Borough to 1865* (Oxford, 1952).

Godsden, P. H. J. H., *The Friendly Societies in England, 1815–75* (Manchester, 1962).

Gould, R. F., *History of Freemasonry* (rev. edn, by Dudley Wright, London, 1931–36).

Guttridge, G. H., *English Whiggism and the American Revolution* (2nd edn, Berkeley, Cal., 1963).

Hadfield, C., *The Canals of the West Midlands* (Newton Abbot, 1966).

—*The Canals of the East Midlands* (Newton Abbot, 1966).

Haight, G. S., *George Eliot, a Biography* (Oxford, 1968).

Hans, N., *New Trends in Education in the Eighteenth Century* (London, 1951).

Harlow, V. T., *The Founding of the Second British Empire, 1763–93* (2 vols, London, 1952).

Hill, J., *The Bookmakers and Booksellers of Old Birmingham* (Birmingham, privately printed, 1907).

Hobsbawm, E. J., *Industry and Empire: an Economic History of Britain since 1750* (London, 1968).

Hobsbawm, E. J., and Rudé, G., *Captain Swing* (London, 1968).

Hopkins, M. A., *Dr Johnson's Lichfield* (New York, 1952).

Jewitt, L., *The Life of William Hutton and History of the Hutton Family* (London, 1872).

Jones, E. L., Mingay, G. E., eds., *Land, Labour and Population in the Industrial Revolution* (London, 1967).

Kilvert, F., *Memoirs of the Life and Writings of the Right Reverend Richard Hurd* (London, 1860).

Knoop, D., Jones, G. P., *The Genesis of Freemasonry* (Manchester, 1947).

Lane, J., *Masonic Records, 1717–1894* (Torquay, 1895).

Langford, J. A., *A Century of Birmingham Life: a Chronicle of Local Events, 1741–1841* (2 vols, Birmingham, 1868).

Langford, P., *The First Rockingham Administration, 1765–66* (Oxford, 1973).

Lincoln, A. H., *Some Social and Political Ideas of English Dissent, 1763–1800* (Cambridge, 1938).

Lutnick, S., *The American Revolution and the British Press, 1775–82* (Columbia, Mo., 1967).

Maccoby, S., *English Radicalism, 1786–1832* (London, 1955).

Mackerness, E. D., *A Social History of English Music* (London, 1964).

Mackesy, P., *The War for America, 1775–83* (London, 1964).

Malcolmson, R. W., *Popular Recreation in English Society, 1700–1850* (Cambridge, 1973).

Mantoux, P., *The Industrial Revolution in the Eighteenth Century* (rev. edn, London, 1961).

Meteyard, E., *The Life and Works of Josiah Wedgwood* (2 vols, London, 1856–66).

Mingay, G. E., *Enclosure and the Small Farmer in the Age of the Industrial Revolution* (London, 1968).

Morgan, E. S. & H. M., *The Stamp Act Crisis, Prologue to Revolution* (2nd edn, New York, 1963).

Musson, A. E., and Robinson, E., *Science and Technology in the Industrial Revolution* (Manchester, 1969).

Namier, Sir Lewis, *The Structure of Politics at the Accession of George III* (2nd edn, London, 1957).

—*Crossroads of Power* (London, 1962).

—and Brooke, J., *The History of Parliament: the House of Commons, 1754–90* (3 vols, London, 1964).

Parish, C., *History of the Birmingham Library* (London, 1966).

Patterson, A. T., *Radical Leicester* (Leicester, 1954).

Poole, B., *The History and Antiquities of the City of Coventry* (Coventry, 1870).

Poynter, J. R., *Society and Pauperism: English Ideas on Poor Relief, 1795–1834* (London, 1969).

Raistrick, A. A., *Dynasty of Ironfounders: the Darbys of Coalbrookdale* (London, 1953).

Ransome, M., ed., *The State of the Bishopric of Worcester, 1782–1808* (Worcestershire Historical Society Publications, n.s., 6, 1968).

Raybould, T. J., *The Economic Emergence of the Black Country: a Study of the Dudley Estate* (Newton Abbot, 1973).

Rea, R. R., *The English Press and Politics, 1760–74* (Lincoln, Neb., 1963).

Read, D., *Press and People, 1790–1850* (London, 1961).

—*The English Provinces*, c. *1760–1960: a Study in Influence* (London, 1964).

Ritcheson, C. R., *British Politics and the American Revolution* (Norman, Okl., 1954).

Roll, E., *An Early Experiment in Industrial Organization: the Firm of Boulton & Watt, 1775–1805* (London, 1930).

Rudé, G., *Wilkes and Liberty: a Social Study of 1763 to 1774* (Oxford, 1962).

Schofield, R. E., *The Lunar Society of Birmingham: a Social History of Provincial Science and Industry in Eighteenth Century England* (Oxford, 1963).

Schuyler, R. L., ed., *Josiah Tucker: a Selection from his Economic and Political Writings* (2nd edn, New York, 1966).

Sedgwick, R., ed., *The History of Parliament, the House of Commons, 1715–54* (2 vols, London, 1970).

Shelton, W. J., *English Hunger and Industrial Disorders: a Study of Social Conflict during the First Decade of George III's Reign* (London, 1973).

Smith, Adam, *An Enquiry into the Nature and Causes of the Wealth of Nations* (Cannan edn, London, 1904, repr. New York, 1937).

Smith, J. S., *The Story of Music in Birmingham* (Birmingham, 1945).

Stewart, W. A. C. and McCann, W. P., *The Educational Innovators, 1750–1880* (London, 1967).

Thale, M., ed., *The Autobiography of Francis Place* (Cambridge, 1972).

Thomas, K. V., *Religion and the Decline of Magic* (London, 1971).

Thompson, E. P., *The Making of the English Working Class* (London, 1963).

Veitch, G. S., *The Genesis of Parliamentary Reform* (2nd edn, London, 1964).

Victoria County History, Warwickshire, vols. VII, *The City of Birmingham*; VIII, *The City of Coventry and Borough of Warwick* (Oxford, 1964 and 1969).

Webb, R. K., *The British Working Class Reader: Literacy and Social Tension, 1790–1848* (London, 1955).

Webb, S. & B., *English Local Government*, vol. 4. *Statutory Authorities for Special Purposes* (London, 1922).

Werkmeister, L., *The London Daily Press, 1772–92* (Lincoln, Neb., 1963).

White, A. W. A., *Men and Mining in Warwickshire* (Coventry, 1970).

Whitley, T. W., *The Parliamentary Representation of the City of Coventry* (Coventry, 1894).

Williams, G. A., *Artisans and Sansculottes: Popular Movements in France and Britain During the French Revolution* (London, 1968).

Works published since the completion of this book:

Brewer, J., *Party Ideology and Popular Politics at the Accession of George III* (Cambridge, 1976).
O'Gorman, F., *The Rise of Party in England: the Rockingham Whigs, 1760–82* (London, 1975).
Thomas, P. D. G., *British Politics and the Stamp Act Crisis: the First Phase of the American Revolution, 1763–67* (Oxford, 1975).
Ward, J. R., *The Finance of Canal Building in Eighteenth Century England* (Oxford, 1974).

SECONDARY SOURCES: ARTICLES

Allen, G. C., 'An eighteenth century combination in the copper mining industry', *Economic Journal*, xxxiii (1923), 74–85.
Anon., 'The lodges and their legend' (review of J. M. Roberts, *The Mythology of the Secret Societies*), *Times Literary Supplement*, 15 December, 1972.
Ashton, T. S., 'Early price associations in the British iron industry', *Economic Journal*, xxx (1920), 331–9.
Bargar, B. D., 'Matthew Boulton and the Birmingham petition of 1775', *William and Mary Quarterly*, 3rd series, xiii (1956), 26–39.
Bladen, V. W., 'The Potteries in the industrial revolution', *Economic History Supplement to the Economic Journal*, i (1926–29), 117–30.
—'The Association of the Manufacturers of Earthenware, 1784–86', *Economic History Supplement to the Economic Journal*, i (1926–29), 357–67.
Blaug, M., 'The myth of the old poor law and the making of the new', *Journal of Economic History*, xxiii (1963), 151–84.
Bowden, Witt, 'The English manufacturers and the commercial treaty of 1786 with France', *Amer. Hist. Rev.*, xxv (1919–20), 18–35.
—'The influence of the manufacturers on some of the early policies of William Pitt', *Amer. Hist. Rev.*, xxxix (1923–24), 655–74.
Bowker, M., review of K. V. Thomas, *Religion and the Decline of Magic*, *Historical Journal*, xv (1972), 363–6.
Brewer, J., 'The misfortunes of Lord Bute: a case study in eighteenth century political argument and public opinion', *Historical Journal*, xvi (1973), 1–43.
Briggs, A., 'Press and public opinion in early nineteenth century Birmingham', *Dugdale Society, Occasional Papers*, No. 8 (1949).
—'Middle class consciousness in English politics, 1780–1846', *Past and Present*, 9 (February 1956), 65–74.
—'The language of class in the early nineteenth century', in A. Briggs and J. Saville, eds., *Essays in Labour History* (London, 1960).
Broadbridge, S. R., 'Monopoly and public utility: the Birmingham canals, 1767–72', *Transport History*, v (1972), 229–42.
Brown, A. S., 'Gustavus Katterfelto, Mason and magician', *Ars Quatuor Coronatorum*, lxix (1957), 136–8.
Carter, T. M., 'St John's Lodge, Henley in Arden, 1791–1811', *Ars Quatuor Coronatorum*, xxxix (1928), 4–60.
Chaloner, W. H., 'Dr Joseph Priestley, John Wilkinson and the French revolution, 1789–1802', *Trans. Royal Hist. Soc.*, 5th series, viii (1958), 21–40.
Chambers, J. D., 'Enclosure and labour supply in the industrial revolution', *Econ. Hist. Rev.*, 2nd series, v (1953), 319–43.
Christie, I. R., 'The Yorkshire Association, 1780–84: a study in political organization', *Historical Journal*, iii (1960), 144–61.
Coats, A. W., 'Economic thought and poor law policy in the eighteenth century', *Econ. Hist. Rev.*, 2nd series, xiii (1960–61), 39–51.

—'Changing attitudes to labour in the mid-eighteenth century', *Econ. Hist. Rev.*, 2nd series, XI (1958–9), 35–51.

—'Plebs, paternalists and political economists', *Past and Present*, 54 (February 1972), 130–3.

Cosson, A., 'Warwickshire turnpikes', *Trans. Birm. Arch. Soc.*, LXIV (1941–2), 53–100.

Court, W. H. B., 'Industrial organization and economic progress in the eighteenth century Midlands', *Trans. Royal Hist. Soc.*, 4th series, XXVIII (1946), 85–99.

Cranfield, G. A., 'A handlist of English newspapers and periodicals: additions and corrections', *Trans. Cambridge Bibl. Soc.*, II, No. 3 (1956).

Ditchfield, G. M., 'The early history of Manchester College', *Trans. Hist. Soc. Lancs. and Ches.*, 123 (1972), 81–104.

Fisher, W. G., 'A cavalcade of Masons in 1731, as recorded in the *Gentleman's Magazine*', *Ars Quatuor Coronatorum*, LXXIV (1961), 32–49.

George, M. D., 'Fox's martyrs and the general election of 1784', *Trans. Royal Hist. Soc.*, 4th series, XXI (1939), 133–68.

Genovese, E. F., 'The many faces of moral economy', *Past and Present*, 58 (February 1973), 161–8.

Gill, C., 'Birmingham under the Street Commissioners, 1769–1851', *University of Birmingham Hist. Journal*, I, No. 2 (1948), 255–87.

Ginter, D. E., 'The Loyalist Association movement of 1792–93 and British public opinion', *Historical Journal*, IX (1966), 179–90.

Henderson, W. O., 'The Anglo-French treaty of 1786', *Econ. Hist. Rev.*, 2nd series, X (1957–8), 104–12.

Kelly, P., 'Radicalism and public opinion in the general election of 1784', *Bull. Inst. Hist. Res.*, XLV (1972), 73–88.

Kettle, A. J., 'Lichfield races', *Trans. Lichfield and S. Staffs. Arch. Soc.*, VI (1964–65), 39–44.

Kiernan, V. G., 'Evangelicalism and the French revolution', *Past and Present*, 1 (February 1952), 44–56.

Koebner, R., 'Adam Smith and the industrial revolution', *Econ. Hist. Rev.*, 2nd series, XI (1958–9), 381–91.

Light, S. W., 'Poet John Freeth', *The Central Literary Magazine* (journal of the Central Literary Society of Birmingham), December 1960.

McKendrick, N., 'Josiah Wedgwood, an eighteenth century entrepreneur in salesmanship and marketing techniques', *Econ. Hist. Rev.*, 2nd series, XII (1959–60), 408–33.

—'Josiah Wedgwood and factory discipline', *Historical Journal*, IV (1961), 30–55.

—'Josiah Wedgwood and Thomas Bentley: an inventor–entrepreneur partnership in the industrial revolution', *Trans. Royal. Hist. Soc.*, 5th series, XIV (1963), 1–33.

Martin, J. M., 'The parliamentary enclosure movement and rural society in Warwickshire', *Agric. Hist. Rev.*, XV (1967), 19–39.

—'The cost of parliamentary enclosure in Warwickshire', *Univ. of Birmingham Hist. Journal*, IX (1963–64), 144–62.

Mitchell, A., 'The association movement, 1792–93', *Historical Journal*, IV (1961), 56–77.

Money, J., 'Taverns, coffee houses and clubs: local politics and popular articulacy in the Birmingham area in the age of the American revolution', *Historical Journal*, XIV (1971), 15–47.

—'Birmingham and the West Midlands, 1760–93: politics and regional identity in the English provinces in the later eighteenth century', *Midland History*, I (1971), 1–19.

—'The schoolmasters of Birmingham and the West Midlands, 1750–90: private education and cultural change in the English provinces during the early industrial revolution', *Social History/Histoire Sociale* (Ottawa, Canada), X, No. 1 (spring 1976), 129–53.

Morgan, P., 'Early booksellers, printers and publishers in Stratford on Avon', *Trans. Birm. Arch. Soc.*, LXVII (1947–8), 55–70.

Musson, A. E. and Robinson, E., 'Science and industry in the late eighteenth century', *Econ. Hist. Rev.*, 2nd series, XIII (1960–61), 222–44.

Norris, J. M., 'Samuel Garbett and the early development of industrial lobbying in Great Britain', *Econ. Hist. Rev.*, 2nd series, X (1957–8), 450–60.

Pelham, R. A., 'The immigrant population of Birmingham, 1688–1726', *Trans. Birm. Arch. Soc.*, LXI (1937), 45–80.

—'The West Midlands iron industry and the American market in the eighteenth century', *Univ. of Birmingham Hist. Journal*, II (1949–50), 141–62.

—'The Worcester to Birmingham canal', *Univ. of Birmingham Hist. Journal*, V (1955), 60–82.

Pope, S., 'The development of Freemasonry in England and Wales, as depicted by graphs from particulars in Lane's *Masonic Records*, second edition', *Ars Quatuor Coronatorum*, 68–70 (1956–58), 129–31.

Roberts, J. M., 'Freemasonry: possibilities of a neglected topic', *Eng. Hist. Rev.*, LXXXIV (1969), 323–35.

Robinson, E., 'The Derby Philosophical Society', *Annals of Science*, IX (1953), 368–76.

—'An English Jacobin: James Watt junior', *Cambridge Historical Journal*, XI (1953–5), 349–55.

—'Boulton & Fothergill, 1762–82, and the Birmingham export of hardware', *Univ. of Birmingham Hist. Journal*, VII, No. 1 (1959), 60–79.

—'New light on the Priestley riots', *Historical Journal*, III (1960), 73–5.

—'Eighteenth century commerce and fashion: Matthew Boulton's marketing techniques', *Econ. Hist. Rev.*, 2nd series, XVI (1963–64), 39–60.

—'Matthew Boulton and the art of parliamentary lobbying', *Historical Journal*, VII (1964), 209–29.

—'The origins and life span of the Lunar Society', *Univ. of Birmingham Hist. Journal*, XI, No. 1 (1967), 5–16.

Rogers, N., 'Aristocratic clientage, trade and independency: popular politics in pre-radical Westminster', *Past and Present*, 61 (November 1973), 70–106.

Rose, R. B., 'The Priestley riots of 1791', *Past and Present*, 18 (November 1960), 68–88.

—'The origins of working class radicalism in Birmingham', *Labour History* (Canberra, Australia), 4 (November 1965), 6–14.

Rosenfeld, S., 'Landscape in eighteenth century English scenery', in K. Richards and P. Thompson, eds., *Essays on the Eighteenth Century English Stage* (London, 1972), pp. 171–7.

Rylands, W. H., 'A forgotten rival of Masonry: the Noble Order of Bucks', *Ars Quatuor Coronatorum*, III (1890), 140–62.

Sheldon, W. C., 'The Birmingham magistrate who suppressed the rioters', *Procs. Wesley Hist. Soc.* (September 1903), 61–4.

Styles, P. M., 'The development of county administration in the late eighteenth and early nineteenth centuries, illustrated by the records of the Warwickshire Court of Quarter Sessions, 1773–1837', *Dugdale Society, Occasional Papers*, No. 4 (1933).

—'The corporation of Warwick, 1660–1835', *Trans. Birm. Arch. Soc.*, LIX (1935), 9–122.

Sutherland, L. S., 'Edmund Burke and the first Rockingham Ministry', *Eng. Hist. Rev.*, XLVII (1932), 47–62.

Thomas, P. D. G., 'The beginning of parliamentary reporting in newspapers, 1768–74', *Eng. Hist. Rev.*, LXXIV (1959), 623–36.

—'John Wilkes and the freedom of the press, 1771', *Bull. Inst. Hist. Research*, XXXIII (1960), 86–98.

Thompson, E. P., 'The moral economy of the English crowd in the eighteenth century', *Past and Present*, 50 (February 1971), 76–136.

—'Time, work discipline and industrial capitalism', *Past and Present*, 38 (December 1967), 57–97.

Underdown, P. T., 'Religious opposition to the licensing of the Bristol and Birmingham theatres', *Univ. of Birmingham Hist. Journal*, v (1957–8), 149–60.

Walker, B., 'Birmingham directories', *Trans. Birm. Arch. Soc.*, LVIII (1934), 1–36.

—'The Anacreontic Society', *Trans. Birm. Arch. Soc.*, LXIII (1939–40), 76–80.

Wedgwood, J. C., 'Staffordshire parliamentary history', *William Salt Arch. Soc., Collections for a History of Staffordshire*, III (1933), 1–122.

Western, J. R., 'The Volunteer movement as an anti-revolutionary force, 1793–1801', *Eng. Hist. Rev.*, LXXI (1956), 603–14.

Wiles, R. M., 'Further additions and corrections to G. A. Cranfield's handlist', *Trans. Cambridge Bibl. Soc.*, II, No. 5 (1958).

Wise, M. J., 'Birmingham and its trade relations in the early eighteenth century', *Univ. of Birmingham Hist. Journal*, II, No. 1 (1949), 53–79.

Wood, A. C., 'The diaries of Sir Roger Newdigate, 1751–1806', *Trans. Birm. Arch. Soc.*, LXXVIII (1960), 40–54.

Wrigley, E. A., 'A simple model of London's importance in changing English society and economy, 1650–1750', *Past and Present*, 37 (July 1967), 44–70.

UNPUBLISHED THESES AND DISSERTATIONS

Bebbington, P. S., 'Samuel Garbett, 1717–1803, a Birmingham pioneer' (Birmingham, M. Comm. 1938).

Ditchfield, G. M., 'Some aspects of Unitarianism and radicalism, 1760–1810' (Cambridge, Ph.D., 1968).

Watson, D. H., 'The Duke of Newcastle, the Marquis of Rockingham and mercantile interests in the provinces, 1761–68' (Sheffield, Ph.D., 1968).

—'Barlow Trecothick and other associates of Lord Rockingham during the Stamp Act crisis, 1765–66' (Sheffield, M.A., 1958).

Walvin, J., 'English democratic societies and popular radicalism, 1791–1800' (York, D.Phil., 1969).

INDEX